Optimizing
Windows NT™

Russ Blake

Microsoft®

WINDOWS NT
RESOURCE KIT

Volume 3 of the 3 volume set

PUBLISHED BY
Microsoft Press
A Division of Microsoft Corporation
One Microsoft Way
Redmond, Washington 98052-6399

Library of Congress Cataloging-in-Publication Data
Microsoft Windows NT resource kit / Microsoft Corporation.
        p.   cm.
    Includes indexes.
    Contents: v. 1. Resource guide -- v. 2. Messages -- v.
3. Optimizing Windows NT.
    ISBN 1-55615-598-0 (v. 1) -- ISBN 1-55615-600-6 (v. 2)
-- 1-55615-619-7 (v. 3)
    1. Operating systems (Computers) 2. Windows NT.   I. Microsoft
Corporation.
QA76.76.O63M5238   1993
005.4'469--dc20   93-4950
                                                     CIP

Printed and bound in the United States of America.

 2 3 4 5 6 7 8 9 FFG 9 8 7 6 5 4

Distributed to the book trade in Canada by Macmillan of Canada, a division of Canada Publishing Corporation.

British Cataloging-in-Publication Data available from Penguin Books Ltd., Harmondsworth, Middlesex, England

Technical Writers: Sharon Carroll, Mark Williams, and Stephen Wood
Database Designer and System Administrator: Cary E. Reinstein
Team Manager: Peggy Etchevers
Technical Editor: Sharon Tighe
Production Team: Donalee Edwards, Wendy Boyd, Risa P. Suzuki, and Yong Ok Chung
Graphic Designer: Sue Wyble
Interface Design Consultant: Bill O'Daly
Technical Consultants: Donald Funk and Chris St. Valentine

U.S. Patent No. 4955066

Contents

Appendixes

Introduction

I encountered my first computer performance problem 25 years ago. A professor at my college wanted to build a tightrope for his children in the backyard. He needed to know how strong the rope would have to be, so he asked if I could help. Eager to brandish my new-found programming expertise, I readily volunteered. He told me the weight of his children and the length he wanted the tightrope to be, and I was off in a rush to the time-sharing terminal. I created the program, punched in the paper tape, and soon returned to him with the answer, gleeful with my success.

A few weeks later, another professor managing our link to the time-sharing computer stopped by and asked me if I knew what had caused the computer service to bill us an extra $600 that month. I knew we were charged for connect time and for computation time, but the bill seemed incredible to me and I could think of no reason for it. A few days later it dawned on me. My little program to compute the tensile strength of the tightrope iterated repeatedly from 0 to degree x, where x was the angle of descent of the tightrope. Then x would be increased, but the program started back at 0 again. A very simple change to the program would have made it hundreds of times more efficient. $600. Ouch.

So my first performance-measurement tool was a bill. Sometimes a bill is still the most effective tool, because poor computer performance costs money. And solving a performance problem by buying the wrong piece of hardware wastes money. But the biggest cost of poor performance is in the productivity of all the people who use our systems and our programs. If we could properly tune all the programs and computers in the country we could pay off the national debt. Well, make a dent anyway.

We want to help you to avoid that $600 bill, which (given inflation) is likely to be somewhat larger today. This book describes the dynamic behavior of the Microsoft® Windows NT™ operating system and its applications, and how that behavior affects their performance.

This book will prove useful to a wide range of computer professionals, including:

- Corporate Information Systems and network administration personnel who evaluate, design, deploy, and administer Windows NT on both servers and desktop computers.
- Corporate departmental administrators who must maintain Windows NT departmental servers.
- Corporate Information Systems personnel who design, implement, and maintain mission-critical applications deployed on Windows NT.
- Independent software vendors who port 16-bit applications to Windows NT, or develop 32-bit applications for Windows NT.
- Windows NT users who make decisions concerning the addition of hardware to their computers to improve performance.

Because we figure that our readers include people with different backgrounds and with exposure to a wide variety of different systems, we have tried to be careful to define our terminology as we go along. If we're going to win this game, we need to start with a level playing field. Hopefully this will not prove too ponderous for those of you well-versed in computer science. Even if you are, you should stay on your toes: like all systems, Windows NT has its own terminology.

Once you have read this book, you will be able to:

- Determine hardware requirements for deploying Windows NT.
- Find bottlenecks in networks, servers, and desktop computers.
- Determine accurately what new hardware purchase will best enhance your productivity.
- Gain an understanding of how various activities affect the performance of your computer hardware.
- Perform capacity planning, to determine your future equipment needs for servers and desktop computers.
- Gain an understanding of the performance-critical features of Windows NT.
- Determine the effect of various design tradeoffs for optimally performing applications.
- Assess the hardware requirements for your applications.
- Determine the bottlenecks in your applications, and remove them if possible.

This book is extremely topical, which is both an asset and a liability. It is tied to the initial release of Windows NT 3.1, and reveals a host of details that are extremely important for you to understand if you are to manage the performance of Windows NT. But such details may change in subsequent releases. If you are working with a later release of Windows NT, you may find that some algorithms have been refined and some counter names have changed, and some of the hints we mention here may no longer apply. We've tried to make sure that you'll have all the tools in your toolkit to characterize any changes clearly for yourself as they emerge in new releases.

As you will discover, optimizing Windows NT is not an issue of tweaking many magic system parameters. Instead you will learn a new set of powerful tools for analyzing system performance. Each tool will lead you to the next until you have decimated the bottleneck demon.

On the floppy disk (or CD-ROM) provided with this book, you will find a synthetic load generator along with quite a few other useful tools. The synthetic load generator, which helps you perform controlled performance experiments on your system, is described in Appendix C of this book. The other utilities have online documentation. We discuss most of these tools in the text as we cover related topics, but you should browse the floppy disk for tools which might be useful in your situation. Give them a try. They don't weigh much, so you might as well carry them around.

There are a few topics we have not tried to cover at all in this book. For example, we have not tried to help you to minimize the disk space required for Windows NT on your computer. As already mentioned, we have not tried to provide an exhaustive treatise on the effects of changing the parameters listed in Appendix B, mainly because we think you'll never need to change them unless your situation is quite unusual. And we have not tried to do an exhaustive comparison of the performance of Windows NT on this or that hardware platform. Instead, we have enabled you to do that comparison in your own environment.

A book like this is the result of an enormous team effort. It is a book built upon a great foundation of software. At the base of that foundation is the dedicated team that built Windows NT (led by Dave Cutler), that tested it (led by Moshe Dunie and Ken Gregg), and that documented it (led by Chris Brown). I designed and helped implement Performance Monitor, but the bulk of the code was written by Hon-Wah Chan and Mike Moskowicz, with a key contribution by Bob Watson, and help from Christos Tsollis and all the NT development team members who added counters to Windows NT. Windows NT also supports a strong set of application performance tuning tools provided with this book and in the Windows NT Software Development Kit and Device Driver Kit. These were implemented by Reza Baghai (lead programmer), with help from Paramesh Vaidyanathan, Lee Smith, Tom Zakrajsek, Mark Leaming, Mark Lucovsky, Lou Perazzoli, Mark Enstrom, and Phillip Marino. And I want to give special thanks to the dedicated editing team for this book. If this book is readable at all, it is due to their many tireless hours, and if it's not it's because I mangled the text hopelessly in the first place.

All these dedicated individuals have toiled long and hard to arm you with the most advanced tools for bottleneck detection and capacity planning. So go forth and slay those bottlenecks. It's a tough job, but somebody has to do it!

Russ Blake
Summer 1993

CHAPTER 1

How to Optimize Windows NT

There are many ways to make your computer go faster—for example, you can drop it from a tenth story window, a temptation we have all had. But it's better to figure out why it is slow, and then do something more reasonable about it.

In this book we'll be picking through the various things that make computers slow, particularly the things that slow down computers running the Microsoft® Windows NT™ operating system. And we'll find out how to fix those problems, because your time, and your computer's or network's time, is precious.

We'll also talk a little about capacity planning, so that the capacity of your computer or network can stay one step ahead of its necessary workload. And we'll cover strategies and tools you can use to make sure the applications you write perform well on Windows NT.

This chapter serves as an overview of Windows NT performance issues, starting with the tools historically available for tuning a system and how Windows NT changes the traditional approach. We'll define performance bottlenecks and how to locate where in your systems they are occurring, and how to anticipate potential bottlenecks so technology managers can accumulate the right equipment for your applications' requirements. We'll take a quick look at what programmers can do with the performance information Windows NT gathers, and finally, we'll glance at the key performance measuring tools included with this book.

Windows NT Is Always in Tune

In the old days, operating systems were built with many tuning parameters that could be adjusted to affect the performance of the system. These parameters frequently had obscure effects deep within the system. Understanding these effects meant grasping subtle design details. In fact, operating system designers became adept at leaving the most difficult decisions about the system's performance to the users.

Unfortunately, the users rarely had the system's source code at hand to help make these decisions. In an effort to keep manuals simple and friendly, the documentation rarely included the information required to set the parameters properly. Tuning an operating system became the arcane art of somehow understanding the many poorly documented values and how they affected the system's performance. This task was made more difficult because the interactions of the parameters were even more obscure than the parameters themselves.

A major design goal of Windows NT was to eliminate the many obtuse parameters that characterized earlier systems. Adaptive algorithms were incorporated in Windows NT so that correct values are determined by the system as it runs. The 32-bit address space removed many limitations on memory and the need for users to manually adjust parameters to partition memory.

Windows NT has fundamentally changed how computers will be managed in the future. The task of optimizing Windows NT is not the art of manually adjusting many conflicting parameters. Optimizing Windows NT is a process of determining what hardware resource is experiencing the greatest demand, and then adjusting the operation to relieve that demand. The system comes equipped with elegant (if we do say so ourselves) tools for accomplishing this task. Teaching you how to use these tools to make your computer run faster is the primary purpose of this book.

Windows NT did not achieve the goal of automatic tuning in every single case. A few parameters remain, mainly because it is not possible for us to know precisely how every computer is used. Default values for all parameters are set for a broad range of normal system use, and they rarely need to be altered. But there are special circumstances when changes might be advisable. In this book we will be sure to mention the few tuning parameters that remain in Windows NT, and when it is appropriate to change them from their default values.

Detecting Bottlenecks

Of course you never drink bottled beer, but if you did you would notice that the neck of the bottle is narrower than the base. When you turn the bottle upside-down, the narrow neck of the bottle restricts the flow so that you can barely get enough beer to quench your thirst.

With computer bottlenecks, the bottleneck is the part of the computer that is restricting the flow of work. But unlike the neck on a beer bottle, the bottleneck in a computer can move around from one part of the system to another.

Bottleneck detection is the process of isolating the hardware component that is restricting the flow of your activities. But because it is generally easier to move software around than it is to move hardware, it is also useful to find the software component that is generating all the activity.

For example, let's suppose you have a computer that occasionally gives a sluggish response. You follow the directions in this book, and quickly determine that the problem is that your main disk is very busy from time to time. You will want to find the source of this disk activity. Depending on the source of the activity, you might be able to move it to a second disk drive and thus reduce the interference with your normal work.

And here's something that you probably didn't know: software sometimes has bugs. These can cause programs to overconsume your hardware. If you find the software is the problem, you can replace it or modify it—it is generally true that it is cheaper to drop your software from the tenth story than your hardware.

Whether you are a single, isolated user with Windows NT on your desktop or you are managing a great many file and print servers, the questions you ask and the methods you use to find bottlenecks in your computer are similar. We will thoroughly discuss bottleneck detection in Chapters 3 through 7. There are a number of special considerations for computers being used in certain ways, and we'll look at those as we move along. But generally we all need to approach bottleneck detection through the same looking glass.

Capacity Planning

Even if your computer is humming along today, you can be sure that at some point in the future you will run out of capacity. That's because newer software often uses more hardware to get its job done. You will find over time that your hardware resources are not keeping up with your use of the system.

Bosses like to have advance notice of any hardware requirements, along with lots of documentation showing the need for new equipment. In Chapter 8 we'll discuss how to collect data on a regular basis so you can predict your future equipment needs. Windows NT includes tools for easily archiving the capacity planning data for your computer or network.

Monitoring your system on a regular basis will also provide you with essential information for bottleneck detection. One of the topics we will cover in detail in this book is the equipment-dependent nature of performance counters. For example, the maximum transfer rate of a disk drive is dependent on many aspects of your system. No one can just provide you with a "good" number. But by having a record of your computer in normal operation, you can build an understanding of reasonable values for your counters. Then, if you make a change or something slows down, you have a baseline against which to compare your new situation. Without this baseline, the detection of bottlenecks can be tricky.

Optimizing Applications

If you are developing software for Windows NT, you will want to take advantage of the advanced features that will make your application hot, hot, hot. It's important to know that much of the lore that guided the development of Windows-based applications for 16-bit computers is no longer relevant to the new, 32-bit architecture of Windows NT. In Chapter 9 we'll cover these issues in some detail.

If you are merely a victim of these ruthless programmers, Chapter 9 will give you a few weapons to defend yourself. You will be able to determine whether they are using the correct techniques to get the most out of Windows NT. Imagine the looks on their faces when you point out to them that they should be mapping the WIZBANG.DAT file. Send us the videotape!

If you are developing software on Windows NT, you immediately have access (through the Windows NT Software Development Kit) to a strong set of tools for application optimization. You can find out how your application is using the system, and whether it is behaving as you hoped. You can acquire intimate knowledge of such details as how long it takes to make any given system call on your computer and how often your program is making that call. For example, you can use the Windows NT API Profiler to determine which files are most heavily accessed and which events and semaphores are causing the most delays within the application. Chapter 10 will give you some guidelines on using these tools wisely, as well as guidelines for other useful tools that are on the floppy disk accompanying this book.

You will also be able to minimize the memory used by your application. A tool for automatic working set tuning is included in the Windows NT Software Development Kit (SDK). Other tools will help you to understand your virtual memory activity in some detail, so you can find memory and virtual memory leaks. Chapter 11 discusses all of this.

In Chapters 12 and 13 we will provide information to help you write your own performance monitor or to incorporate the monitoring technology into your application so you can produce information about the system's behavior along with statistics about your application's progress. And you will find out how to add counters from your application to the performance monitor so that your users can remotely monitor the progress of your application and correlate that progress with computer resource usage.

Performance Monitor and Other Cool Tools to Use

On Windows NT your primary tool will invariably be the Windows NT Performance Monitor or a similar product. Performance Monitor is designed to pinpoint the majority of performance problems. You can think of Performance Monitor as a broad, horizontal tool that lets you look at a wide range of system components. But some problems require other tools, which you can think of as specialized, vertical tools for intensive monitoring of specific aspects of your system or application. Performance Monitor can lead you to the correct tool for the next phase in your investigation. This method of using Performance Monitor first, and then a more specialized tool, will always save you time.

Another tool that is quite handy for quickly assessing the status of programs on your system is PView, available on the floppy disk provided with this book. PView shows what programs are currently running and gives some basic information about each. With the exception of a few items included in PView to aid in debugging applications, all the data items in PView are also available in Performance Monitor. But PView is a bit simpler to start and displays data in a different way that's quite handy for a quick glance at system status.

As mentioned above, additional tools exist for tuning individual applications. Some of these can also be an aid to tracking down performance problems. So be sure to familiarize yourself with these tools even if you do not plan to write any applications yourself.

Performance Monitor Is a New Breed of Application

The microcomputer industry has been built upon a few application types. Word processors and spreadsheets make up the majority of applications sold. Other popular application categories include databases, desktop publishing, presentation graphics, drawing, and myriad games.

Windows NT Performance Monitor is not like any of these. It is an entirely new type of application, so we are all amateurs in its use. If you invest the time to learn how to use Performance Monitor, you will be repaid with knowledge of a powerful tool. You will be able to understand a computer running Windows NT in a way that few people ever understood the computers they have used. This knowledge will enable you to do your job more effectively, or at least provide you with a great conversation topic at parties.

In Chapter 2 we will discuss the rationale behind the Performance Monitor feature set. This goes beyond just listing features to indicate how and why each one is useful. In the following chapters we will explore what you can measure on Windows NT, and what those measurements tell you. Reading this will empower you to hunt bottlenecks in the densest, darkest networks of computers!

CHAPTER 2

Zen and the Art of Performance Monitoring

Computer performance bottlenecks are usually typified by the overconsumption of some hardware resource. Generally this results in the underconsumption of other hardware resources. If a particular piece of equipment is the bottleneck in a computer, it is usually true that by purchasing more of that resource you can eliminate the bottleneck. But buying more of a different resource will not help, and although we all like to help the economy whenever possible, it is best not to spend the boss's money needlessly.

To determine the precise location of the bottleneck in your computer, you must become as one with the computer. There can be no distinction between you as an individual and the computer as a machine. To achieve this state requires years of meditation, prayer, and insanity.

Luckily we have an alternative approach, which requires only a little insanity: Windows NT Performance Monitor. Performance Monitor is an excellent tool for optimizing computer performance. With a little background information on how computers work internally and how Performance Monitor measures performance, you can make sure you are getting as much as possible from your computer.

You might think that a great deal of complex mathematical theory is required to work on computer performance, but luckily that is not the case. If you can do simple arithmetic, you can understand bottlenecks and capacity planning. We'll present some of the basics in the next few chapters. Anyway, even if you never use this stuff, you'll have some new terminology to use to impress your boss.

In this chapter, we'll start with some of the basics of computer architecture, and then go over the features of Performance Monitor and how you can use them to solve various problems. Performance Monitor has online Help to explain how to invoke its features using various keystrokes and mouse clicks, so we usually won't repeat those details here. Instead we'll focus on why the various features exist, their intended use, and their limitations. As any woodworker with fewer than ten fingers will tell you, it's worth spending some time getting to know your tools.

Computer Architecture 101

To get a handle on the bottleneck issue, we need to understand just a little about how our computer is organized internally. Figure 2.1 is a block diagram of the hardware organization of the original IBM® personal computer. Modern systems may partition things a bit differently, but the basic idea has not changed much since the early 1980's.

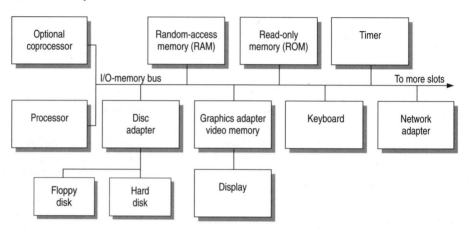

Figure 2.1 Block diagram of the original IBM personal computer

Actually, Windows NT will not execute on one of the original PCs, because those PCs used a processor that's just too puny—a 16-bit processor, instead of a 32-bit processor. A more modern system, based on the Intel® 486 chip, is shown in Figures 2.2 and 2.3.

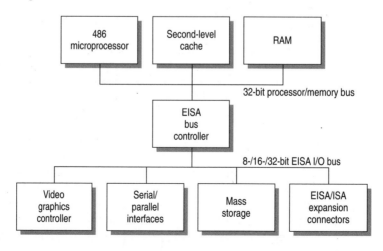

Figure 2.2 Block diagram of a current Intel 486-based computer

Just as some perfectly competent auto drivers don't know how spark plugs work, some perfectly competent computer users might not know how programs execute on the architectures represented by the illustrations in this section. Programs are composed of instructions that reside initially on the disk drive or across the network on some other computer's disk drive. The processor executes these instructions and follows their logic. It is typical for Intel 486 processors to take about 2.75 processor cycles per instruction, on average. The processor is running at a cycle rate determined by the system clock. Typical cycle rates today vary from 25 MHz to 66 MHz, (megahertz, or millions of cycles per second). A 33-MHz 486 executing at a rate of, say, 2.75 cycles per instruction will observe an instruction rate of approximately

$$\frac{(33,000,000 \ cycles/sec)}{(2.75 \ cycles/instruction)}$$

or 12,000,000 instructions per second.

In RISC architectures, the design goal is to execute one or two instructions in every clock cycle. The price for this speed is a simpler instruction set, and hence a compiler needs to generate about 20% more instructions to do a given job. Achieving this design goal is also heavily dependent on the effectiveness of the cache hierarchy, and RISC systems tend to benefit from large caches. Because caches are cheaper than processor chips, this is a reasonable approach.

When told to execute a program, Windows NT must bring the program into RAM. Windows NT does this in *pages* so the whole program does not have to be in memory at one time. This is called *demand paging*. Why use paging at all? To efficiently use a scarce resource—RAM.

Control is transferred to the instructions in the program. Instructions are brought from RAM into the processor and tell the processor what to do next. The program can ask Windows NT to read file data from or write file data to the disks or the network. This causes the data to pass from RAM to the adapter, which takes care of transferring data to or from the media. On completion of the operation, the adapter interrupts the processor.

The program can ask Windows NT to draw text or graphical images on the display using the graphics adapter. In this case, the bits flow from RAM memory to the video memory on the graphics adapter, or else the image is drawn directly into video memory. Whatever is in video memory is automatically displayed on the monitor by the graphics adapter hardware. The program can also ask Windows NT to notify it when you press a key on the keyboard or move the mouse, which can also be attached to the I/O-memory bus.

You may have guessed by now that all this movement of data is on the I/O-memory bus. This is not a wheeled vehicle inside your machine that ferries data around, but there is absolutely nothing wrong with thinking of it as one. The bus is really a collection of printed circuit board traces along which electrons scream at about half the speed of light. Unfortunately, the circuitry controlling the bus access and routing slows things down quite a bit. In the design in Figure 2.1, the processor and the I/O-memory bus run at the same rate: 8 MHz. One big difference between Figures 2.1 and 2.2 is the partitioning of the system hardware into two separate buses, so slower I/O traffic does not interfere with the high-speed processor memory traffic of today's systems. These buses are fast enough that they are seldom a computer system bottleneck. There are exceptions, however, and we'll mention a few later on.

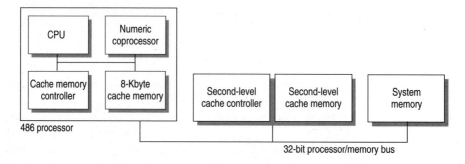

Figure 2.3 Memory bus organization of a current Intel 486-based computer

The two memory caches detailed in Figure 2.3 help form a memory hierarchy, which speeds system operation considerably while also reducing bus traffic. The cache built into the 486 processor is 8K and holds recently used code and data. This exploits a well-known property of programs—a program uses many of the memory bytes that it has used in the recent past. This is called *locality*. By keeping these bytes near the processor in high-speed (expensive) memory, access to them is much more rapid. Usually it takes one processor cycle to fetch something from the first-level cache. The second-level cache is larger, slightly cheaper memory that is not in the processor chip itself. The second-level cache can usually be accessed in two processor cycles. It is not unusual for a main memory access to take around 10 processor cycles, so you can see the caches provide a huge performance win when the data is present there. The presence of the cache hierarchy in the 486 is the main reason for its large performance improvements over the 386. Now that it is commonplace in the industry, it will be a while before we again see such a large leap in processor performance from one generation to the next.

The block diagram in Figure 2.4 shows a Reduced Instruction Set Computing (RISC) system. One important difference between the designs shown in Figures 2.3 and 2.4 is the inclusion of video memory on the high speed memory bus instead of on the much slower I/O bus. This is a great benefit to graphics performance, typically improving graphical performance by a factor of between 5 and 10. This design is beginning to appear in 486-based systems as well as RISC systems.

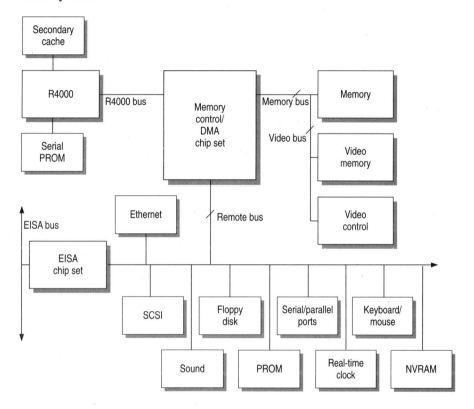

Figure 2.4 Block diagram of a RISC-based personal computer

The main difference between Figure 2.5 and its predecessors is the addition of multiple processors. This permits multiple programs (or parts of programs, called *threads*) to execute simultaneously. Because they are all using the same memory, cache design is very important to reduce memory traffic and the potential for memory to be a bottleneck in such systems. The common memory usually will limit the amount of useful concurrency (ability of the multiple processors to work together) such a design will yield in practice, and the limits are very application-dependent. Although it may be difficult to predict the common memory-imposed limit, you will at least be able to determine how effective adding a new processor is once you've done it, so don't stop reading yet.

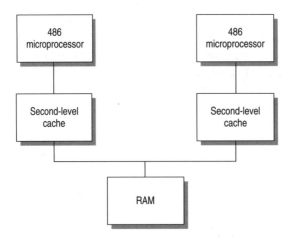

Figure 2.5 Block diagram of a multiprocessor computer

Bottleneck Defined

Think of an *interaction* as a unit of work on the system. This could be a user interaction with an application, a reading of a file from a network server, or a sending of e-mail across the network. It is best if you define this action yourself, because you know what your computer is being used to accomplish. (Well, maybe you don't. But we certainly don't know.) If we know just a few things about this interaction, there are a lot of things we can say about the performance limitations of the system.

The first thing we want to know is the total time the interaction uses on each unit of hardware on the computer. Call this the *demand* for the device, and measure it in seconds.

If *demand(processor)* is the processor time used by the interaction, and *demand(disk)* is the disk time used by the interaction, we can invent a natural law called the Consistency Law that states:

$$\frac{util(processor)}{util(disk)} = \frac{demand(processor)}{demand(disk)}$$

where *util(device)* is the utilization of the device (either the disk or the processor in this case). *Util(device)* is a number from 0 to 1 which is generally expressed as a percentage from 0 to 100%. This tells us that the devices will be busy in relation to the demand for them. A consequence of this law is that a device may not necessarily be at maximum utilization in order for a system to be achieving maximum *throughput*, defined as interactions per second.

If a device can achieve utilization of 1 (for reasons why a device may not be able to achieve utilization of 1, see the discussion of sequencing in Chapter 7), the maximum throughput for that device is:

$$max\ throughput(device) \quad = \quad \frac{1}{demand(device)}$$

Clearly, the device with the smallest *max throughput* in the system for this interaction will determine the maximum throughput the system can achieve. This device is the bottleneck. Notice that making any other device faster can never yield more throughput; it can only make the faster device have lower utilization. This is why it is so important to discover the bottleneck in a system before signing the purchase order for new hardware!

For example, suppose that an interaction requires .3 seconds of processor time and .5 seconds of disk time, and no other device time. The processor can handle 3.3 interactions per second, while the disk can handle 2 interactions per second. So the overall system can handle only 2 interactions per second, at which point the disk will be *saturated* (utilization = 1). By the Consistency Law, the utilization of the processor at that point is .3/.5 = .6, or 60%. Pretty cool, huh?

This gives rise to a general observation known as the Throughput Law, which says that for all devices, the overall throughput of the system is measured by the following:

$$throughput \quad = \quad \frac{util(device)}{demand(device)}$$

For certain devices, it is useful to define the demand for the device in terms of the number of times the device is used by the interaction, and the average amount of time the device is used on each visit, known in queuing theory as the *service* time of the device:

$$demand(device)\ =\ visits(device) * service(device)$$

Windows NT Performance Monitor is based on these simple yet powerful principles. For each device, it counts and displays such basic elements as the utilization, visits, and service time. Sometimes it displays only some of these values and you can easily compute the others. This is done in those cases when we must leave it to you to define what constitutes an interaction on your system.

But we also use a simple trick. Because we don't know what your interaction is, we define the default interaction on the system as whatever took place during the last second. With this definition of interaction, *demand(device)* expressed as a fraction of a second is the same numerically as *util(device)* expressed as a number from 0 to 1. So if you don't care to define your interaction too precisely, you can use our default definition and get meaningful results..

Soon, you will easily be able to toss these simple formulas around. Your friends will be amazed.

What a Counter Counts

Someone once said that if you can't measure it, you can't manage it. Unfortunately, just being able to measure something does not guarantee that you can manage it. But it's a start.

Fundamental to Performance Monitor is the concept of a *counter*. On hardware devices, counters count visits to the device (in the fancy parlance of the previous section, *visits(device))*. The Physical Disk device has, for example, a count of disk transfers made, expressed as Transfers/sec. The *service(device)* is sometimes also provided, as in Avg. Disk sec/IO in the case of Physical Disks. Often we break down these visits into categories to better indicate the cause of the activity. To continue the example, we provide the counters Disk Reads/sec and Disk Writes/sec so you can gain a better understanding of the cause of disk congestion.

We have a strong bias for expressing counters as rates per second, and timers as the fraction of time that a device is used (expressed as a percentage). The advantage of this approach is that if a counter is observed over a five-minute period and then compared to its value over a 10-second period, the numbers are comparable if they are expressed as a fraction of time or a rate over time.

You'll have to deal with this a lot, so let's take an example to make this concept clear. Suppose we have one counter that is timing disk operation, and another that is counting disk transfers. Table 2.1 shows a simple case with absolute counter values.

Table 2.1   Absolute Counter Values

	10-second interval	5-minute interval
Disk time	8.654 seconds	225.621 seconds
Disk transfers	258 transfers	9024.8 transfers

Looking at these two sets of data, it is actually a bit difficult to see which one has the busier disk. Look at the same situation in Table 2.2, expressed as rates and utilizations:

Table 2.2   Relative Counter Values

	10-second interval	5-minute interval
Disk time	86.54%	75.20%
Disk transfers	25.800 Transfers/sec	30.080 Transfers/sec

Now we can see that over the five minute interval the disk was slightly less busy, yet handled more transfers. How can this be? Either there was less seeking/rotation on each transfer, or fewer bytes per transfer. To determine which, see the Average Disk Bytes/IO counter for this disk. But we won't fuss with that now because the real point here is that Table 2.2 is directly relevant, and Table 2.1 is not. Now you can see why Performance Monitor will display nearly all of its data in the form shown in Table 2.2.

Why You Can't Always Get Easy Answers About Performance

You might want to know what a good value is for Physical Disk: Transfers/sec. We'd love to give a simple answer, but we can't. We don't know anything about your hardware or applications software, and there are many factors that affect the answer.

So now you'll ask about the maximum Physical Disk: Transfers/sec. We don't know that either, for the same reason. Do you know the maximum speed your car can attain? How would you find out? By driving as fast as you could, of course. But where? Up a hill, or down? Around a Formula I race car track, or the Daytona Speedway? All these factors affect the highest speed you can attain with your car.

Similarly, a large set of factors determines the normal operating range for each Performance Monitor counter. You'll have to drive your system through a large number of conditions, or at least those of interest to you, and develop a sense for normal operating ranges for your equipment. You should record these typical values in Performance Monitor log files for future reference. Then, as you make changes in your workload or your hardware, you can refer to your earlier experience as a baseline.

We can help a little if you want to know the maximum values you can attain on various counters. Included on the disk that accompanies this book is a utility called Response Probe. Response Probe lets you place known, pure, predefined loads on your equipment. You can then characterize, in a disciplined way, the *response surface* of your computer—its response to pure loads. You can max out your disk drive, no problem, and in several different ways. By using Response Probe you can establish maximum counter numbers under a variety of known conditions and then use that logged information later when assessing real data.

The only counters that we can say much about immediately are the queue length counters. A little later on we talk about the relationship between queue lengths and utilization. But here we can make a simple statement: the apparent speed of the device is inversely proportional to the length of the waiting line. It's just like at the grocery store or the bank. In general, waiting lines longer than 2 are bad.

How Performance Monitor Sees a Computer

We need to descend from this ethereal realm of generalizations into the realities of performance monitor construction. Software performance monitors are great tools, but they have certain limitations we can't ignore. They measure what they can without disturbing the system under measurement too much. And some elements cannot be measured because the current generation of hardware does not support counters or timers on those elements.

Here's an important example: the processor and the cache/RAM memory hierarchy are busy during the execution of instructions. Because we don't have an inexpensive way to partition the activity among these tightly knit elements, we consider them as a unit when we think of the processor as a device doing work in the system. When we become concerned about memory being a bottleneck in the system, we usually are concerned about its size, not its speed. On single processor systems we just lump memory speed into processor speed, and we won't say much more about it. From now on when we speak of the processor being busy, we will be speaking of the group of hardware devices shown in Figure 2.3.

Note The new Intel Pentium™ processor and other new processors have counters on some of these low-level items. We should see a Performance Monitor extended object for these counters in the near future. (Extended objects are explained in Chapter 13 of this book.) In particular, these new counters should help with finding memory speed bottlenecks in multiprocessor systems.

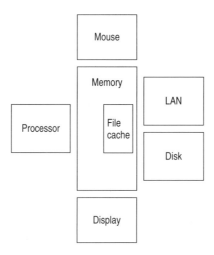

Figure 2.6 Performance Monitor view of personal computer hardware

So, what does happen when memory is too small? Then there is not enough room in memory for all the needed pages of program code and data. The system starts to spend a lot of time moving pages between disk and RAM. Bummer. What you see is loads and loads of disk utilization. By the definition of bottleneck, you might be tempted to rush out and buy a faster disk drive. Bad decision! What you really need is more memory. Although the disk is, strictly speaking, the bottleneck in the system, the reason it is the bottleneck is lack of memory. There is a Windows NT counter (Memory: Pages/sec) that clearly shows this to be the case, and a number of other counters to help you back it up.

Lack of memory is by far the most common cause of serious performance problems in computer systems. If you stop reading here, you can do better than you should just by saying "Memory!" whenever someone complains about performance. But if you have the integrity your parents raised you to have, you'll want to understand enough about how the system works to draw reasonable conclusions about what you observe. Don't worry; by the time we're done, you'll be downright dangerous.

Performance Monitor Overview

We can't really say much about Performance Monitor unless we first give a brief overview of how you can view its data.

You can chart a counter. This will display the counter's values over time. You can chart many counters at one time. A chart of two counters is displayed in Figure 2.7. The horizontal axis is time.

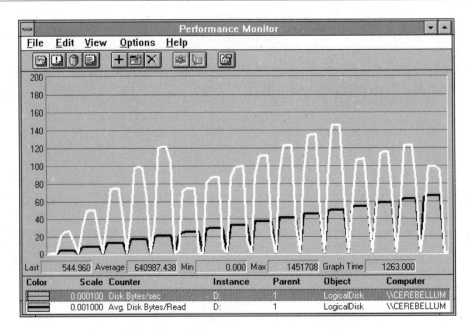

Figure 2.7 Performance Monitor Chart view

You can report on a counter. A report shows the value of the counter. You can create a report of all the counters in Performance Monitor. There are many; you'll have to scroll to see them all. Figure 2.8 shows a report.

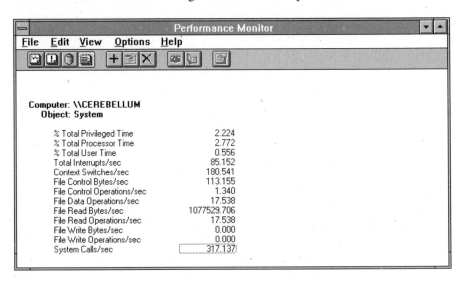

Figure 2.8 Performance Monitor Report view

You can set an alert on a counter. This causes the display of an event when the counter attains a specified value. You can monitor many alerts at one time. Figure 2.9 shows some alerts.

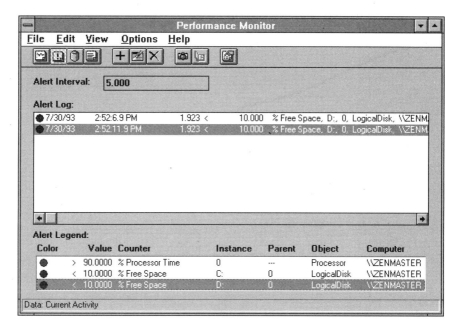

Figure 2.9 Performance Monitor Alert view

You can (best of all) log counters. Logging causes the counters to be recorded on disk for further analysis. You can feed log files back into Performance Monitor to create charts, reports, or alerts from the logged data—and that's just the tip of the iceberg. Figure 2.10 shows some data being logged.

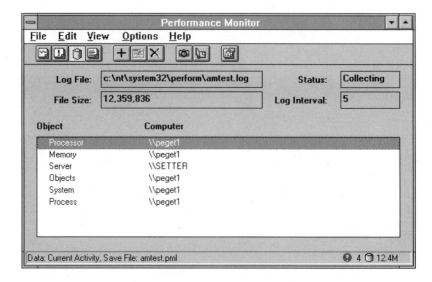

Figure 2.10 Performance Monitor Log view

If this range of formats does not immediately meet your needs, you are a chronic malcontent. In this case you can export Performance Monitor counter data to other products such as spreadsheets and databases for further data reduction and analysis. Figure 2.11 shows an Excel chart of exported performance data.

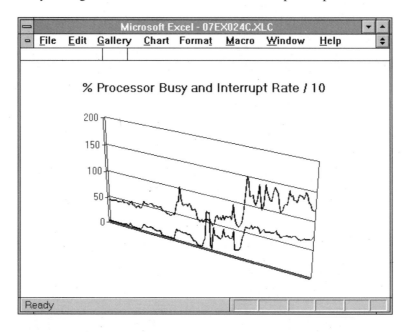

Figure 2.11 Excel chart of exported Performance Monitor data

How Performance Counters Are Structured

If you've played around with Performance Monitor at all, you've noticed it has a few counters. And a few more. And then some. To cope with this flood of data, the counters are organized into a logical hierarchy. This hierarchy is defined by the structure of the (measurable) hardware equipment and (measurable) software elements.

At the top of the hierarchy is the Domain. Each Domain contains computers. For our purposes, each computer has distinct elements called *objects*. There are objects for physical components such as Processors, Physical Disks, and Memory. There are other objects, such as Process and Paging File. Each object has a set of *counters* defined for it. An object's counters record the activity level of the object. We use the following typographical convention to name a counter of a particular object: *object: counter*

Some objects have multiple *instances*. For example, a computer can have multiple physical disk drives. Each such disk drive is an instance of the Physical Disk object. Each such disk drive has a name; in the case of Physical Disks it is its physical unit number. All the instances of a particular object have the same counters defined for them. The % Disk Time counter is the main indicator of how busy a disk is. Each physical disk drive has a counter that measures % Disk Time. We use the following typographical convention to denote a particular counter of an object with instances: *object: counter[instance name]*

This structure is used in the dialog box where you select counters for measurement. This dialog box is shown in the following section.

Selecting Computers

The first step in selecting a counter for measurement is to choose Add To Chart from the Edit menu in Performance Monitor.

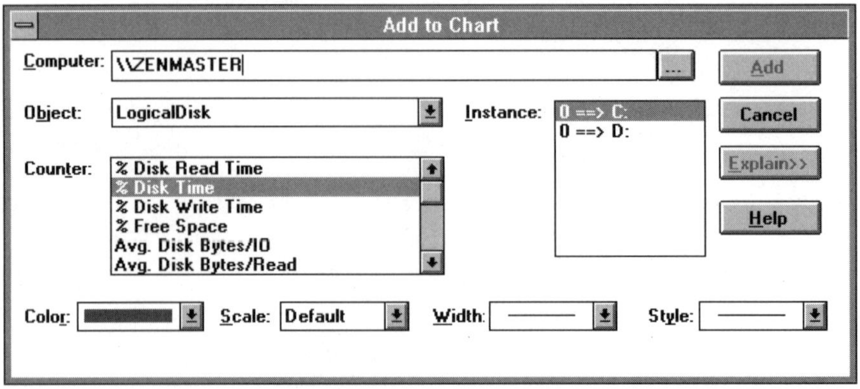

Figure 2.12 Add To Chart dialog box

Each time you select a counter you must provide the name of the computer you want to measure. By default, this is your local computer.

If you don't want to look at an object on your local computer, you can enter the name of another computer. You must have the Access This Computer From Network right on that other computer, or you will be unable to monitor it. To select the computer on which you want to monitor this counter, type its name in the Computer box. If you type in the name of a Windows NT computer, be sure to enter the leading backslashes (\\). These are not supplied automatically by Performance Monitor because they might not be included in the name of foreign (non-Windows NT) computers. (Extensible objects can be created for measuring objects on foreign computers. For more details, see Chapter 13, "Adding Application Performance Counters.")

If you can't remember the name of the Windows NT computer you want to monitor, you can choose the ellipsis button to the right of the Computer box. This brings up the Select Computer dialog box. The computers in your own domain are automatically listed for selection. You can double-click icons representing other domains to see a list of computers in those domains.

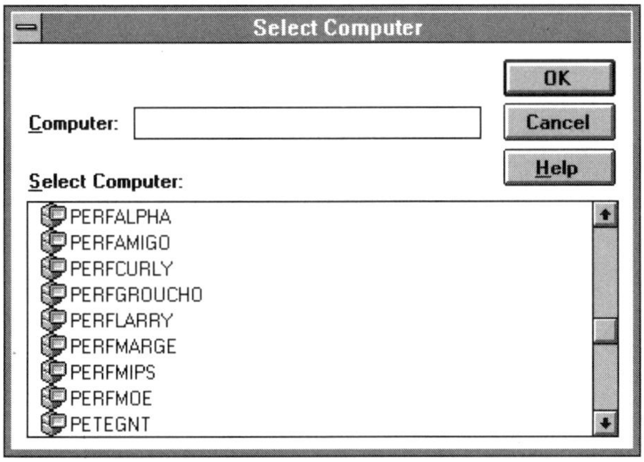

Figure 2.13 Computer Selection dialog box

You can collect data simultaneously from as many computers as you want. You must point at each computer to select the data you want to collect from it. Obviously it can be a lot of work to perform this selection process. You can save your selections in a *settings* file, and reload those settings later. We'll go into that in "Saving Settings," later in this chapter.

Remote measurement does not carry a large overhead. Even better, you can measure that overhead. You should do so to become aware of what you are doing when you collect data from a remote computer. Each time interval, you will be visiting that remote computer and gathering data on the objects that you specified. We call each such visit a snapshot. You can use Performance Monitor to determine the overhead of a snapshot. You can monitor the network protocol objects to determine the number of bytes being transferred across the network, and the processor overhead on each machine. See Figures 2.14 and 2.15 for examples of overhead.

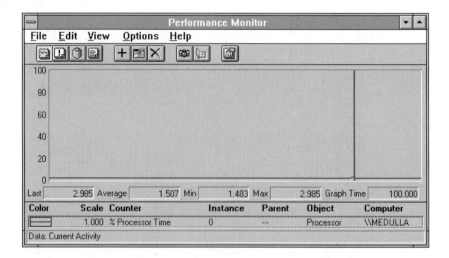

Figure 2.14 Overhead of remote monitoring on the monitored computer

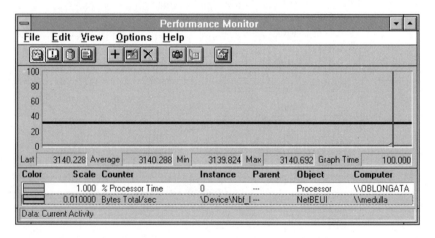

Figure 2.15 Overhead of remote monitoring on the monitoring machine

If a computer is shut down while you are monitoring it, Performance Monitor receives a time-out while attempting to access that computer. Later, it will retry the access. When the computer starts again, Performance Monitor succeeds during the operation. During the initial failure and unsuccessful retries, Performance Monitor stops data collection while it times out.

Measuring Many Computers Without Affecting Performance

When you measure data from many computers, Performance Monitor begins by obtaining data from the first computer you selected. It then goes to each subsequent selection. Even though the data is shown as though it was collected concurrently, this is only approximately true. It's a fine point, but that's why you're reading this, right?

There are no intrinsic limits on the number of computers you can monitor simultaneously, but limited hardware resources can make measuring too many at once impractical. If you find you are clogging your computer or network with measurement data, there are a number of tricks you can employ to reduce your overhead.

First, collect data less frequently by increasing the time interval of your data collection. Overhead is inversely proportional to the time interval, so doubling the time interval will halve the overhead. This relationship between time interval and overhead is a basic design principle of Performance Monitor. You can make an explicit trade-off between the overhead and the resolution of your measurement. Greater resolution (smaller time interval) has greater overhead and thus affects the measured system's performance more.

Next, reduce the number of objects you are monitoring. The Thread object is the most expensive to monitor, because a plain vanilla Windows NT system has over 100 threads. Next in line in amount of data collected is the Process object. Remove objects in a disciplined manner, watching the effect on your network protocol byte counters. This tells you the impact of your changes.

This brings us to Rule #1. Along the way in this book, we have included a lighthearted "10 Rules of Bottleneck Detection." These rules are simple guidelines or reminders about what you should do or watch out for when you hunt bottlenecks on your computer systems. And Rule #1 is: When hunting for a bottleneck, make only one change at a time.

Rule 1.

Make only one change at a time.

If the overhead of graphing counters on your system is too high, consider using alerts instead of charts to monitor a large number of computers simultaneously. The same amount of data is transferred across the network, but the local cost to display is lower as long as the alert thresholds are not triggered too frequently. Again, by measuring your overhead, perhaps with another copy of Performance Monitor, you can determine the effects of your changes.

If you are charting data from many computers, you may find it useful to run more than one copy of Performance Monitor. Each copy could be monitoring a particular type of counter. One could monitor Processor: % Processor Time from each computer, another could measure Memory: Pages/sec, and so on. This permits deviant behavior to be spotted easily.

Selecting Objects

In the Add To dialog box, if you click the arrow to the right of the Objects box you see an alphabetized list of the objects being measured on the computer you selected. You will have to scroll up to see them all, because Processor is the default object and it is fairly far down the list alphabetically. The Processor is the object selected by default, because it is the most commonly selected object. Different computers have different lists, depending on the hardware and software installed. All Windows NT systems always have a core set of objects installed. These are listed in Table 2.3.

Table 2.3   Core Objects in Windows NT Performance Monitor

Object name	Description
Cache	File system cache used to buffer physical device data
Logical Disk	Disk partitions and other logical views of disk space
Memory	Random-access memory used to store code and data
Objects	Certain system software objects
Paging File	File used by system to back up certain virtual memory allocations
Physical Disk	Hardware disk unit (spindle or RAID device)
Process	Software object that represents a running program
Processor	Hardware unit that executes program instructions
Redirector	File system that diverts file requests to network servers
System	Counters that apply to all system hardware and software
Thread	Software object inside a process that uses the processor

You use the Add To dialog box to select an object for measurement (see Figure 2.18).

Performance Monitor automatically displays any *extended objects* successfully installed on your computer. These are objects added after Windows NT was shipped to you. Extended objects for Performance Monitor are typically installed automatically when the object manager software for the object is installed. The ability to add new objects to Performance Monitor is one of its most powerful features. In Chapter 13 we explain how to create extended objects for your own applications.

If you are in the Log view you can select multiple objects for measurement (Figure 2.16). In the other views you can only select one object at a time. This determines the contents of the Counter and Instance boxes so you can complete your selection.

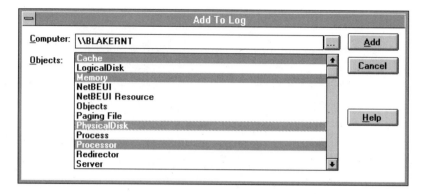

Figure 2.16 Selecting multiple objects for logging

Selecting Counters

If you are in the Chart, Report, or Alert view, you next designate a counter to measure by choosing its name in the Counter box. For each object, what we consider to be the most important counter is the default selection. The counters are listed in alphabetical order.

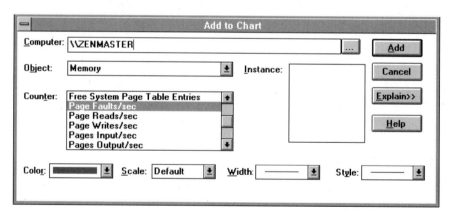

Figure 2.17 Selecting a counter for measurement

If the name of a counter is longer than the box can accommodate, a horizontal scroll bar appears so you can view the entire name. Once you have clicked anywhere in the Counter box, you can press the first letter of the counter name to move to its name more rapidly. Repeatedly pressing a letter scrolls sequentially through multiple counters that begin with that letter.

You can select more than one counter at one time. Hold down the CTRL key and click the counter names to select noncontiguous counters. Then use the Add button to add them to your view.

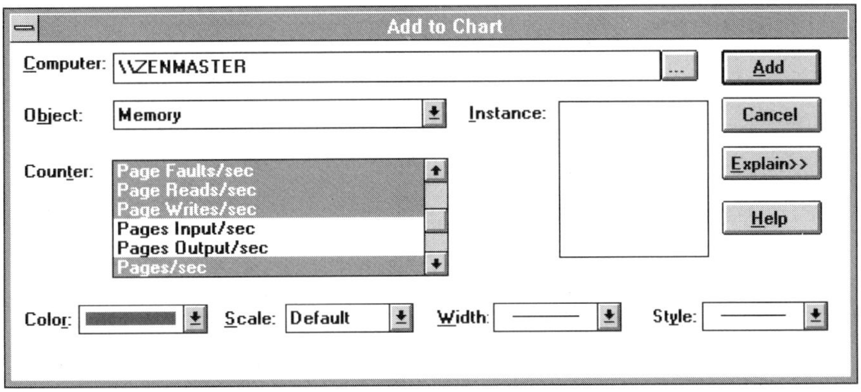

Figure 2.18 Selecting multiple counters for measurement

We have said just a bit about selecting multiple counters. How certain options apply to multiple counter selections is "intuitive," which is a programmer's word for "not obvious, but easy to understand once you know it." We'll cover these details as we explore the various views later on.

How do you know which counters to measure? Good question!

We'll go into detail about the counters in the next few chapters. Each counter tells a story about the system's operation on your hardware. Once we understand that story, selecting a counter is pretty easy.

Selecting the default counter for any given object is often an excellent idea. We made each of these counters the default because it tells the most about the object's activity.

Click the Explain button whenever you are looking at a new counter. This explains the nature of the counter and its role in monitoring system activity. After you click the Explain button once, you see the Explain text for every counter you select until you close the dialog box. See Figure 2.19.

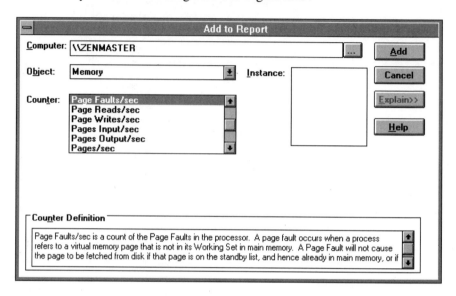

Figure 2.19 Using the Explain text

Appendix A contains a list of the objects, their counters, and their Explain text. When all you want to do is peruse the names and Explain text of counters in the system, you may find the appendix easier to use than scrolling through the counters on-screen.

Sometimes it is desirable to select all counters for an object. It makes sense to do this in the Report view. Looking at all the counters at one time in the Report view can illustrate how the counters vary during an operation. To select all counters for an object, drag all their names with the mouse, or press HOME and then SHIFT+END.

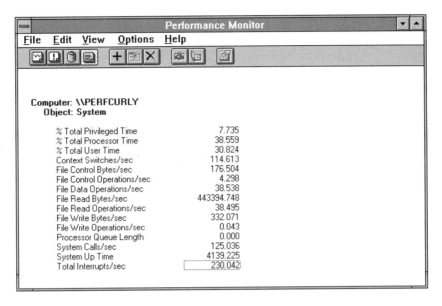

Figure 2.20 Viewing all the counters for an object at one time

Selecting Instances

If you selected an object with instances, you're not done selecting yet. Many objects do have instances, which are individual occurrences of the object type. For example, if you have more than one disk partition on your system, you will have one instance of the Logical Disk object for each partition. Similarly, each running program is represented by a Process instance.

Every instance has the same counters defined for it, but each instance has its own private copy of those counters so you can observe their behavior individually. In a few cases there are summary counters in another object giving a sum of the collected instances' counters. One example is the System: % Processor Time which is an average of the Processor: % Processor Time for all processor instances on a multiprocessor system.

Some instances have a *parent instance* that helps to identify them. The Logical Disk instance has as its parent instance the Physical Disk on which it resides. Each Process object has one or more threads of execution. Each Thread instance has as its parent the Process instance that contains it. Instances with parents are denoted in the list box by the following notation: *parent instance ==> child instance.*

In the Instance box in the Add To dialog box, the default instance is the one that is alphabetically first, because we just can't guess which one you care most about. You often may want to select a different instance, or multiple instances, to examine. Do this just as you did for multiple counters, by holding down the SHIFT or CTRL keys and clicking the contiguous or noncontiguous instances you want to select. Once you have clicked anywhere in the Instance box, you can press the first letter of the name of the instance you want to select to move there more rapidly.

If the name of the instance is larger than the Instance box can display, a horizontal scroll bar appears so you can view the entire name.

Instances are usually identified by name or, if there is a parent, by the parent==>child name. This makes it impossible to successfully select more than one instance of an object if there is more than one instance with the same name. Suppose you have a program named SPLENDID.EXE. If you run two copies of SPLENDID.EXE and attempt to select them both, Performance Monitor will get confused about which one you mean. If you run into this relatively rare situation, you will have to make a copy of the program and give it a different name; say, EXCELLENT.EXE. Then you will have no difficulty distinguishing between them, and neither will Performance Monitor.

Some instances are called *mortal instances* because they are born and then die during system operation. Typical examples are processes and threads. A mortal instance must be alive in order for it to appear in a menu and be selected. If you want to measure your program, you must first start it up. How, then can you measure startup behavior of a mortal instance? Well, once you have selected your living mortal instance, it remains selected even if it dies. When dead, all counter values go to zero. On each snapshot, Performance Monitor continues to look for that instance. If you start another application with the same name, Performance Monitor automatically begins measuring it on the first snapshot in which it appears. There are cases when you may need to log the data in order to capture all the instances you need to see. When an object is logged, all the instances of that object occurring in any snapshot are logged. You can then explore the log file to find the instances of interest.

There are some special considerations for charting and reporting multiple instances. We'll discuss them as we explore the views in more detail later in this chapter.

Custom Displays

Read this section if you want to astound your coworkers with your Performance Monitor expertise. Figure 2.21 shows Performance Monitor in Report view with its several display options marked.

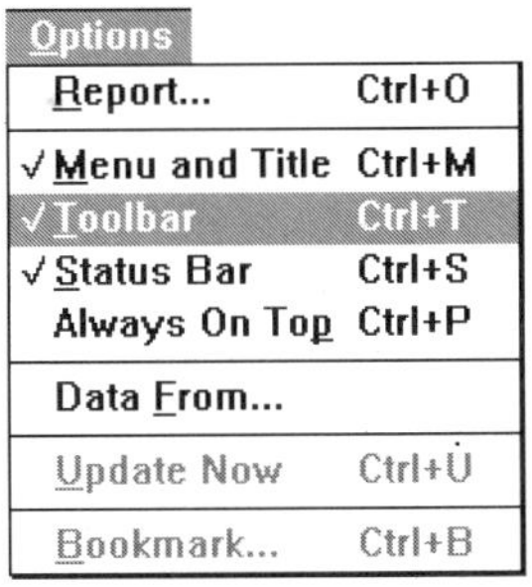

Options	
Report...	Ctrl+O
√ Menu and Title	Ctrl+M
√ Toolbar	Ctrl+T
√ Status Bar	Ctrl+S
Always On Top	Ctrl+P
Data From...	
Update Now	Ctrl+U
Bookmark...	Ctrl+B

Figure 2.21 Performance Monitor display options

Performance Monitor has a flexible display format you can customize to suit your needs. These options are available in all views. The options permit you to reduce the size of Performance Monitor to occupy just a small part of your screen. You can keep an eye on performance activity while you are working on some other task. Many of us place Performance Monitor in our Startup Group so it always starts in a certain spot when we log on to Windows NT. For more details about this option, see "Saving Settings," later in this chapter.

Performance Monitor has a toolbar to speed execution of the most common operations. Table 2.4 is a list of the toolbar icons and their equivalent menu operations. You can remove the toolbar by choosing the Tool Bar command from the Options menu.

Table 2.4   Performance Monitor Toolbar Icons

Icon	Equivalent menu command
	Chart, from the View menu
	Alert, from the View menu
	Log, from the View menu
	Report, from the View menu
	Add To, from the Edit menu
	Edit Chart Line or Edit Alert Entry, from the Edit menu
	Delete, from the Edit menu
	Chart, Alert, Log, or Report, from the Options menu
	Update Now, from the Options menu
	Bookmark, from the Options menu

By default, there is a status bar at the bottom of the window. It displays a brief explanation for each menu selection, including the current settings file you are using and the name of the log file you are playing back, if any. If you are logging data from real-time activity, the current log file size in kilobytes appears here. A count of any alerts triggered since the last time you looked at the Alert view appears here. You can remove the status bar by choosing the Status Bar command from the Options menu.

You can use similar commands from the Options menu to remove the title and menu bars. You can get them back by double-clicking any portion of the dialog box that is not otherwise responsive to the mouse. The various hot keys defined in Performance Monitor menus are still active even if the menu bar is not displayed. This permits ready access to most of the menu functions.

If you have removed the title bar, you can still move Performance Monitor by dragging it. Hold the left mouse button down on the portion of the window that is not otherwise responsive to the mouse and move it.

By removing all these options you can permit Performance Monitor to occupy the minimum real estate on your display. Figure 2.22 shows two Performance Monitors running with a minimal chart and report arranged on the screen for handy viewing.

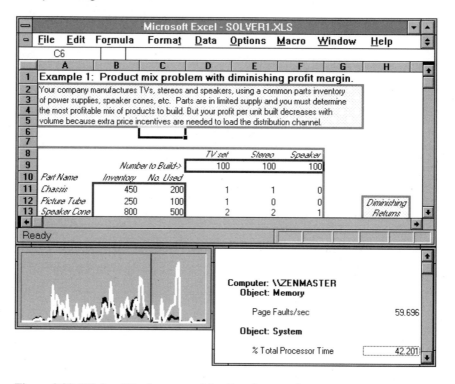

Figure 2.22 Minimal Performance Monitor chart and report arrangement

Always On Top is another Performance Monitor Option. It keeps Performance Monitor visible even if you move to another application. This is useful for watching the performance of full-screen applications. This uses the hot key CTRL+P, so you can click out of this mode quickly when you need to see the whole display.

Now you're an expert!

The Four Performance Monitor Views

We have already introduced the four Performance Monitor views. In this section we discuss the details of each view and what each brings to the party. First we will explore the views as we observe current activity in real time. Then we'll note how things change when the same views are applied to an existing log file.

The four views operate independently and concurrently, but you can only look at one at a time. They each fetch data independently from the target computers, so looking at a counter in all four views is four times the overhead of looking at the same counter in just one view. Luckily, this overhead is designed to be small, so concurrent use of views is not a problem. Although this may seem like a design flaw, in practice the views typically are looking at different computers or counter instances so the practical savings of combining data retrieval are not typically impressive.

To switch between the different views, choose the view you want from the View menu.

We discuss two other features of Performance Monitor in depth at the close of this chapter, but we introduce them here briefly. These are the Settings Files and the Export command, both of which are in the File menu.

When you use Performance Monitor, you choose which counters to look at. You also make decisions about the features of the display, the frequency of counter updates, even the position of Performance Monitor on your screen. All the attributes of your measurements can be saved in settings files and opened later for instant use. In fact, whenever you start to make choices in Performance Monitor, it is building up a record of your selections that you can save at any time. You can save the settings file of any particular view, such as a chart, independently of the settings of your other views. You can also save the settings of all your views at once in a special settings file called a workspace. You will find settings files to be an important time saver when using Performance Monitor, and we discuss using them in some detail in "Saving Settings," later in this chapter.

We like to think Performance Monitor will provide an acceptable interface for viewing data most of the time. But every tool has its limitations. We have therefore included the capability for exporting performance data, as either tab- or comma-separated ASCII files. You can then feed these files into spreadsheet or database programs, as well as editors or custom programs you may want to write. Using these other programs, you can decorate, analyze, and present the data in any way you choose. Export capability helped us keep the Performance Monitor interface relatively simple. We'll discuss exporting in more detail in "Exporting Performance Data," later in this chapter.

Chart View

In some sense, the Chart view is the most interesting view. Seeing the system counters respond in real time as the computer operates is both educational and visually interesting.

To select various options that govern how the chart appears on the screen, choose Chart from the Options menu. This brings up the Chart Options dialog box. One option you can choose here is to select between two basic modes: graph and histogram. Graphs are useful for looking at a counter value over time. Histograms lose the historical perspective but are useful for looking at many counters at one time. First let's take a look at a full-blown graph in all its glory.

Anatomy of a Graph

In Figure 2.23 we show a chart in graph mode. All chart display options are active.

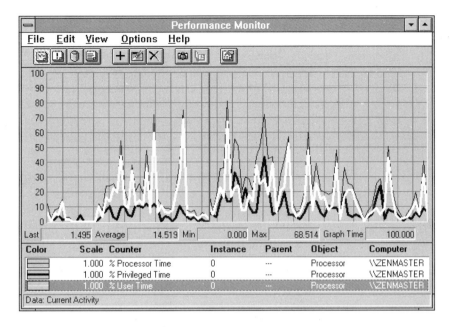

Figure 2.23 All chart display options in graph mode of current activity

A Performance Monitor chart always displays between 0 and 100 data points for each counter shown. This is a key attribute of these charts.

Notice the vertical line in the middle of the chart. This is the Time Line. It is always red and it occupies a space just beyond the last observed value. It moves to the right when the display is updated at the end of each Time Period. It wraps to the left edge of the chart at the end of the Time Period following the 100th data point plotted. This scheme is different from many performance monitors, which scroll the display to the left on each data point. This scrolling is resource-intensive, adding to the monitor overhead. Windows NT Performance Monitor works like a hospital's heart monitor, and causes much less overhead than scrolling.

The vertical scale to the left of the chart is displayed by default. It always starts at zero. If you want to have it start elsewhere, export the data to a spreadsheet for analysis. By always starting at zero, this axis always has a clear meaning. The default upper limit of this axis is 100, but you can change this by selecting Options from the Chart menu, then typing a different number in the Vertical Maximum box. For your vertical maximum, you can use any positive number from a decimal number less than one up to about two billion.

You can add horizontal and vertical gridlines, if you want. You can choose one or the other or both. They add to the cost of updating the display, and so are not activated by default. The horizontal gridlines are sometimes useful, but the vertical gridlines are rarely interesting. To add or remove gridlines, choose Options from the Chart menu, and then check or clear the Vertical Grid and Horizontal Grid boxes.

The legend below the chart is displayed by default, but you can remove it if you want by clearing the Legend box in the Chart Options dialog box. The legend describes each chart line. The legend shows the following pieces of information about the line:

- Color and Width
- Scale Factor
- Counter Name
- Instance Name
- Parent Instance Name
- Object Name
- Computer

When you add a new counter to a chart, that legend item is automatically selected.

Note By pressing BACKSPACE you can highlight the chart line corresponding to the current Legend selection. The selected line becomes a wide white line. If you change your legend selection, the new selection is highlighted. You can change your legend selection by scrolling with the arrow keys. HOME, END, PAGEUP, and PAGEDOWN also work within the Legend window. Pressing BACKSPACE a second time removes the highlight. This is extremely useful if you are charting multiple lines.

For the counter currently selected in the legend (whether or not it is highlighted), the counter's last value, average, maximum, and minimum are shown in the value bar. The value bar is displayed by default.

The counter's average, maximum, and minimum are calculated using only the values currently shown on the chart. When you graph real-time activity, once the Time Line wraps around and starts overwriting previous counter values, these statistics reflect only the last 100 observations. If you need more history than this, you should be logging the data (see "Log View," later in this chapter).

If you add a counter while a chart of real-time data is displayed, the zero values up to the first valid value are not counted in the value bar statistics. If a data value is too large to fit in its value bar window, it is displayed in scientific notation.

You have to have the Legend displayed in order to display the value bar, because the Legend is used to select the line displayed by the value bar.

If you make the Performance Monitor window small enough, the Legend (and hence the value bar) are not displayed. Increasing the size again causes them to reappear. Try it. Pretty cool, eh?

As you know, you can change the time interval at which the chart is updated. To change the time interval, choose Chart from the Options menu, and then type the interval in the Interval box.

Because there are at most 100 data points, you can multiply 100 times the time interval to get the number of seconds displayed on the full chart. This product is shown as the Graph Time in the value bar. Graph Time indicates the time span (in seconds) the chart currently is capable of displaying.

In the Chart Options dialog box, you can select the Manual Update option instead of specifying a time interval. In this case, the chart updates only when you specify taking a snapshot. This is useful for observing counters during a particular event. You take a snapshot of the counters, then cause the event of interest to occur. Then take another snapshot. The counter values you observe apply to the event bracketed by the snapshots. To take a snapshot, choose the Update Now command from the Options menu, or click the camera icon on the toolbar, or use the CTRL+U hot key.

Even when you are charting data at a regular interval, you can also obtain manual snapshots between the regular time interval snapshots. If you have time interval currently set to one minute, for example, you might want to see data sooner if you notice a particular slowdown.

You can clear the current chart data with the Clear Display command from the Edit menu. This leaves your selections in place but starts the chart over again from the left edge. You can clear all your selections and stop charting altogether by choosing the New command from the File menu. This creates a new settings file and clears your old settings.

How Graphs Are Drawn Initially

Here's a fine point for the record. When you add a counter to a chart, you'll notice a slight delay before the chart begins to draw. In order to display the first point on the chart, two data snapshots are required. This is because most of the counters are displayed as a rate or a percentage, as discussed in "What a Counter Counts," earlier in this chapter. To form a rate or a percentage, we need the value of the counter at the start and at the end of a time interval:

$$rate \quad = \quad \frac{counter[end] \; - \; counter[start]}{timer[end] \; - \; timer[start]}$$

What happens is this: you press the Add button and the first snapshot is taken at the end of the first time interval. The second snapshot is taken at the end of the second time interval. Thus the first data point requires two time intervals to elapse before it can be displayed. After the first point displays, the start of the next time interval is the end of the previous one. So a new data point displays when each time interval elapses.

Anatomy of a Histogram

The other primary mode of looking at counters is a vertical bar chart, the histogram. This is very useful for looking at many instances of a given counter at one time. Take a look at Figure 2.24.

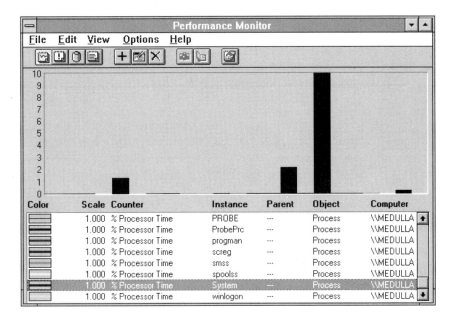

Figure 2.24 Chart histogram mode: a view of many processes' % Processor Time

In Figure 2.24 you see the % Processor Time of many processes. This might be something we would do if we wanted to see how much the various processes on our computer were using the processor. What the histogram mode gives up in history, it makes up for by clarifying the values of many similar counters.

An especially useful feature in histogram mode is the highlighting mentioned in the previous section. By pressing BACKSPACE, you can turn the bar belonging to the currently selected counter to white. Because this color is not otherwise used, it will help you to locate the instance you're interested in.

All the other display options for charts apply to both graph mode and histogram mode. Mercifully, we won't repeat our descriptions of them.

Formatting Chart Lines

When you select a counter to chart, you can also specify how the line or bar representing the counter displays. To do so, use the Color, Scale, Width, and Style boxes at the bottom of the Add To Chart dialog box, which was shown in Figure 2.12.

The Color box specifies the color representing the counter. When you add a counter to the chart, the selection in the Color box automatically advances to the next color. This lets you add several counters at once, and each is assigned a new color.

Tip If you are adding many counters at once, the color selection wraps and thus is reused. Each time the colors wrap, the line width increases automatically. So although there may be two red counters, the second one is thicker. This creates a potentially annoying side effect: when you select the black color at the end of the Color list box, the width will increment automatically for the next color. To manually choose a counter line's width, use the Width box.

If you have a line that is one pixel wide (the default width), you can assign a line style to distinguish it from other lines.

Our stingy boss won't buy us a color printer, so we have to print all the examples in this book in black and white. I'm sure your boss is more magnanimous, but in the off chance that is not the case, you can use line style and width to great advantage in preparing a chart for printing. You will notice us doing so throughout this text.

Line width and style are ignored in histogram mode. If you have multiple red counters, you will want to use the BACKSPACE highlighting feature mentioned above to distinguish between them.

We've saved the best for last: the scale factor. Performance Monitor multiplies the scale factor times the counter value and the resulting product is charted instead of the original counter value. This applies to both graphs and histograms. The default scale factor for a counter is assigned by the counter's designer. This multiplier is chosen so that typical values plotted lie between 0 and 100 and the counter can be easily viewed on the default vertical axis. For example, Processor: Interrupts/sec is typically a counter in the range from 125 to 1000. By having a default scale of 0.1, this counter usually appears in the visible portion of the chart, from 12.5 to 100. The default scale is only a guess, however, and you may need to adjust a counter's scale to your situation.

The value bar data are not scaled, so you can always find the unscaled value of a counter in the value bar.

The scale factor selected when the Add button is pressed is applied to all the counters currently selected. So if you are selecting multiple counters, the scale factor is applied to all of them. If the Default scale is chosen, they are all charted with their individual default scale factors.

The scale factor does not change after adding a counter to the chart. Therefore, if you select a value of 0.001 for the scale of some counter, remember to change it to something reasonable for the next counter you select.

The only way to determine the default scale factor for a counter is to chart it. Then you can read the default value from the Legend. This is usually not a problem, but in case it is, you can find the default scale factors for the counters included in Windows NT in Appendix A.

If you select a counter in the legend, you can alter its display properties by choosing the Edit Chart Line dialog box from the Edit menu or the toolbar. You can only alter the properties of one counter at a time.

You can delete a chart counter by selecting the line in the legend and then choosing Delete from the Edit menu.

Report View

The report is useful for observing the values of many counters at once. It is helpful in deciding which counters to place on a chart. As an activity progresses, you can see how the many values change and which ones are key to the activity you are observing. Figure 2.25 shows a report with counters from multiple computers.

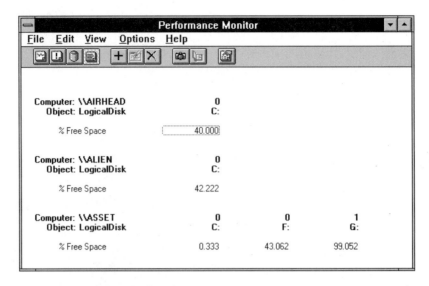

Figure 2.25 Report with counters from multiple computers

You can select multiple counters and multiple instances for a report just as you can for a chart. But unlike charts, there are no special display features for reports. In particular, there is no scale factor because you can always observe the entire counter value.

As you add objects and counters, they are added to the bottom of the report. Very soon they will extend beyond the windows, and you will get a vertical scroll bar which you will have to use to see them. Instances are added to the right, with their names (and, if present, their parent's names) above them. When they will no longer all fit in the window, you get a horizontal scroll bar. If you want to see many instances at one time, you might have to start multiple copies of Performance Monitor and watch several instances in each. At about this point you should consider using logging, or exporting of the report data, but you'll be sacrificing the real-time view. Tradeoffs!

The only option in Report view is for the time interval. The default time interval is five seconds. This gives you time to read several values before they change. You can set this to any value you want, and as with the chart, you can choose Manual Update mode. As always, there is more overhead if you update more often.

You may notice a delay before the first counter values appear. In the meantime, you will see minus signs, indicating that data is missing. As with the chart, a report needs the snapshot of the counters at the end of two time intervals before you see any data. By default, it is 10 seconds before you see values. If you get impatient, take a couple of snapshots with the camera icon on the toolbar to get some preliminary data.

All the counters for a particular computer are grouped together. Objects reported for that computer are listed in the order you select them. Counters for each object are listed from top to bottom in the order you select them. If you select multiple counters of an object and then choose Add, they are listed in alphabetical order. Instances for each object are listed in the order in which you select them for measurement. Likewise, if you select multiple instances of an object and then choose Add, they are added in alphabetical order.

By heeding these properties, you can arrange reports to your liking. If this lacks the flexibility you need, you should choose the Export command from the File menu for manipulation by a spreadsheet or database report writer (for details, see "Exporting Performance Data," later in this chapter).

You can delete a report counter by selecting it with the mouse and choosing Delete from the Edit menu, or by using the appropriate toolbar icon. To prevent accidental deletion, there is no hot key. If you delete all the counters for an instance, the instance is deleted. If you delete all the counters for an object, the object will be deleted. But there is no way to select multiple counters to delete.

You can clear the current report data by choosing Clear Display from the Edit menu. This leaves your selections in place but starts the report over again from the left edge. You can clear all your selections and stop reporting altogether by choosing the New command from the File menu. This creates a new settings file and clears your old settings.

Alert View

The Alert view helps you keep an eye on many counters with minimal overhead. This view is particularly useful for watching a large number of computers on a network.

You add counters in the Alert view much as you would to a chart or a report. But the Alert view has a few unique attributes.

For each counter for which you want an alert, you must supply a threshold value. For most counters, you want to be alerted if the counter becomes greater than some value. For a few, you want to be alerted if the value falls below a certain value. These are counters like Logical Disk: % Free Space, or Memory: Available Bytes.

In Alert view, the alerts you have created are shown in the legend at the bottom of the display. You can select an alert counter from the legend and change its properties.

When an alert is triggered, it displays a line in the alert log explaining the condition that caused the alert. The latest alert is at the bottom of the alert log, which can contain up to 1000 entries. After 1000 entries are logged, earlier entries are discarded as new entries are added.

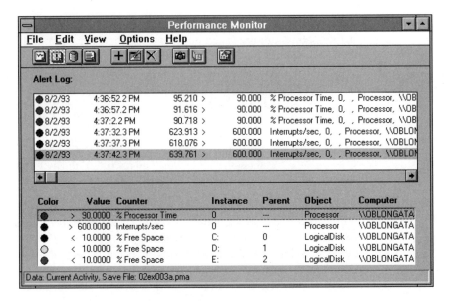

Figure 2.26 Some common alerts and their alert logs

You can designate a program to be run either the first time or every time each different alert is triggered. This program receives the alert log entry on its command line, and the alert log entry appears in a Unicode™ space-separated format. What you have your program do at this point is quite open. It might log the data to some special database, activate a program on a remote computer, or even start another copy of Performance Monitor to monitor the condition more closely. For more information, see "The GUI Batch Processor," later in this chapter.

The alert condition applies to the value of the counter over the time interval you specify. The default time interval is five seconds. If you set an alert on Memory: Pages/sec > 50 using the default time interval, the average paging rate for a 5-second period has to exceed 50 per second before the alert is triggered.

If you select Manual Update mode instead of having data collected at intervals, the alert is checked only when you take a snapshot of the data. The interval in this case is the time since the last manual snapshot. As with the other views, you can take a manual snapshot between time interval snapshots to see if any alert conditions have been triggered.

When you monitor a remote computer, the performance data traverses the network each time interval, and the alerts are checked on the local computer. It would have been more efficient to have a remote agent checking the alerts, and only sending the data if an alert condition occurs. This is a significantly more complicated design and was beyond the scope of the initial release of Windows NT Performance Monitor. Everything can be improved, even Performance Monitor!

You should use another copy of Performance Monitor to determine the overhead of your alert setup, and then increase your time interval until the overhead is acceptable.

You can configure your alerts to send a network message which will appear as a pop-up window at a chosen location on the network. The destination can be the name of a computer or the name of a user. If you choose the name of a user, the alert appears on the first Windows NT computer that user has logged on to, because the name must be unique in the network. Perhaps more practical is the use of an arbitrary name. Suppose you choose the name "PerfAlert." When you have chosen the computer that should receive the alerts, you can enter the following command on that system to receive the pop-up windows there:

net name perfalert

Caution Generating a large number of remote pop-ups is irritating to the recipient, who must close each one manually. Furthermore, the alert log is a fairly processor-intensive display to update because of the fancy spacing of the elements on each line. You should select your alerts so that pop-up windows do not flood the alerted computer, and so the alert log is not being updated rapidly, or you will be surprised at the processor overhead of using the alert feature. Because alert values are chosen precisely because they are urgent bottleneck indicators, this is not a real problem in practice, but is still worth noting.

You can choose the color assigned to an alert. When an alert is triggered and you are in another view, you can observe the colored alert icon in the status bar. The count of alerts since the last visit to the Alert view is also shown, along with the colored icon of the most recent alert. As you add alert conditions, the color advances automatically as an aid in distinguishing multiple alert conditions.

If you select multiple counters simultaneously, they must be similar in meaning because the same alert condition will be applied to each of them. (To set alerts on multiple counters with different thresholds, set the alerts one at a time.) It is, however, reasonable to add multiple instances at one time. Setting an alert on all Logical Disk: Disk Queue Lengths at one time is a reasonable operation, because the threshold could meaningfully apply to all instances. See Figure 2.27.

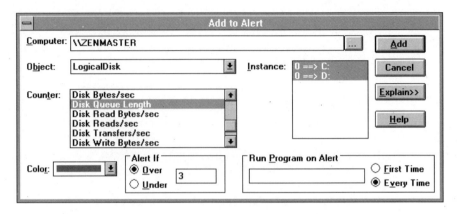

Figure 2.27 Setting an alert on multiple instances

You can clear the current alert data by choosing the Clear Display command from the Edit menu. This leaves your selections in place but starts the alert log over again from the top. You can clear all your selections and stop alerting altogether by choosing the New command from the File menu. This creates a new settings file.

Log View

When you really get serious about looking for bottlenecks, or doing anything about capacity planning, or even looking closely at an application's performance, you're going to be logging the data, possibly in addition to using the other views. The log permits you to peruse the data at your leisure, rather than perform a complete analysis before the data disappears from the screen in real time.

Figures 2.28 and 2.29 diagram how logging works. You ask Performance Monitor to place data in a log file. When it is done writing data to the log, you can read that log file back into Performance Monitor. Now you can chart, report, alert, and even relog any portion of that log file. You can also export those views of the log file data for further reporting.

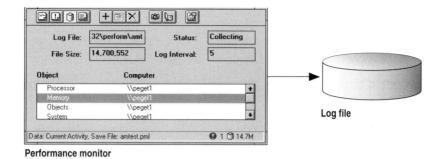

Performance monitor

Figure 2.28 Creating a log file

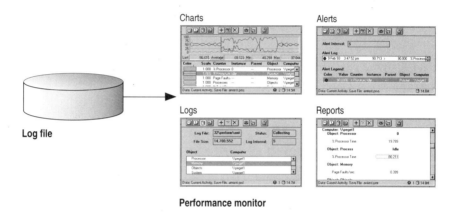

Performance monitor

Figure 2.29 Analyzing data from a log file

To create a log file, switch to the Log view, and then choose the Add To Log command from the Edit menu to select objects to log.

In the Add To Log dialog box, you can log data from many computers into a single log file. This lets you see how the computers' activities correspond. All you have to do is enter the name of the computer you want to monitor. Choosing the ellipsis button brings up a Select Computer dialog box to aid in browsing the network for likely suspects. We discussed this earlier, as you may remember.

You can select one or more objects to log. Use the SHIFT and CTRL keys as you did for selecting multiple counters or instances. All the counters for all the instances of each selected object are logged. This means that you cannot log individual counters or individual instances. Trust us, this is okay.

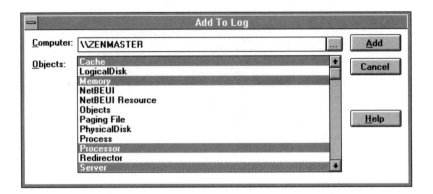

Figure 2.30 Add To Log dialog box

Once you have selected the computers and their objects to log, you can choose the Log command from the Options menu. This brings up the Log Options dialog box, which you can use to specify the name of the log file. This can be on a local computer or across the network. You can use the Network button to connect to a remote computer for logging to a remote file.

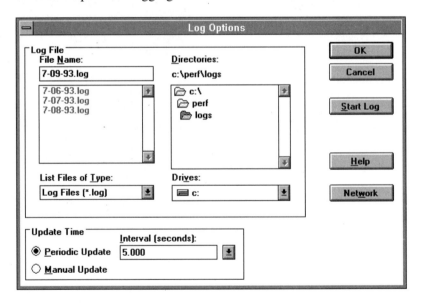

Figure 2.31 Log Options dialog box

If you specify the name of an existing log file, the new data is appended to the end of the log file. This is a powerful feature which permits the creation of long-term archives. We'll say more about this in Chapter 8, "Capacity Planning."

You can use the Log Options dialog box to change the time interval, which has a default of 15 seconds. You can also switch to Manual Update mode, but in this case nothing is logged unless you choose the Update Now command from the Options menu, or use the camera icon.

You must remember to press the Start Log button to start logging. If everything is set up right, the Log view then displays Status: Collecting. Otherwise, if you just press OK, you return to the Log view, but the Status displays Closed. If the status is closed, doing one or more of the following starts the logging process:

- Select at least one object to log

- Provide a log file name

- Choose the Start Log button

If your Start Log button is dimmed, go back and pick at least one object to log. Once you do that, Start Log becomes active.

To stop logging, choose the Stop Log button in the Log Options dialog box.

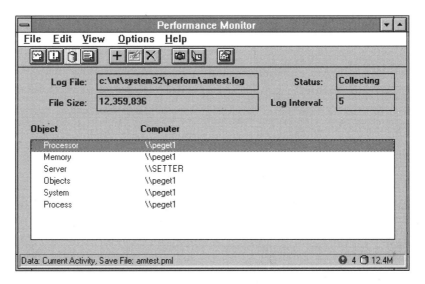

Figure 2.32 Log view during data collection

The Log view shows the name of the log file and the log status. Although it looks like an inactive window, you can click in the Log File box and use the HOME, END, and arrow keys to scroll through the log file name, if it is too long to see at once in the box. The Log view also shows the file size in bytes and the time interval in seconds.

You can change the time interval during logging without stopping the log file. So if you need to bump up the resolution, just do it! But remember, you are using more disk space, so lower it when you are done.

Because the log file size is displayed in the Log view, you can quickly determine how much data you are collecting on each snapshot. From the Options menu, choose Log and then choose Manual Update. Return to Log view by choosing the OK button. Click the camera a couple of times to take a couple of snapshots. Record the file size. Click the camera again. Record the file size. The difference is the amount of data collected in each snapshot. Now try it again to see if you get the same answer. If its different, the reason is that Performance Monitor occasionally writes out an index record which you may not want to include in the size of every snapshot. This certainly occurs on the very first snapshot in the file, which is why we had you start with a couple of initial snapshots. (Counter names are also written with the initial snapshot.) These index records are infrequent; one is written every 100 snapshots.

Other information, in particular counter names, also appears at the start of the log file, and some new ones may appear when you add new systems to the log. We mention these details just for completeness.

By adding and deleting objects, you can determine the byte cost of each. Fun and games!

When you are logging data, you can use the Bookmark command from the Options menu command and its equivalent icon from the toolbar. These allow you to insert a comment into the Log File. Such comments can be used later as indexes to different points in the file. They help you to locate the start or end of interesting events you have logged. Use them freely, they are cheap. They automatically include the date and time, so don't bother to type those into your comment. If you append data to a log file by supplying the name of a pre-existing log file when you start logging, an automatic bookmark is placed at the start of the new data. It reads, "New set of Log data."

The current log file size appears on the status bar if you are collecting data, no matter what view you are in. Keep an eye on this. We're talking disk space here.

You can delete objects from the list of logged objects while you are logging. Select the object in the Log view legend and use the Delete From Log command from the Edit menu, or use the equivalent toolbar icon. After you do so, there will be no more data on that object until you add it back in. It is not terribly likely that you will need to delete an object, but you can.

Loading and Viewing Log Files

It's sort of boring to log data, but it's very exciting to play it back. To play back a log file, choose Data From in the Options menu, then choose Log File and type the log file name or choose the ellipsis button to access the Open Log File dialog box.

Note If you are monitoring current activity, switching to playing back a log file causes the monitoring of current activity to stop. So if you have spent time setting up your current measurements, be sure to save your workspace (as explained in "Saving Settings," later in this chapter) before viewing the log file. Or start another copy of Performance Monitor to view the log file. Then you can watch the cost of viewing log files. (Is there no end to this? Don't worry, it's job security.)

Viewing data from a log file is very similar to viewing current activity. You can create charts, alerts, reports, and even new log files. But because the data already exists, you don't have to wait for it to materialize, and this changes the views in subtle but important ways.

Graphing of Logged Data

You select objects, counters, and instances for charts of logged data just as you do when charting current activity. But the display of time on the chart is different.

First consider charting in the graph mode. (We talk about histogram mode in "Histograms of Logged Data," later in this chapter.) There is no vertical time line in charts of logged data. Instead, Performance Monitor attempts to graph 100 points, which fills the chart window. If there are fewer than 100 data snapshots in the log file, you will see every point graphed, and the graph will not reach the right hand edge of the window. If you look at the Chart Options dialog box, you will see that the Update Time group is unavailable because it is not relevant when playing back a log.

Log files are self-contained. You can take them to any Windows NT machine for viewing. However, there is no Explain text in the log file, a decision we made to conserve log file space. To see counter explanations you have to use Performance Monitor on Current Activity (or see Appendix A of this book).

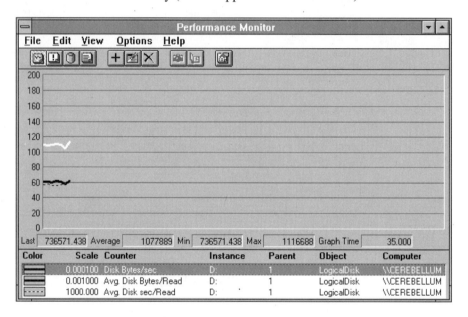

Figure 2.33 Chart of a log file with fewer than 100 snapshots

If there are more than 100 snapshots in the log file, the graph fills the window. Suppose you have a log file with 1000 data points; every tenth point will appear on the graph. If you need to see every point, you can look at portions of the log file by choosing the Time Window command from the Edit menu, or you can export the chart. (For more information on exporting, see "Exporting Performance Data," later in this chapter.)

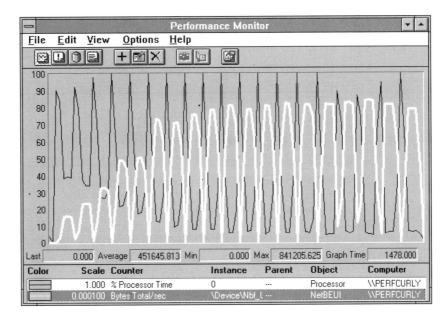

Figure 2.34 Chart of logged data with more than 100 snapshots in the log file

Selecting the Time to View in a Log File

To move around in time in a log file, choose the Time Window command from the Edit menu. This brings up the Input Log File Timeframe dialog box. Use the slider bar in this dialog box to change the time window shown in the chart. You can change the starting time and the ending time of the time window by dragging the start and end panels of the slide bar. You can move the whole time window by dragging the center section of the slide bar. You can also click the portions of the slide control not covered by the current time window to page through the file. The times above the slide bar are the start and end times of all the data in the log file. The times below the slide bar are the current start and end times.

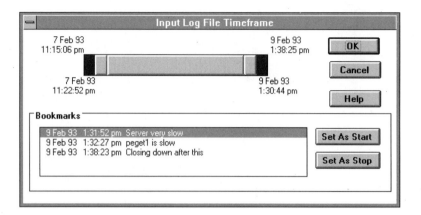

Figure 2.35 Anatomy of the Input Log File Timeframe dialog box

When you move the left end of the time window slide bar, you can see a gray bar move across the chart. It shows the current location of the time window start that will be set if you press OK. Set the end of the time window the same way.

Below the slide bar control is a box displaying any bookmarks you've placed in your log file. You can select a bookmark and assign it to be the start or the end of the current time window. You can't set the end of the time window to be earlier than the start. Magic it's not.

The time window is very important because it determines the start and the stop snapshots for all of the following:

- Charts
- Reports
- Alerts
- Relogged data

This means that changing the time window on the chart is how you manipulate which data is visible in all four views.

Gory Details on Charting Log Data

You'll remember that some instances, like those of the Process or Thread objects, are called mortal instances because they start and stop while the system is running. Anyway, this can be a bit of a problem, because you need to have your time window start while they are alive if you want to see them in the Add To dialog boxes. This is one good reason to insert a bookmark saying "Application started" in your log file. This will help you to set the time window to a period of time when the application is running.

Once you have selected the application instance, you can move the time window freely. Counters will appear to go to zero during those time intervals when the application is not running.

Now we're going to touch on an even more obscure point regarding the display of logged data. As mentioned above, in those cases where there are more than 100 data points in the log file, you are missing some data in the initial chart because some snapshots are skipped over and not displayed.

To be certain of what you are seeing, you will want to mentally separate counters into two types: those which are averages over time, and those which are instantaneous values. Most counters are time averages, such as Server: Bytes Total/sec or Processor: % Processor Time (which is the ratio of time used to the time interval, expressed as a percentage). Counters like these, that are an average over time, continue to be proper averages over time even if some time intervals are skipped. This is equivalent to smoothing the data by computing a simple average. So if you have more than 100 data points, that is, your chart fills its window, you can properly think of the chart as smoothing the data in the log file.

But there are a few counters, such as Memory: Available Bytes, that are not averages, but instantaneous values. We call these instantaneous counters. We try to be careful about noting that a counter is instantaneous in its Explain text. This fact is also noted in Appendix A, where such counters have the counter type Raw Count. An instantaneous counter is not an average over the time interval, but rather the value of the counter at the end of the time interval. Therefore, skipping data points can hide peaks and valleys that might be important.

There are three things you can do about this. Number one is to just forget about it, under the assumption you have enough real problems. Number two is to change the time window you are viewing in the log file to see fewer than 100 data points. Number three is to choose Export from the File menu to export the chart. When you export a chart of logged data, all the data points inside the current time window are exported whether they appear explicitly in the graph or not. More about this in "Exporting Performance Data," later in this chapter.

Histograms of Logged Data

As when viewing current activity, histograms of logged data are useful for looking at the data from many instances. But the height of each bar in the histogram is a function of the time window. If the counter is a time average, the height indicates the average over the current time window. If the counter is an instantaneous value, the bar height indicates the value at the end of the time window.

The value bar numbers pertain to the 100 or fewer data points you see when you switch to graph mode. The histogram itself is based on the snapshots at the start and end of the time windows. If there are more than 100 data points, and the counter is a time average, the histogram displays the correct average, and the value bar displays an estimate based on the 100 data points you see in graph mode. So if these differ, don't panic.

If you need to be picky about these numbers, you might want to export the data and process the values in a spreadsheet. For more fine points on exporting data, see "Exporting Performance Data," later in this chapter.

Reports of Logged Data

Reports of logged data are the numerical form of histograms of logged data. For time-average counters the counter value at the start of the time window is subtracted from the counter value at the end of the time window, and the result is divided by the time span of the time window. This means all of the considerations just mentioned concerning histograms of logged data apply to reports of logged data. Suffice it to say that the reported number is an accurate average, whereas the graphed number and the value bar values can be estimates because of skipped data points.

For the most part you can ignore these issues. Just set the start of the time window on the start of the event of interest, and the end of it at the close of the event. Voilà.

A comment was made in the earlier section "Gory Details on Charting Log Data" about selecting mortal instances. That note applies equally to reports on mortal instances.

Alerts of Logged Data

If you have a lot of logged data, you might want to find the hot spots quickly. You can use alerts on logged data to do this. Usually, you would first chart the data, and set the time window to some period of interest. Then choose Alert from the View menu and set the alert condition you are concerned about. Perhaps this is some indicator of heavy load, such as System: Processor Queue Length > 3. The logged data is scanned and the alert conditions located and placed in the alert log on your screen. You can export the alert log entries for further processing.

Unlike charts and reports, the time interval is relevant here. Suppose you have logged data at a 15-second time interval. You can look for an alert condition at, for example, a one-minute time interval. In this case, the Alert view scans the logged data looking for a snapshot that is at least one minute past the start of the time window. It then computes the time average for the counter over that minute and checks against the condition. Then, using the ending snapshot as the start of the next time interval, it looks for another snapshot that is at least one minute later. This continues to the end of the log file. If you have set an alert on an instantaneous counter, the value at the end of each time interval determines if the condition is met.

Logging Logged Data

Once you have chosen a log file in the Data From dialog box, your data source is that log file. You can then select the Log command from the View menu and relog that data to a new log file.

Why on earth might you want to do such a thing? Actually, there are a number of good reasons for relogging. The first is to create an archive. If you have a file of logged data you really care about, you might want to append it to an archival log for long-term storage. You can do this, as we mentioned, by supplying the name of the archive file as the output log file. This keeps you from having to save lots of individual log files, which can be a nuisance.

You can select a longer time window when you relog. This permits you to condense your data. If you collect data at a one-minute time interval, and relog at a five-minute time interval, you condense your data to use only 20% of the space. For this, your boss should give you a bonus!

When you relog data, you can use the time window to limit the data. This means that you can log a 24-hour period, but archive only that portion of the day that has peak activity. Looks like another bonus!

A log file of relogged data is just like a log file of new data. Such a file can be designated in the Data From dialog box, and can even be relogged itself.

Saving Settings

You've picked your way through all 400-plus counters and innumerable instances, and configured your measurements with great care. Do you want to do it again tomorrow? No way!

This is what the settings files are all about. You can save what you are measuring and how you are measuring it in a settings file by choosing Save or Save As from the File menu. The first time you save your settings, you are prompted to assign a name to your settings file. The name of your settings file appears in the status bar. You use Open from the File menu to install a previously saved settings file. The name of your opened settings file appears in the status bar. You can remove all your current settings by choosing New from the File menu.

Usually, you will save your current view. The following file suffixes are, by convention, used for the settings files, but you can save and open settings files with different extensions.

Table 2.5   Settings File Suffixes

Suffix	Settings-file type
.PMC	Chart
.PMR	Report
.PMA	Alert
.PML	Log
.PMW	Workspace

If you choose Save Workspace from the File menu, the current settings for all four views are saved in the Workspace settings file. Opening this file restores all four views. In addition to the four views, the current screen size and position of Performance Monitor are saved in the Workspace. (Otherwise, Performance Monitor starts up in the position it held when you last quit.)

You can move settings files from one computer to another. However, if the computers have different hardware and software, the settings file might not apply fully on the new machine. For example, if the original machine has one disk partition, and the new one has two, the second disk partition is not in the settings file. If you want it to be, simply add the second partition to the measurement and choose Save from the File menu to save the settings file.

What if you now move the settings file back to the first machine? The second partition will not be found, but it will still appear in the measurement. Because no such object or instance could be found, the counters will all drop to zero just as though it were a deceased mortal instance. The nonexistent object will remain in the measurement and in the settings file even if the settings file is saved again on the first computer. Thus you can build up settings files from multiple computers with ghosts of mortal and even immortal instances, and share them around with your friends. It's like sharing a little bit of heaven. Sort of.

You can specify a settings file on the command line of Performance Monitor by typing:

perfmon *settings-file-name*

Performance Monitor starts up with that settings file loaded. If it's a chart, report, or alert settings file, the appropriate view starts data collection as specified in the settings file. If it's a Log view, however, you will have to supply a log file name and start the logging yourself. We do not want to cause automatic consumption of disk space by accident. If you need to automate this, see "The GUI Batch Processor," later in this chapter.

If you specify a workspace on the command line, Performance Monitor loads the settings for all four views, but only starts data collection on charts, alerts, and reports.

If there is no settings file specified on the command line, Performance Monitor searches its working directory for the file _DEFAULT.PMC. If found, it loads this settings file and it becomes the current view.

Tip Here's a trick you can use: although the .PMC suffix is used, this file could actually be from any view or even a workspace. This is one reason why we do not enforce the suffixes: there are times like this when you want to fake them out.

If you have a settings file that you can see in File Manager, you can drag it to a running copy of Performance Monitor and it will start running. This clears out the current settings file in that view (or in all four views for a workspace), so be sure to save your current settings if necessary.

Here is another neat thing you should try once you have a few settings files created. Start File Manager from Program Manager's Main group, and then select the Associate command from the File menu. Press the New Type button. In the File Type box, type **Performance Monitor Charts**. In the Command box, type **perfmon.exe**. In the New Extension box, type **PMC**, and then press the Add button, and the OK button. Do the same for alerts, reports, logs, and workspaces, using appropriate file types and extensions. Once this is done, you can double-click a settings file in File Manager, and Performance Monitor starts, executing that settings file.

Now some more legerdemain: go back to Program Manager and create a new program group called PerfMagic using the New menu command on the File menu. (It can be either a personal or common program group. If you want other people to be able to use it, it must be a common program group. You must be an administrator on your computer to create a common program group.) Now restore File Manager and Program Manager so that you can see your settings files in File Manager, and your new PerfMagic Group in Program Manager. Now you can drag your settings files to the PerfMagic Group from File Manager. They are Performance Monitor icons and you can double-click them to execute them. Now that's cool!

Exporting Performance Data

Data export is the Performance Monitor general purpose escape hatch. Just about every time we run into a limitation of Performance Monitor, we tell you to export the data and use some other tool to format or analyze it.

This is not necessarily bad. The ability to use software as building blocks was one of the fundamental principles in the construction of the very successful UNIX operating system. We have used that concept here, and it will serve you in good stead. Examining or analyzing the standard deviation of the numerical values of many chart points, printing lots of alert log entries or a large report, and making a list of all the computers being logged in a large network all rely on data export. These are normal activities of performance monitoring, and it is the explicit design of Performance Monitor that you export the data to accomplish these activities. So don't struggle, export!

The Export command on the File menu permits you to create either tab-separated or comma-separated ASCII files for use by other applications. Which you choose depends on which format your other application will best accommodate. If you want to look at the data with a simple text editor, tab-separated (the default) is the easiest to read.

Note It's worth repeating that the export of a chart of a large log file does include every data point in the time window, even though the visible chart displays only 100 data points. If you want to export the data in a log file, you must first chart that data. Once you have set up a complex chart for export, consider saving your settings in a settings file so you can reuse them.

Performance Monitor Limitations

As with any real product, Windows NT Performance Monitor has a few, well, warts. We can explain, justify, and rationalize until we're blue in the face, but this does not make the warts disappear. We might as well talk about them, or you'll get even more annoyed with us. Anyway, we hope you'll forgive us.

Why You Don't See Any Disk Data

The disk utilization on Windows NT is measured by measuring each disk transfer with a high-precision timer. This gives very accurate results, but does have some overhead associated with it. In addition to the calls to the timer routines, measurement of disk activity involves adding an extra disk driver to the I/O system. All this spells overhead. On a 20-MHz 386 this was observed to cost up to 1.5% of the disk throughput. On a 33-MHz 486 there is no measurable impact.

We decided not to burden the system with disk performance measurement unless you really want it. Which, believe me, you do. So right away you should activate disk performance measurement on your computer of interest by executing the following command:

diskperf -y

If you need to look at a remote system named, say, \\cerebellum, try

diskperf -y \\cerebellum

Unfortunately, that's not the end of the cure. You must now shut down Windows NT on the system you are measuring. Next time you start it, you will have operational LogicalDisk and PhysicalDisk counters.

Why the Processor Queue Is Always Empty

We haven't talked about all Processor Queue counters yet, but if we're going to talk about gotchas, we might as well come clean now. The Processor Queue Length is a measure of the number of threads ready and waiting to execute program instructions when there is no free processor. Because there is only one such queue, the counter belongs to the System object (as opposed to each processor object).

You might be watching a uniprocessor system with lots of threads running and be disappointed to see that the Processor Queue Length counter is always zero. The reason is that in Windows NT 3.1, this counter is measured by counting ready threads. This cannot be done unless you also select at least one thread for measurement. Once you include some counter from some thread in your measurement, the count for the Processor Queue Length will be valid. This is mentioned in the Explain text for the Processor Queue Length, but this is a very important counter and a pretty subtle wart, so we thought we'd better tell you.

Ways to Print Performance Data

Can't find a Print command on the File menu? That's because it isn't there! All of the screen shots of Performance Monitor that you see in this book were made by pressing the ALT+PRINT SCREEN key on the keyboard. This places the screen image of the active application in the clipboard. You can then start Paintbrush (it's in the Accessories Group) and chooses Paste from the Edit menu. Then you can save the image as a file or print it directly.

Pressing ALT+PRINT SCREEN places the entire screen's contents into the clipboard for similar processing.

You may not be happy with this clever trick. In that case, you might consider exporting Performance Monitor data using the Export command on the File menu. The resulting file can be printed by your favorite spreadsheet program.

The GUI Batch Processor

You may want to automate use of Performance Monitor beyond what is possible in settings files. If this is the case, we direct your attention to a product known as Microsoft Test, known affectionately around here as MS Test. MS Test records your keystrokes and mouse movements to drive GUI applications like Performance Monitor.

You need to use the 32-bit version of MS Test to drive Performance Monitor, because the latter is a 32-bit application. This is provided in the Windows NT Software Development Kit (SDK).

There is really no limit to what you can do now. You can use MS Test to start and stop Performance Monitor at particular times of the day or week, or to change the time interval of observations as the day progresses. It can start multiple copies of Performance Monitor, setting up measurements for a whole network with ease.

As we promised, you'll be dangerous!

TCP, SNMP, and Thee

There are a number of objects associated with the TCP/IP protocol. The SNMP protocol routines are used to retrieve the statistics for the TCP/IP objects. To see any of them, you must install the SNMP protocol as well as the TCP/IP protocol. Use the Network option in Control Panel to install SNMP.

Crucial Hot Keys

There are a few hot keys that make using Performance Monitor a breeze.

Hot Key	Function
BACKSPACE	Highlight current selection in legend
CTRL+P	Always on top
CTRL+U	Update now
CTRL+E	Bring up time window
TAB	Add To command from the Edit menu

Here is a list of the remaining hot keys.

Hot Key	Function
CTRL+C	Switch to Chart view
CTRL+A	Switch to Alert view
CTRL+L	Switch to Log view
CTRL+R	Switch to Report view
CTRL+O	Bring up Options dialog box
CTRL+W	Save workspace
CTRL+B	Create bookmark
CTRL+M	Display or hide menu and title bars
CTRL+T	Display or hide toolbar
CTRL+S	Display or hide status line
CTRL+F12	Open file
SHIFT+F12	Save file
F12	Save As file
F1	Help

CHAPTER 3

Detecting Processor Bottlenecks

If you've read the first two chapters, you should be an expert on the use of Windows NT Performance Monitor. It's time to go out and slay those bottleneck dragons!

There is never a shortage of dragons—every computer doing any work at all always has a bottleneck. You can see this if you review the definition of bottleneck presented in Chapter 2. The device for which there is the greatest demand is the bottleneck. This is the device with the greatest utilization during an activity's execution.

It isn't hard to see that there is frequently a second bottleneck lurking beneath the first. This is usually the device with the next lower utilization. We say "usually" here because if you remove the first bottleneck, the one to surface could change, depending on how the first one is removed. The important thing to remember is that just removing one bottleneck does not always turn the dragon's lair into a palace. You sometimes have to slay another dragon.

This leads us to our second rule of bottleneck detection.

Rule 2.
One bottleneck may mask another.

Bottlenecks Are Moving Targets

The other thing to keep in mind is that during processing, the bottleneck may shift around from one piece of equipment to another. Each second of operation might yield a different bottleneck if looked at in isolation. If you want to improve the situation as a whole, you'll need to look at the big picture. And even then the situation can be tricky. Let's take a look at a real example to illustrate these points.

The first thing we have to do is run the **diskperf -y** command to enable disk performance counters, as discussed at the end of Chapter 2. (You did read Chapter 2, didn't you?) After running **diskperf**, you'll have to reboot the computer being monitored before the disk performance counters can be activated.

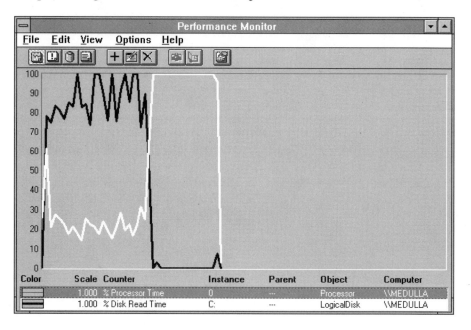

Figure 3.1 Chart of processor and disk usage

In Figure 3.1 we have charted data from a Performance Monitor log file. The black line is the Logical Disk: % Disk Read Time, and the highlighted, white line is the Processor: % Processor Time. Activity is divided into two distinct phases. During the first phase, the disk is clearly the bottleneck, with the processor a somewhat distant second. During the second phase, the processor becomes the bottleneck, with the disk even less in use. The overall data is provided in Figure 3.2.

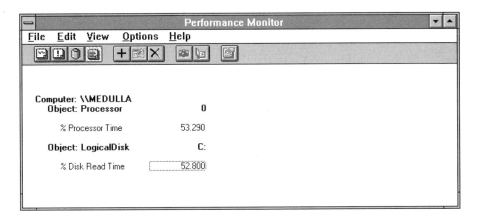

Figure 3.2 Report of processor and disk usage

This disk is utilized at 52.8% and the processor at 53.3%. Because the time
window is 44 seconds, this means we used 23.23 seconds of disk time (this is
demand[disk]) and 23.45 seconds of processor time (*demand[processor]*). In the
formal terms of the last chapter, the maximum throughput at which the disk can
accomplish this task is 1/23.23 * 3600 = 155.0 times per hour, and for the
processor 153.5 times per hour. Technically, the processor is the bottleneck. In
reality, both components are nearly equally to blame.

One way to think of this is to imagine how much faster this task would go if either
component were infinitely fast. In this case, the activity would be accomplished in
half the time if either component were blindingly fast. Is there a bottleneck? Yes,
it is the processor. Could you improve performance by attacking either
component? Yes. But you could only improve the first phase if the disk were
improved, whereas in this case a faster processor would help the second phase a
lot, and the first phase a little bit. Which brings us to Rule #3 of Bottleneck
Detection.

Rule 3.

The bottleneck depends on when you look.

Getting Started: Making an Overview Settings File

Before diving in to understand any performance problem it is always best to take a step back and get the broad picture. When we first see a problem, we tend to try to solve it instantly. A common failing is to dive too deeply, too quickly, and thus miss the real problem altogether. We might backtrack and find it eventually, but we'll waste time. This gives us Rule #4.

Rule 4.

Get the big picture first.

On computers running Windows NT, there are a number of essential objects and counters for those objects you should check out first for any problem. We'll go into detail about these counters later, saying just enough here to provide an overview.

Consider building an OVERVIEW.PMW workspace settings file for each computer. In the following paragraphs we discuss useful counters to include in this file to monitor the computer's basic hardware components. To have Performance Monitor start up automatically using OVERVIEW.PMW whenever anyone logs on at the computer, do the following steps.

1. Create a Startup group in Program Manager, if there isn't already one.

2. With the Startup group selected, choose New from the File menu.

3. Type a description in the Description box. In the Command Line box, type **perfmon overview.pmw**. In the Working Directory box, be sure to specify the directory containing the OVERVIEW.PMW file.

4. Choose OK.

In the overview settings file, measure Processor: % Processor Time. This tells you how much processing is happening. If there is work being done and the processor is idle, you can be sure there is some other object causing delays. If you have a multiprocessor system, you might want to measure System: % Total Processor Time. This combines the average processor usage of all processors into a single counter. If you have many processors, this is the way to go.

You may want to measure System: Processor Queue Length. This is a key measure of processor congestion. We mentioned in the last chapter that you must include the measurement of at least one thread in order for this counter to operate. (Stop complaining: this is the type of knowledge that makes you an expert.)

The next counter to include in your OVERVIEW.PMW is Memory: Pages/sec. This tells you how many pages are being moved to and from the disk drives to satisfy virtual memory requirements. If the computer does not have enough memory to handle its workload, this counter will be consistently high. You will learn later how to distinguish between paging activity caused by program code and data accesses and paging caused by file accesses. Few computers have room for all their disk files in RAM, and paging allows code and data to get into memory initially. But sustained paging of code and non-file data because of a memory shortage yields particularly poor performance.

The next counter to include is Physical Disk: % Disk Time, for each physical disk unit. This will tell you how active the disk subsystem is. If there is excessive paging, it will show up as high disk utilization. General disk activity will also show up here.

Next to consider is networking. Here, what you measure depends on what protocol(s) you have installed on your system. It also depends on whether the computer is primarily a client, a server, or both.

If you are measuring a client and have NetBEUI installed, you can look at NetBEUI: Bytes Total/sec. If you have TCP/SNMP installed, you can look at Network Interface: Bytes Total/sec. If you have extended object counters for other protocols, they will probably have counters indicating total throughput. If you have extended object counters for your network adapter cards, you can look at byte transfer rates on those objects.

What you are looking for here is an indication of network activity, because on a client you usually deduce a network bottleneck rather than see it. For example, suppose that on a client, the processor and disk are not busy and the network is active. You are probably waiting for the network. If the problem is out on the network rather than in the local computer, it could be just about anywhere in the world, depending on your network. So let's try first to make the decision about local versus remote problems when we get the overview. We can search out the real culprit later.

If the computer is primarily a server, you might want to use Server: Bytes Total/sec to monitor your network activity. This will give you a single counter that shows most of your significant network activity. You will want to know how close the server's adapters are to being fully utilized. We'll discuss how to determine this below. It is also useful to watch Server: Context Block Queue Time, Context Blocks Queued/sec, and System: Total Interrupts/sec.

There are many other counters you could look at, but this set makes a pretty strong OVERVIEW.PMW. You don't want too many counters here because you want to get the broad picture. Once you have that, your chances of running off in the wrong direction are greatly reduced.

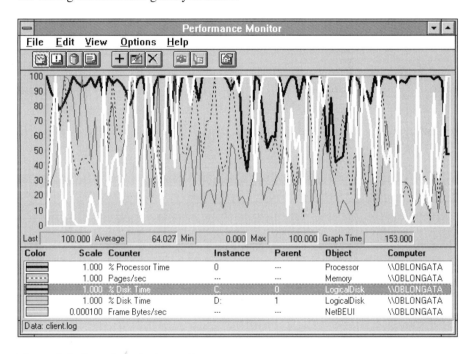

Figure 3.3 Overview of a busy client

What a jumble! Can we make sense of such a mess? (Yes, we can, as you'll see.)

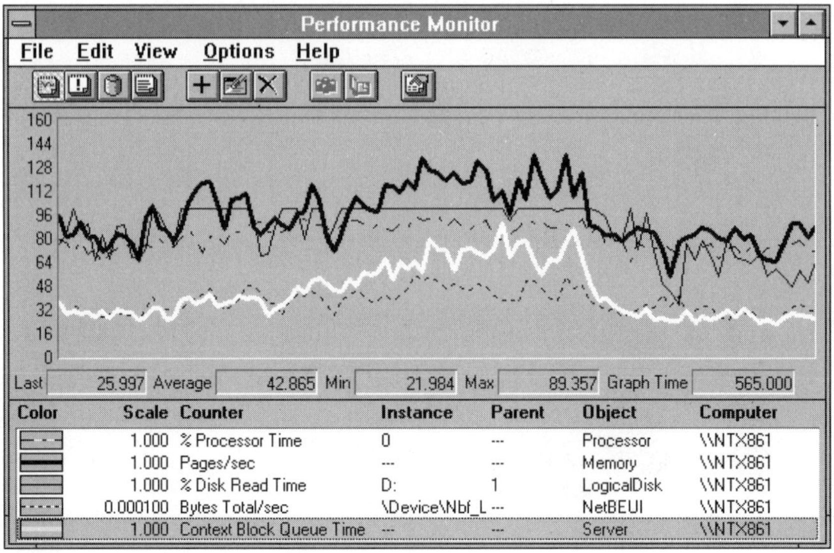

Figure 3.4 Overview of a busy server

That's one busy server! There is a memory bottleneck to the right of center on the display. Can you see it? Maybe not yet. This is the kind of problem we will learn how to solve.

These pictures can get pretty confusing, as even the simple example that opened this chapter showed, never mind these spaghetti charts. To get a better idea of how to approach more complex issues, let's look at each system component in turn, exploring how the counters behave under known, well-defined workloads. This will help us view the complexities of the real world from a platform of knowledge.

Charting the Response Surface

Computers are only one kind of system; there are many other electrical, mechanical, biological, and social systems around us. One favorite method of characterizing systems is called the Stimulus-Response model. The system is treated as a black box, and stimulated in a known way. The resulting response is noted, and a new stimulus is tried. In this way you gradually chart what is called the *response surface*.

We can do this with the computer. By applying known workloads and observing the response, we can learn about the system, and also about how it is viewed by the measurement tool. The program we use to apply known workloads to the computer system is called Response Probe.

We have included a copy of Response Probe on the floppy disk that accompanies this book. Appendix C explains how to use Response Probe.

Analyzing Processor Performance

Let's first take a look at a simple processor bottleneck. Figure 3.5 shows a processor being used to maximum capacity for a while.

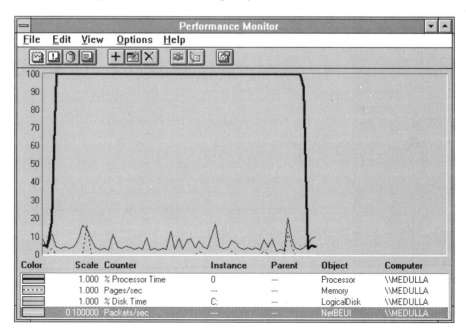

Figure 3.5 Bottleneck on processor utilization

Processor utilization is 100%. Most of our other overview counters are percolating at a low level. Why? Because we are logging the data, in this case at the rather rapid rate of once per second. The paging and disk activity is to the Performance Monitor log file. Later we'll discuss how to determine this. If we do not want this disk activity to interfere with the data, we could log over the network (then NetBEUI: Frame Bytes/sec would be non-zero), but because the disk activity is not really interfering much here, we won't bother this time. Chapter 2 discussed some other ways to reduce interference.

This interference is just the performance monitoring embodiment of the Heisenberg Uncertainty Principle: if you measure it, you change it. To make sure you don't forget this, we'll make it Rule #5!

We do not prevent you from collecting lots of data at a very high rate. There are occasions when you may legitimately need to look at something at very high resolution. But if you use Performance Monitor in such a way that it becomes your bottleneck, we'll tell your boss.

When we uncover a processor bottleneck, we always want to find out more. Is this just one process, or several? If one process, which one? And does it have just one thread, or several? Answers will tell us what we can do to solve the problem. This leads us to Rule #6.

Rule 6.
Any discovery raises
new questions.

So the next step is to look at System: Processor Queue Length to determine how many threads are contending for the processor. Luckily we logged the Thread as well as the System object, so we get the picture in Figure 3.6.

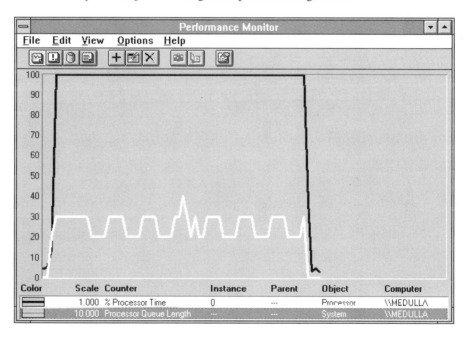

Figure 3.6 Processor Queue Length with a processor bottleneck

The Processor Queue Length here is scaled by 10 so we can see it better. It looks like it has a base of two, which alternates with three, with a peak at four. What are these threads? Figure 3.7 shows a chart in histogram mode, selecting the Processor: % Processor Time for all processes.

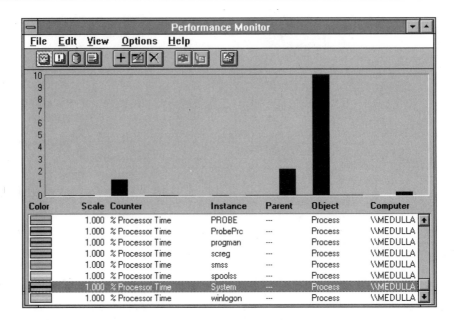

Figure 3.7 Processes active during a processor bottleneck

The culprits are cast appropriately in black. Here we have changed the Vertical Axis Maximum to 10. If we had left it at 100, you would have seen that the tall bar has 96.34% of the processor. So using this axis maximum lets us look at the remaining amount. On the left is the system graphics process, the Client-Server Runtime Subsystem (CSRSS) which has 1.408%. The bar to the left of the tall one is perfmon, the Performance Monitor executable, with 1.99%. The one on the far right is the System process, with 0.253%. It handles the lazy writing of data from the file system cache to the log file and other system functions. These processes are all involved in writing the log file. Heisenberg rides again! The overhead would have been lower if we had followed our own advice and minimized Performance Monitor while logging this data. You should try this and see if you can measure the improvement.

These values total 99.991% of the processor usage. The main culprit, of course, is the Response Probe process called ProbePrc, with 96.34% of the processor. If it were a real application, we'd rewrite it to use less processor time. Next we see perfmon, CSRSS, and finally the System process.

But Figure 3.6 has a strangely periodic, sawtooth flavor. In order to understand what we are seeing here, we need to digress for a moment and discuss how the % Processor Time is measured on Windows NT, and how the processor is scheduled. Then we'll know enough to pursue the Mystery of the Sawtooth Queue Length.

Why Performance Monitoring Is Free (Not!)

One design goal of software performance monitors is to keep their overhead low. Figure 3.8 shows a chart of the processor used by Windows NT Performance Monitor observing an idle system. Look at the value bar. Because the graph time is 100 seconds, we know the time interval is one second, so the chart is being updated every second.

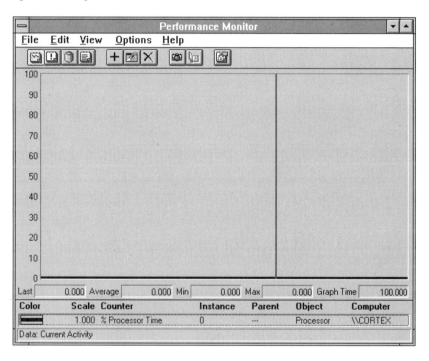

Figure 3.8 Windows NT Performance Monitor overhead (not!)

Notice how the value bar entries are zero. Wow, no overhead! What a tool! Do we think Windows NT Performance Monitor is free? Fat chance! It is good, but it is not free. It does have very low overhead, because it was used to tune itself, and we also followed all the guidelines we will mention in later chapters about how to write fast Windows NT applications. But it is also true that processor utilization on Windows NT 3.1 is sampled, not measured; the sample rate depends on the hardware platform. Sampling whether the processor is busy is much less expensive than timing every processor thread dispatch, because only more advanced processors include cheaply readable timers. On the 486 and earlier processors, time must be obtained from a relatively slow outboard Timer (See Figure 2.1.)

Anyway, what sampling means to you is that a process can execute a few instructions and stop—all in between samples—and thus not be observed. This places a lower bound on the resolution of this counter. On 486 systems in the initial release of Windows NT, the sample rate is once every 15 milliseconds. On MIPS systems, the sample rate is every 10 milliseconds. When the timer ticks, the interrupt looks to see what the current process and thread are, and then effectively bills them for a sample interval's worth of time as though they had executed for the entire sample interval. Clearly, this scheme can overcharge if the thread started just before the interrupt, or undercharge if the thread stops just before the sample interrupt (as is the case repeatedly in Figure 3.8). In aggregate, the counter will be correct. The counter is designed to tell us about which processes and threads dominate the processor, and it can certainly do that with low overhead using this scheme. But if we try to look too closely at thread behavior, we will see the limits to the resolution of this counter.

Processor Scheduling on Windows NT

In order to understand how processors are used in Windows NT you need to understand how they are scheduled. This is typical of what we will find throughout this book: we need to know how the system works and how it is measured to properly interpret the data. Otherwise, we're just guessing. Let's avoid that, it's what our boss does!

Windows NT schedules processors using symmetric multiprocessing with soft affinity and preemptive multitasking. What a mouthful! Read on to find out what it means.

Let's look first at a single-processor computer, which is scheduled by preemptive multitasking. This means that the highest priority thread that is ready to run will execute processor instructions. If another thread is waiting, what happens depends on its priority. If it is a lower priority than the executing thread, it will mostly wait, only occasionally getting processor time to prevent total starvation. If it has the same priority as the executing thread, the two will share the processor. The system will periodically switch from one thread to the other in order to let them both have processor access.

Priorities are assigned at two levels. The process is assigned a priority class based on how the user starts and interacts with it. Then, within the process's priority class, its threads are assigned priorities that can change depending on requests by the thread itself, or because of interactions with peripherals or with the user. When the thread uses the processor, its priority is lowered; when it accesses peripherals, it is raised, and when it accesses such peripherals as the keyboard it is boosted even more. But to gain this boost, peripheral access must be through direct communication with Windows NT Executive. Windows applications are treated somewhat differently, as described shortly.

If a computer has multiple processors, a ready thread can run on any of them. The system attempts to run a thread on the same processor it last ran on, all other things being equal. (This is soft affinity.) This helps reuse data left in the processor's memory caches from the previous execution of the thread. A thread could be restricted to run on only certain processors, but this is not done by any subsystem in the initial release of Windows NT.

Most applications started by users during system operation run in the Normal Priority class. When a user is interacting with an application using the keyboard and mouse, that application is in the foreground. The foreground application processes get an elevated base priority of nine instead of the level eight assigned to other Normal Priority class processes. (A higher number has higher priority.) When an application relinquishes the foreground, it becomes a background process and is given a base priority of seven.

What all this means is that when the foreground application uses the processor heavily, it can lock out all lower priority processes from execution. Because responding quickly to the user is usually the goal of the system, this is the chosen default for Windows NT operation. If you want to alter this behavior, choose the Tasking button in the System option in Control Panel. The setting of Best Foreground Application Response Time is the default. If you change this to Foreground Application More Responsive Than Background, foreground processes will be given a priority of eight. Setting this to Foreground And Background Applications Equally Responsive assures that both foreground and background processes get priority level seven.

The following table lists all possible thread priorities.

Table 3.1   Thread Priorities in Windows NT

Base	Priority class	Thread priority
31	Real-time	THREAD_PRIORITY_TIME_CRITICAL
26	Real-time	THREAD_PRIORITY_HIGHEST
25	Real-time	THREAD_PRIORITY_ABOVE_NORMAL
24	Real-time	THREAD_PRIORITY_NORMAL
23	Real-time	THREAD_PRIORITY_BELOW_NORMAL
22	Real-time	THREAD_PRIORITY_LOWEST
16	Real-time	THREAD_PRIORITY_IDLE
15	Idle, Normal, or High	THREAD_PRIORITY_TIME_CRITICAL
15	High	THREAD_PRIORITY_HIGHEST
14	High	THREAD_PRIORITY_ABOVE_NORMAL
13	High	THREAD_PRIORITY_NORMAL
12	High	THREAD_PRIORITY_BELOW_NORMAL
11	High	THREAD_PRIORITY_LOWEST
11	Foreground normal	THREAD_PRIORITY_HIGHEST
10	Foreground normal	THREAD_PRIORITY_ABOVE_NORMAL
9	Foreground normal	THREAD_PRIORITY_NORMAL

Base	Priority class	Thread priority
9	Background normal	THREAD_PRIORITY_HIGHEST
8	Foreground normal	THREAD_PRIORITY_BELOW_NORMAL
8	Background normal	THREAD_PRIORITY_ABOVE_NORMAL
7	Foreground normal	THREAD_PRIORITY_LOWEST
7	Background normal	THREAD_PRIORITY_NORMAL
6	Background normal	THREAD_PRIORITY_BELOW_NORMAL
6	Idle	THREAD_PRIORITY_HIGHEST
5	Background normal	THREAD_PRIORITY_LOWEST
5	Idle	THREAD_PRIORITY_ABOVE_NORMAL
4	Idle	THREAD_PRIORITY_NORMAL
3	Idle	THREAD_PRIORITY_BELOW_NORMAL
2	Idle	THREAD_PRIORITY_LOWEST
1	Idle, Normal, or High	THREAD_PRIORITY_IDLE

The Mystery of the Sawtooth Queue Length

Now let's go back to the sawtooth behavior of the processor queue length. Now we know enough to understand that % Processor Time may not show the bottleneck. One reason is that some of the processes might be so quick that they do not register any processor usage. Another reason is that a process in the queue might never execute because higher priority processes are dominating the processor. The Processor Queue Length counter's Explain text tells us that this counter tracks the threads in the Ready State. If we want to know what is in the processor queue, we need to look directly at the threads and their thread states. All the possible thread states are listed in the following table.

Table 3.2 Thread States in Windows NT

Thread state	Meaning
0	Initialized
1	Ready
2	Running
3	Standby
4	Terminated
5	Wait
6	Transition
7	Unknown

The easiest way to analyze what is happening in Figure 3.6 is to first bracket the time period of interest with the time window. Then add the counter Thread: Thread State for all threads in the system. This will take a while for Performance Monitor to draw, and the resulting picture is not too illuminating. However, we can now export the data and use a spreadsheet to analyze it. We look at the thread states of all the threads, and eliminate those threads that never have Thread State = 1 (that is, ready on the processor queue). We change all the thread states that are not 1 to 0, so the remaining thread state 1s really stand out. Now we can really see what's happening, looking at Figure 3.9.

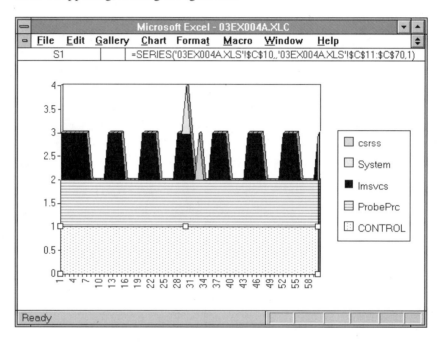

Figure 3.9 Components of processor queue length

The ProbePrc process is our processor hog. The Control process is Control Panel, which attempts to wake up and do housekeeping about six times per second. Because it is in the background, it virtually never executes—it is not getting enough of a priority boost to get much processor time—but it sits on the processor queue trying to run. The System process is rarely queued, mainly because it runs briefly when it runs. CSRSS is rarely active when Performance Monitor is actually retrieving data. It updates the log file size after the data is written to the log file, and that is way after the data is collected and the Processor Queue Length is observed.

We can now see quite clearly that the sawtooth queue length is caused by the periodic nature of the LAN Manager Services (LMSVCS) process. LMSVCS handles the Server, the Redirector, the Browser, some TCP/IP functions, and so on. This process has a thread that wakes up to do housekeeping once per second. If it cannot run right when it wakes up, it goes into the processor queue. Now that we know what to observe, we can look at this thread in more detail.

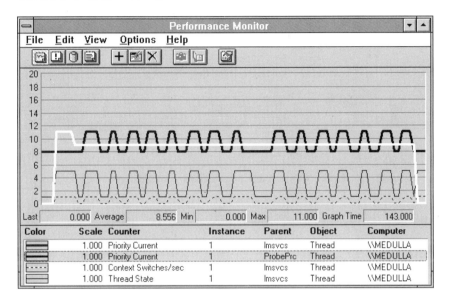

Figure 3.10 Anatomy of a periodic, blocked thread

Figure 3.10 shows where the sawtooth comes from. The heavy black line is the Thread: Current Priority of LMSVCS thread 1. It starts at 8, below the highlighted foreground priority 9 of the Response Probe process, ProbePrc. It is in Thread State 1, Ready. After a while, the system boosts the priority LMSVCS thread 1 to 11 so it can get some processor time. At this point several things happen at once. The thread state switches to 5, because the thread is usually idle when the snapshot is taken. The Thread: Context Switches go from 0 to 1 per second. (A context switch is when the processor switches from executing one process or thread to another.) After some of this level of activity, the thread is returned to its base priority of 8. The next time it tries to wake up, it goes onto the processor queue, and the cycle repeats. We have solved the mystery of the sawtooth.

The threads that are observed to be busy when there is a long processor queue may not be the ones that are in the queue. This may be because they are too quick to be seen by the timer interrupt that is sampling the processor usage, or they may be at too low a priority to capture any processor cycles, in spite of any priority boost. The next figure shows the threads that are observed to be getting processor cycles during this experiment. Note the use of scale factors to show all these threads on one chart.

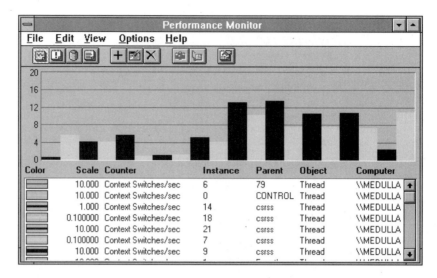

Figure 3.11 Threads active during a processor bottleneck

User Mode and Privileged Mode

Windows NT uses a couple of different protection mechanisms, and at the root of them all is the distinction between user mode and privileged mode. In user mode, the application is restricted in a number of ways. It cannot access the peripherals directly, but must call Windows NT to get or change peripheral data. This lets Windows NT assure that one application will not destroy data for another. When an application is in user mode, it also cannot read or change data maintained by Windows NT itself. This prevents applications from corrupting Windows NT either inadvertently or intentionally. When an application needs Windows NT to do something, it calls one of the system routines. Many of these make the transition into privileged mode, perform the required operation, and return smoothly to user mode.

Other protection mechanisms in Windows NT, such as the subsystem model, are built on the transition between user and privileged mode, and we'll explore that shortly. The highest level of protection is provided by the Windows NT security model. We measure it when necessary by looking at these lower levels on which it is built.

Figure 3.12 shows the processor modes in the previous example. The dotted line is Processor: % User Time, or the percentage of time spent in user mode. The thin black line at the bottom of the chart is Processor: % Privileged Time. Almost all of the processor time is being spent in user mode, and there is very little privileged mode activity. This application is chewing up the processor in user mode and requires very few system services.

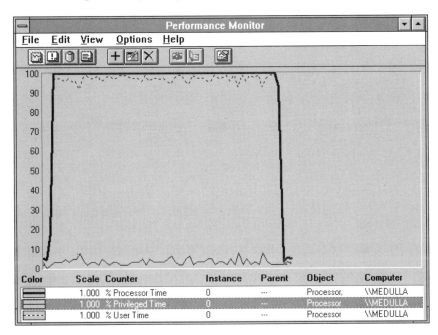

Figure 3.12 A self-absorbed application obsessed with user-mode processing

Figure 3.13 tells a different tale. Here we have measured a single process that is retrieving file data, and consequently spending most of its time in privileged mode. This is not necessarily bad, it just means that the application is getting its work done by calling the operating system. When user mode time goes up, privileged mode time goes down. Together they add up to all the processor time being used, if we got our arithmetic right when we built Performance Monitor. (And we did; we checked.)

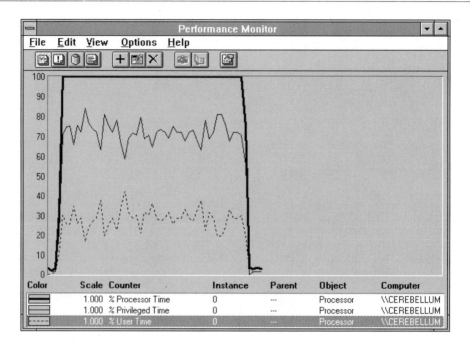

Figure 3.13 A process wisely using Windows NT to get its work done

Performance Monitor enables you to get an overview of a few basic areas where an application might be spending its time when it is using the system in this fashion. Figure 3.14 shows some of the key counters to note in this situation.

You may notice that % Processor Time appears in the report before % Privileged Time. This is logical, which is why we have done it here, but it is not what you get if you just select all Processor counters and add them to a report. Report counters appear in the order selected. If you select all counters at once, they appear in alphabetical order. By first selecting % Processor Time, adding it, and then selecting all Processor counters and adding them, you will get the report shown here. Adding the % Processor Time a second time has no effect because duplicate additions are ignored.

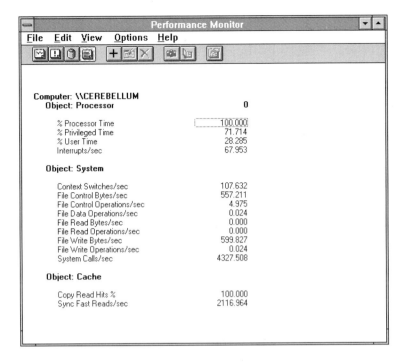

Figure 3.14 Some key indicators of system call activity

The Processor: Interrupts/sec counter is near its rest state of 66.667 on the x86 processor. (This rate reflects the rest state because the processor clock interrupts every 15 milliseconds on x86 computers.) It is a bit higher because we are logging performance data once each second. A large number of interrupts could press privileged time up, but that is not happening here. Windows NT is capable of sustaining thousands of interrupts per second; that's how we know this number near 66 is low.

The Context Switches/sec rate is quite low, so the application is not switching to another process, or switching among multiple threads within itself. This is another counter capable of being in the thousands; we'll see examples of this later.

All the file operation counters are very quiet as well, so we're not beating on the Windows NT file system for data. (How could that be, when we were getting file data? Hang on and you'll see.) System: System Calls/sec measures the number of times the application is calling Windows NT, and thus counts the transitions into and out of privileged mode from user mode. We can compute the amount of time between each call:

Time / System Call = 1 / (System Calls/sec) = 1 / 4327.508 = 0.000231

or 231 microseconds. User time per system call is the ratio of % User Time (expressed as a number from 0 to 1, this is the fraction of each second in user mode) to System Calls/sec

User Time / System Call = 0.28285 / 4327.508 = 0.000065

or, 65 microseconds. And, finally

Privileged Time / System Call = 0.71714 / 4327.508 = 0.000166

or, 166 microseconds.

All this tells us that the application is making a very large number of system calls each second (on average), and each one is quite fast.

We turn our attention to another key Windows NT component, the file system cache. Windows NT uses a single cache for all file systems. Before going to fetch the data from disk or LAN, the file system first asks the Windows NT I/O Manager if the data is in the cache. If it is, the file system bows out and the request is fielded by the cache manager. We'll say more about all this later, primarily in Chapter 6, "Detecting Cache Bottlenecks."

What we see here is a 100% hit rate in the cache for copy reads, meaning every time the cache manager is asked for such data, it is there. Copy reads are those in which the cache manager is directed to satisfy the request by copying the data from the cache to the application's buffer. (Reminder: this sort of information is in the Explain text for the counter.) We also see a high rate of Sync Fast Reads/sec. This is the key to the absence of file system activity in the file counters. Sync here means the application will wait until the request is finished. Fast reads are special I/O Manager operations which bypass the initial call to the file system and go directly to the Cache manager. So the file system never got called, and never had a chance to bump its File Read Operations/sec counter.

We can see how these cache requests relate to the overall system calls by forming another ratio:

System Calls / Cache Request = 4327.508 / 2116.964 = 2.04

Just about every other call is a call to get data from the cache. To get more detail on the calls and the amount of time spent in them, you would use the Call/Attributed Profiler (or a similar tool), which is described in Chapter 10, "Tuning Windows NT Applications."

We've gotten a pretty good idea what is going on here, and we know what tool to use to get more information. We've also exposed another important Rule:

Rule 7.

Counter ratios reveal bottlenecks.

What Multiple Processes and Threads Look Like

In this last example, we saw what the system looks like when we have a single process that is hogging a single processor. What if we had more than one process active? This is visible in the next few figures, starting with Figure 3.15.

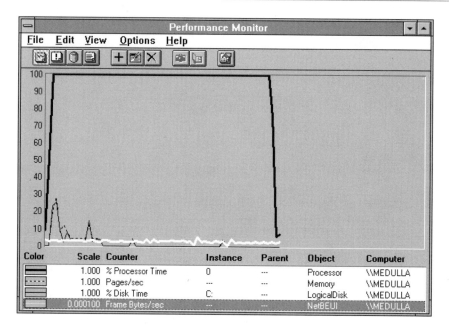

Figure 3.15 Multiple processes in a processor bottleneck

Contrast this with Figure 3.5. The only change is in the background activity, and this is different because we have decided to place the log file on a remote computer, instead of on the local disk. We thought you would like to see the difference in usage this would cause. After some initial activity, the disk becomes quiet, and you see a steady stream of NetBEUI Frame Bytes/sec (the white line at the bottom). We are still logging this data at a one-second time interval. (This is a very high rate for logging. Except for making illustrations like this, we do not recommend it.)

To see how this situation is really different from Figure 3.5, we can compare Figures 3.6 and 3.16, which show the processor queue length.

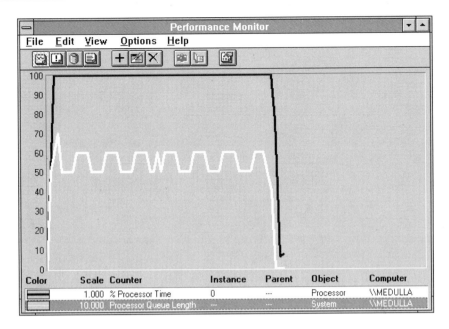

Figure 3.16 Processor queue length with multiple processes consuming the processor

The highlighted queue length in Figure 3.16 is much longer than the one in Figure 3.6. It goes as high as 7 and never drops below 5. Suppose we find the average queue length in each case. Let's start two copies of Performance Monitor, each looking at its own log file. We move the time window in on each one to bracket the time when the processor is 100% utilized. Then we select the Processor Queue Length in the legend, and note the average value in the value bar. See Figure 3.17. The average values are 2.5 in one case, and 5.5 in the other. So we would guess there are three more processes in Figure 3.15 than in Figure 3.5.

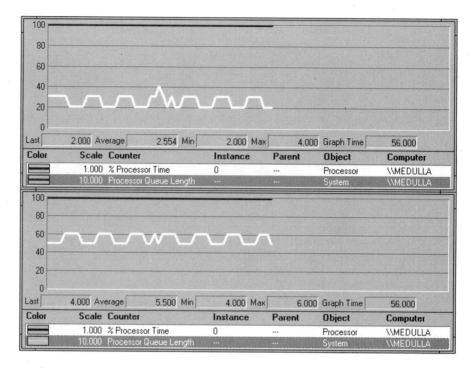

Figure 3.17 Comparing processor queue lengths

This is a certain clue that there is more than one culprit hogging the processor. What are these masked processes? We expose them in Figure 3.18.

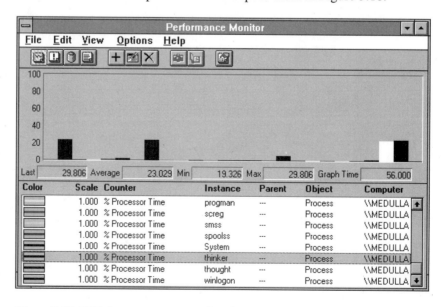

Figure 3.18 Which processes are eating the processor

Clearly, four processes are consuming the processor in this case. They are sharing it equally. We see minor usage by two others, the CSRSS and Performance Monitor. So, we have found the bottleneck!

How would this look different if we had just one process, but with multiple threads? At this point you can probably guess. Take a look at Figures 3.19 through 3.22. This time we have placed Performance Monitor on a remote system. You see the same network traffic in the background that you saw last time. But Performance Monitor is remote. We can see the consequence of this indirectly in Figure 3.20.

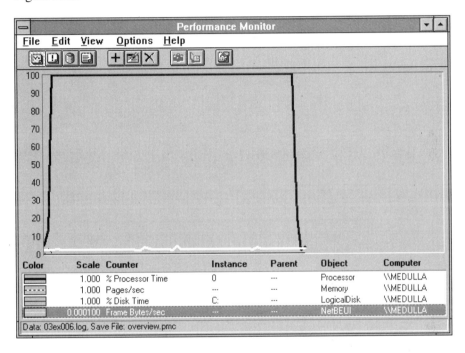

Figure 3.19 Processor consumption by multiple threads

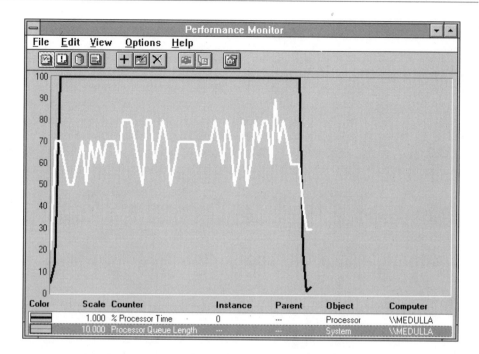

Figure 3.20 Processor time and queue length with multiple threads (remote measurement)

The Processor Queue Length is more erratic and longer than before. We can analyze this as we did previously, by exporting the Thread: Thread State for all threads, and finding those with Thread State 1 (Ready). What we see is that there are two new, multithreaded processes participating when we do remote measurement. The first is the Network Server, which we know only by a number because it is started without a name. The second is the Service Controller and Registry process (SCREG). Both participate in handling the remote request for performance data, and both have multiple asynchronous threads that contribute erratically to the queue length.

So we've muddied the waters a little by changing both the way we are collecting the data as well as the experiment itself, in violation of Rule # 1 of Bottleneck Detection. But this way we've convinced you of the value of Rule #1, right?

You can look at Figure 3.21 to see which processes are participating in this bottleneck, and you can see from Figure 3.22 that the Thinker process has four active threads.

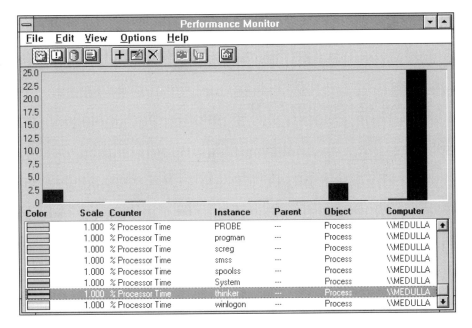

Figure 3.21 Processes in a multithreaded processor bottleneck

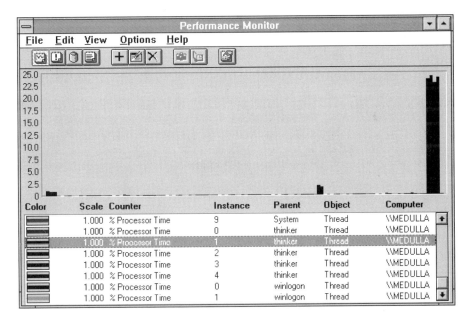

Figure 3.22 Threads in a single process in a multithreaded processor bottleneck

What you want to remember is that although we tend to think of processes as the executing programs on a system, it really is the threads that use the processor. The process is the address space, and the threads inside that process share that address space and actually execute the instructions.

Bottlenecks at Lower Utilization

Does a device have to be at 100% utilization to be the bottleneck? Unfortunately, no, or our lives would be much simpler.

Two important issues contribute to the relationship between queue lengths and utilization. The first is the arrival patterns of requests for the device service, and the second is the amount of work the device is requested to do on each arrival.

Suppose we had ten threads that each wanted exactly 0.9 seconds of processor time in a continuous block, just once every 10 seconds. Further imagine that exactly 1 second after the first one arrived to ask for its 0.9 seconds, the second one arrived, and in the next second the third one arrived, and so on. The processor would be 90% busy, and there would be no queue. If each thread needed precisely 0.95 seconds of processor time, the processor would be utilized at 95%. If 0.999, then 99.9%. Note there is no queuing in this situation, and no interference between the threads.

In queuing theory this is called a constant arrival and constant service distribution. In a carefully engineered situation, a device can be nearly 100% busy without creating a queue. How delicate the balance between arrivals and service to achieve this state!

It is not hard to see that, if the second thread arrives just a little bit early, it has to wait for the first one to at least complete a time slice before it can run. Likewise, if the first thread requires just a little more than a second of processor time, it will get in the way of the next thread. A processor queue will start to form. Once arrival rates and service requests become unpredictable, a queue can build up, and there can be delays.

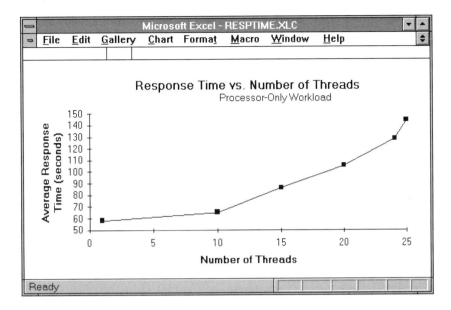

Figure 3.23 Response time to a randomized processor load

Figure 3.23 shows how the response time can grow for a number of threads if the arrivals and service requests are less regular. These threads ask for a somewhat random amount of processor time after an irregular delay. The utilization of the processor in the 25 threads on the right was 76%. Yet the delays experienced were almost three times that of the stand-alone thread. This means the length of the processor queue was almost 2.

According to queuing theory, if the arrival pattern is random and the service pattern is random, the length of the queue is 2 when the device utilization is 66%, or two-thirds utilized. We are using the word "random" somewhat loosely to mean unpredictable. For example, in a large telephone exchange, the length of the phone calls is found to be random in this way. (In fact, what we mean is that interarrival and service distributions are exponential, but that is more formal than we need to be here.)

Distributions can be worse than this, in the sense that queues can form at even lower utilizations. The most commonly occurring situation like this is a bi-modal distribution of service, when most requests are very short or long with few that are medium length. We don't see these too often in computer systems, but they do occur. If your queue length is large and the utilization is low, you may be experiencing this type of usage pattern. If you want to impress your boss, say that your device is experiencing hyper-exponential service distributions.

So how a device is used determines the length of the queue that will form for a given utilization of the device. When looking for bottlenecks in real systems, you must be aware of this. It won't be hard to remember because it will apply at the bank and the supermarket as well as on your computer. So next time you are standing in line somewhere, you can quote Rule #8:

Rule 8.

Random usage forms longer queues at lower utilization.

How the Graphics System Uses the Processor

We mentioned in passing that the client-server runtime subsystem, affectionately known as CSRSS, handles graphics on Windows NT. Actually it handles all window manipulation as well as graphics, and thus makes up an important portion of processor activity on the system. This architecture is illustrated in Figure 3.24.

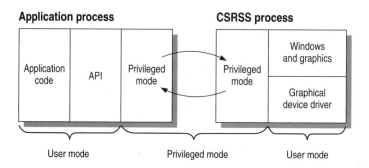

Figure 3.24 Graphics architecture on Windows NT

The Windows NT SDK contains a graphical device interface demonstration program called Gdidemo. As shipped in the SDK, Gdidemo pauses between drawings. For this experiment, we modified the Gdidemo program to remove that pause so that it will spend all its time drawing. Figure 3.25 shows processor utilization for the processor, the modified Gdidemo program bouncing balls around the screen, and the CSRSS process.

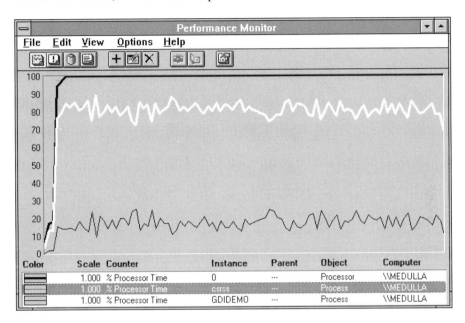

Figure 3.25 Processor utilization by a graphics program pumping pixels

The processor is 100% busy, and most of the time is in CSRSS, which makes sense because it is doing most of the work. On Windows NT you need to think beyond the application process itself and look at other processes in the system that the application may be using. CSRSS is a primary candidate for consuming processor cycles on behalf of an application. Usually this is pretty obvious, because the display changing rapidly is a primary clue. But some tasks that manipulate windows do not change the visible display: they may be operating on windows that are hidden behind others. So taking a look at CSRSS is a good basic policy.

The graphics application communicates with CSRSS using a fast form of the local interprocess procedure call. What makes it fast is dedicating one thread in CSRSS for each application thread that communicates with CSRSS. So you'll see lots of CSRSS threads. An application sends graphics commands to CSRSS in batches to amortize the cost of the process switch over a number of graphical operations. Each such context switch is counted by System: Context Switches, and by Thread: Context Switches as well. You can see from the report in Figure 3.26 that the context switches between Gdidemo and a thread in CSRSS account for nearly all the context switches in the system. (Remember Heisenberg: Performance Monitor is logging at one-second intervals here. You can see its communication with CSRSS in the two threads at the right of Figure 3.26.)

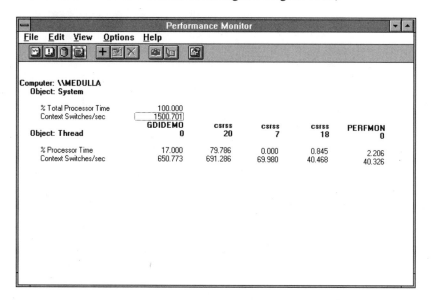

Figure 3.26 Thread context switching during graphics processing

Thread 7 of CSRSS is waking up about 70 times per second to do some housekeeping, but shows no processor activity. This thread is slipping through our processor usage sampling crack. Context switches are a more positive indication of activity than processor utilization because they are always counted. Look at them if you want to know for certain whether a thread is active. We used this technique in Figure 3.11.

Processor Usage by 16-bit Windows Applications

All of the 16-bit Windows applications are run as separate threads in a single process named NTVDM (NT virtual DOS machine.) This process is known as the WOW subsystem, which stands for Windows-16 on Windows-32. This architecture permits 16-bit applications to share the address space the same way they did under 16-bit Windows. It is illustrated in Figure 3.27.

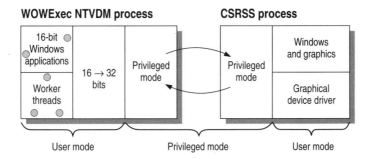

Figure 3.27 16-bit Windows applications on Windows NT

Unfortunately, the architecture obscures Performance Monitor's measurement of these applications in two ways. First, the name of all such applications is that of the single process, NTVDM. Second, if you have two or more such applications running, it is hard to tell them apart because they are identified only by thread number inside that NTVDM.

It can require a little disciplined experimenting to determine which thread is which application. The NTVDM process that handles 16-bit Windows applications is started automatically when Windows NT starts. Before starting any 16-bit applications, use Performance Monitor to look at the NTVDM to see how many threads it has initially. Figure 3.28 shows such a report.

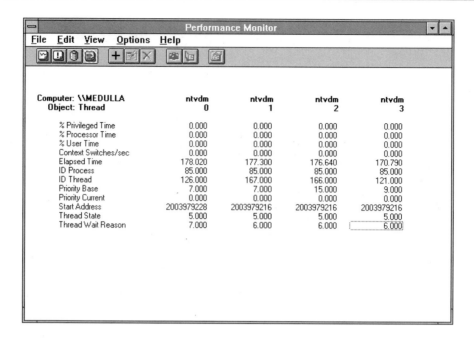

Figure 3.28 16-bit Windows NTVDM before application execution

Now let's start another thread, 16-bit Excel. Here's what we see as a result:

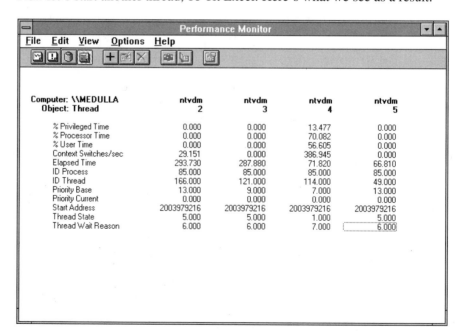

Figure 3.29 16-bit Excel in the WOW NTVDM

There is not room in the illustration for all the threads, so we show the last four. The last two are new. Thread 4, with ID Thread 114, is actually Excel. We can tell this because it is looping. We might as well 'fess up now: this is a bug (oh, no!) in 16-bit Excel 4.0, which causes it to consume processor cycles needlessly under some conditions, one of which is startup. (Because of the Windows NT preemptive multitasking ability, this looping activity is not a problem. Just put Excel in the background and carry on.) Notice the high Context Switch rate of Thread 4. Excel is talking to CSRSS (which is not shown here). Moving the focus to Excel and away again removes the loop. Figure 3.30 shows Excel in the NTVDM after it has stopped looping. (Of course the next version of Excel will not do this. By the way, this bug in Excel was discovered with Windows NT Performance Monitor.)

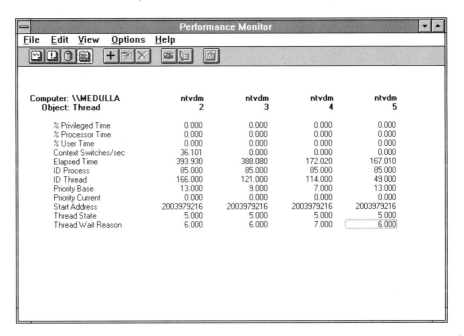

Figure 3.30 16-bit Excel has calmed down now

Looking at Figure 3.30 you can see that the elapsed times for Threads 4 and 5 are shorter than those of 2 and 3 because the application was started after WowExec was executed. This is another clue about which application thread is which in the WowExec NTVDM. Now let's stop Excel and look at what changes.

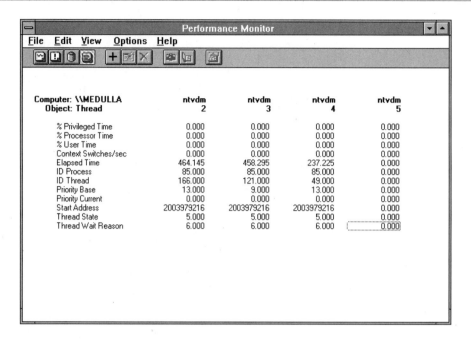

Figure 3.31 16-bit Excel has stopped

Can you see that ID Thread 114 is gone now? Notice that Thread 4 is still there, but it is now the thread that was Thread 5 before (its ID Thread is still 49). In Performance Monitor, threads are named sequentially, starting with 0. If one in the middle disappears, the numbers of following threads decrease. So you should use ID Thread to make a positive identification. Because ID Thread numbers get reused, they won't be proof positive, but they do last for the life of the thread, at least. In this example, there is no longer a Thread 5, as indicated by its zeroed counters. Performance Monitor continues to search for any instance selected for measurement, but if an instance cannot be found, its counters are all set to zero.

You can use the PView tool to stop the WowExec NTVDM if you want to get a fresh start on identifying 16-bit Windows applications. Be sure to stop the NTVDM with at least 4 threads! Other NTVDMs run non-Windows MS-DOS® applications, as we'll discuss shortly. You can restart the WowExec NTVDM by using CTRL+ESC to bring up Task Manager, pressing TAB to get to the Run box, and entering **wowexec**. WowExec will also start automatically when you run the first 16-bit Windows application.

In Figure 3.32 we show what happens if we start 16-bit Excel again. Here you'll
see a new Thread 5 with ID Thread 163. Notice that the ID Thread is not 114 as
before. The ID Thread assignments appear somewhat arbitrary. But here, as long
as we keep Excel alive, it will retain the ID Thread 163.

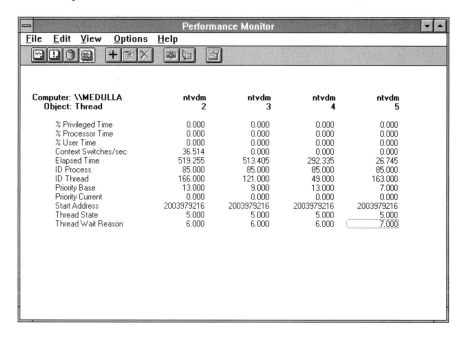

Computer: \\MEDULLA	ntvdm	ntvdm	ntvdm	ntvdm
Object: Thread	2	3	4	5
% Privileged Time	0.000	0.000	0.000	0.000
% Processor Time	0.000	0.000	0.000	0.000
% User Time	0.000	0.000	0.000	0.000
Context Switches/sec	36.514	0.000	0.000	0.000
Elapsed Time	519.255	513.405	292.335	26.745
ID Process	85.000	85.000	85.000	85.000
ID Thread	166.000	121.000	49.000	163.000
Priority Base	13.000	9.000	13.000	7.000
Priority Current	0.000	0.000	0.000	0.000
Start Address	2003979216	2003979216	2003979216	2003979216
Thread State	5.000	5.000	5.000	5.000
Thread Wait Reason	6.000	6.000	6.000	7.000

Figure 3.32 WowExec NTVDM threads after restarting 16-bit Excel

Okay, let's start another application. We have a copy of Word for Windows
handy, so we'll fire that up.

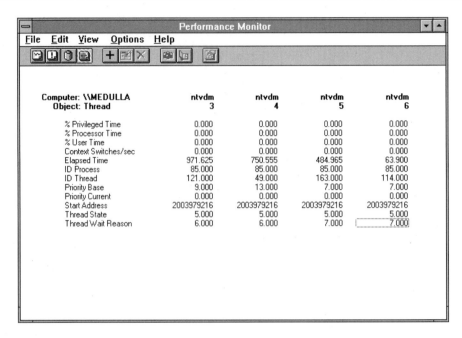

Figure 3.33 WowExec NTVDM threads after starting Excel and Word for Windows

So we see the new Thread 6 with ID Thread 114. This must be Word for Windows. By looking at Thread: Elapsed Time, we can tell which thread belongs to which application.

You get the idea. By executing or stimulating the application of interest and watching the reaction in Performance Monitor, you can isolate which WowExec NTVDM thread is executing its code. From that point until you exit the application, you have a positive identification of the thread.

Processor Usage by 16-bit MS-DOS Applications

Each MS-DOS application runs in its own NTVDM process on Windows NT. If you have been following along carefully you will realize that this creates a bit of a challenge for us, because we can only monitor one program of a given name at a time. Not only are all MS-DOS applications given the same name, they have the same name as the process running all the 16-bit Windows applications. Could it get any worse than this?

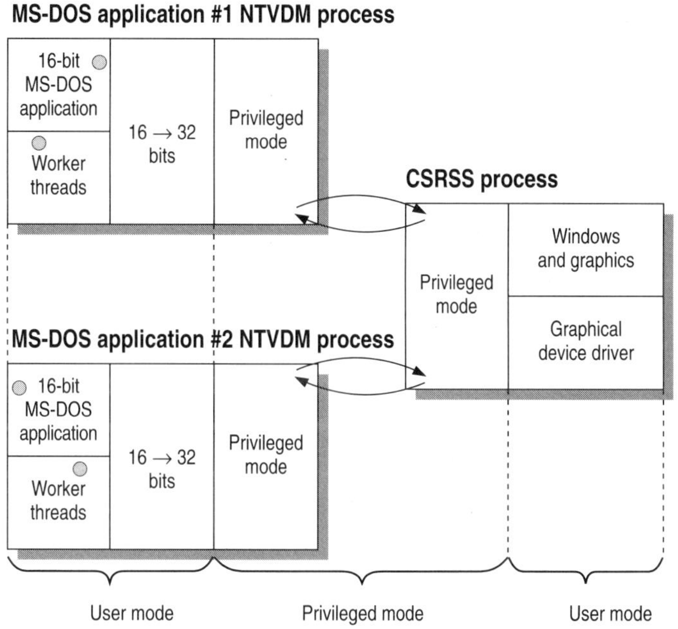

MS-DOS application #1 NTVDM process

| 16-bit ○ MS-DOS application | 16 → 32 bits | Privileged mode |
| ○ Worker threads | | |

CSRSS process

| Privileged mode | Windows and graphics |
| | Graphical device driver |

MS-DOS application #2 NTVDM process

| ○ 16-bit MS-DOS application | 16 → 32 bits | Privileged mode |
| ○ Worker threads | | |

User mode   Privileged mode   User mode

Figure 3.34 16-bit MS-DOS applications on Windows NT

Yes, it could, because this isn't really so bad. What we can do is change the name of the program used to execute MS-DOS applications. Go to the directory %SystemRoot%\SYSTEM32 on the volume holding your copy of Windows NT. Copy NTVDM.EXE to a file name of your choice. (Be sure to copy it to another filename instead of renaming it, because you want to leave NTVDM.EXE around for WowExec to work with.) You then tell Windows NT to use the new program copy for executing MS-DOS programs. You do this by making a slight change in the Configuration Registry using the Registry Editor, REGEDT32.EXE. You can do this between starting the applications, and you do not have to shut down the system to have this change take effect. The value to change is

```
HKEY_LOCAL_MACHINE
    SYSTEM
        CurrentControlSet
            Control
                WOW
                    cmdline:
```

Double-click the **cmdline** entry to change it. Modify the spelling of
NTVDM.EXE to that of your copied NTVDM.EXE. Then start an MS-DOS
application. If you need to start another one and measure it separately, you can
repeat this process. You can leave the Registry Editor running and positioned at
the cmdline value to make repeated changes easy. Figure 3.35 shows the Registry
Editor in this position.

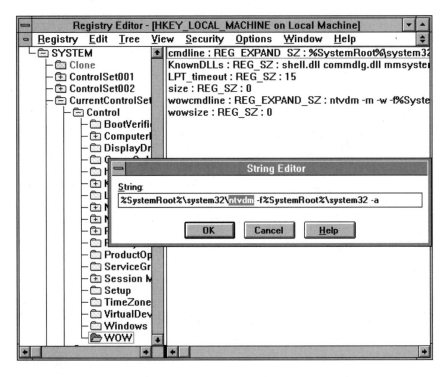

**Figure 3.35 Registry Editor set to change name of NTVDM for running MS-DOS
programs**

Note We recommend that you set cmdline back to NTVDM.EXE when your
experiment is over. If you are very ambitious and this is a big issue for you, you
might want to write an application to perform these changes before and after the
execution of your MS-DOS applications.

Figure 3.36 shows two MS-DOS applications being monitored concurrently by Performance Monitor using this technique. The threads in one of them are shown in Figure 3.37. There are two worker threads and one for the application. By stimulating the application you might be able to distinguish between them, but this is not really crucial because unlike in WowExec, there is only one application per process, and you know what the process is.

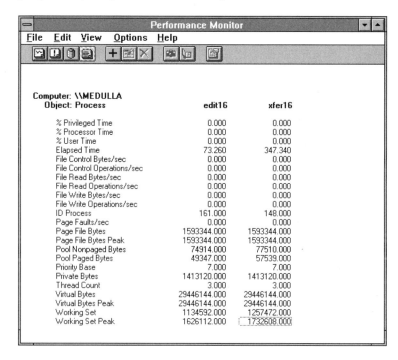

Figure 3.36 Two MS-DOS applications monitored using renamed NTVDMs

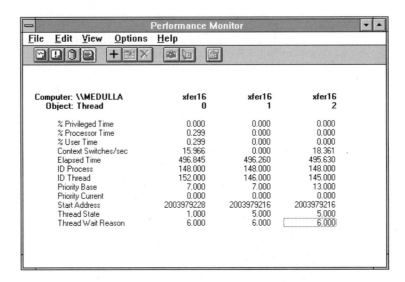

Figure 3.37 Threads in a renamed NTVDM executing an MS-DOS application

See? Piece of cake.

Who Started All These Processes?

Maybe you thought all you wanted to do was run a program, but Windows NT starts many processes as a normal matter of doing business. Few of these ever become a system bottleneck because all they do is provide numerous housekeeping and bookkeeping functions in the background. Figure 3.38 shows the number of each of several important object types, as counted in the Object object.

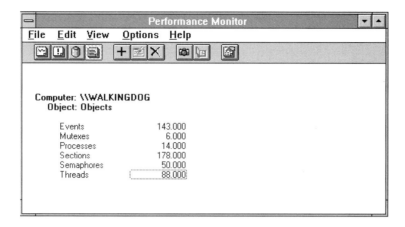

Figure 3.38 Object counts on a Windows NT system

Here's a brief introduction to those objects not already mentioned. *Event objects* are used by Windows NT and its applications to synchronize operations by permitting a thread to suspend execution until an anticipated event occurs, such as the completion of an asynchronous file operation. *Mutex objects* are used to assure that only one thread is executing a particular piece of code at a time, such as updating a common data structure. *Section objects* are areas of memory that can be viewed as a contiguous sequence of addresses. A s*emaphore object* grants a limited number of threads concurrent access to a shared resource, such as a buffer pool with limited entries; if more threads than the specified limit try to access the resource, they are automatically suspended until a resource becomes available. If these objects are given a name when they are created, they can be shared by multiple processes.

Object counts are important because each object takes space in nonpaged memory, which we'll talk about more in Chapter 5, "Detecting Memory Bottlenecks." Also, we unfortunately don't have a counter for Open File objects. However, the Server object does have an Files Open counter, and we have a tool which monitors application file activity. We'll discuss that tool in Chapter 10, "Tuning Windows NT Applications."

There are 14 processes and 88 threads in Figure 3.38. That's just about as few as you can get, because this snapshot is taken on a laptop that is not connected to a network. One of these processes is Performance Monitor, so let's be sure we understand who the others are, and what role they play in the operation of Windows NT.

Table 3.3   Processes in Windows NT with No Network Connection

Process name	Function
clipsrv	Clipbook Server
csrss	Client Server Runtime Subsystem, handles windows and graphics functions for all subsystems
EventLog	Fields all requests to enter events into the system event log
Idle	Provides an idle thread for each processor that gets control when the processor is not executing programs
lsass	Local Security Administration Subsystem, handles certain security administration functions on the local computer
nddeagnt	Network DDE Agent, handles requests for network DDE services
netdde	Handles requests for network DDE data
progman	Program Manager handles application startup, switching, and termination functions
screg	Service Controller/Registry, handles network API service control functions and remote Registry and Performance Monitor data requests
spoolss	Spooler Subsystem handles despooling of printer data from disk to printer
System	Contains system threads that handle lazy writing by the file system cache, virtual memory modified page writing, working set trimming, and similar system functions
winlogon	Handles logon and logoff of users

When connected to a network there are additional processes, one of which is identified only by a number. This is the File Server, which handles remote network file system requests. The number varies from system to system.

Getting Rid of a Processor Bottleneck

What can you do once you determine you have a processor bottleneck? The answer depends partly on the context.

You can try to fix the application, using the tools we discuss in Chapter 10. Let's assume you've already done this.

If you have an 386 processor, you can upgrade the computer to one with an 486, Pentium, or RISC processor.

Assuming you have at least a 486, if you are in a server environment, part of your problem may be the network or disk adapter cards you have chosen. 8-bit cards use more processor time than 16-bit or 32-bit cards. The number of bits here refers to the amount of data moved to memory from the adapter on each transfer. The most efficient cards use 32-bit transfers to adapter memory or direct memory access (DMA) to move their data. Adapters that don't use memory-mapped buffers or DMA must use processor instructions to move data, and that makes the processor busy. DMA uses the memory, and that can slow the processor down, but it is still more efficient than individual instructions.

If you have fixed the adapters and you still have a problem, you might be able to increase the processor clock speed. One method is to multiply the processor clock speed while leaving the rest of the memory and I/O bus speeds alone. Clock doubler and tripler processors do this. This can be very beneficial, although the results in practice are usually less than the multiplier, because real applications do more than just use the processor.

Another thing you can do is increase the size of your secondary cache. Many computers accept a range of secondary cache sizes, and those that do so seldom ship with the maximum installed.

Adding memory without upgrading the secondary cache size sometimes degrades processor performance. This is because the secondary cache now has to map the larger memory space, usually resulting in lowered hit rates in the cache. This slows down processor-bound programs because they are scattered more widely in memory after memory has been added. If you suspect such a slowdown, create a processor-bound test with Response Probe that touches a lot of memory, but fits in the original memory size without sustained paging. Run this test before and after adding the memory, and you may well see that the test is slower with more memory. Disable the secondary cache using the BIOS setup utility, and repeat the experiment with both memory sizes. They should now perform the same. If they do, you have isolated the problem to the secondary cache design.

Finally, you might benefit from adding additional processors. This will help only if you have a bottleneck involving more than one thread capable of asynchronous execution. To the extent that threads can execute in parallel, adding processors provides relief.

Monitoring Multiple Processors

In the previous chapter we illustrated multiple processors as just additional hardware resources, and so they are. If you are a product of the personal computer era, thinking of multiple processors as you think of multiple disk drives might be a bit of a strain at first, but you'll get used to it. In the next example we are running eight processes on an eight-processor system, which we started artificially with only one processor running, and we see the expected contention.

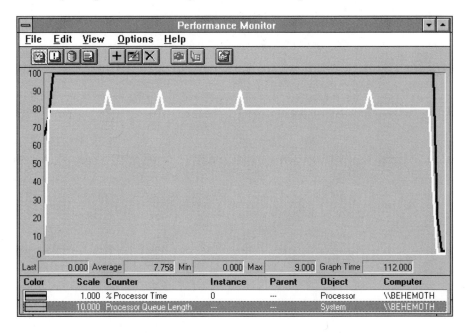

Figure 3.39 Eight processes in one processor

We see the processor utilization at 100% in black and the highlighted queue length in white. In the next figure, we see the processor is indeed shared equally among the eight processes. Unfortunately they are all running at about 12.5% of full speed, and if we were waiting for them we'd probably be complaining about how slow they were. The output from Response Probe tells us that on average they are taking 8.05 times longer than the response time of a single process running in a single processor doing the same amount of work.

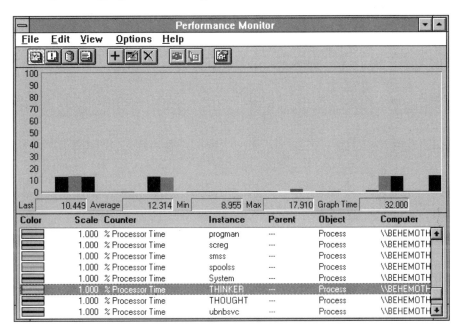

Figure 3.40 Processor time distribution among eight processes in one processor

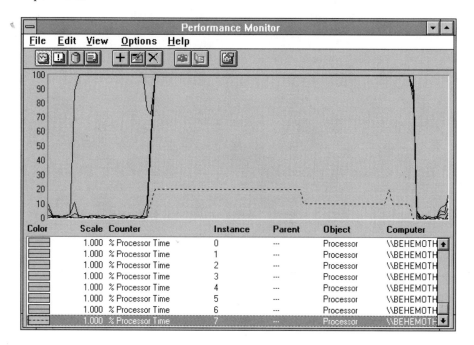

Figure 3.41 Eight processes on eight processors

The first processor busy at 100% is a single processor handling Response Probe while it is doing its processor calibration. During this phase, Response Probe determines the number of times it must execute its basic computation loop to use up one millisecond of processing time. Later it will use this information to apply the amount of processing you request. Once it has calibrated, the probe starts the eight processes. Each one starts executing. The processor queue length (the dotted line) goes way down from our last example. On closer inspection, we'd find that the threads waiting in the processor queue are system processes waiting to complete housekeeping functions at a lower priority.

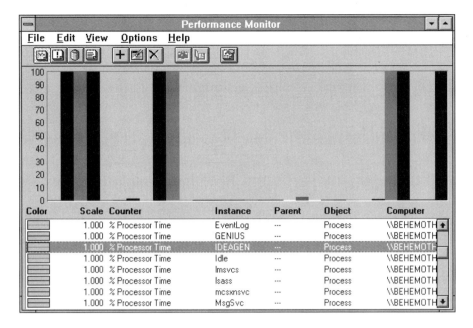

Figure 3.42 Processor use by eight processes on eight processors

Figure 3.42 shows that each process is using 100% of a processor. This time the output of Response Probe tells us that each one is getting exactly the same response time as a single process running on a single processor. We are getting eight times the work done.

For each processor we added, we got 100% of a processor's worth of work done. Life is not always this rosy in multiprocessor land. There are a number of reasons why adding processors might not yield the response time improvements we see in this idealized experiment. For example, if the bottleneck is not in the processors at all, adding more does not help. If the disk subsystem is maxed out, adding a processor does not increase work done. (If this isn't obvious to you, it's time to reread the beginning of this chapter.)

More subtle problems can occur. These all revolve around the contention for shared resources. The processes in the example above were selfish in the extreme: the only thing they shared was their code. Because code is only read and not written, each processor can have a copy of the code in its primary and secondary memory caches; as they execute they don't even have to share access to the RAM that holds the code. Programs frequently operate independently like this, but unlike this example they tend to use shared system resources and thus mutually develop bottlenecks as they contend for those resources.

Here's a different example that quickly illustrates the contention for shared resources. We again use our modified copy of Gdidemo that draws balls continuously on the screen. This program does minimal computation and maximal drawing. Because there is only one display subsystem, contention develops for resources surrounding writing on the display. We'll start eight copies of this program, one after the other, and see how they fare on the eight-processor computer. But let's be clear: eight-processor computers do not normally sit on a desktop and get used for drawing pictures. This is not something you'll normally do but it serves to illustrate the conflicts that can arise.

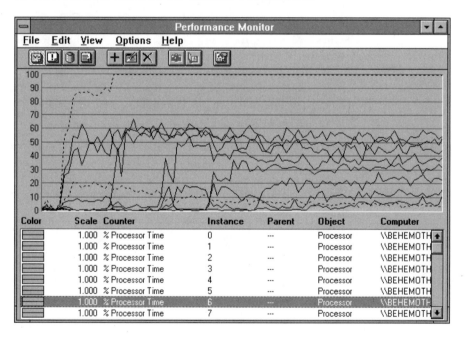

Figure 3.43 Resource contention by eight graphics programs on an eight-processor computer

Spaghetti? No, poetry! The thin black lines are the utilizations of the eight-processors. The high black dotted line is the processor utilization of CSRSS, the graphics subsystem process. The first program starts and two processors leap into action, with a third contributing a little effort, around 8 to 9%. When the second program starts, the third processor picks up considerably. Now CSRSS is using 100% of a processor. As each program gets going, another processor kicks in, although at decreasing utilization.

The next figure shows that by the time we have four drawing programs running, we have reached a firm bottleneck. The heavy black line is the System: % Total Processor Time. This is the aggregate sum of processor utilizations. By the time the third program starts, we are nearly maxed out. With the fourth program, it's the end of the line. The highlighted line is System: Context Switches/sec. This reaches a maximum (see value bar) of 14,256 switches per second. Because there is a context switch each time a program sends a batch of drawing commands to CSRSS, this is a pretty good measure of drawing throughput. It is not quite as jittery as the total processor utilization, and shows the bottleneck very clearly. After the fourth program, even though we are adding more processors, there is no more work getting done. Bottleneck defined. Once we get to this point we could add processors all day.

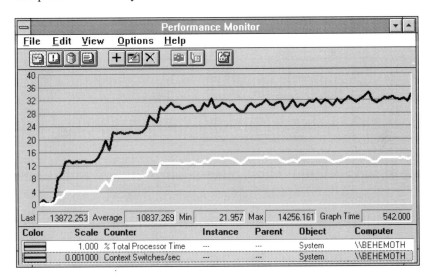

Figure 3.44 After the fourth process is added, no more work gets done

What is the cause of this bottleneck? CSRSS has to protect the common data structures that surround drawing on the display. This includes the video RAM itself which holds the drawn images for the display, but also numerous internal structures involved in drawing. Once these are 100% in use, we're at maximum throughput.

We noted that when the second drawing program started, CSRSS jumped to using 100% of a processor. Untrue. Actually, it is using more. On a multiprocessor computer, 100% is not really the maximum percentage of processor time that a process can have, but Performance Monitor artificially restricts the value to 100% anyway. It takes the meaning of "percent" a bit too literally. Are we embarrassed? A little. Will we survive? Probably. Anyway, to see how busy such a process really is on a multiprocessor system, you have to look at the utilization of processors by a process's individual threads. This we do in the next figure.

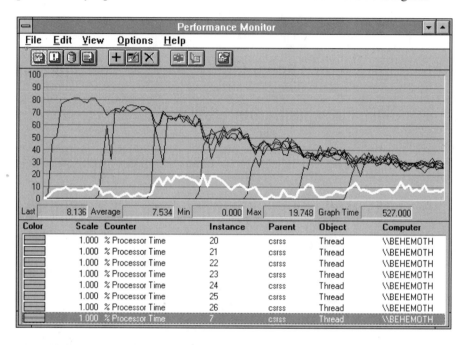

Figure 3.45 CSRSS threads with eight graphics programs and eight processors

This shows thread 7 highlighted and solves the minor mystery of who it was that used the 8 to 9% of a processor when we first started. This is a CSRSS housekeeping thread doing background work as a result of the primary activity.

Now when the second drawing program starts, we see two CSRSS threads equally active at about 72.5% processor utilization. That's almost 150% for the CSRSS process as a whole even if we ignore thread 7. We know the bottleneck is at four programs, and at that point the four CSRSS threads are at a little over 50% utilization, or 200% for CSRSS as a whole.

This shows that system hardware or software resource contention can lead to a bottleneck in a multiprocessor system. To understand what is going on you need knowledge of the application, the hardware, and the operating system. Unfortunately, there is no substitute for this knowledge. If you don't know what's going on inside, all guesses are equally poor.

Here is another example of how contention can arise in multiprocessor systems. This example is extreme but again illustrates the point nicely.

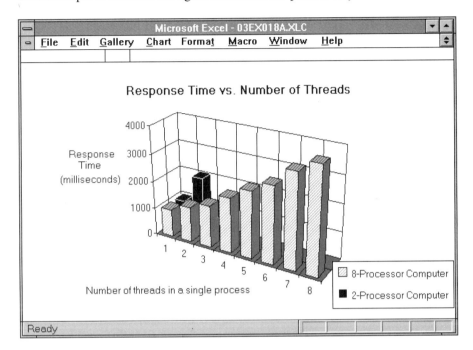

Figure 3.46 Memory contention in multiprocessor systems

This figure shows the output of Response Probe in two different computers: a two-processor system and an eight-processor system. Each thread of the probe is being asked to compute for one second, with no file or special memory activity, and to measure the time it takes to do that one second of computation. Remember that the number of instructions the probe needs to execute to use up a second of computation is determined by the main probe process before starting the child process that applies the load. This number is then communicated to its children.

In this experiment there is only one process. In successive trials, a thread is added to the process. The response time is observed each time.

In the first experiment in this section, we saw that eight probe processes doing this same workload got the same response time on eight processors as one process did. Here, this is not so. Each thread added slows the aggregate down. The response time grows. Moreover, it degrades more on the two-processor computer than on the eight-processor.

Why are the results for multiple threads in one process different from multiple threads in separate processes? Because they are in the same process, these threads are sharing the same address space. They are writing frequently to the same memory location. This is a big bummer for multiprocessor systems.

First let's take a brief look at how Response Probe works and the source of all this contention. Response Probe is basically in a loop trying to determine how much of what load to place next on the system. It uses a normal number generator to find out how much processor load is being requested. The normal number generator returns a number which, over a sequence of calls, will be normally distributed (on a bell-shaped curve) with the mean and standard deviation you supply (see Appendix C for details). Inside the processor load loop, Response Probe looks at where in the pseudo-code space the next read from "code" memory is to take place. Then it generates another normally distributed number and looks at where in its data space you want the next words to be written. This causes yet another call to the normal number generator. Each call to the normal number generator causes seven calls to a random number generator. And each call to the random number generator returns a random number which, as a side effect, is stored in a global cell of memory for use on the next call. This memory cell is the spot where all the contention takes place.

When a memory cell is written in a multiprocessor system, care must be taken to make sure that cell is kept consistent in the memory caches of each processor. This is done by the cache controller hardware in the multiprocessor computer. A number of algorithms can do this, and they vary in cost of implementation. The idea is the same in each, however: when a processor needs to write to memory, the hardware must determine whether that memory location is in the cache of some other processor(s). If so, the other caches must be invalidated (cheap solution) or given the new data (expensive solution).

At this point, the cache controller writing the data may update main memory so that other caches will get the updated data from memory if they need that word in the future; this is called *write-through caching*. Alternatively, the cache controller can wait to update main memory until it needs to reuse the cache location. This is called *write-back*. If the location is rewritten frequently, write-back caching obviously can cause fewer writes to main memory, and thus less contention on the memory bus. But if another cache needs the data (as is increasingly likely as we add threads in this case), it must have the logic to get the data from the other cache instead of from main memory. In this case, the original cache must listen in on bus requests and respond before main memory to requests for data which it has but which is not yet valid in main memory.

This is the briefest possible introduction to the rich and interesting topic of multiprocessor cache coherency. There are lots of schemes with varying tradeoffs in cost and performance. Obviously, two quite different schemes were used in the two-processor and the eight-processor computers measured here. In fact, we get no particular benefit from adding the second processor in the two-processor system for this test. That does not mean that this is a bad implementation of multiprocessors, although it is likely a cheap one. You need to keep in mind that this is an extreme example. The test of multiple drawing programs ran quite well on this two-processor computer, and because it was designed more to handle this sort of desktop application, all is well. But this example illustrates that the investment in more sophisticated hardware in the eight-processor system paid off in improved performance when memory contention is a big factor. It also shows that Response Probe is a pretty brutal test of cache coherency hardware designs.

It is quite difficult to see cache and memory contention with Performance Monitor because the conflicts are in hardware at a level where there are no counters visible. It just looks like the processors are busy. It is not possible to see that they are being stalled on cache and memory accesses. The only test that works is the addition of a processor and the observation of throughput or response time. And being sure the problem is cache/memory and not some other resource is also tricky. There is just no substitute for doing controlled experiments like those in this section to characterize the system. Alternatively, you can buy another processor and hope for the best.

C H A P T E R   4

Detecting Disk Bottlenecks

Disks store programs and the data that programs process. When you are waiting for your computer to respond, it is frequently the disk that is the bottleneck. And if memory is tight, it is the disk that takes the beating. In this chapter, we'll take a look at how disks behave when they are used heavily, and how you can spot a disk bottleneck.

Making Sure Disk Performance Statistics Are Collected

First let's review the important point we covered briefly in Chapter 2: you must run the **diskperf** utility to activate disk performance statistics on your computer. To activate disk performance statistics on the local computer, type the following, and shut down and restart the computer.

diskperf -y

To activate disk performance statistics on a remote computer, specify the computer name when you start **diskperf**; for example, to collect statistics on a computer named AARDVARK, you would type:

diskperf -y \\aardvark

After typing this, you must restart the remote computer before disk statistics are collected.

You must be a member of the Administrators local group on a computer to run **diskperf** on it.

The **diskperf** utility installs the disk performance statistics driver, DISKPERF.SYS, in the I/O Manager's disk driver stack. See Figure 4.1, showing the stack with the disk performance statistics driver installed.

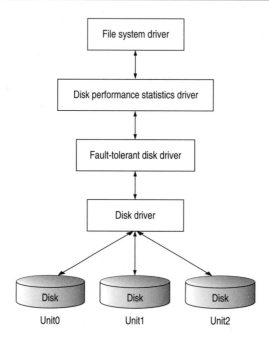

Figure 4.1 Disk driver stack with disk performance driver installed

The reason we put you through the bother of installing **diskperf** manually is because it causes a little performance-degrading overhead that you may not always want. Let's use Response Probe to do a quick experiment to see if it's worth it.

Note By the way, be sure when doing these experiments to let your Windows NT computer settle for a while after logging on. Various background startup activities can interfere with your experiment. You might also want to disconnect the network if it is not involved in the experiment. Network drivers may respond to network events even if they are not directed to your computer.

By setting the FILEACCESSMODE parameter in Response Probe to UNBUFFER, we are guaranteed to bypass the cache and go directly to disk. (For more information about Response Probe and its parameters, see Appendix C, "Using Response Probe.") We'll set up Response Probe to do 100 reads of 512 bytes from a file. We want to transfer a small amount of data because we want to see the maximum distortion caused by the **diskperf** overhead. Unbuffered access to disk must be a multiple of a sector in size, so 512 is as small as we can go.

We'll use a file that is 100K in length. To create the file, we'll use the **createfil** utility, which is on the floppy disk provided with this book. To create a 100K file with the name FILENAME.EXT, type:

createfil filename.ext 100

We'll set the Response Probe FILESEEK to a mean of 100 and a standard deviation of 30. Because this is in units of 512-byte records, it means our accesses will be normally distributed around a point near the middle of the file. It is a property of normal distributions that about 99% of the access will be within plus-or-minus 3 standard deviations, so we should get a nice bell-shaped distribution of accesses across the length of the file. (For more information about using bell-shaped distributions in Response Probe experiments, see Appendix C of this book.)

On our 486 computer with a 50 MHz clock, we get consistent average times from Response Probe of 1666 milliseconds for the 100 reads, or 16.66 milliseconds/read, with **diskperf** enabled. This is probably close to the rotation time of the disk. The standard deviation of the response time to the 100 reads is 1 millisecond, so this is a very repeatable experiment. With **diskperf** disabled, we get the same number: 1666 milliseconds. There's no visible degradation in performance! So why did we make **diskperf** optional? Because if you do this same experiment on an 386 20 MHz computer, you see a degradation in disk performance of about 1.5%. On a 386/25SX laptop computer we observe a 0.9% (nine-tenths of 1%) degradation in disk throughput. Because we don't know what sort of system you are going to place Windows NT on, we prefer that you elect whether to collect disk performance statistics, rather than force you to do so by default.

Busy Disks Are Happy Disks

Let's take a look at the damage we inflict on a disk with the preceding Response Probe experiment. Naturally, we crank up Performance Monitor, and we'll set up Performance Monitor to write its log file on another disk, to minimize the interference it might cause.

Figure 4.2 shows Processor: % Processor Time as a thin black line, and Logical Disk: % Disk Time as a thick black line during the above experiment. To get this data, you must have installed **diskperf**, or the % Disk Time will remain at zero.

What is the difference between a physical disk and a logical disk? A physical disk is the unit number of a single physical disk unit, while a logical disk is the drive letter of a disk partition. (For example, a single disk drive with two partitions would be a single physical disk instance, such as 0, with two logical disk instances, such as C and D.) The parent instance of a logical disk is the unit number of the physical disk on which it resides.

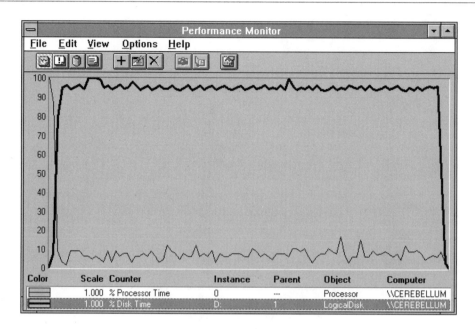

Figure 4.2 Processor and disk behavior during disk bashing

One thing that is pretty clear is that the processor is no longer the bottleneck, and the disk certainly is. Boy, this is easy!

In Figure 4.3 we show a bit more detail about overall performance. Average Processor utilization is only 7.2%, but the interrupt rate is well above the 66.667 Interrupts/second we expect from the clock on an idle system isolated from the network. We see an additional 60.194 Interrupts/sec. Could they be from the disk? Let's find out.

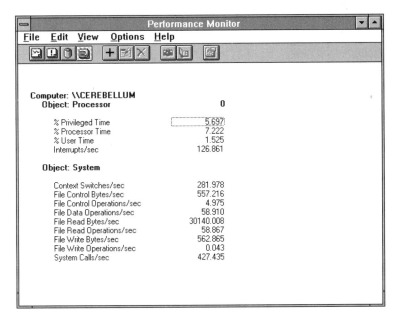

Figure 4.3 Processor and system activity when reading small records from disk

If we divide File Read Bytes/sec by File Reads/sec, we get 30140/58.867 = 512 bytes per read, which is what we told Response Probe to do, so this is good. Other than the elevated system call rate, the remainder of the System counters show a small amount of background activity, which we shall not explore further.

Figure 4.4 contrasts the activity on drive D, from which we are reading the 512 byte records, and the C drive, on which we are logging the Performance Monitor data. (We omitted the % Free Space and Free Megabytes counters because they don't play a role here.)

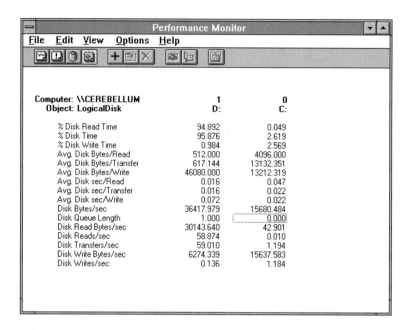

Figure 4.4 Disk activity while reading short records, logging elsewhere

Drive D is, basically, pegged to the wall and preoccupied with reading. Drive C is barely perturbed and focused on writing. What a grand study in contrasts! There's really quite a lot to look at here. In both cases, we see that % Disk Read Time and % Disk Write Time sum to % Disk Time. You might have expected this but it is not always true, as we will see shortly.

Remember the 60.194 extra interrupts discovered in Figure 4.3? If we add the Transfers/sec from Drive D and Drive C, we get 60.204. This is close enough that we should suspect more than a coincidence. Why aren't they identical? When collecting data, the system polls each object manager in turn for its statistics. Because the system is still running during this process, we might expect System counters to be off slightly from Disk counters. So now you know a new Rule.

Rule 9.

Close counts in horseshoes and bottleneck detection.

Average Disk Bytes/Read on drive D are 512 as expected in this experiment. On drive D we see an Avg. Disk sec/Read of 0.016, quite near the 16.85 milliseconds observed by Response Probe in this case. This means Performance Monitor interferes with the experiment only 1.1% as measured by the time to do the 100 unbuffered disk reads. Because we were logging at a one-second time interval, this is impressively low.

This number of 0.016 Avg. Disk sec/Read is bothersome. Because the counters of average disk transfer times (such as Avg. Disk sec/Read) are rounded to the millisecond, some interesting details may be omitted. What can you do? Remember that the % Disk Read Time is 100 times the average number of milliseconds the disk was busy during a second. So we can eke out a few more digits of precision:

Avg. Disk sec/Read = % Disk Time / Disk Reads/sec = .94892 / 58.874 = 0.016118

So we were quite close to 16 milliseconds after all. There are times when it is worth checking. But a word of caution is definitely in order: this calculation only works when the queue length is one or less, as we see shortly.

Reversing our perspective for a moment, we see a very small Disk Writes/sec on drive D (0.136), but a very large Avg. Disk Bytes/Write (46080). We don't write very often, but when we do, it's a whopper! This gives an Avg. Disk sec/Write of 0.072 (72 milliseconds), much larger than the 0.016 Avg. Disk sec/Read. This activity is due to system directory maintenance. It's unclear whether this large 72 millisecond transfer time is due to the large transfer size or to the disk having to do a seek operation away from our experimental file. How could we find out? Construct a quick experiment to read 46080 bytes repeatedly.

Let's look into this a little further, because we sense another Rule about to emerge. Let's plot the Avg. Disk Bytes/Write on drive D and see what is happening here. Take a gander at Figure 4.5.

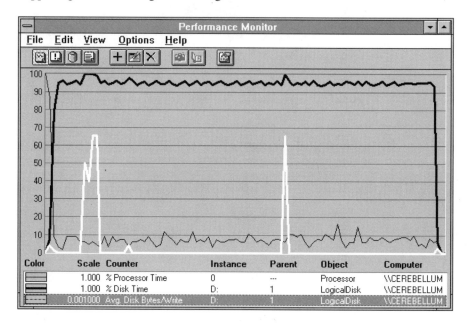

Figure 4.5 Background disk writing while reading short records

The 40K number reported in Figure 4.4 did not give us much of a clue. Now we can see that what is really happening here is that 65K writes are taking place, along with some smaller ones. The file system is updating its directory information during our experiment, and there's really no stopping it. This is not significant, as far as interference with our experiment goes. But the 40K number is a bit misleading, and the rate of 0.136 writes/sec contains no clue that this is really a few isolated large writes instead of a steady stream of writes of various sizes. Because Performance Monitor is built on lots of averages, it is wise to remember Rule # 10:

Rule 10.

Averages reveal basic truths while hiding crucial details.

You can divide Disk Read Bytes/sec (30143.640) by Disk Reads/sec (58.874) to get the Avg. Disk Bytes/Read of 512.002. This differs from the 512.000 reported, because the reported numbers are truncated to 3 decimal digits. There's no point in getting bogged down in the fine print—what's 0.002 bytes among friends?

There is an interesting difference between the data on drive D and that on drive C. Look at Figure 4.6, which isolates the issue.

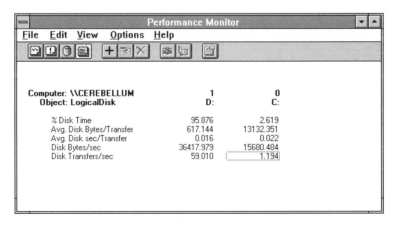

Figure 4.6 Study in contrasts: disk transfer rates

Drive D is 96% busy, doing 59 transfers and moving 36K a second. Drive C is 2.6% busy, doing 1.1 transfers a second, and still moving almost half as many bytes per second. Clearly drive C is operating more efficiently. The reason is that Drive C has a higher value for Avg. Disk Bytes/Transfer, 20 times higher. Yet each transfer is taking only 6 milliseconds more time. When you try to locate a disk bottleneck, after noting that the disk is busy, look at the average transfer size. It is a key to efficient use of the disk.

Looking again at Figure 4.4, the Disk Queue Length on drive D is 1. This is an instantaneous count—just the value at the endpoint of the time interval of the report. But the probability that there is someone in the disk queue is 95.876%, the same as the disk utilization. Unlike System: Processor Queue Length, the Disk Queue Length counter includes the request in service at the disk as well as any requests that are waiting. In fact, all the disk statistics are collected by the DISKPERF.SYS driver, which is located above the normal disk driver in the driver stack. When a file system request comes into DISKPERF.SYS, it gets a time stamp and is added to the queue count. Then it gets handed to the next level of driver. This may be a fault tolerant (software RAID) disk driver, or the "real" disk driver. Any processor cycles consumed by the drivers go into % Disk Time.

Given the low processor utilization shown in Figure 4.2, it seems obvious that we have plenty of spare horsepower to drive the queue length up. Let's get five processes to do the same experiment at once and see what happens to the disk statistics.

Figures 4.7 through 4.9 show five processes doing the same thing the one did above: unbuffered reading of 512 byte records from a small file. Figure 4.7 includes the Disk Queue Length, which varies between 4 and 5, depending on when we take the snapshot. The % Disk Time is now pegged to the max. Comparing Figures 4.3 and 4.8 shows they are remarkably similar.

We have chosen to use the System counters instead of the Processor counters in Figure 4.8, but because this is a single processor system the processor statistics for processor 0 are the same as those for the system overall. In a sense Figure 4.8 is the "correct" style, because if we had a multiprocessor system Figure 4.3 would be showing the data for just one of the processors. And yes, we have manually placed Total Interrupts/sec out of order to make comparing these two figures easier.

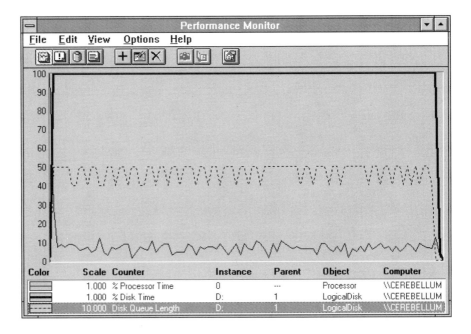

Figure 4.7 Five processes reading small records at once, or trying to

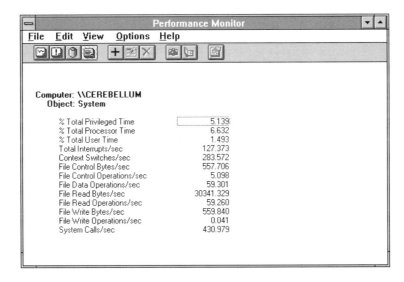

Figure 4.8 System overview of five processes reading small records at once

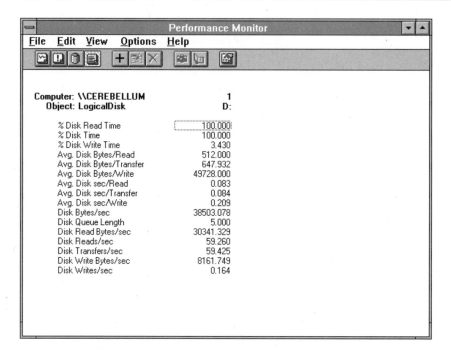

Figure 4.9 Disk behavior of five processes reading small records at once

But we digress. The main point here is that the statistics are nearly identical, even though we have added four more processes to the mix. But this should not surprise you. This is what we mean by the word bottleneck! The disk statistics don't change because the disk was already maxed out. All we have really done is dumped these poor processes into the disk queue. Figure 4.7 shows that this has taken up the remaining 4% slack in disk utilization, yielding about 1/2 more transfer per second.

So we see pretty much what we might expect in Figure 4.9, except for one thing. The sum of the % Disk Write Time and the % Disk Read Time exceed the % Disk Time. This is because DISKPERF.SYS begins timing a request when the request is delivered to the next driver layer. You can see this pretty clearly by comparing Avg. Disk sec/Read in Figure 4.9 to that in Figure 4.4. Let's use the trick we learned above to get a more accurate number for read transfer time:

Avg. Disk sec/Read = % Disk Time / Disk Reads/sec = 1 / 59.260 = 0.016875

Wow, this result of 16.875 milliseconds is very different from the Figure 4.9 Avg. Disk sec/Read of 0.083. What's going on? The 16.875 millisecond number is the time it is taking us to get each request from the disk. But the reported 0.083 number is the time spent in the queue plus the time to get the data from the disk. Dividing 0.083 by 0.016875 gives 4.9, which is an excellent measure of average queue length, and a better one than the instantaneous counter value Disk Queue Length.

Uncovering High Disk Throughput

To tell you the truth, we've been slacking. This disk is capable of much more than this level of throughput. Let's build a large file so we can simulate a more realistic load with more seek operations. We'll use **createfil** to make a 500-MB sandbox for us to play in. We'll turn on Performance Monitor while we're at it to see what **createfil** is doing.

Figure 4.10 was logged at five-second intervals while we created the 500 MB file. Obviously the disk was quite busy, and the processor was loafing. Must be its day off.

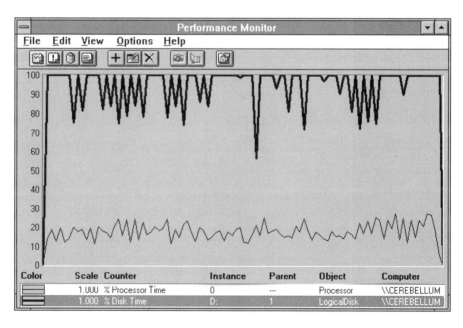

Figure 4.10 Creating a 100-MB file

The system overview in the next figure reveals a rather surprising lack of file activity. File bytes are being written at about 51K per second. We knew from the Graph Time on the value bar in the chart represented by Figure 4.10 (value bar not shown) that it takes about 722 seconds to create this file. (We subtracted one time interval, or five seconds, from each end because the chart starts before and ends after the file is created.) Multiplying the File Write Bytes/sec times 722 seconds give us a result of only around 37 million bytes. But the file is over 524 million bytes in length. We've seen this before, right? This must be the old fast path to the cache that bypasses the file system altogether. While we can tell Response Probe to use unbuffered access, **createfil** always uses buffered file system calls. In fact this is the default, and because it is almost always faster, almost all applications use buffered file access. The principal exceptions are network server applications which do their own caching.

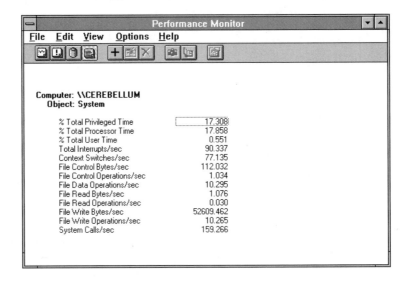

Figure 4.11 System overview of creating a 100-MB file

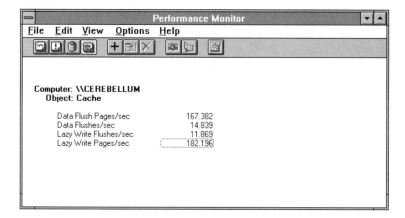

Figure 4.12 Cache behavior when creating a large buffered file

The cache statistics in Figure 4.12 show that the lazy writer is launched frequently to help clear the cache, and in addition the cache is rapidly flushing dirty pages to make room for new ones. (Lazy writes and data flushes have an interesting relationship, detailed in Chapter 6, "Detecting Cache Bottlenecks.") Multiplying the number of Lazy Write Pages/sec times the page size (4096 bytes on this machine), we see a byte rate of 746,275 bytes/sec. This is close to the disk transfer rate we see on drive D in the next figure.

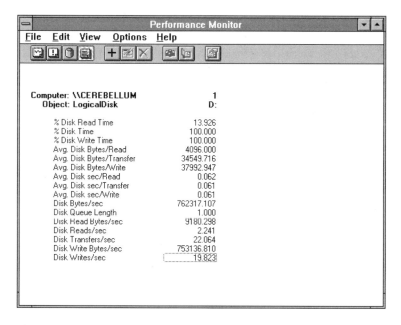

Figure 4.13 Disk behavior when creating a large buffered file

Now we've got a disk really pumping bytes. Compare this to the rate achieved by reading small records in Figure 4.7. The large transfer size here, 37993 bytes per write, is the key to the high efficiency the system achieved. And we can do even better than this.

Uncovering Even Higher Disk Throughput

Let's try to discover the maximum rate at which we can get data from this disk. We'll read the same record over and over, increasing its size, until we maximize throughput. We'll read from the beginning of the file so we know we will be starting at the same point on the disk every time. We'll start by reading 1 page, and increase the size of the read 1 page at a time until the reads reach 64K. The results appear in Figure 4.14. The highlighted (white) line is the disk throughput in Disk Bytes/sec, while the black line is the size of the record that is read. This goes from 4096K per read (1 page) to 65536K per read (16 pages).

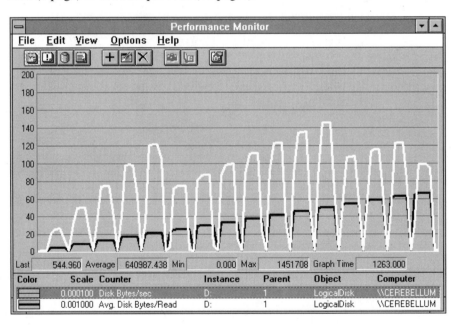

Figure 4.14 Transfer rates achieved by various-sized reads

Its not hard to see the highest transfer rate occurs in the case of 12-page records. As the size of the read operations grows, the transfer rate climbs, but something happens between the record size of 5 pages and that of 6 pages. Then it rises to a peak at 12 pages, and falls again for 13. It rises thereafter until the final fall at 16 pages. Very suspicious. Anyway, the maximum throughput we have achieved (see the value bar) is 1.4 MB per second. Finally, some decent throughput!

Now let this sink in: in this situation the disk is nearly 100% busy and transferring 1.4 MB/sec, while in Figure 4.2 the disk is nearly 100% busy and transferring 36K/sec. You may be able to tell how busy the disk is by looking at the utilization, but you don't know how much work it is doing unless you look at the transfer rate. In this respect, disk performance isn't that different from employee performance. We all have a coworker or three who is frantically busy all the time but doesn't get much actual work done. How hard a disk or person labors and how much they achieve is not always directly related.

The next figure shows pretty clearly why our transfer rates are not increasing monotonically.

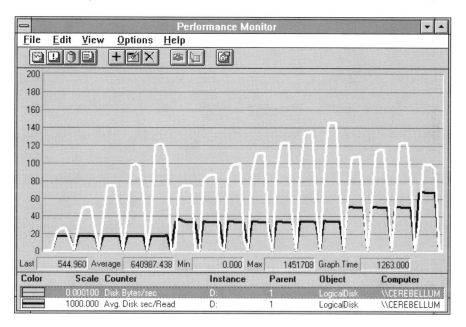

Figure 4.15 Transfer rates and transfer times achieved with various-sized reads

Aha! The transfer times are jumping just when the transfer rates fall off. And if you look closely you can see that they jump by 16.7 milliseconds each time. We've seen this number before, and here's why. Many disks rotate at 3600 rpm, or 60 revolutions per second. That's one revolution every 16.666 milliseconds. When we go from 5 to 6 page records, we suddenly need an extra revolution to read the entire record. This is quite damaging to our transfer rate.

The next two figures show the system overview and disk data for the read operation using 12-page records. We got this data by shrinking the time window to the case of interest, then viewing the report. The system data shows that all the bytes are going through the file system because we are unbuffered. The results are quite a contrast to those in Figure 4.3.

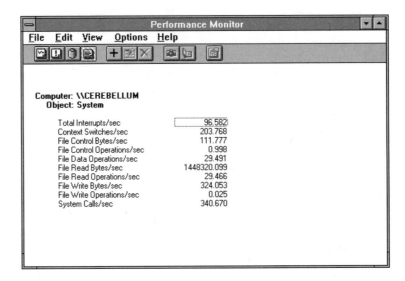

Figure 4.16 System overview during maximum disk throughput

The file statistics are just about as good as they get on this computer. Transfer size is exactly 48K per second, giving throughput of 1.4 MB per second. This puppy is hummin'!

But is this realistic? Recall that we are reading the same record over and over again, something we're not likely to see in the real world. Let's take another look at maximizing disk throughput, but this time let's use all of the 500 MB file we took so much time to create.

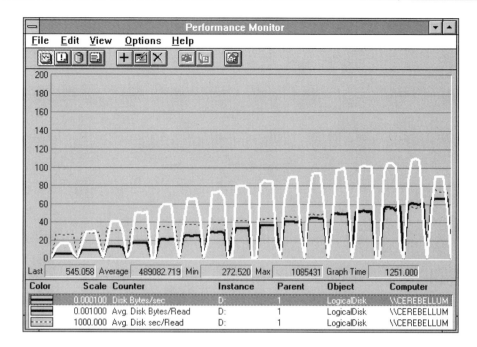

Figure 4.17 Randomly reading successively larger records of a 500-MB file

Now when we integrate seeking across the disk we see a linear increase in disk throughput as a function of record size, until we reach 64K. In this case, we lose another rotation every time, and throughput falls off accordingly. If we are not forcing a rereading of the same record over and over, we do not have to wait for the disk to rotate around to the start of the record each time. By accessing more randomly, the cost of the extra rotations that do occur is too small to notice.

In Figure 4.18 we narrow the time window to the case where throughput is maximum. Now we see all the data points collected during this time, and a slightly higher maximum is uncovered. If you really care about the details, be sure to narrow your time window to fewer than 100 data points so you don't skip any data points.

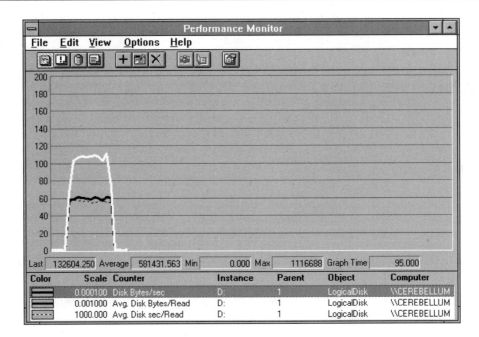

Figure 4.18 Narrowing down to the case of maximum throughput

Now we'll reveal a step we have been doing in many of these experiments, especially when we've shown you reports. This step is the further narrowing of the time window to include only the data of interest: the actual transfers themselves. If we fail to do this, the next few figures would include the end regions of Figure 4.18, and the averages would be lower. Always be careful to set the time window to include only the data of interest before looking at your detailed reports.

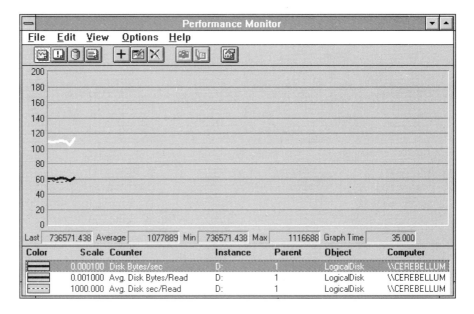

Figure 4.19 Setting the time window to exclude extraneous data points

Now we are set up to produce the usual detailed reports.

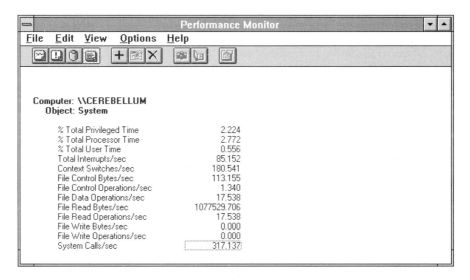

Figure 4.20 System overview reading across a 500-MB file with 60K records

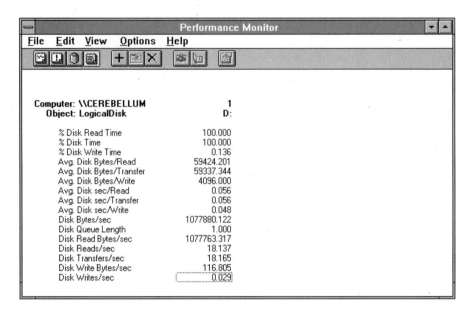

Figure 4.21 Disk statistics reading across a 500-MB file with 60K records

What do we learn from all this? This tells us that 56 milliseconds is a reasonable transfer time for large records with fairly substantial seek activity. Because Response Probe distributes access normally (a bell-shaped curve) across the 500 MB file, this might be considered an easier task than real random seek activity. We could repeat the experiment with real random seek activity, but by now you get the idea. You need to characterize the performance of your processor/disk adapter/drive subsystems in this sort of controlled fashion if you want to understand the bottlenecks on your systems. Response Probe permits the construction of a wide range of access patterns, as this and the previous example show. You can use these controlled experiments to understand observations from real-life systems.

Let's try one more experiment to make this point clear. We'll set up an experiment that does read operations in 60K chunks, but instead of distributing the read operations normally across the 500 MB, we'll distribute them randomly. We do this by increasing the standard deviation of the file seek position in Response Probe, making it equal to the mean. (Response Probe folds any attempts to access the disk beyond the end of the file back into the file. For more information on this, see Appendix C, "Using Response Probe.") The result of this change is displayed in Figure 4.22.

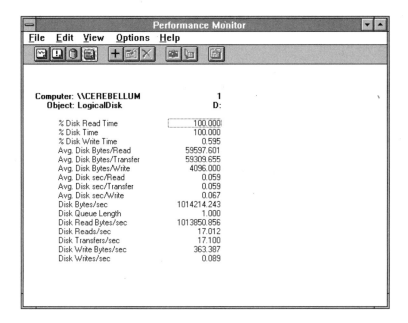

Figure 4.22 Disk behavior reading 60K records more randomly

The average time per read operation has gone from 56 to 59 milliseconds, and the throughput has fallen from about 108 MB per second to about 101 MB per second. That's a pretty substantial loss of throughput—about 6%. If we were to increase the file size, we would see more erosion in throughput as the disk spends more time seeking. Keep up this sort of nonsense, and you'll really know your disk!

Getting Rid of a Disk Bottleneck

If you discover a disk bottleneck, what can you do? The first thing you need to determine is whether it's really more memory that you need. To restate a critical truth, if you are short on memory, you will see the lost performance reflected as a disk bottleneck. We'll take a look at that issue in the next chapter.

If memory isn't the problem, there are a number of possible avenues to pursue to improve disk throughput. First, think about your controller card. Find out from the manufacturer if it does 8-bit, 16-bit, or 32-bit transfers. The more bits in the transfer operation, the faster the controller moves data.

Your I/O bus architecture comes into play here. EISA and MCA buses transfer data at much higher rates than ISA buses. Some computers also have a "turbo switch" that affects bus speed. Make sure it is set to on if you have such a switch. ISA buses cannot see above 16 MB of RAM. To place data above 16 MB of RAM, the driver must arrange a copy of the data from the area below 16 MB. This can slow you down. Changing the bus within a computer is usually not an option. But it's about time you got that new computer anyway, and now if you've isolated your performance problems to the bus, you have a reason!

Also determine if your disk adapter uses direct memory access (DMA) or not. DMA can noticeably improve transfer speeds.

Some disk adapters feature built-in caches. The benefit of this depends a lot on the access patterns of your system. If you are going to purchase the RAM anyway, you might want to consider putting it in the computer's main memory instead of on the adapter card. Because Windows NT features adaptive disk cache size, when memory is needed for something besides disk caching, it is available. It is also available to disk drives on other adapters, as well as to the LAN file systems. But some computers are limited on the amount of main memory they can use, in which case adding memory to a disk adapter may be just the ticket.

If you've done the best you can with your adapter, you might want to think about your disk subsystem configuration. If you have all your activity focused on one disk and one adapter, consider getting a second disk and even a second adapter. Try to spread the load across them. This idea segues into our next topic.

Looking at Redundant Arrays of Inexpensive Disks

What we touch on here is how Performance Monitor sees various redundant arrays of inexpensive disks (RAID) and fault-tolerant disk configurations. We'll also mention some issues relating to their relative performance as observed on one computer, but it would be an error to extrapolate these results to some other system. You need to perform these experiments on your own configurations and under your own real or anticipated workloads to make judgments about optimal disk configuration.

In our example, we have (as physical unit 0) a hardware RAID array of 4 spindles and 800 MB capacity. We partitioned this into drive C (300 MB), and drives F and G, which are 250 MB each. We also have three other disk units with about 340 MB capacity each to play with. We created a 200 MB file on a single partitioned drive D, and another one on a mirrored partition on the other two disks, drive E. After we finished the experiments on drives D and E, we rearranged those three spindles as a single striped partition for drive D (no parity) and created a 200 MB file on that.

We had two disk controllers, one for the hardware RAID array, and another for all three of the other disk units.

All the 200-MB file creation times were 420 seconds, except for the striped partition on drive D which created itself in 314 seconds. In the next two figures we show the difference in behavior of drive D as a single drive and as a striped volume.

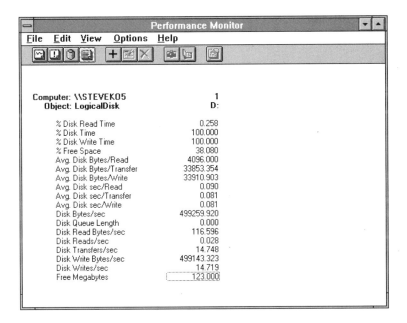

Figure 4.23 File creation on a single spindle

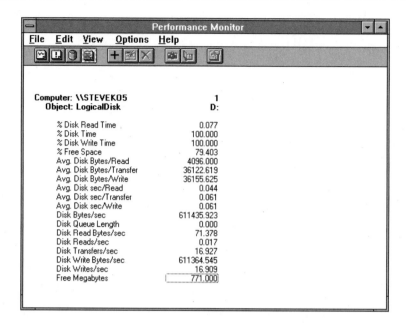

Figure 4.24 File creation on a three-spindle striped volume without parity

Notice the Avg. Disk sec/Write is 0.081 for the single unit and 0.061 for the striped set. This results in higher Disk Bytes/sec. Striping reduces seeking and therefore improves performance.

In Figure 4.24, drive D is striped across units 1, 2, and 3. Let's look at the performance of the Physical Disks.

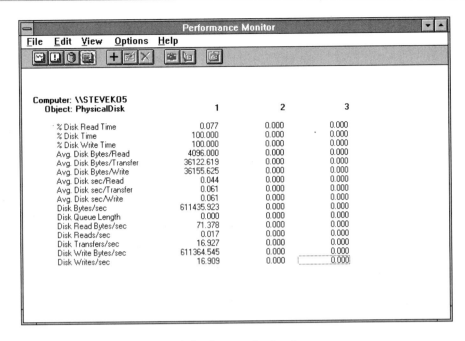

Figure 4.25 Physical disk statistics for a striped volume

Whoops. What happened to units 2 and 3? Well, DISKPERF.SYS cannot see
which physical volume the write operation executes on. This is because
DISKPERF.SYS is located above the fault-tolerant disk driver FTDISK.SYS in
the driver stack, as shown in Figure 4.1. The decision as to which spindle will get
the data is made by FTDISK.SYS and therefore is invisible to DISKPERF.SYS.
The only way to get visibility would be to add another measurement driver below
FTDISK.SYS on the stack. But this would increase the overhead, and we elected
not to do it. The additional information is not important enough to warrant the
overhead.

Mirrors, stripes, and hardware RAID devices all share this Performance Monitor
characteristic: Performance Monitor summarizes all Physical Disk statistics under
the first unit assigned to the disk array.

The next experiment was to read 100 unbuffered (with no file system cache),
normally distributed records of 8192 bytes from the file on each drive type.

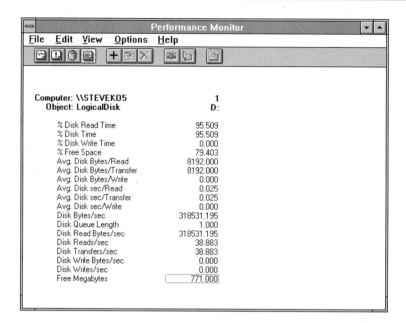

Figure 4.26 Reading from three-spindle striped volume

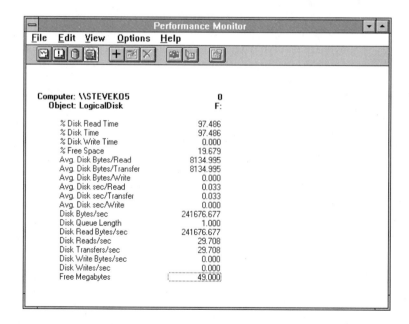

Figure 4.27 Reading from four-spindle hardware RAID

The hardware RAID is slower at this, for some reason. Perhaps its physical drives are slower. The next two figures show our old test of rereading records of various sizes to determine maximum disk throughput. The first figure shows the striped volume, the next one shows the hardware RAID.

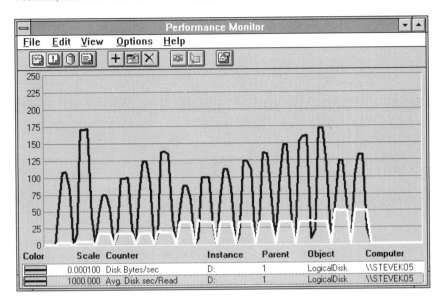

Figure 4.28 Disk throughput test for a three-spindle striped volume

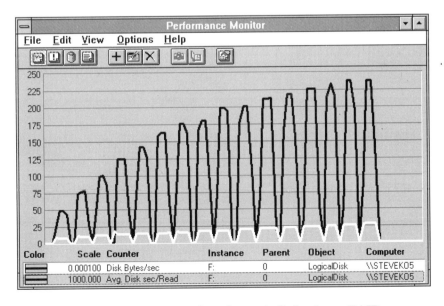

Figure 4.29 Disk throughput test for a four-spindle hardware RAID

Well, now isn't that interesting! The RAID device is quite impressive at higher transfer sizes, and increases monotonically in performance as the transfer size does. The striped volume is not so pretty. It has spots where the performance degrades due to missed revolutions. (Because we are rereading the same record over and over, only one spindle participates in this test.) But there is a serendipitous node at the 8192 transfer size, which just happened to be the size in our test case.

Which of these two technologies would you rather spend your money on? You need to understand the transfer size characteristics of your traffic to be sure. For 4096- or 8192-byte transfers, the striped volume wins; for transfers larger than 5 pages, the hardware RAID is the clear winner. Now don't get us in trouble by trying to use these results directly in your shop. There are a lot of variables. With a different controller, drive, or processor you get different results.

Another way to alter the outcome is to try writing instead of reading. When we substitute writing for reading in the above test, we get 0.016 seconds per record for the striped volume, 0.028 for the single spindle, 0.030 for the hardware RAID, and 0.041 for the mirror. Writing is slower on the mirror because both spindles must be written. If we had another controller for one half of the mirrored pair we would have possibly seen an improvement, not to mention better fault tolerance.

CHAPTER 5

Detecting Memory Bottlenecks

Memory shortage leads to poor performance faster than any other single resource shortage. Why? Memory shortages can cause the computer to have to read and write from the disk more often, and accessing the disk is much slower than just executing instructions in the processor.

We briefly mentioned in Chapter 2 that Windows NT is a virtual-memory system and uses paging so when it executes a program it doesn't have to store the entire program in memory at one time. Instead, only part of the program, divided into chunks of memory called pages, is in memory at any one instant. When the program instructions call for a page of code or data that is not currently in memory, Windows NT must bring in that page from somewhere, usually a disk. It is possible that a single instruction execution can cause one, two, or more page I/O operations.

The average instruction in today's computers takes something in the order of a hundred nanoseconds to execute. (A nanosecond is one-billionth of a second.) We saw in Chapter 4 that disk accesses range in orders around tens of milliseconds. Even one missing page per instruction would make the machine run 100,000 times slower than normal. Now that would be the mother of all bottlenecks!

Things do not usually get that bad. But they can get very bad, and when they do you need to know what you can do about it. (Besides find another job; our boss calls this Option 7, because if we haven't solved a problem in six tries, we're told that Option 7 is no longer optional.)

How the Windows NT Virtual Memory System Works

You probably know that Windows NT is a 32-bit operating system that runs both 16-bit and 32-bit applications. Even the system calls of 16-bit applications are translated to 32 bits.

What does this mean? A program can see 32 bits worth of address space. This translates to 4 gigabytes (4 billion bytes) of virtual memory. The upper half of this is devoted to system code and data and is only visible to the process when it is in privileged mode. The lower half—2 billion bytes—is available to the user program when it is in user mode, and to those user-mode system services called by the program.

Furthermore, the RAM on your Windows NT computer is divided into two categories: *nonpaged* and *paged*. Nonpaged code or data must stay in memory and cannot be written to or retrieved from *peripherals*. Peripherals include disks, the LAN, a CD-ROM, and other devices. Paged memory is RAM which the system can use and later reuse to hold various pages of memory from peripherals. Paged memory is divided into *page frames*, that hold various pages from time to time much as a picture frame can hold various pictures.

Page size varies with the computer's processor type. Page size is 4096 bytes (4K) for 386, 486, and Pentium processors, the same for MIPS® processors, and 8192 (8K) for DEC® Alpha processors. Varying page size is the reason many Performance Monitor counters are in bytes: 100 pages of data is not the same amount of data on all computers.

When a page of code or data is required from a peripheral, the Windows NT memory manager finds a free page frame in which to place the required page. The system transfers the required page, and processing can continue. If no page frame is free, the memory manager must select one to reuse. The memory manager tries to find a page frame whose contents have not been referenced for a while. When the memory manager finds a suitable page frame, it discards the page in it if that page has not been modified since it was placed into RAM. Otherwise, the changed page must be written back to its original location on the peripheral before the new page can replace it. The memory manager has lots of tricks to minimize and anticipate the flow of pages and thus reduce the possibility that paging traffic will beat the peripherals into abject misery. We'll discuss a few of these as we go along.

Normally, programs execute by fetching one instruction after another from a code page (a page that contains program instructions) until they call or return to a routine in some other code page, or make a jump to code in another page. Or, they can simply run off the end of the current page and need the next one. Such a transfer of instruction control to a new page causes a *page fault* if the needed page is not currently in the *working set* of the process. The working set of the process is the set of pages currently visible to the process in RAM.

A page fault can be resolved quickly if the memory manager finds the page elsewhere in RAM. It might be in the working set of some other process or processes, or it might have been removed from this process's working set by the memory manager in an overzealous attempt to keep the process trim and fit. The memory manager places such pages on a list of page frames called the standby list, and they can be reinserted into a process's working set lickety-split. But if the page is not in RAM somewhere, the memory manager must find a free page frame, or make one free as described above, and then fetch the required page from the peripheral. One characteristic of code pages is it isn't normal for code to be modified while in RAM, so code pages can be discarded without being written back to disk.

Data pages, which contain data used by a program, are accessed in a somewhat more random fashion than code pages. Each instruction in a program can reference data allocated anywhere in the address space of a process. The principle, however, is much the same. If an attempt is made to access a data page not in the working set of the process, a page fault occurs. From that point on, the process is just as described for code pages. The only difference between data pages and code pages is that data pages are frequently changed by the processes that access them, and so the memory manager must take care to write them on the peripheral before replacing them with another page. A general page fault handling diagram appears in Figure 5.1.

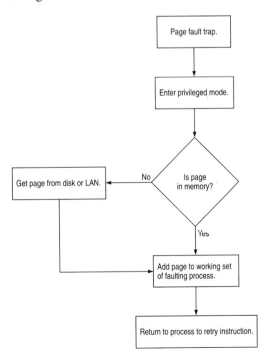

Figure 5.1 Handling page faults on Windows NT

Configuring Available Memory in Windows NT

To see how much RAM Windows NT thinks your system has, switch to Program Manager and choose About Program Manager from the Help menu. For testing purposes, you can reduce the amount of memory that Windows NT thinks you have by modifying the BOOT.INI file. This file has protected attributes. If you want to modify it, make a copy of BOOT.INI first, and then use **attrib** to turn off the Read Only, Hidden, and System attributes for BOOT.INI.

Caution By turning off the protected attributes, you can now overwrite BOOT.INI. Some mistakes written to BOOT.INI can prevent Windows NT from starting.

To observe paging in action, it's useful to fool your system into thinking it has less memory. This forces the memory manager into more activity that we can easily observe. Find the line indicating the Windows NT operating system you want to boot with. We'll add a **/MAXMEM**=n parameter to the end of your Windows NT version line. The n is the number of megabytes you want to test. It is important that you do not make this less than eight. Following is an example of a BOOT.INI file set up with four versions of Windows NT, each configured to use different amounts of memory.

```
[boot loader]
timeout=30
default=multi(0)disk(0)rdisk(0)partition(1)\winnt

[operating systems]
multi(0)disk(0)rdisk(0)partition(1)\winnt="Windows NT Version 3.1"
multi(0)disk(0)rdisk(0)partition(1)\winnt="Windows NT 3.1, 12Mb" /MAXMEM=12
multi(0)disk(0)rdisk(0)partition(1)\winnt="Windows NT 3.1, 10Mb" /MAXMEM=10
multi(0)disk(0)rdisk(0)partition(1)\winnt="Windows NT 3.1, 8Mb" /MAXMEM=8
c:\="MS-DOS"
```

Examples of Memory Activity and Paging

This has been a fairly abstract discussion, so let's look at some concrete examples. We'll start Clock, a Windows NT accessory, and see what kind of memory activity occurs. Starting applications is relatively quick, so we'd better log at one-second intervals if we want to see what's happening. We'll let the system settle down for a few seconds, and then choose Clock from the Accessories Group.

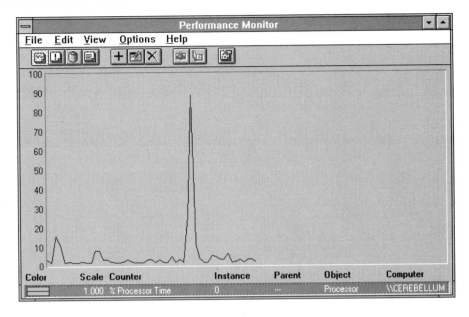

Figure 5.2 Processor activity while starting Clock

Now let's add Memory: Page Faults/sec to the picture in Figure 5.3, it's the thick black line. There are two bursts of page faulting, a large one followed by a small one.

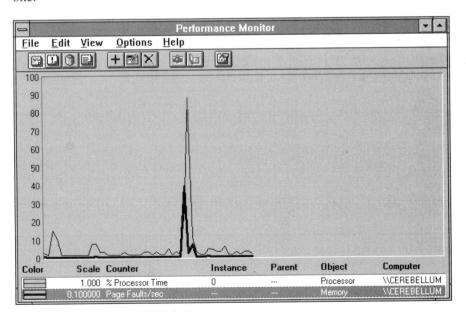

Figure 5.3 Page faults while starting Clock

Because page faults may not involve peripheral activity, it is important to look at how many of these pages faults actually resulted in pages coming in from the disk. In the next figure we have Page Faults/sec in a solid black line, and Pages Input/sec in a dashed line. During the first peak of activity, there is a lot of page fault action that does not result in disk activity. In the second peak, however, every page fault seems to need a new page from disk.

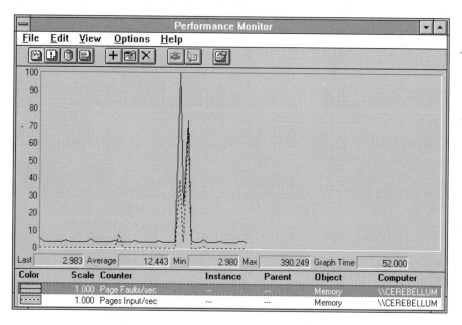

Figure 5.4 Pages input while starting Clock

In the next figure, we can see how many times per second the memory manager asked the disk driver for pages. We can see that this is less than the number of pages input. The memory manager is asking for multiple pages on each request to the disk driver. We told you the memory manager was tricky!

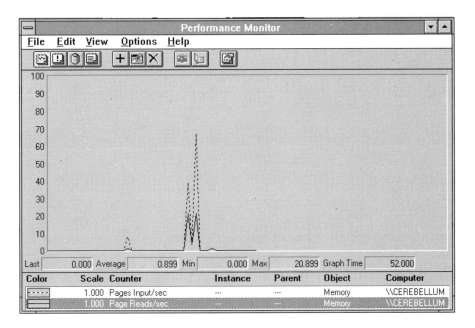

Figure 5.5 Page reads while starting Clock

Presumably Clock causes all this activity, but we'd better check. We can switch over to Report view and look at page faults committed by all the processes. When we do this we see there are three processes that have page faults during this time: Program Manager, Clock, and our old buddy CSRSS. Their faults are charted in Figure 5.6. Clock is highlighted, Program Manager is the thick black line, and CSRSS is the thin black line.

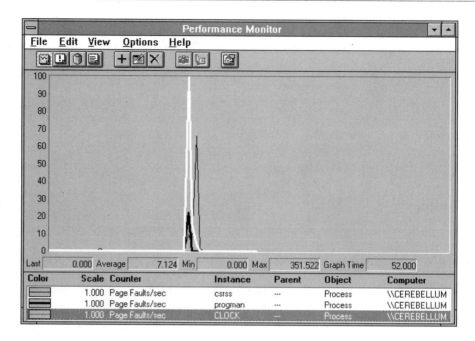

Figure 5.6 Page faults by process while starting Clock

Now we are getting somewhere. First, the little blip on the left is CSRSS. These page faults occurred when we switched focus to Program Manager to get ready to select Clock. Apparently not all the pages needed to perform this action were in the CSRSS working set at that point. It is also clear that the first peak of page fault activity was caused by Clock and to a much lesser extent, Program Manager. During this period we saw that most of the pages faulted were already in memory and we did not have to go to disk for them. How can that be? Clock is likely to use a lot of system windows and graphics routines which are already in use by other processes. These get put into the Clock working set through the page fault process, but they are probably already in memory because other processes are using them.

CSRSS is generating a few page faults during the first peak, but it is largely responsible for the second peak. Because we saw that page faults and pages input were closely correlated during the second peak, we can deduce that the pages that CSRSS needed to bring in to handle the Clock startup were not in memory. This makes sense, really, because Clock uses a very large font for its digits, and such a large font is not likely to be lying around in memory.

Now let's look at the disk activity this set of actions causes. We'll narrow our focus to the period of active paging, and look at some memory and disk statistics.

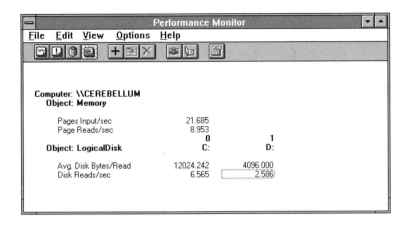

Figure 5.7 Memory and disk reports when starting Clock

By adding the values of LogicalDisk: Disk Reads/sec from the two drives involved we see their sum is just a little higher than the value of Memory: Page Reads/sec. On drive C we are reading almost 3 pages (12K) on every read request. Multiplying three times the Disk Reads/sec and adding the drive D Disk Reads/sec, we get the total Pages Input/sec of 21+. So the paging statistics from the disk and memory are pretty closely related. Close enough for bottleneck detection, according to Rule #9. We had narrowed the time window down to five seconds here, so we have brought in about 105 pages.

But we're just getting started! Let's take a look at the working set sizes of these processes. If they are faulting in a lot of pages, they are probably increasing their working sets. Figure 5.8 shows the working set sizes for each process that is causing page faults.

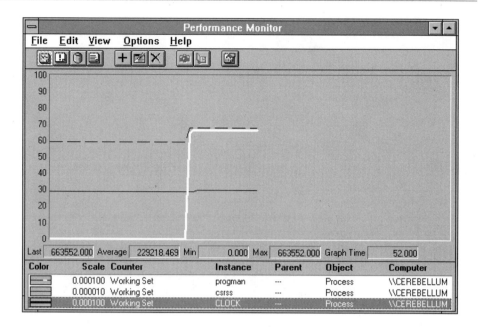

Figure 5.8 Working set size growth when starting Clock

Pay close attention to the scale factors used in this chart. Both Program Manager and Clock have working sets that rise to about 600K, but CSRSS is up to nearly 3 MB. Sure enough, the working set sizes rise just as one might expect. At the start of the test, Program Manager has a fair number of pages lying in memory. The first thing that happens in our experiment is Program Manager brings into its working set whatever pages are required to launch Clock. Total growth in working set is 84K (21 pages), which we can calculate by subtracting the Minimum from the Maximum on the value bar when selecting Program Manager.

Then Clock, starting at ground zero, brings in its working set. A lot of these pages were already in memory, and are just being added to the Clock's working set so Clock can share them. Or perhaps they are fresh data pages that Clock needs, in which case the memory manager will provide Clock with a zeroed page frame, which also does not require disk input.

As soon as Clock starts to use CSRSS to draw the large numerals on the clock face, CSRSS starts to bring in its pages. Although it looks like CSRSS has not increased much here, in fact it looks that way because its scale factor is ten times smaller; it has grown here by 88K, or 22 pages. Recall from Figure 5.4 that most of the CSRSS fault activity resulted in real pages from disk. Because we faulted in a total of 105 pages and we know that 22 went into CSRSS, we calculate that 83 went in to Clock and Program Manager. Because we know that Program Manager's working set grew by no more than 21 pages, that leaves at least 62 pages brought in from the disk by Clock itself.

Can these processes really need all this space? Perhaps not all at once. The memory manager lets processes grow their working sets until memory pressure develops. This is indicated by the decline of another key counter, Memory: Available Bytes. In the next figure we add Available Bytes to the above chart to see how much free memory we have before and after the test.

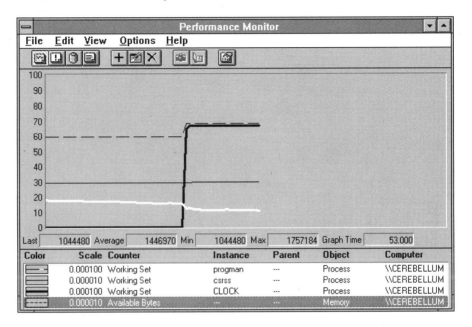

Figure 5.9 Available bytes decline when Clock starts

From the value bar you can see that Memory: Available Bytes starts at about 1.7 MB and ends right near 1 MB. When Memory: Available Bytes gets too low, the memory manager begins to take pages more aggressively from the working sets of inactive processes. It also makes different choices in which pages it replaces. Instead of allowing the working set of a process to grow and use up the remaining free memory, it takes pages from other parts of the working set of that process.

This is a change from a *global* page replacement policy to a *local* one. When enough space becomes available, the memory manager again reverts to global replacement. To some extent, you can fine-tune at which point this transition occurs. To do so, choose the Network option in Control Panel, and then select Server in the Installed Network Software list and choose Configure. You can play with the various options, but for normal system use we recommend using the Balanced option. We ran this experiment on a server system tuned to Maximize Throughput For File Sharing. We'll discuss the implications of the settings when we cover server bottleneck detection.

Until memory pressure is significant, working sets grow and you can't tell by looking at them how much space they actually need. But we can create memory pressure, and we can empty memory fairly effectively with a little utility we call **clearmem**. The **clearmem** utility, which is on the floppy disk provided with this book, determines the size of your computer's RAM and allocates enough data to fill it. It then references all this data as quickly as possible, which will toss most other pages out of memory. It also accesses files to clear the cache, in case that is important to you. Let's run **clearmem** on a system after we start Clock and see how large the working sets are after we have taken away all the unused pages.

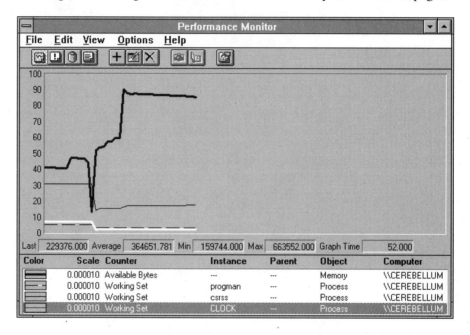

Figure 5.10 Working sets reduced to operating minimums by the clearmem utility

You can see Available Bytes, the thick black line, really climb as a result of **clearmem**. Clock, highlighted, is reduced from its initial 648K to 224K. That's quite a difference. Program Manager has followed a parallel path. CSRSS has dropped back to 1.7 MB, about half the space it occupied previously.

So we can see that the working sets were much larger than they needed to be to run Clock (and Performance Monitor). Isn't all this inefficient? No, it's not. The memory manager constantly makes tradeoffs between using the processor cycles to keep working sets trimmed up, and not using those cycles when it is not necessary. If there is plenty of memory, there is really no point in consuming processor time to trim working sets. You can see from this figure that, when memory is in demand, the trimming process occurs in high gear.

Let's return to the issue of starting Clock. We have left something out. We brought in a bunch of pages. It looked like they went into free page frames, because we saw the Available Bytes drop. But we have looked only at pages brought in to memory. What about the pages memory manager ejects? Figure 5.11 shows all page traffic, in and out, during and around the startup of Clock.

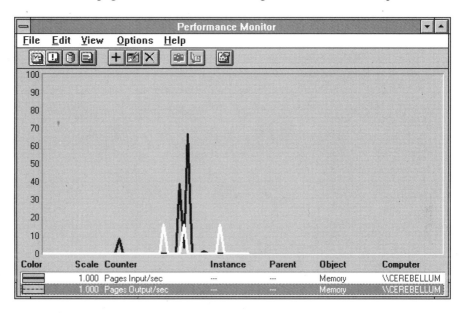

Figure 5.11 Both input and output page traffic during the startup of Clock

The input pages are the wide black line and the pages being written are the highlighted white line. It looks like some pages were written in response to our starting clock, right in the center of the figure. But it also looks like some were written both before our activity and after. What's going on? Pages that have been changed in RAM but are not yet updated on the peripheral they came from are called *dirty pages*. When changed pages are removed from a working set when there is not much memory pressure, the memory manager may not write those pages back to disk right away. Instead they are placed on a *modified page list* maintained by the memory manager. Periodically a thread in the System process, called the *modified page writer*, examines the modified page list and writes some of the pages out to free up the space. This strategy prevents excessive writing of pages that are removed from working sets, only to be quickly reclaimed by the process using them. As free space becomes scarce, the modified page thread is awakened more often.

We went through the working sets of all the processes in the system during this test. We found only one that had been trimmed during the test: the lmsvscs process. This process controls LAN Manager services such as the Workstation service, and is the agent for starting, stopping, and querying the status of such beasties. It has been idle on this system for quite some time, and the memory manager has removed a few pages from its working set just as we started logging activity. Clean pages went to the *standby list*, from which lmsvcs could retrieve them if they were needed. Those which are dirty go to the modified page list. When free page frames become scarce, pages on the standby list are cleared and added to the *free list*. If they are needed after that, they must come from the peripheral source. When the writing of a modified page is completed, the page—now clean—goes onto the standby list.

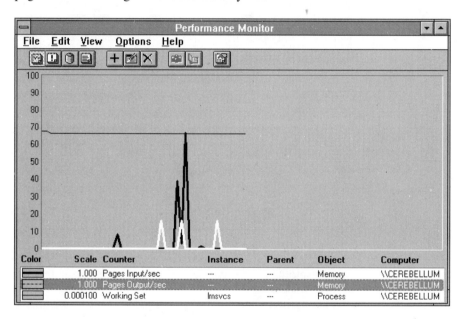

Figure 5.12 A working set is trimmed because it is inactive

To see all the page traffic in both directions, use the Memory: Pages/sec counter. This counter indicates the overall level of paging activity. It is important to watch both input and output pages, even though a page fault only results directly in page input. This is because a process could be flooding the system with dirty pages (which is what **clearmem** does to the extreme) and this can cause the memory manager to trim the working sets of lots of other processes.

Paging with Lots of Processes

When we start Clock, it has to get into memory somehow (assuming it is not already there). When not in use, the program and those mondo fonts it uses are certainly better left on disk. Paging is the price we pay for being able to execute and address much more memory than will fit in RAM at one time. Usually, the price is quite reasonable, as in this case. Where is the bottleneck? Take a look at the next figure, where we've narrowed the time window to the three seconds of Clock startup activity.

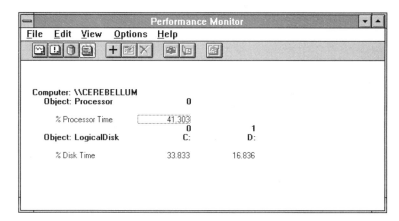

Figure 5.13 Nested bottlenecks during the startup of Clock

The combined disk activity is 50.669%, while the processor is a close second at nearly 41.303%. The disk is the bottleneck. The system is fairly balanced, and if we got a faster disk subsystem we would quickly hit the processor bottleneck. We use 3 * 0.50669 = 1.520 seconds of disk time and 3 * 0.41303 = 1.239 seconds of processor time. The real elapsed time for Clock to start is the sum of these, or 2.759 seconds. A bit more than half of that is disk time. Paging has certainly cost us something here but we're not going to hit the boss up for a new disk drive to solve this particular bottleneck.

This is an important point. Paging is not inherently evil. It provides a very flexible system that uses memory in a reasonable way. It relieves the programmer of lots of memory management tasks—tasks which, if not performed carefully, can lead to unreliable programs that are difficult to maintain. But there are times when the computer simply does not have enough memory for all the necessary pages. Then we're in trouble.

Let's take a look at a more extreme case. We'll crank up the old Response Probe and start adding processes to the mix. We'll set up each one to write to one megabyte of memory in a bell-shaped distribution of references. This should give us some idea of what things look like when life is not so rosy. Figure 5.14 shows processor usage and page traffic during this experiment.

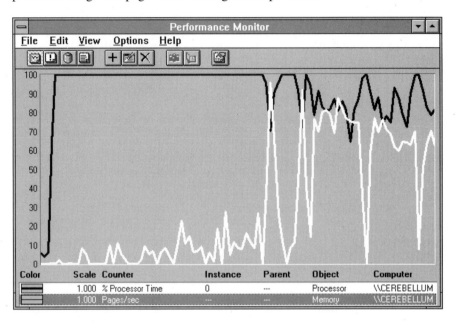

Figure 5.14 Processor usage and page traffic under increasing memory pressure

As the experiment proceeds, we see processor usage start to fall and Memory: Pages/sec start to rise. These trends are not even because if a process can get enough pages into memory to make some progress it will grab the processor and execute for a while. Overall, however, things are going from fine on the left to awful on the right.

But there's something else going on here which we should mention. On the right you can see some downward spikes in paging traffic. In the next figure we focus in on this section of activity.

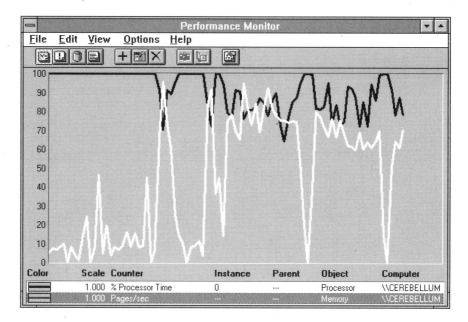

Figure 5.15 System usage at the onset of paging

The downward spikes in paging activity are accompanied by periods of full processor utilization. This is where a new copy of Response Probe is starting and calibrating the processor. Because this occurs at High Priority class, the other probe child processes are pretty much brought to a halt and their paging activity stops. When calibration completes, the child processes begin to compete for pages again.

In the next figure we show the working sets of these processes as they apply increasing pressure on the system. By the time the third process has entered the mix, it looks as though they are settling down at their desired working sets, which seem to be at about 1.2 MB. Things go pretty well until the eighth process enters the mix, and then they degrade badly. To the right of the chart some processes are being forced out of memory for a while, and others are taking over. If we let them fight it out they would equalize to some extent, but the fact is there is just not enough room for everybody. From the previous chart we see that Pages/sec winds up in the 70s for sustained periods; that's just about as fast as this machine can execute page transfer.

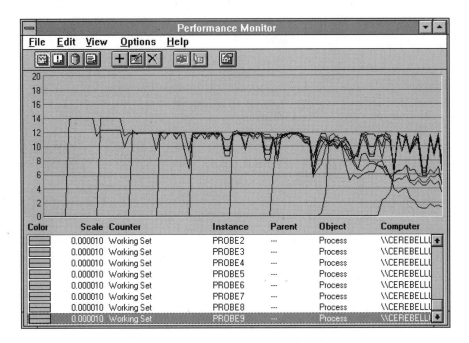

Figure 5.16 Response Probe working sets as memory pressure increases

We need to focus on some of the activity on the right of the chart and look at the Memory object data that indicates excessive paging.

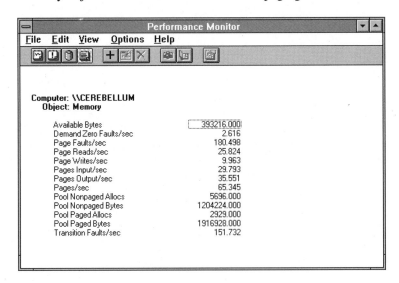

Figure 5.17 Memory statistics when paging is excessive

We've already said that Pages/sec is a key indicator and here we see 65 per second moving to and from the disk. Paging rates like this, when not due to file activity, are more than a system can sustain and still perform well. Available Bytes are down to 400K. Because the memory manager likes this number to hover in the 4-MB range, this is another indicator that we are extremely short of memory.

There are 180 Page Faults per second. Notice that there are 151 Transition Faults per second. This means that most of the page faults are being resolved by retrieving a *transition page*—a page that is in memory but is being written to disk to update the disk copy at the time of the fault. Why does this happen here?

Each probe process writes to a 1 MB data space with a normal distribution of references. As the memory manager attempts to retrieve space from the probe processes, it trims some pages from their working sets and, because the pages are dirty, the memory manager puts them on the modified page list. Because memory is so tight, it starts to write them to disk right away in hopes of freeing the frames holding them and satisfying the backlog of page faults. Once a write starts on a page it becomes a transition page. But the probe processes quickly re-reference many of the pages, because the bell-shaped reference pattern causes many pages in the middle of the curve to be touched repeatedly. A re-reference of such a page causes a page fault, because the page was trimmed from the working set. The page is found by the memory manager on the transition list, and replaced in the process's working set. The disk write process may stop if caught in time; in this case, most of them are caught in time, as we'll see shortly. This is why the modified page writer tries to delay the writes, so it doesn't have to rewrite the pages, but when there is so little free memory it has no chance to delay. It must write pages to free up space as quickly as possible.

Of the 180 Page Faults/sec, 151 are satisfied by these Transition Faults/sec, and 29 of them are satisfied by Pages Input/sec. This is close enough to count in horseshoes and bottleneck detection.

The demand zero faults come from the startup of new processes which require new cleared memory pages for their stacks and global data areas. These are satisfied by finding free page frames and filling them with zeros. We see that Page Reads/sec and Pages Input/sec are about equal, which means the memory manager is not having much luck bringing in multiple pages on a page fault. On the output side, however, the Page Writes/sec of 9.9 is causing Pages Output/sec of 35.5, or about 3.5 pages on each page write.

Monitoring the Nonpaged Pool

Pools are where the operating system and its components obtain data storage, and we need to divert our attention to them for a moment. The data structures that represent system objects created and used by applications (and by the system itself) reside in these pools. Pools are accessible only in privileged mode, so you must transition to the operating system to see the objects stored in the pools.

The paged pool is where the system allocates data that can be paged out to disk. In the nonpaged pool, pages do not leave memory. Space is obtained here if the data structures stored there can be touched by interrupt routines or inside the spinlock critical sections which prevent multiprocessor conflicts within the operating system. These pages must remain in memory because page faults are not permitted within interrupts or spinlocks.

Uncontrolled growth in nonpaged pool space is a bug which you must watch for. If a computer is short of memory, you should check nonpaged pool size. This can vary quite a bit from one computer to the next, depending on the use of system services. You should note the nonpaged pool size at system startup, and compare that to its present value. It should not grow spontaneously during system operation, although each new object a program creates will use some nonpaged pool space. Gradual growth of nonpaged pool space is called a *pool leak* but, unlike pool leaks in the backyard, these pools get larger if there is a leak: stuff leaks in instead of out. A typical cause for a pool leak is an application's repeated inadvertent opening of a file or some other object.

The Memory: Nonpaged Pool Allocs indicate the total number of allocations currently in the pool. A division indicates the average size of the allocations, 211 bytes in this case. This quotient trends in the direction of the size of a leak if there is a pool leak. If there is a pool leak, the current number of allocations rises. Total allocations will certainly grow. You may have to watch these values for hours before you catch a pool leak.

Luckily, each process also has counters for Pool Nonpaged Bytes and Pool Paged Bytes. These are not precise counts, but rather estimates by the system Object Manager, which bills for pool usage based on object addressability rather than creation and destruction. In other words, a process is billed for the space to hold a thread object when the object is created and also when the handle to the object is duplicated. So process pool statistics tend to be overestimates, which we tell you so that you don't expect them to add up to the totals of the pool counters in the Memory object. The important thing is that if you have a pool leak you probably are able to discover which process is leaking by looking at the Process pool statistics.

As well as watching for leaks, we recommend you don't add protocols and drivers to your computer unless you need them. Windows NT is so easy to configure it is sometimes tempting to start everything possible. But there's no free lunch. Even idle protocols use pool space.

Lack of Memory Causes Disk to Suffer

When your computer is memory poor, it's the disk that pays. Look at the poor C drive in the next figure.

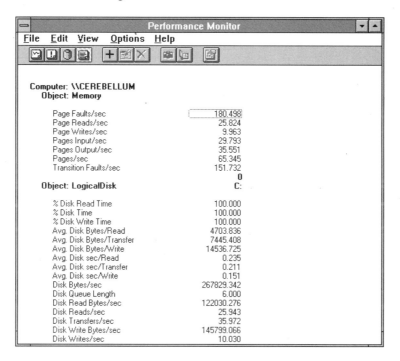

Figure 5.18 Lack of memory causes excessive disk usage

Did your eyes snap first to the disk utilization, then to the queue length? This disk is maxed out. And look at those transfer times. Almost a quarter of a second on average. This disk is seeking its brains out.

There are 9.963 Page Writes/sec, and 10.030 Disk Writes/sec. Once again, values this close are good enough for bottleneck detection. Similarly we see 25.824 Page Reads/sec and 25.943 Disk Reads/sec. Looks like the memory manager is certainly dominating the use of this disk drive, and that all its activity is directed to this volume. This situation would be a good candidate for splitting the paging file onto separate volumes, to reduce the excessive seeking that we see.

There are some related figures. Dividing the value of Pages Output/sec by Page Writes/sec gives 3.578 pages per write. Multiplying that by 4096 bytes per page gives us 14655 bytes per disk write, which is remarkably close to the 14537 value of Avg. Disk Bytes/Write. You can't expect these to match perfectly, because Performance Monitor is writing to this disk once every ten seconds. Similarly, dividing Pages Input/sec by Page reads/sec yields a result of 1.154 pages per read. Multiplying this by the bytes per page gives us 4726 bytes per read, which is very close to the 4704 value for Avg. Disk Bytes/Read.

What a Memory Hog Looks Like

A memory hog is an application that either through self-indulgent design or sheer complexity of mission, absorbs large amounts of memory. Let's take a look at a memory hog application, in Figure 5.19. There is a little paging activity on the left (highlighted in white) and then the processor (thin black line) saturates for a bit, and then kablooey, the disk is pegged and Pages/sec goes crazy, while the processor is suppressed and only gradually regains some ground as paging subsides a bit.

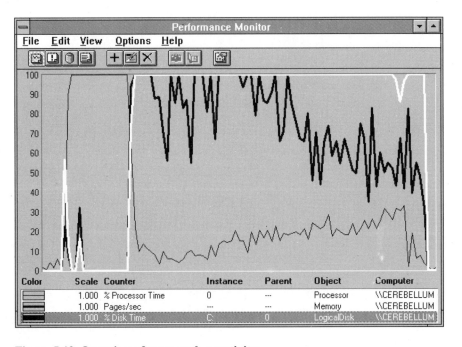

Figure 5.19 Overview of memory hog activity

We know enough already to know that this system is memory bound. The sustained high paging rate is the only clue we need. But who's the culprit? Let's take a closer look.

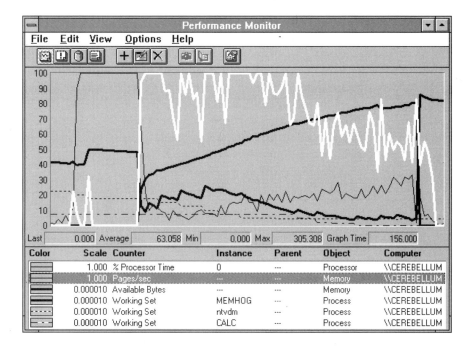

Figure 5.20 Memory hog innards exposed

On the left we see the processor utilization (thin black line) shoot up to the max during Response Probe calibration. There is some paging activity (highlighted) as Response Probe is first brought into memory. The NTVDM running Word for Windows loses a bit of its working set at this time as indicated by the black dotted line. During calibration there is some more paging activity as the memory manager seeks to get back to 4 MB of free space. The NTVDM loses a bit more, and presumably some other process not shown because we see a nice gain in Available Bytes (thick black line). Things are pretty quiet during calibration, but when the probe starts the MemHog process, life gets exciting.

Pages/sec goes wild, up to 305 as the value bar indicates. The rising thick black line of the MemHog working set creeps up across the display, destroying everything in its path. The working sets of NTVDM and Calc get trimmed, as well as those of other processes not shown. This causes some momentary increases in Available Bytes (the other thick black line), which are short lived as the counter eventually succumbs to memory demands and yields most of its gains to the MemHog. In the face of all this paging activity, the processor usage has dropped quite low. This is more typical of severe paging than the previous example, where some of the probe processes were able to make some processor headway in between page faults. This example illustrates the inability of the applications to use the processor in the face of the heavy disk demands imposed by excessive paging.

Calc has the working set indicated by the dashed black line. Notice that it is level until about halfway across the screen. Why? Because Calc was in the foreground before the test started. The memory manager favors the working sets of both the foreground process and the process that was previously in the foreground. Both Program Manager and, in particular, CSRSS get favored treatment also. The memory manager waits until things are quite desperate before trimming pages from the working sets of these favored processes. In this case, the memory manager is forced eventually to abandon this policy and give the memory used by the Calc working set to MemHog. Bummer. Now when you switch back to Calc, expect a delay and some disk rattling.

As MemHog builds up its working set, paging softens a bit and the processor utilization improves. But there is no real relief until the MemHog program ends. Then Available Bytes soars as all that memory is returned for other uses. What a relief!

C H A P T E R 6

Detecting Cache Bottlenecks

On MS-DOS systems, the primary tuning parameter in the system is the size of the disk cache. Recent versions of MS-DOS and Windows have reduced the need for you to tweak this parameter because they adapt a bit to the memory size of the machine. Still, few users of those systems can resist the temptation to display their computer prowess by tuning the cache size.

As we shall see shortly, the Windows NT cache adapts itself automatically to memory size and pressure in the computer and has few tuning controls. In this chapter we'll explore how the file system cache works on Windows NT and show how you can determine if it is the primary focus of system activity.

File System Cache Overview

The file system cache is a buffer that holds data coming from or destined for disks, LANs, and other peripherals (such as CD-ROM drives). Windows NT uses a single file system cache for all cachable peripheral devices. For simplicity we'll refer primarily to the disk as the source of data, but keep in mind this is a simplification, and any time we use the word "disk" in this chapter you may substitute LAN or CD-ROM or the high speed peripheral of your choice.

Unless an application specifies the FILE_FLAG_NO_BUFFERING parameter in its call when opening a file, the file system cache is used when the disk is accessed. On reads from the device, the data is first placed into the cache. On writes, the data goes into the cache before going to the disk.

Unbuffered I/O requests have a quaint restriction; the I/O must be done in a multiple of the sector size of the disk device. Because buffering usually helps performance a lot, it is rather unusual for a file to be opened without buffering enabled. The applications that do this are typically server applications (like SQL Server, for example) that manage their own buffers. For the purposes of this chapter, we will consider all file activity to be buffered by the file system cache.

When Windows NT first opens a file, the cache maps the file into its address space, and can then read the file as if it was an array of records in memory. When an application requests file data, the file system first looks in the cache to see if the data is there, and the cache tries to copy the record to the application's buffer. If the page is not in the working set of the cache, a page fault occurs, as shown in Figure 6.1.

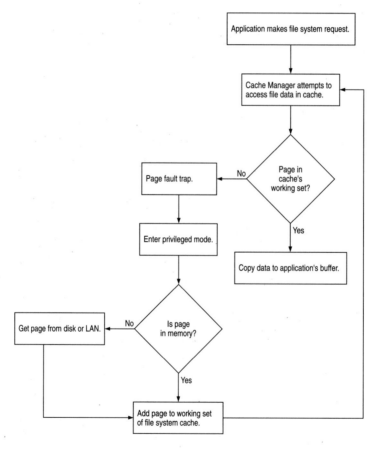

Figure 6.1 Cache references to absent file pages are resolved by the memory manager

If the page is in memory, it is mapped (not copied) into the cache's working set. This means a page table entry is validated to point to the correct page frame in memory. If the page is not in memory, the memory manager gets the page from the correct file on the peripheral. This is how the cache manager uses the memory manager to do its input. The cache is treated much like the working set of a process. It will grow and shrink as demand dictates.

Let's see how this looks to Performance Monitor.

Basic Cache Experiments

The experiments in this chapter were done on a 386SX/25 laptop with 12 MB RAM and a 120-MB hard drive. The first thing we do is see how the disk performs.

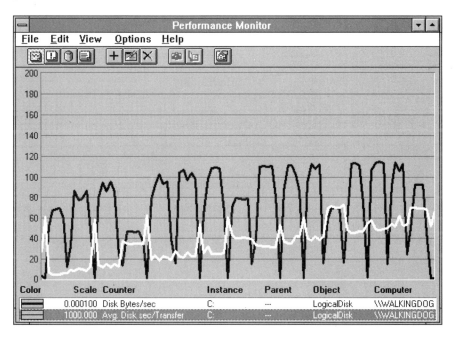

Figure 6.2 Disk performance of an example 386SX/25 laptop

Hey, that's not bad performance for a carry-on.

Let's take a quick look at why we might want to use caching in the first place. We'll do some tests, and run **clearmem** before each trial to make sure the cache is clear of file data before the test begins. In the first, we'll read a 1 MB file sequentially using 4096 byte records. In the second, we'll write the same file sequentially. (When Response Probe reaches the end of the file while doing sequential disk access, it restarts at the beginning.) In the third test, we'll read the file randomly with our usual bell-shaped normal distribution. In the last we'll read a record under normal distribution, and then write that record. In the next table we see the results of these tests, expressed as the response time to do one file operation of the type specified.

Table 6.1   Cached vs. Non-cached File I/O Times in Milliseconds per Record

Type of file access	Operation	Non-cached time	Cached time
Sequential	Read	6.58	1.32
Sequential	Write	22.91	1.70
Random	Read	20.45	1.51
Random	Read/Write	40.66	3.16

Okay, you were probably convinced anyway, but now we know for sure. Caching is good for performance.

So now let's take a look at what's going on inside. We'll create a 10 MB file and we'll read from it 8192 byte records spread over about 4 MB in the middle of the file in, you guessed it, a normal distribution. The following picture emerges.

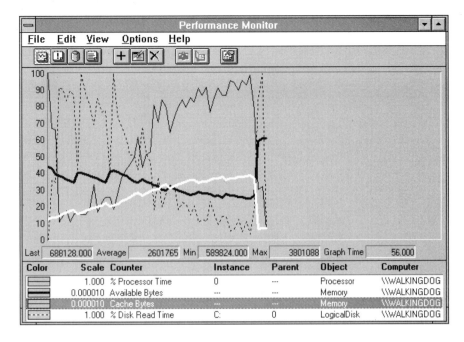

Figure 6.3 System behavior during cached reading of a large file

At the beginning, the processor utilization goes way down and the disk utilization goes way up, while the cache (highlighted in white) grows. When the cache gets to about 4 MB, the disk and processor utilization lines cross, disk activity drops off, and the processor activity picks up.

The dark black line is Memory: Available Bytes. There is meaning behind the sawtooth in this line. When Available Bytes drops below 4 MB, the memory manager wanders about the system trimming working sets in the off chance that some pages are not in active use. You can see the cache is also trimmed. Available Bytes jumps as a result of the trimmed pages becoming available. The cache quickly recovers its trimmed pages because they are in active use. It continues to expand and takes more of the Available Bytes as it does. As the cache settles to its necessary size, it has suppressed Available Bytes to about 2.75 MB, and the system stabilizes here until the experiment ends.

The next figure shows the cache statistics for this test case. Starting at the top, the asynchronous counters show activity for asynchronous I/O requests (you could have guessed that, right?). When it does asynchronous I/O, an application fires off a file request and keeps on processing other stuff, checking the status of an event to determine completion of the request. This permits applications to overlap file operations with each other and with other processing. This could also be done by assigning a separate thread to handle the file operation, but that is quite expensive in terms of memory used compared to asynchronous I/O. Many applications do synchronous file operations, in which case the application waits until input data is available, or output data is copied to the disk.

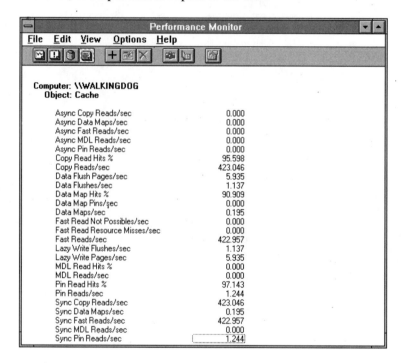

Figure 6.4 Cache statistics during the reading of a large file

The first counter with activity is the hit ratio for copy reads, Copy Read Hits %. This is the normal file system read. It causes data to be copied from the cache to the application buffer. A hit occurs when a request is made by the file system for data and the data is already in the cache. We see a high hit rate and an impressive number of operations per second. We'll take another look at this.

There is a little bit of file output activity, indicated by the two Data Flush counters monitoring cache output. Data flushing occurs when the cache manager is told to make room by writing some modified pages out to the peripheral(s). There are a number of code paths that can trigger a data flush:

- The cache manager's lazy writer thread (in the System process) wakes up periodically looking for modified cache pages to flush to disk. The two lazy writer counters reflect this activity.

- The memory manager's *mapped page writer* can cause data flushes if memory becomes tight or if the number of modified pages mapped into the cache's address space becomes large. (The mapped page writer is a System process thread that handles dirty file pages mapped into the address space of some process or the cache. The mapped page writer thread is kin to the modified page writer mentioned in the previous chapter. The difference is the modified page writer writes dirty pages only for the paging files. We'll say more about mapped files shortly.)

- An application can instruct the file system to flush the cache for a particular file.

All of these actions call the data flush operation, which in turn invokes a memory manager routine to build an output request for the file system to actually place the data onto the peripheral(s). By the way, it's Performance Monitor that is writing the data here. Heisenberg in a laptop!

Look at the high percentage of Data Map Hits. Wow, what a great cache hit rate! Wrong! True enough, the hit rate is high, but the operation count as measured by Data Maps/sec is small. It is very important to watch the operation counts when trying to interpret the hit rates. Data maps are used to map in file system metadata such as directories, the File Allocation Table in the FAT file system, Fnodes in HPFS, or the Master File Table in NTFS. If this count is high, you are burdened with directory operations and the like. This may indicate the copying of many small files, for example. You'll see Data Map Pins when the mapped data is pinned in memory preparatory to writing it, indicating the system is making changes to file system data structures.

To emphasize the importance of looking at both the hit rate and the operation frequency, in the next figure we illustrate the relationship between Copy Read Hits % and Copy Reads/sec. On the far left there is a spike in Copy Read Hits % but the low operation rate renders this unimportant. Then, as the cache grows in size to accommodate the file, the counters rise together. The result is the lower disk traffic and better processor utilization numbers seen on the right half of Figure 6.3.

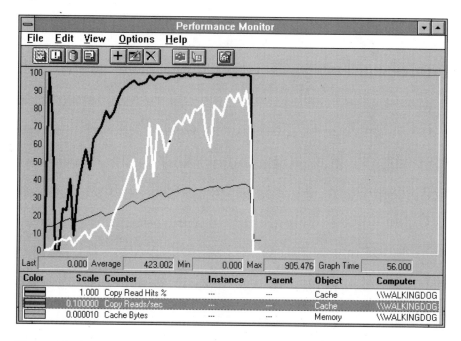

Figure 6.5 Copy Read Hits % and Copy Reads/Sec during reading of a large file

We mentioned in an earlier chapter that Fast Reads are the I/O manager look-aside mechanism which can bypass the file system and obtain data directly from the cache. Ideally, most application file requests are handled in this fashion because it is very efficient.

A multiple data list (MDL) request is a way for a file system to deliver large blocks of cache data using direct memory access (DMA). The MDL provides a physical memory address for each page involved in the transfer. The Windows NT server process sometimes uses this method for large transfers of data from cache.

In a Pin Reads operation, the cache is reading data with the objective of writing it. To do the write to a partial page, the cache must first read the entire page off the peripheral. The page is "pinned" in memory until the write takes place. The hits occur when the data is already in the cache at the time of the read request. Because of pinning, writes always hit the cache, or else go into new page frames materialized for the purpose when written to new space.

The Sync counters exist just to break out which requests are synchronous versus which ones are asynchronous, as described previously. This breakdown is not going to be of vital concern to you often. If you have a lot of cache activity and you have an application mix that uses these two different access modes, the hit rates of the two might give you a clue as to which applications were hitting the cache and which were missing. Usually your powerful server application will be using asynchronous file access to get the best concurrency for the least system cost, and you will be able to determine if that application is the one that is getting the cache hits (or misses).

The upshot of all this is that for normal file read operations you watch Copy Read counters to judge activity. For normal file write operations you watch the Data Flush counters to judge activity. Data Map operations generally indicate directory activity, or activity on lots of files. It's really not as complicated as it looks.

Sequential Reading and Writing

Let's take a look at another very common case. Let's process this file sequentially, first reading a record and then writing it. We'll set the record size to 512 bytes this time. We still have a 10-MB file. The next figure tells the tale.

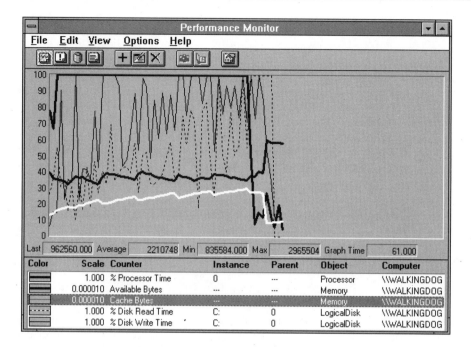

Figure 6.6 Cache and disk activity while reading and writing a large file sequentially

Processor utilization is the heavy black line at the top of the chart: it's pinned at 100%. The disk is quite busy both reading (dotted line) and writing (thin black line). The cache does not grow as large even though we are processing the entire 10 MB file, much more data than in the last example. Why? The cache manager detects that the file is being read sequentially and realizes that retaining lots of file data in the cache will not help much, because it is probably not being re-referenced. The next figure shows the cache statistics for this case.

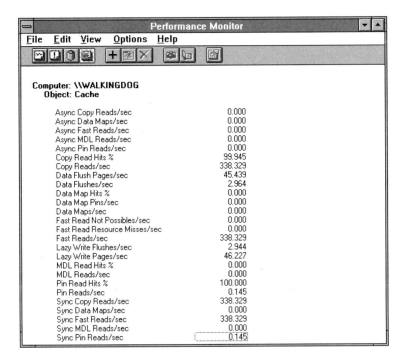

Figure 6.7 Cache statistics for read/writing a large file sequentially

The high Copy Reads/sec of the example in the previous section are lower here because now we are writing the data as well as reading it. There are 45 Data Flush Pages/sec, but the flush is only occurring 2.9 times per second. This means we are sending out 45/2.9 or about 15 pages on each flush. This also tells us that the cache manager has discovered the sequential nature of our file access and is grouping together lots of pages to expel at once. As we have seen previously, large transfer blocks are very efficient. The lazy writer would like to write the sequential data in 64K chunks. However, the lazy writer is not doing all the writing here because there are just a few more Data Flushes/sec than Lazy Write Flushes/sec. This means the mapped page writer has become concerned about memory from time to time and does a little page output of its own. This can interfere with the sequential nature of the lazy write output and slightly reduce the number of pages per write.

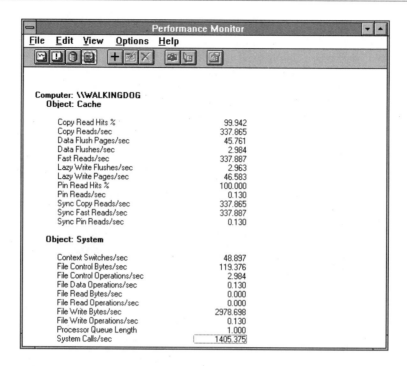

Figure 6.8 Cache and system statistics for read/writing a large file sequentially

We can tell for sure from Figure 6.8 that we are on the fast read path because the file operation counts in the System object are nearly all zero. This means the I/O manager is diverting requests to the cache and it rarely needs to get the file system involved in data retrieval or deposit. We see 1405 system calls for every 338 reads, for four system calls per read. We happen to know that there is a write for every read because that is what we told the probe to do, and we'll get a seek for every read because that's what the general algorithm in the probe does.

The system needs to perform a seek for the write to get back to the start of the latest read so we can rewrite the record. It's not hard to see why there are four system calls per read. The WAP tool we discuss later in Chapter 10 would be a more direct way to determine application file activity.

Look at how efficient data flushing is. Although we are doing almost 338 reads per second and the same number of writes, the lazy writer is only waking up about 3 times per second and writing 15 pages each time. The System process is only using 3.3% of the time to do all this. The following figure shows the threads of the System process. That process is using very little processor time to eject these pages. The threads most involved here are the lazy writer thread, the mapped page writer thread, and the modified page writer thread (clearing memory for the cache). If the system is creating a file, the demand zero thread works to create page frames filled with zeros. If memory is tight, the working set manager thread works to trim working sets to make space.

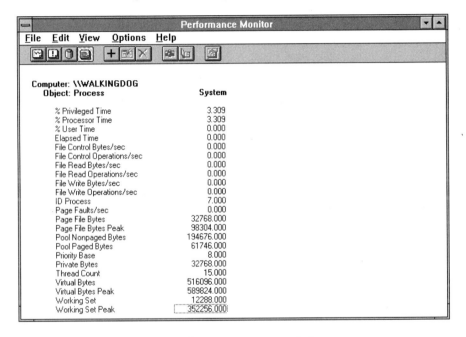

Figure 6.9 Lazy writing by the System process is truly lazy

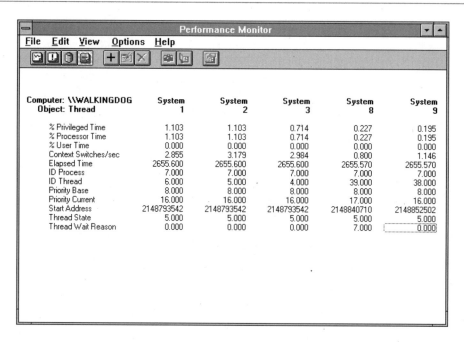

Figure 6.10 System process threads divide the lazy work up

Let's see how the disk fares under all this pressure. Figure 6.11 shows disk behavior and how that behavior relates to cache and virtual memory activity. Let's continue to look at the output side. If we add Cache: Data Flush Pages/sec and Memory: Output Pages/sec we get 50.605 per second. Multiplying by 4096 bytes/page gives 207208 bytes per second, quite close to the 210955 Write Bytes/sec the disk drive is seeing. The reason the lazy writer thinks more pages are written is that after they have been handed to the data flusher, they are handed to the memory manager. It's the memory manager that makes the ultimate decision about whether the page is still dirty or not. So some lazy write flushed pages may already have been written by the memory manager by the time the data flusher tries to write them.

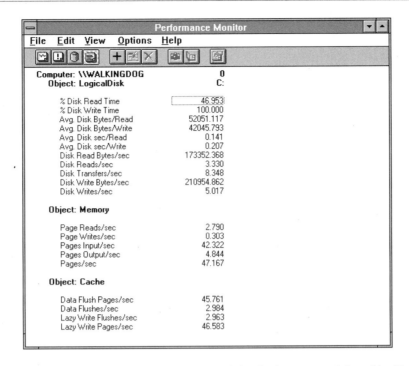

Figure 6.11 Disk response to cache activity during sequential read/writing

On the read side of the fence, we see the Memory: Pages Input/sec = 42.322, which, multiplied by the page size, gives 173392 bytes input per second. This is so close to the 173352 Disk Read Bytes/sec that we are in ecstasy (recall the 9th Rule of Bottleneck Detection).

Looking at Avg. Disk Bytes/Read and Avg. Disk Bytes/Write we see fairly high numbers, which is good. But because the lazy writer is trying to write 64K chunks on sequential output, it's a shame the Avg. Disk Bytes/Write are not that high. What's going on here? The next figure really ties a bow around this issue.

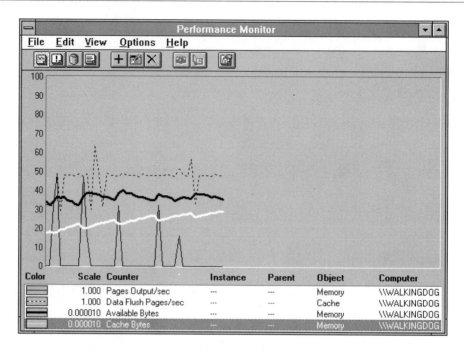

Figure 6.12 Memory manager and cache manager make sweet music together

The memory manager's work is shown as Memory: Pages Output/sec in the thin black line. Notice how it has five spikes. Let's consider them one at a time, moving from left to right. The first spike emits 48 pages (in three writes but we can't show everything on one chart), adds to Available Bytes, and takes little from the cache. The cache manager is trying to write 48 pages each second (also in three data flushes, as we have seen) but right after the memory manager writes its 48 pages, the cache manager backs off to 30 pages for a second. In the next spike, the memory manager writes some more data, this time having taken some pages from the cache (white line). But we know it took pages from other working sets as well because the increase in Available Bytes is greater than the decrease in Cache Bytes. In reaction the cache manager again writes fewer than the normal 48 pages as a net result of the next three seconds of activity.

In the third output, the memory manager backs off to writing out only 32 pages. This time the cache supplied most of the Available Bytes. In the fourth spike of 32 pages, nearly all of the memory taken comes from the cache. The memory manager sees that it is not making headway, but gives it one last try, extracting 16 pages from the cache, and a few seconds later the cache manager again writes fewer pages to the disk in its flush.

Reading and Writing Randomly

So much for sequential file processing, now that we understand its cache behavior better than we ever wanted to. Let's look at how the cache behaves when we access about 3 MB of this file with a normal distribution, first reading a 4096 byte record and then writing it. This wreaks the havoc shown in Figure 6.13.

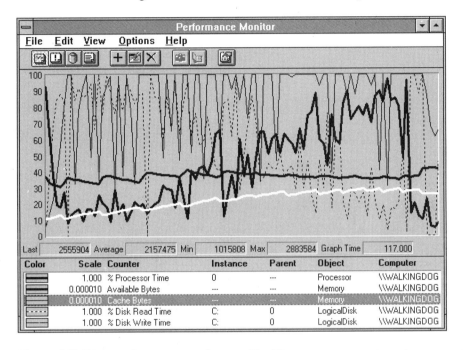

Figure 6.13 Havoc reigns over random read/writing

The scary thing is that Figure 6.13 might make sense to you now. The highlighted line is Memory: Cache Bytes and we see the cache growing as the test case proceeds. The dotted line is % Disk Read Time. It starts out at a quite busy level and, as the cache is filled with data, it drops off. The thin black line is % Disk Write Time. It spends more time near 100% as the cache is filled with data. This is because the less time we spend going to disk to read the data (because it is in the cache), the more rapidly we write the records, and the more output activity we create. The heavy black line measuring % Processor Time increases steadily as we fill the cache and we wait less for the disk. The other heavy black line measuring Available Bytes stays relatively level, indicating the cache is getting its new space from inactive working sets, as shown in the next chart.

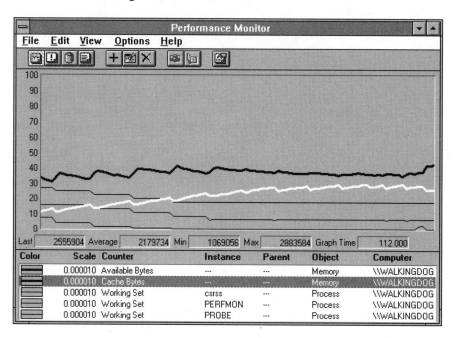

Figure 6.14 The cache steals much needed pages from other working sets

In Figure 6.14 it is clear where the cache is getting its space. You can see that each time space is trimmed from the working sets, it is added to Available Bytes. The CSRSS working set is reduced in size until it is held by the memory manager at about 2 MB to assure some screen responsiveness. The working set of Performance Monitor is reduced until it reaches the level it needs to maintain logging. The working set is trimmed a bit too far, and you can see a little blip where a few pages are retrieved (by a soft fault) back into the working set. Pages trimmed after that are immediately retrieved so we see no further trimming. The Probe process is the master process controlling Response Probe, and is inactive during the test, so it completely loses its page allocation. We see the process wake up and bring them back in (causing page faults) at the end of the test on the right of the chart.

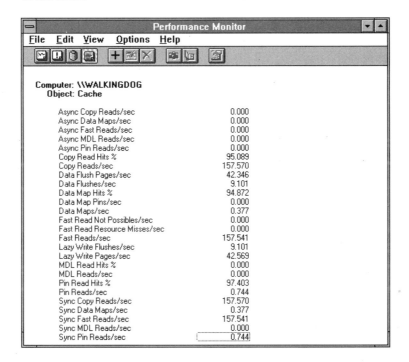

Figure 6.15 Cache statistics for normally distributed read/writing

The next two figures display cache statistics. We see a lower Copy Reads/sec in this case than during sequential reading, because the cache manager can anticipate sequential read requests more effectively than this normal distribution. Figure 6.15 is also a strong exemplar of the 10th Rule of Bottleneck Detection: Averages reveal basic truths while hiding important details. Figure 6.16 shows why.

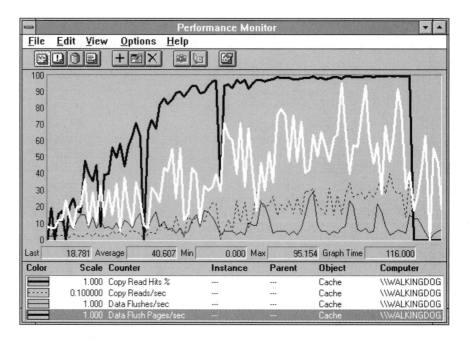

Figure 6.16 Cache statistics during normally-distributed reading and writing

Here we can see the heavy black line of the Copy Read Hits % rising nicely as the experiment progresses. The Copy Reads/sec starts out quite low, but rises as the hit rate improves. Likewise, the Data Flush Pages/sec (in white) rises on the right side of the chart. They also continue beyond the end of the experiment as the lazy writer clears the cache of dirty data.

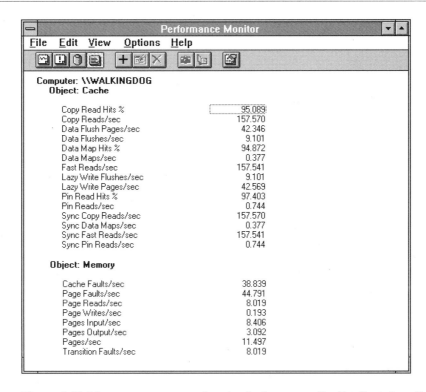

Figure 6.17 Memory manager and cache during normally-distributed reading and writing

Figure 6.17 shows how the memory manager's statistics compare to those of the cache. Cache Faults/sec are a subset of the Page Faults/sec. You can tell the bulk of the memory management activity is due to the cache activity because the Cache Faults/sec at 38.8 account for most of the 44.8 Page Faults/sec. Obviously, quite a few of these are soft faults, because the number of Page Reads/sec is only 8.0. Furthermore, we can see the lack of sequentiality in the read operation because there are 8.4 Pages Input/sec. Not many pages are being acquired on each read.

Looking at the output side, because Data Flush Pages/sec is at 42.3 and Pages Output/sec is at 3.1, the cache is clearly doing almost all the output. In fact, we have seen this pattern before: because Page Writes/sec is only 0.2 and Pages Output/sec is 3.1, there are really 3.1/0.2 or 15.5 pages written on each memory management output. The memory manager is getting in there and occasionally trimming working sets again, and getting almost 16 pages to write each time to disk.

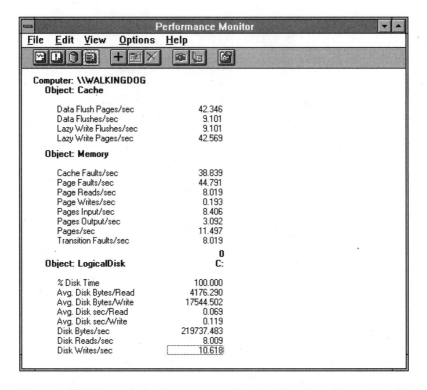

Figure 6.18 Disk statistics during normally-distributed reading and writing

Disk statistics for this test are illustrated in Figure 6.18. Notice the relatively long Avg. Disk sec/Write. Hey, it's just a laptop, remember? But looking back to Figure 6.2, when we characterized the disk speed by reading a single record, we can see that simple read time is not bad. Looks like it's seeking that slowed us down here. In the design of this laptop, the manufacturer made a tradeoff to seek a little less quickly than on desktop systems. Just think of all those extra hours of battery life they got in return for this decision!

Mapping Files Into Memory

There is a way for applications to access file data that is even faster than using the file system cache. By mapping a file directly into its address space, an application can access the data in the file like an array and need never call the file system at all. This avoids all the overhead associated with the file system call and the search of the cache. The next table shows our little laptop's performance while accessing the file as we did earlier in the chapter, this time adding memory mapping as an access mode. The times shown are

Table 6.2   Memory Mapped vs. File I/O Times in Milliseconds per Record

Type of file access	Operation	Non-cached time	Cached time	Mapped time
Sequential	Read	6.58	1.32	0.75
Sequential	Write	22.91	1.70	0.64
Random	Read	20.45	1.51	0.97
Random	Read/Write	40.66	3.16	1.31

File activity just doesn't get any faster than that! But memory mapping of files is not always advisable. For one thing, you'd have to recode an existing application to get rid of all those old-fashioned file system calls. Although the resulting code would be simpler, you must weigh this against taking the time and effort to recode an existing application. Another tricky tradeoff occurs when access is strictly sequential; the cache uses much less memory to read the file, as we have seen. Also, using memory mapping means that you lose access to the file system synchronization modes such as file locking or the more exotic opportunistic locking. This means that any multiple writers of the file, whether they be threads inside a process or multiple processes sharing the file, must coordinate their access using mutexes. And if there is any possibility that the file might be remotely accessed by multiple processes which are writing to the file from different computers, you must invent an inter-process synchronization mechanism which might obviate the performance advantage you got from memory mapping in the first place.

In cases where you decide to map files into memory, it's a clear winner in speed. Performance Monitor uses memory mapping for accessing the log file when it is reading it for reprocessing. Because access to the file might be random, this is just the sort of task which benefits from memory mapping. Conversely, output of log files is done through the normal file system calls because the cache can detect the sequential nature of the output and can therefore use memory more efficiently writing files created in this fashion.

The principal difference in the behavior of the system between using mapped and unmapped files is that mapped files go directly into the working set of the process, while, as we have seen, buffered files go into the "working set" of the file system cache. When a process maps a file into its address space, it might use quite a bit of RAM to hold the file. But from the memory manager's viewpoint, it really doesn't make too much difference whether the working set of the process or the working set of the cache gets the page that's faulted in. The real elegance of the memory management scheme on Windows NT is exemplified in this point, which is illustrated by the next experiment.

We start two processes, each accessing a file with normally distributed record access. First the distribution covers 1 MB, then 2 MB, 3 MB, and so on up to 8 MB. One process reads the file using the file system calls, and the other maps the file into its address space. The results are displayed in the next two charts. The first four trials with working sets from 1 to 4 MB are shown in Figure 6.19, and the next four trials with working sets from 5 to 8 MB are shown in Figure 6.20.

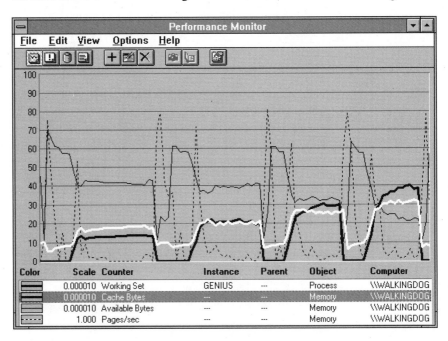

Figure 6.19 Competing processes using mapped and file system reads

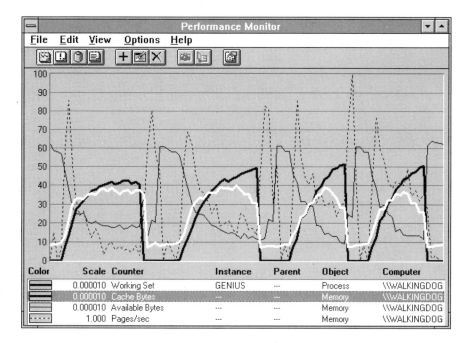

Color	Scale	Counter	Instance	Parent	Object	Computer
	0.000010	Working Set	GENIUS	---	Process	\\WALKINGDOG
	0.000010	Cache Bytes	---	---	Memory	\\WALKINGDOG
	0.000010	Available Bytes	---	---	Memory	\\WALKINGDOG
	1.000	Pages/sec	---	---	Memory	\\WALKINGDOG

Figure 6.20 More competing processes using mapped and file system reads

In the beginning, the highlighted cache has a slight size advantage, but as the working sets get larger, the process in heavy black begins to get ahead. The thin black line shows Available Bytes declining, and the dotted line shows that Pages/sec are rising as the experiment progresses. By the time the normal distribution covers 8 MB, the paging rate on this laptop is shaking it right off your lap.

These charts seem to indicate that the memory manager is favoring the process's working set over that of the cache. To some extent this is true. In general, the code and data referenced directly by processes is more crucial to good application performance than the file data in the cache. The cache tends to get the space not needed by processes. It certainly gets any unused space, as we saw when it took pages trimmed from inactive working sets. When processes are active, however, they tend to do a bit better than the cache, as in this case. But the result is not overwhelmingly in favor of the process, as the next figure shows.

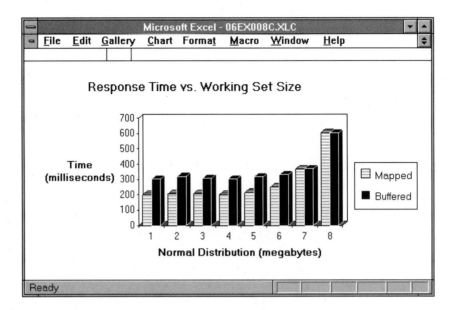

Figure 6.21 Response time for mapped and buffered competing processes

Figure 6.21 shows each process's response time as measured by Response Probe during this experiment. The mapped access is faster in the beginning, as we saw in Table 6.2. Then, as the paging increases, and disk access time becomes a significant component of the response time, the two processes' performance evens up. The fact that the working set of the process doing mapped access is a bit larger is not a significant advantage. This indicates that the policy of the memory manager is perfectly balanced.

In the next chapter we discuss how you tune memory manager to favor either the cache or the application in specific circumstances.

C H A P T E R   7

Detecting Network Bottlenecks

When Pandora opened her box, the first form of Chaos to emerge was the computer network. To begin with you've got your client and your server, or possibly hundreds or thousands of them. To this you add the transmission media, the network adapter cards, and possibly multiple network protocols. Inside this complex mixture of equipment and logic lurks the bottleneck.

One good thing about searching for network bottlenecks is that everything we have covered in the previous chapters of this book still applies. A server that has a disk bottleneck because memory is too tight is still a computer that has a disk bottleneck because memory is too tight. The fact that it is a server just makes it more annoying because more people are affected. So what you've learned thus far is not wasted, we just have to add a bit more knowledge. We need to look at the counters that reflect on network traffic and gain some understanding of their capacities under various configurations. Only then can we submit our application for the Nobel Prize for Bottleneck Detection.

We are limiting the scope of this chapter so it does not become a book in itself (which it easily could be). We want to cover the principles and techniques of network bottleneck detection for a few common cases so that you will be able to apply these techniques in your own case. For example, we won't be trying to cover wide-area networks (WANs). The analysis of WANs is much the same as the analysis of local-area networks (LANs), although the choice of a protocol's *window sizes* (the number of packets within which a response is expected) is a crucial determinant of performance when crossing from LANs to lower-bandwidth WANs.

The most common transmission media of LANs are Ethernet and token ring. We'll only look at Ethernet here but the principles also apply to token ring.

In Appendix B we list the Configuration Registry parameters that control many details of how the network runs. These are only provided for reference. In general you will never have to change these values. If you suspect you might want to adjust a value listed there, we urge you to experiment with your configuration using the techniques and tools presented here.

Windows NT ships with a number of protocols. The ones with counters in Performance Monitor include NetBEUI, TCP/IP, and a Novell® NetWare®-compatible protocol providing NWLink IPX/SPX capabilities. Mostly we'll be using NetBEUI for illustration but we'll glance briefly at the counters used by the other two. You may even be using a protocol that had extended object counters added into Performance Monitor when it was installed. If so, you will undoubtedly find that the guidelines discussed here apply to your situation.

We also cannot possibly discuss all the counters in all the network protocols. We will try to expose the essential counters. Then you will be able to solve the important problems, and become familiar with the other counters over time as they vary in your environment.

A Profile of Network Throughput

First, let's see how the client and the server look when we have an isolated network with just the two computers connected. We want to use unbuffered reads from a file so we can bypass the cache on the client side. This will not bypass the cache on the server, however, so if we reread the same record over and over, we'll hit the cache on the server side every time. By increasing the record size we can get a pretty clear view of how much data a single client can pump across this isolated network. The server is a 100-MHz MIPS 4000 with a 1-MB secondary cache, a 50-MHz memory bus, 32 MB of RAM, and a Sonic DMA Ethernet controller on the motherboard. The client is a 486/33 with 16 MB of RAM and a 16-bit memory mapped network adapter. The media is thin cable Ethernet. We've selected the NetBEUI protocol for now.

Since we are doing unbuffered reading, we must read in multiples of our disk sector size. We'll start with 512-, 1024-, 2048-, and 4096-byte reads, and then increase in 4096-byte increments up to 64K records. The resulting NetBEUI: Bytes Total/sec from the client's side is shown in Figure 7.1.

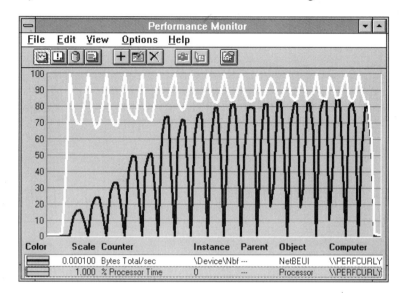

Figure 7.1 Client's view of a network throughput test

The throughput as measured by NetBEUI: Bytes Total/sec climbs as we increase the record size. (If we had multiple network cards installed, each would be an object instance and we would see a different such value for each card.) The spikes in client processor usage are the times when Response Probe is calibrating. During application of the test cases, the processor usage rises to a plateau.

Before we take a closer look at what is going on here, let's see how the server fares.

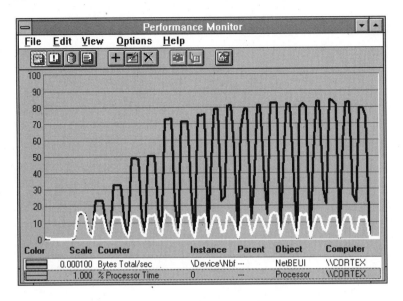

Figure 7.2 Server's view of a network throughput test

Notice the throughput matches the client side (it had better!), but the processor utilization is much lower on this side. Unlike on the client, the processor utilization on the server is pretty constant.

Let's begin by explaining what is in these throughput charts. The throughput rises in an almost linear way up to a record size of 4096 bytes. Then at 8192 bytes we get just little more throughput than at 4096 bytes. This is because the Redirector file system treats a request of 8192 bytes as two 4096-byte requests. Since we don't have to go back through the application program and the I/O system for the second 4096 bytes, we get only a very slight boost over the 4096-byte case. But with 3-page transfers we get a significant jump, because the protocol switches to what are called large reads. This is a more efficient protocol as long as the server has buffer space to handle the request, which is surely the case in this test. We'll look closely at a case of large reads later in this chapter.

First let's look at the 2048-byte transfer. We narrow the time window to focus in on the 2048-byte case. In the next two figures we present first the client's view of this activity, then the server's view.

Note For NetBEUI we are showing only the non-zero counters in these illustrations. This does not mean the other counters are not useful. In fact, knowing that the failure counters are zero removes an important potential bottleneck source from consideration. It just means these counters are not useful for the analysis of this rather sterile environment test case.

NetBEUI: Bytes Total/sec normally includes both frame-based activity and datagram activity. (When *frames* are sent across the network, they are expected to be acknowledged by the receiver, and are re-sent by the sender if not acknowledged, while *datagrams* are just sent with no expectation of an acknowledgment and no retransmission in case of failure.) Datagram counters can be a major indicator of activity. By knowing which applications use datagrams, you can get a clue about which ones are causing the majority of your network activity. Because no process is sending datagrams in our example, we omitted the datagram counters from Figure 7.3.

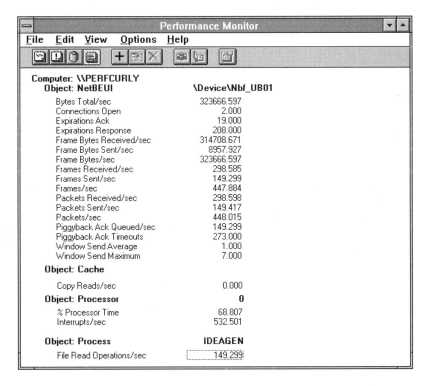

Figure 7.3 Client's view of unbuffered reading of 2048-byte records

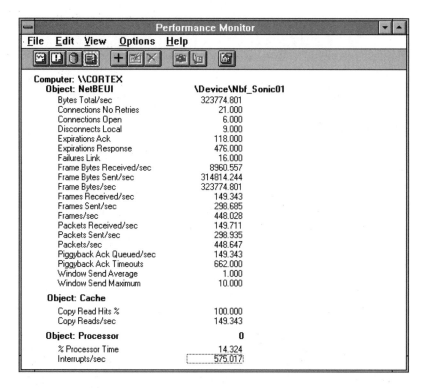

Figure 7.4 Server's view of unbuffered reading of 2048-byte records

NetBEUI: Bytes Total/sec is a key indicator of network throughput. This only includes bytes in data frames and not other bytes sent as part of the protocol, such as stand-alone acknowledgments (called ACKs). Bytes Total/sec includes both incoming and outgoing data frame bytes. As an average, it's a victim of Rule #10: it reveals basics while hiding details.

We have called the Response Probe process that's generating all this activity Ideagen. Since it does not use the cache on the client side, its Process: File Read Operations/sec value gives us a clear indication of the file read activity. Dividing Frame Bytes Sent/sec by the Process: File Read Operations/sec we get 59.9999; perhaps we can take a risk and invoke Rule #9 and call that 60. This is the basic minimal data frame for NetBEUI. This frame holds the entire request for our data. Similarly, dividing Frame Bytes Received/sec by Process: File Read Operations/sec we get 2107.9, which is 2048 + 60, our requested record size plus the basic frame size.

There is one packet sent for each frame sent, but there are two packets received for each read request (298.598/149.299 = 2). That's because Ethernet has a maximum packet size of 1514, so it takes two packets to send the 2108 bytes back.

Average packet size received is Frame Bytes Received/sec divided by Packets Received/sec, or 1053.95, or about half of the 2108 as we might expect for an average. We can also see that we are not hitting the cache on the client at all, which is good, because that is what we want to do in this experiment. We are using 68.807% of the client processor to do all this, and have a pretty healthy interrupt rate (the at-rest interrupt rate on this system with Performance Monitor running at five-second intervals is 80 interrupts per second). We'll get back to the issue of interrupts in a moment. It turns out to be a key point.

Let's take a look at the server. The server side is a close mirror of the client side. We did not collect both systems' data into one log file because we did not want to add to the network traffic during this test, so the two time windows do not coincide precisely. (Even if we had, exact synchronization of Performance Monitor data from two computers is not possible, as we noted in Chapter 2.) Nonetheless, we see pretty good agreement between the client and the server, as we expect in such a steady-state test. The server is hitting the cache on every read request. It is getting just a few more interrupts but has significantly lower processor utilization.

The next two figures show how the redirector and the server software see this activity. On the client side we divide the Redirector: Bytes Received/sec by Redirector: Packets Received/sec and get 2108, which must be the 2048 bytes we are requesting plus the 60-byte basic frame. The redirector considers the whole request and the whole reply as a single "packet." This is obviously not a packet in the NetBEUI sense. Keep this in mind when looking at these statistics.

The redirector is also not a separate process. Very nearly all the % Processor Time spent in processes is accounted for by the Ideagen process, which is the name of our probe application process reading the records. The redirector is just a file system invoked by the I/O manager inside the address space of Ideagen. Yet there is a large gap between the Processor: % Processor Time and the Process: % Processor Time of Ideagen. We'll have to come back to this, but let's take a look at the server software's view first.

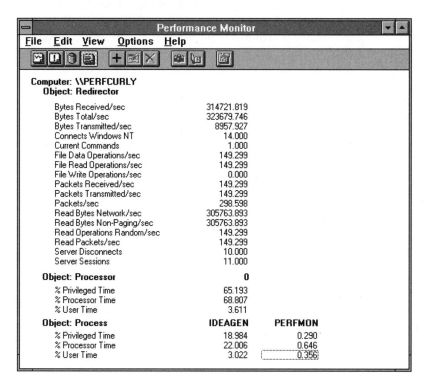

Figure 7.5 Redirector's view of reading 2048 bytes

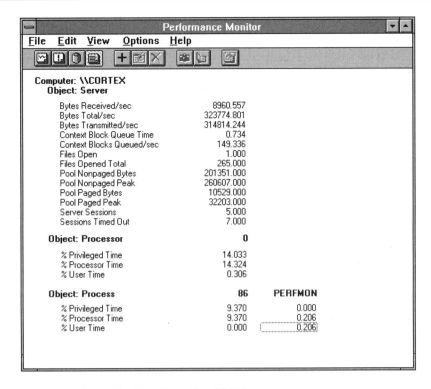

Figure 7.6 Server's view of reading 2048 bytes

The server's side of things holds no surprises. As we noted in an earlier chapter, the server process has no name and just goes by a number, which is the same as its Process ID and which is different from one system to the next. Dividing the Bytes Transmitted/sec by the Context Blocks Queued/sec gives the number 2108. By now, this is a familiar number. The Processor: % Processor Time is over 50% higher than that of the server process, so we see a gap similar to the one we saw on the redirector side. Take a look at Context Block Queue Time, which is measured in milliseconds. This is the time it takes to respond to requests, and you'll never see it smaller than this simple retrieval from cache.

A Simple Model of a Network Bottleneck

Figures 7.3 and 7.4 correspond to the third peak on the left of Figures 7.1 and 7.2. (The first two were for 512 and 1024 bytes, respectively, and this one is for 2048 bytes.) Clearly, if we increase the record size requested, throughput increases. Can we determine what the bottleneck is from this data? Let's give it a try. (If you thought Rule #7 about counter ratios wasn't important before this, just wait!)

Let's define our interaction as one read. The time for this read is one divided by the Process: File Read Operations/sec, or 0.006698 seconds. A simple model of this interaction would be:

- Some processor time on the client
- Some media time to transmit the data request to the server
- Some processor time on the server
- Some media time to transmit the 2108 bytes back
- Finally, some processor time on the client to get the data into the application's buffer.

Assuming for the moment there is no overlap between media transmission and processor time, this reduces to just (client processor time) plus (media time) plus (server processor time).

The server processor time used in one second is just the Processor: % Processor Time expressed as a number between 0 to 1, or 0.14324 seconds. On the client this is 0.68807 seconds. Dividing each of these by the number of reads per second gives the server and client processor time per read as 0.000959 seconds and 0.004609 seconds, respectively.

Each read transfers 2168 bytes, as we have seen above (we get this by dividing Bytes Total/sec by Frames Total/sec). The media (Ethernet in this case) transmits at 800 nanoseconds per byte, so we multiply that by the number of bytes per read and get 0.001734 seconds per interaction. Now, summing server processor time, client processor time, and media time, according to our simple model, we get 0.007302. This is 0.000604 or 604 microseconds more than the time for each record, indicating that our assumption there was no overlap was slightly inaccurate.

The Mystery of the Missing Time

This is all well and good, but we don't yet know who is really using all that processor time. We can see that it is used, but we can't see it in any process. The answer is in the high interrupt rates observed during network or serial data communications activity. Time in interrupts is not billed to the thread or process that is running, but it is counted in overall processor usage. When there are lots of interrupts, this can grow to be the majority of the Processor: % Processor Time. In the following figure we show the relationship between overall processor usage and time in the user process, as well as interrupt rate. Since most of the time is in privileged mode, we can use privileged mode time to eliminate those annoying user mode spikes caused by the Response Probe calibration.

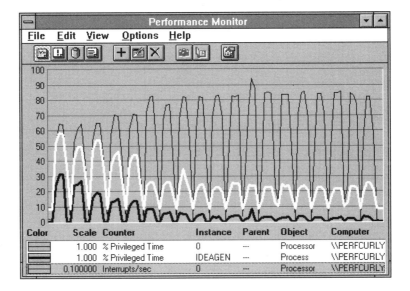

Figure 7.7 Processor usage on the client side of a 2048-byte read

We see the Ideagen processor time (thick black line) and the interrupt rate (white line) fall off as the record size increases. But overall processor utilization increases. We can conclude from this that we are spending more and more time in each interrupt. Why? The larger records must be copied to Ideagen's buffer, and this is done at interrupt time. As the average transmission size increases, so does the amount of time in the client's interrupt handler. Now let's take a look at the server to see what's happening there.

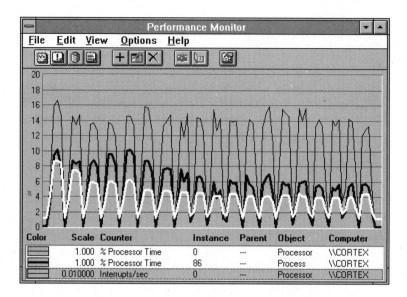

Figure 7.8 Processor usage on the server during 2048-byte reads

Did you notice the change in the vertical maximum on this chart? Qualitatively, the picture is similar to the picture of the client side; more work in the interrupt handler when the records are longer. But the work split is not quite so dramatic.

Where is the bottleneck here? The definition of bottleneck is the device with the most demand during the interaction. In this case, the bottleneck is the client processor with 0.004609 seconds per interaction. It is not, however, utilized 100%, but only 68.807%.

Why? Its activity is in sequence with the media and the server. *Sequencing* is an important limitation on the utilization rate of hardware components. When devices operate in sequence, they cannot be fully utilized. Or, looking at it another way, 68.807% is in this case fully utilized if the other devices are held constant, because the other two devices take 1 - 0.68807 = 0.31193 seconds out of every second. And until they finish, the client is in a forced idle state. When there is sequencing, the bottleneck is still the device with the greatest demand. Making one of the other devices faster can improve throughput, but to a lesser degree.

Generalizing Network Bottleneck Detection

Stay with us for a moment longer and we'll get the rest of this network bottleneck detection sorted out. Let's take a look at those interrupt rates. Let's assume for a moment that the interrupts always occur when the processor is idle. This is not a good assumption in all cases, but it mostly holds in this experiment.

On the server side we have total processor utilization of 14.324%, and processor utilization by the server process of 9.370%. Subtracting the utilization by the server process from the total processor utilization tells us that the interrupts took 0.04954 seconds. Since there were 575.017 interrupts per second, we can divide 0.04954 by this amount and get 0.00008615 seconds, or 86.15 microseconds per interrupt.

On the client side we saw 68.807% processor utilization with 22.006% in the Ideagen process, giving us 0.46801 seconds of interrupt time. Performing the same calculation we did for the server side gives us 878.89 microseconds per interrupt. The reason this is so much larger is because on the client side the data must be copied to the application's buffer, whereas on the server side the data can be read onto the network directly from the file system cache. They are also different processors, which is something we want to revisit in a moment.

It's worth mentioning that most of this interrupt time does not actually occur in the interrupt handler itself. That would delay lower-priority interrupts for a prohibitively long period of time. The Windows NT interrupt architecture permits the bulk of work normally done in an interrupt handler to be handled instead at a level just between interrupts and threads called the deferred procedure call or DPC level. The interrupt handler puts into a queue a DPC packet that describes the work to be done and then exits. When there are no more interrupts to service, the system looks for DPCs to execute. A DPC executes below interrupt priority and thus permits other interrupts to occur. No thread executes any code until all the pending DPCs execute. This design gives Windows NT an extremely responsive interrupt system capable of very high interrupt rates.

Let's now take a look at a case on the right hand side of Figure 7.1 and see how the result changes. We've chosen the 14-page transfer because it is in fact the one with the greatest throughput, although all the cases on that side of Figure 7.1 are pretty near the maximum.

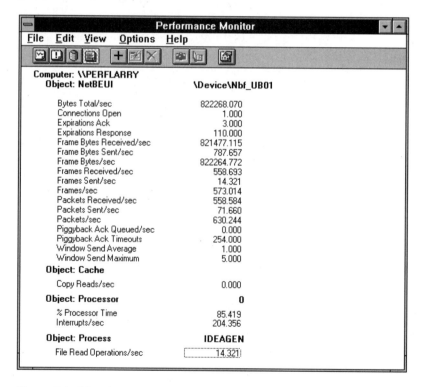

Figure 7.9 Client's view of 14-page reads

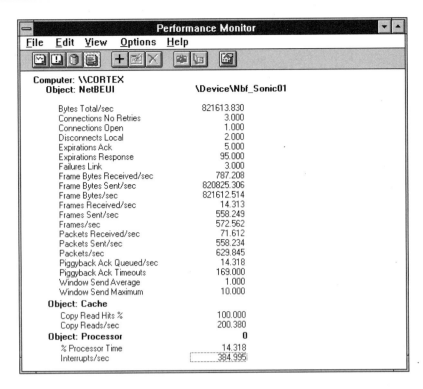

Figure 7.10 Server's view of 14-page reads

Looking at client File Read Operations/sec, we are getting 14.321 reads per second. The inverse, which is the time per read, is therefore 0.069828 seconds. Can we account for the time?

On the server side we are using 14.318% of the processor, so dividing this by the client's File Read Operations/sec gives us 0.0099979 seconds per read. On the client we are using 85.419% of the processor or 0.059646 seconds per read. Accounting for the network media, we divide the client's NetBEUI: Bytes Total/sec by 14.321 to get 57417 bytes per read, which is just 73 bytes over the 57344 requested per read. (You might recall that at 12K we saw a shift to a more efficient protocol for large transfers.) And multiplying 57417 by the Ethernet transmission time we mentioned previously gives 0.0459336 seconds per read. Adding client, server, and media gives 0.115578 seconds.

Whoops. This is much larger than the time per read of 0.069828 we computed by simply inverting the read time. Why? Our more efficient protocol combined with the fact that we have many packets per read is now permitting an overlap of processing time on the server with transmission and processing time on the client. The data transfer is now broken up into 558.693 / 14.321 = 39.012 frames. (Be generous, invoke Rule #9, and call it 39 frames.) So transmission of these frames on the server is overlapping with receipt on the client side.

Now let's take a look at how this larger transfer size affects time per interrupt. Continue to assume the interrupts occur when the server and Ideagen processes are idle, although the assumption is becoming dubious. On the server, we see 384.995 interrupts per second. Knowing we are using 14.318% of the processor, and subtracting 6.232% spent in the server process (not shown), gives us 8.086% in the interrupts. Dividing that number by interrupts per second gives us 0.00021003 seconds. This is over two times the 0.00008615 seconds for the time per server interrupt during the 2048-byte transfer.

On the client side we have 85.419% of the processor with only 3.892 % of the processor time in Ideagen (not shown). This means 0.81527 seconds of each second are in the interrupt handler. Since the client is seeing 204.356 Interrupts/sec, the same calculation that we performed for the server side gives us 0.0039895, or 3.99 milliseconds/interrupt. This is over 4.5 times the 878.891 microseconds per interrupt we saw in the 2048-byte case.

Using Role Reversal to Compare Platforms

Let's take a step back for a moment. We see a big difference in the processor usage on the client and the processor usage on the server. This is reflected in overall processor usage as well as in such details as the estimated time in the interrupt handler. There are two fundamentally separate sources for this difference, and we should try to separate them. One is that the client and the server are not doing exactly the same work. The other is that they have different hardware: one computer has a MIPS processor with a DMA network adapter, and the other is a 486 with a memory-mapped adapter.

One way to get a handle on how these separate factors influence what we are seeing is to reverse their roles. Windows NT is pleasantly flexible in this regard. We can make the 486 computer be the server and the MIPS computer be the client with a couple of mouse clicks in File Manager.

The next figure shows the client side of the 2048-byte read case when the client is the MIPS computer. It is followed by the server's view of the same case with the server being the 486 computer.

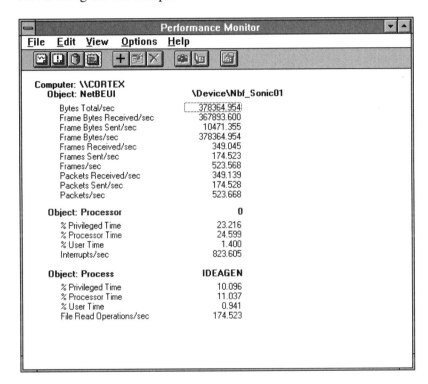

Figure 7.11 MIPS client statistics for 2048-byte reads

Looking at NetBEUI: Bytes Total/sec, we see an increase of about 50K per second. Sure, you say, because the bottleneck was the client processor and we replaced it with a faster one. But we also violated Rule #1 because we changed the server at the same time. To some extent, we just got lucky.

What we wanted to do was distinguish between the change in the roles of client and server and the different processor types. How can we do this? When the MIPS computer was the server, we saw that it handled 149.299 reads per second using 14.324% of the processor, which gave 959 microseconds per read. Now that it's the client, we are doing 174.523 reads using 24.599% of the processor, or 1409 microseconds per read. We have almost 47% more processor cycles being used on the client side of the transaction. Clearly it is more expensive to be a client than to be a server. Let's double-check this on the other side of the fence.

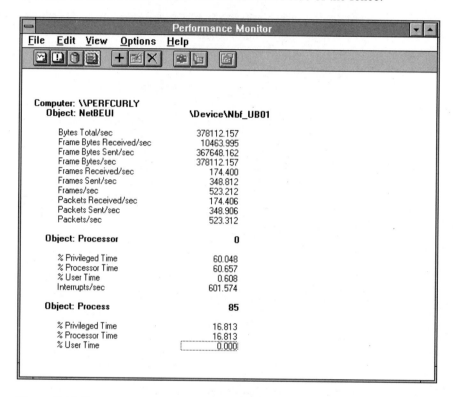

Figure 7.12 Server statistics when the server is a 486/33

We can just glance at this to see the server load is lighter than the client load was. The processor utilization has dropped from 68.807% to 60.657%, but the number of reads per second has increased. Do we see the same shift on this processor that we saw on the MIPS? The per read processor time in this test is 3478 microseconds. Before, it was 4609. The increase caused by doing client work instead of server work is 33% on the 486/33 and 47% on the MIPS. In both cases it is more expensive to be a client than a server.

This means that some of the client/server difference we saw in processor usage is definitely due to the more burdensome nature of client work (at least in this simplified test when we are fetching a record from the server's cache). What can we say about the relative behavior of the two processors?

The MIPS is 3.3 times faster at doing the client work because it uses 1.409 milliseconds per read, versus 4.609 on the 486/33. And the MIPS is 3.6 times faster at doing this simple server work than the 486/33 (959 microseconds versus 3.478 milliseconds for the 486/33). You might be inclined to make some decisions based on this fairly consistent result, but don't get carried away just yet. For example, the Response Probe calibration loop is 5.5 times faster on the MIPS, because it pretty much fits into the MIPS cache.

Relative processor performance—or relative hardware computer performance in general—is extremely sensitive to the workload applied. Here we are using a simple synthetic workload, so generalizing it to a real application workload would be improper. Once you get your own applications running on these servers, you can compare the processors in the way we have here. At that point other important mitigating factors like disk subsystem performance will enable you to get a realistic picture of relative platform performance. What we've tried to do here is make sure that when you get to that point, you'll know precisely how to proceed.

And finally, where is the bottleneck now? Well, the media time hasn't changed; it is still taking 1.734 milliseconds per read. We have shifted the bottleneck over to the server, or left it on the 486/33, depending on how you want to look at it.

Adding Clients to a Test Server

Let's have several clients simultaneously access our server to test its mettle. We'll revert to the 2048-byte transfer case, since it seems a bit more realistic for normal network traffic than the 14-page transfer. But it's not entirely realistic, because all the clients will simultaneously try to copy the same record from the server, over and over, without causing any server disk activity or doing any processing on the client side. So we'll be hammering the server in an unrealistic manner, but we'll see how the additional clients affect overall performance. We'll add two, three, four, and then five clients, each doing the above unbuffered read over NetBEUI on the Ethernet network.

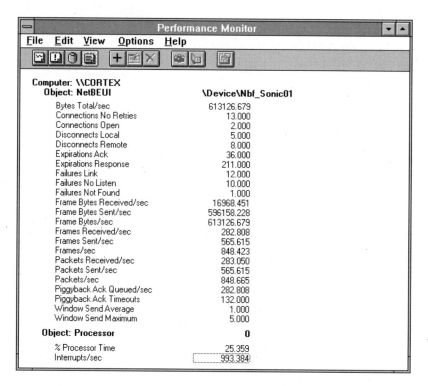

Figure 7.13 Two clients on a server, NetBEUI view from the server's perspective

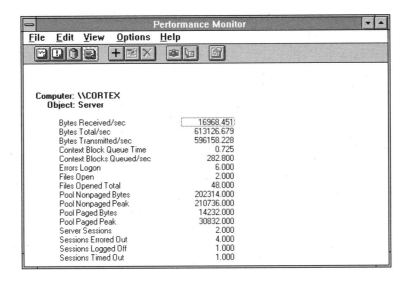

Figure 7.14 Two clients on a server, Server statistics

Let's look first at the two-client case. What we see is nearly double the throughput of the single client case. Boy, how we love these controlled experiments! The interrupt rate is also nearly doubled, but the processor time has increased by only 77%, so there must be some economy of scale at work here. When there is more concurrent activity it is sometimes possible to get more work done with less effort, such as fielding two client requests on a single thread switch.

The Server: Context Block Queue Time has not changed from Figure 7.6. Server: Context Block Queue Time indicates how long a server request must wait in the server while it is being processed. This is a good indicator of how busy the server itself is. It is a primary parameter to watch to detect busy servers. Queue time is unchanged here, so there is no interference between the clients.

Let's add another client.

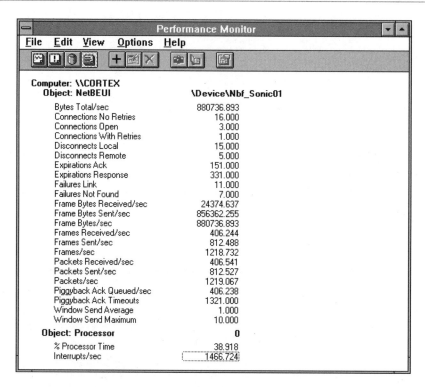

Figure 7.15 Three clients pile on, NetBEUI statistics on the server

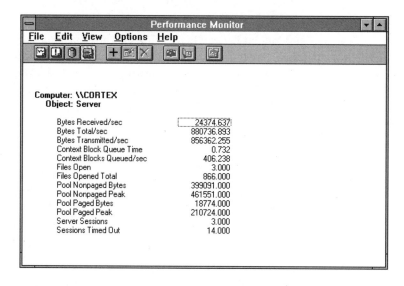

Figure 7.16 Three clients pile on, Server statistics

We already see something interesting with just three clients. Note that the NetBEUI: Bytes Total/sec is not three times the individual client transfer rates of 323666.597 we saw in the single-client case. Also the Server: Context Block Queue Time, which is expressed in milliseconds, has not changed much. So the three clients are experiencing little additional conflict within the server itself. There should be some new conflict. Is this reasonable?

Let's look first at the server's processor usage. The processor itself is now 38.918% busy handling the server work. This is quite a bit more than we had in the single-client case, but unlikely to be the bottleneck. Why? Because the more concurrency we have, the less sequencing we have, and the utilization of the bottlenecking device should be closer to 100%.

Now let's take a look at four clients.

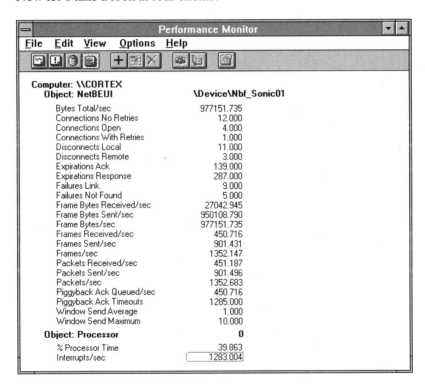

Figure 7.17 Four clients pile on, NetBEUI statistics on the server

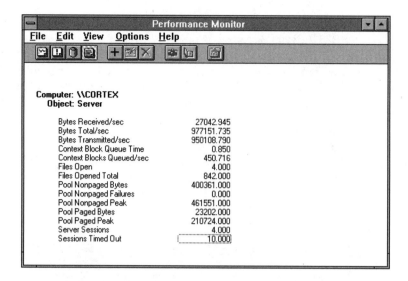

Figure 7.18 Four clients pile on, Server statistics

The total byte throughput is up somewhat, although certainly not by another 323,667 bytes per second, which is what our new client would like to be doing. The % Processor Time is within a Rule #9 of being unchanged, and the interrupt rate has actually fallen. The Context Block Queue Time is up a bit, but it is not a big jump. We have not been able to add a lot of work to this mix, even though we have added more clients. We would probably have guessed that the queue should have increased more than this. By now it should begin to dawn on us that the queue might be forming outside the server.

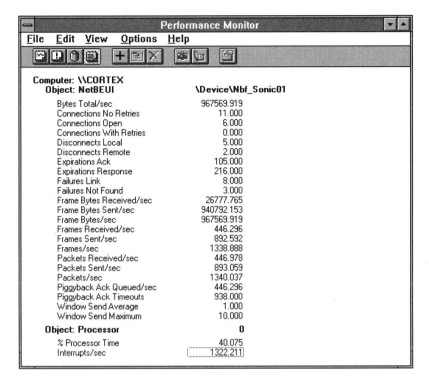

Figure 7.19 Five clients pile on, NetBEUI statistics on the server

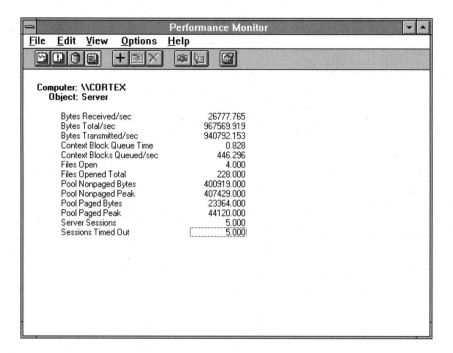

Figure 7.20 Five clients pile on, Server statistics

Now we actually see a slight decrease in byte throughput. The % Processor Time and the interrupt rate have risen a bit, but not enough to get excited about. There has been a decrease in Context Block Queue Time, but it is a small decrease. None of these changes is very significant. Have you figured out the truth yet?

What is happening here is we have saturated the network media. How can that be, you say? We are not yet transmitting 1.25 million bytes/second, which is the capacity of an Ethernet network. There are two reasons why we are not reaching the theoretical maximum.

- Frame Bytes/sec does not include all the bytes on the wire. Performance Monitor doesn't count low level protocol bytes, just the bytes in frames associated with data transfer.

- We are starting to experience collisions on the wire, which the adapter cards detect. A collision on Ethernet causes the adapter to retry the transmission after a random delay. Lore has it that Ethernet networks start to have significant collisions at about 66.67% utilization, or 833375 bytes per second. This is derived from the same considerations from queuing theory that we discussed early in Chapter 2. Our network throughput is quite a bit higher than that here, but our traffic pattern is quite regular so we can do a bit better than one might expect in the general case. (Recall Rule #8: if our traffic were random instead of regular, there would be trouble.)

The total number of bytes on the wire are not available to Performance Monitor as shipped. Neither are the Ethernet collisions. These you can obtain by using a network protocol analyzer.

We hope it will not be long before a network protocol analyzer is added to Performance Monitor as an extended object. Until then, you can sum the Bytes Total/sec from each card and each protocol on each server. You do this by first exporting the data from Performance Monitor. Then you can use a spreadsheet or database program to form the sums. It may not be elegant, but it works.

Server Disk Activity

Up to now we have looked at some pretty simplistic stuff. Now let's add some serious server disk activity. Let's get Response Probe to read a large file, say 40 MB, using the normal distribution on 512-byte records to span the file. The reason we choose this file size is that our server has 32 MB of RAM and we would like to keep the experiment from fitting the whole file into the file system cache in RAM.

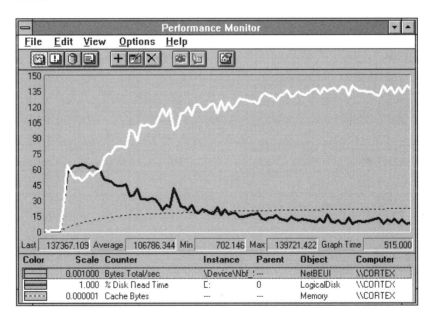

Figure 7.21 Server activity while reading a large file

The heavy black line shows the % Disk Read Time, while the highlighted white line shows NetBEUI: Bytes Total/sec. At the left of the figure, the disk is quite busy, but as the cache (the dotted line) fills, the disk activity falls off and the NetBEUI: Bytes Total/sec rises to a maximum near 140,000 bytes per second. Referring to Figure 7.1, we can see the 512-byte read case gives a maximum of about 150,000 bytes per second. Disk activity never quite dies out, but it does taper off as the cache fills with the center records of the file where the normally distributed access is concentrated.

Let's focus on the period of heavy file usage on the left of the chart. The next two figures display the statistics during this phase.

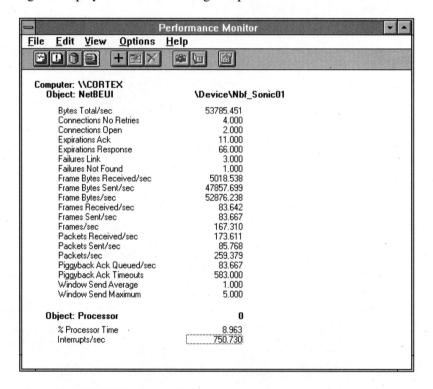

Figure 7.22 NetBEUI view of disk access on the server

We are getting only one-third of the NetBEUI throughput possible at this record size from this client. The processor is not very busy, and the interrupt rate is moderate.

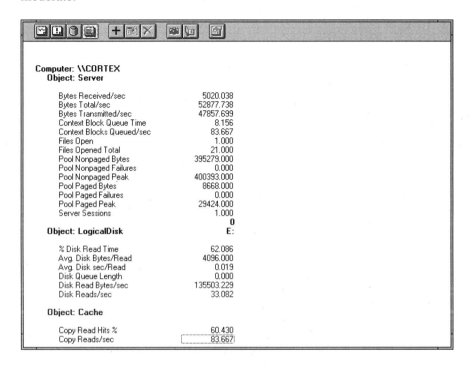

Figure 7.23 Server and disk view of disk access on the server

We can see that every record goes through the cache. The cache hit rate is 60.430%. So the miss fraction is 0.3957, and 0.3957 times the Cache: Copy Reads/sec rate gives us 33.107, which is within Rule #9 of Disk Reads/sec. In other words, when we miss the cache we go to disk. This is not a surprise. We are getting full pages off the disk, and we can tell we are reading randomly because the memory manager cannot find any opportunity to do sequential I/O. Let's take a quick look at the memory manager's statistics, too.

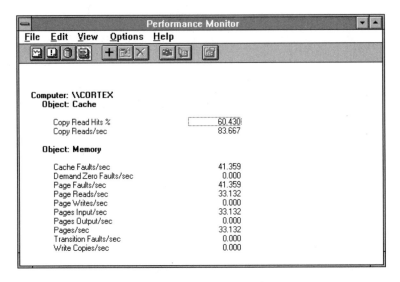

Figure 7.24 Memory manager's view of disk access on the server

All page faults are for cache activity, and the number of Pages Input/sec matches the Disk Reads/sec.

What about the bottleneck? Well, the disk is busy 62.086% of the time, or 0.62086 seconds out of each second. If we divide this by the number of reads from the client each second, we get 0.0074206 seconds of disk activity per interaction. The inverse of the interaction rate is 1 divided by Cache: Copy Reads/sec, or 0.011952, so we already have over half of the time spent going to disk. This makes the disk the bottleneck, even without going into all the other pieces of this particular puzzle.

But we can only make this declarative statement because all the pieces of the puzzle are in sequence. Because of sequencing, once we find a device with over half the time, we know no other device can have more than half. If there were any chance of parallelism among the processors, media, and disk, then we would have to look more closely at the demand for each device.

Copying a Directory from Server to Client

Let's look at a more realistic case. We'll have a client copy the SYSTEM32 directory from the Windows NT server, and see what the result looks like. The first three figures are for the server side, and the next three are for the client side.

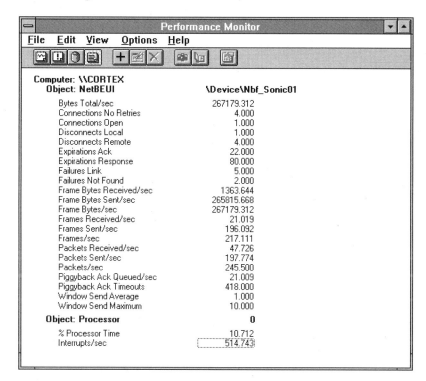

Figure 7.25 NetBEUI on the server during directory copy

The first thing to note is the number of bytes sent per frame is 1356, which (you know by now) we get from dividing the Frame Bytes Sent/sec by the Frames Sent/sec. But actually, when we divide Frame Bytes Sent/sec by Frames Received/sec, we find we are getting a fairly amazing 12646 bytes per request. Pretty good bang for the buck.

The observable processor time is low, and the value of Interrupts/sec is moderate. Whatever else we have done, we have not saturated the server's processor.

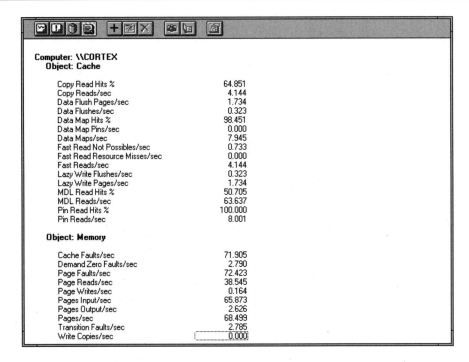

Figure 7.26 Cache and memory on the server during directory copy

The cache statistics show something we have not seen before. The bulk of the activity is in multiple data list (MDL) reads. MDL reads use the physical memory locations of cache pages to obtain multiple disk pages from disk in one operation. The server used MDL reads to get data from the disk. About half of these requests are satisfied by data already in the cache, as indicated by the 50.705 MDL Read Hits %. The Data Map Hits % is high at 98.451%, for 7.945 Data Maps/sec. These are probably directory operations, which is not surprising since we are reading a large directory that contains many small files. You can also see the interaction of the cache with the memory manager. Most of the Page Faults/sec are Cache Faults/sec. Many are resolved in memory with soft faults, but some 38.545 Page Reads/sec result from the 72.423 Page Faults/sec. Dividing the Pages Input/sec by the Page Reads/sec shows 1.7 pages are being read each time the memory manager goes to disk. So let's take a look at the disk.

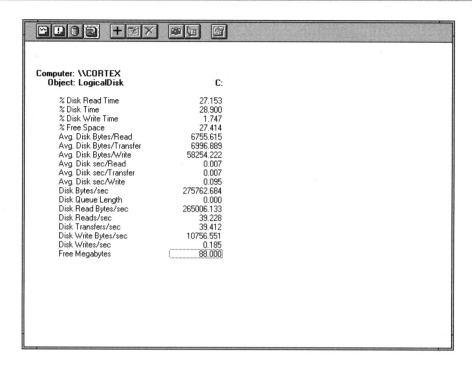

Figure 7.27 Disk activity on the server during directory copy

We see right away that there are 39.228 Disk Reads/sec, within a 9th Rule of Bottleneck Detection of Memory: Page Reads/sec. Also Avg. Disk Bytes/Read are quite close to 1.7 times the page size which the memory manager was reading.

To make our bottleneck detection a little less painful, let's just see how much of each resource is used per second. For the processor we saw 0.10712 seconds, for the disk it's 0.28900, and for the media we multiply the media transmission speed by Bytes Total/sec to get 0.21374 seconds. So far, the vote is for the disk. But that's just the server side. Let's take a look at the client, too.

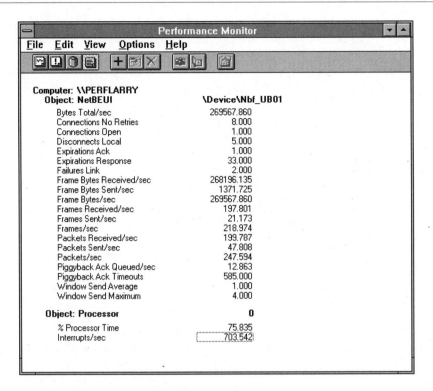

Figure 7.28 NetBEUI on the client during directory copy

These statistics naturally mirror the ones on the server side. There are some slight differences since we are not looking at precisely the same time intervals. The interrupt rate is a little bit higher here, and the processor usage is right up there at 75.835%.

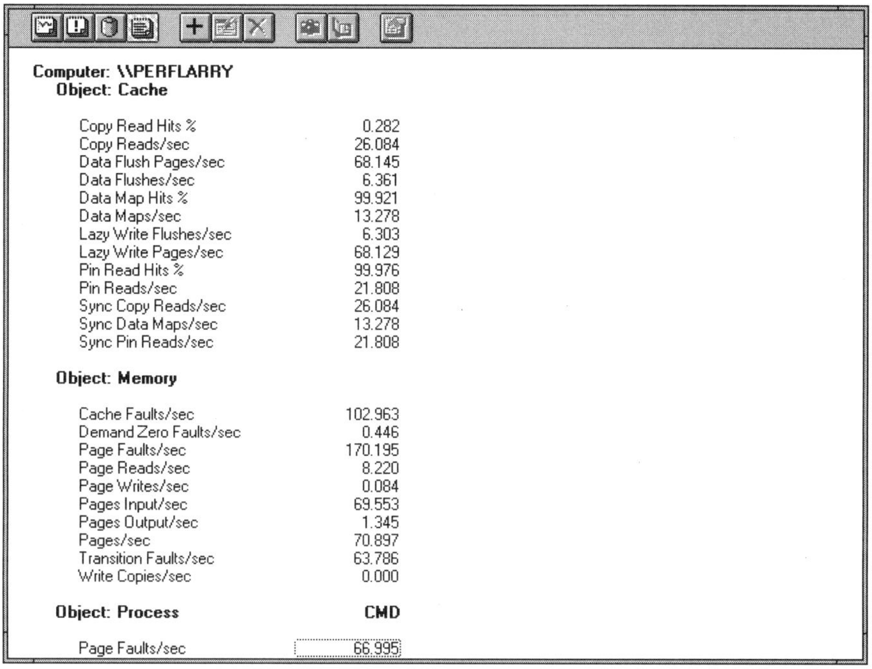

Figure 7.29 Cache and memory on the client during directory copy

On the client side, the cache- and memory-management story is a bit more complex. That is because we are reading into the cache across the network, into the application (in this case, CMD.EXE for the copy command), and then writing the data back into the cache to get it on the disk. This involves directory operations (Data Maps/sec) for both the server's directory and the client's, and we see the client rate is about double that of the server's. The hit rate on these directory operations is very high.

There are 26.084 Cache: Copy Reads/sec by CMD.EXE. Very few hit the cache, which means one or more cache page faults are taken to resolve them. It looks like more than one, because the Memory: Cache Faults/sec is quite high at 102.963. The other Page Faults/sec are coming from CMD.EXE. A little careful thought sorts this all out. Many of the faults are resolved by mapping in existing page frames into the cache's working set, since they result in only 8.220 Page Reads/sec. This is because the memory manager and the cache manager are working together to bring sequential groups of pages into memory in single operations. It is also because over half of the faults, 63.786/sec, are being resolved by transition faults, meaning they are pages which had been flushed from the cache and were being written to disk.

The 8.220 Page reads/sec result in 69.553 Pages Input/sec, which when multiplied by the page size is 284889 bytes/sec, very close to the input NetBEUI data rate of 268196 bytes/sec. These 8.220 Page Reads/sec turn into 21.173 NetBEUI Frames Sent/sec since directory operations are intermingled with the requests for file data. We conclude that only a few of the pages are coming from the client's disk. We see that CMD.EXE is generating soft faults at the rate of 67 Page Faults/sec, accessing buffers allocated and deallocated for the transfer of each file in the directory. This is also equal to Page Faults/sec – Cache Faults/sec, so CMD.EXE accounts for all the page fault activity outside the cache.

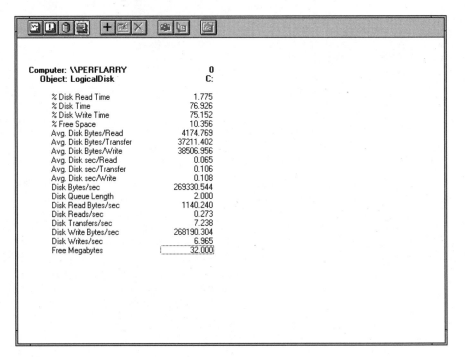

Figure 7.30 Disk activity on the client during directory copy

The disk itself on the client side is rather busy at 76.926 % Disk Time. The Disk Queue Length is 2. Remember that this is an instantaneous counter, so in a report it is just the value at the end of the time interval (in this case, the end of the transfer). We can't read much into that. But the disk is busy, that's for sure.

The 38506.956 Avg. Disk Bytes/Write is quite high, and the 6.965 Disk Writes/sec come from the 6.361 Cache: Data Flushes/sec. The values of Disk Write Bytes/sec and NetBEUI: Frame Bytes Received/sec are almost identical. This disk is a lot busier than the one on the server side because the Avg. Disk sec/Write is 0.108, compared to an Avg. Disk sec/Read of 0.007 on the server. Even though there are more reads on the server per second, its overall access is more efficient. This may be for a variety of reasons: disk layout of the files, disk hardware, controller hardware, and who knows what all else. To isolate the issues, we'd have to study the disk subsystems as we did in Chapter 4, "Detecting Disk Bottlenecks."

What about bottleneck detection on the client side? We've got processor utilization of 75.835%, and disk utilization of 76.926%. In a second of activity this means 0.75835 seconds of processor and 0.76926 seconds of disk. The disk wins the bottleneck award by a small margin. A classic case of one bottleneck masking another (remember the 2nd rule of Bottleneck Detection?) In both cases the device demands are larger than the demands on those devices on the server. This is as one might hope, since the server clearly has bandwidth to serve other clients simultaneously. Notice in passing the excellent overlap of processor and disk activity, since the sum of these device demands is just about 1.5 seconds/second.

Let's pause for a moment and regroup. We are now able to look at real systems doing real work and identify the bottleneck in a simplified client-server environment. We see it is seldom the media that is the bottleneck. We have found we must keep an eye on the disk and on the processor. We have learned when disk activity is the result of cache activity and we can recognize when it is not. We know enough to be able to look at statistics on a server and determine, by looking at processor, disk, protocol bytes, and interrupt rate, whether it is creating a bottleneck.

Monitoring TCP/IP Performance

Lest we wax overconfident, let's take a quick look at how life might change if the protocol were different—TCP/IP, for example. (Recall that we must have SNMP installed to see the TCP/IP counters in Performance Monitor.) If there are multiple protocols installed, the client must have TCP/IP as the highest priority protocol, or it must be the only one available on the server. The highest-priority protocol is the first protocol the workstation uses when it attempts to make a connection.

▶ **To set protocol priority**

1. In Control Panel, choose the Network option.

2. In the Network Settings dialog box, choose Bindings.

3. In the Network Bindings dialog box, choose Workstation in the Show Bindings For box.

   The protocols currently being used on the workstation are listed in the large box. The one on top has the highest priority.

4. To change the priority of a protocol, select it and use the arrow buttons at the right of the dialog box to move it up and down in the list.

5. When finished, choose OK.

In Figure 7.31, we show the throughput chart for TCP/IP from the client's perspective. Again we are bypassing the cache on the client side and are reading 512-, 1024-, 2048-, and 4096-byte amounts, and then page size increments of record sizes up to 16 pages. We've reversed which line is highlighted for clarity.

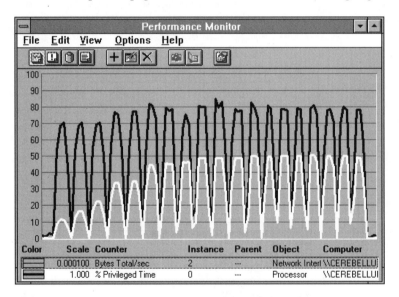

Figure 7.31 Throughput chart for TCP/IP

We don't get quite the throughput with TCP/IP as we did with NetBEUI in Figure 7.1. The implementation of TCP/IP uses the Streams environment, which permits the rapid and reliable development of new, portable protocols at some expense in processor overhead. This gives us the convenience of TCP/IP communication without the years of development and debugging normally associated with a new implementation. It is common for implementations based on Streams to be replaced by higher-performance implementations as soon as they become available.

The TCP/IP counters in Performance Monitor implement Management Information Base II (MIB-II) for use with protocols in TCP/IP-based internets. So we can get some idea of what is happening here, let's look more closely at the 2048-byte read (like we did for NetBEUI). First we look at the Network Interface level. This is the closest to the media that we get with the TCP/IP counters.

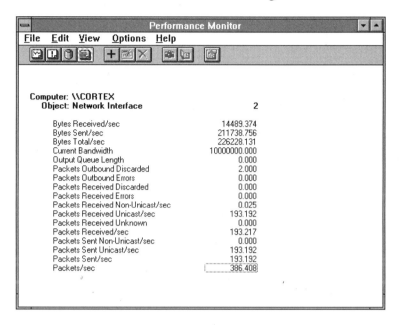

Figure 7.32 Network Interface of TCP/IP doing 2048-byte reads, server side

Dividing both Bytes Received/sec and Bytes Sent/sec by Packets Sent/sec, we find that the packets are 75 bytes each on the receiving side and 1096 bytes on the send side. The value of Bytes Total/sec is somewhat below the comparable values for NetBEUI, as already mentioned. The Current Bandwidth is a constant for Ethernet measured in bits per second. The term "Unicast" means the packets were addressed to this particular computer (as opposed to "broadcast to all on the subnet" or "multicast to several on the subnet"). The other packet categories refer to undelivered packets. Protocols sometimes discard packets even if there are no errors; for example, to free up buffer space. Errors indicate the packet contained problems that prevented the delivery to a higher level protocol (meaning IP). The Output Queue Length refers to the current number of packets pending output and is an instantaneous counter.

As you can see from Figure 7.31, processor usage for TCP/IP is higher than it is for NetBEUI, as we would expect for the Streams implementation. Interrupt rate is moderate.

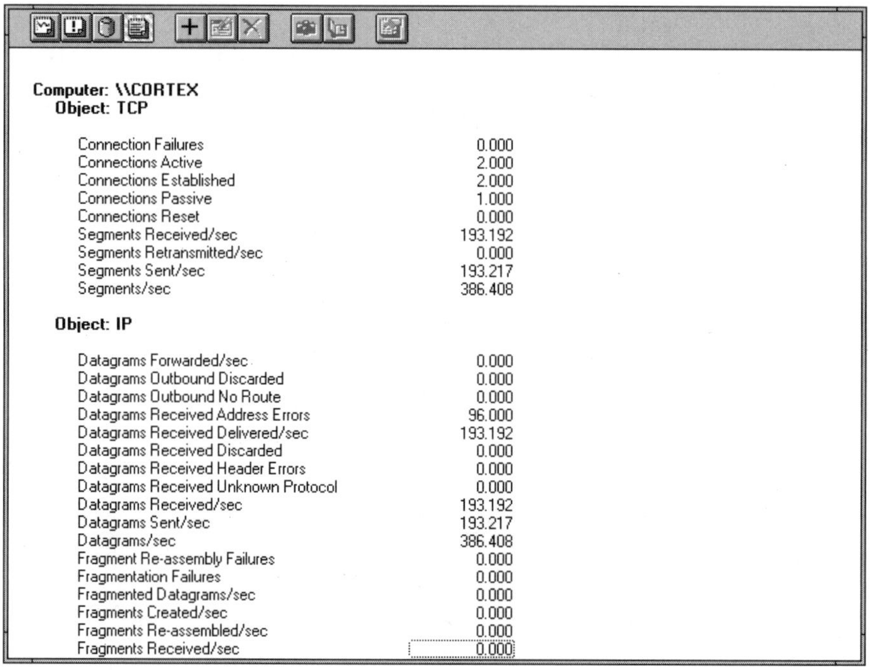

Figure 7.33 Server TCP/IP counters during 2048-byte reads

The next layer above the Network Interface is the IP (Internet Protocol) layer. This layer sees only datagrams. Higher-level protocols (TCP in this case) supply the end-to-end integrity to assure there are no out of sequence or missing packets. At this level, a variety of different dispositions of datagrams are counted. If there are data integrity problems you can often detect them here.

Datagrams Forwarded/sec is the rate at which this node is acting as an IP gateway, forwarding packets received by, but not addressed to, this node. This includes any for which No Route could be found and so were discarded (DataGrams Outbound No Route.) The IP layer can reassemble long transmissions sent as fragments, and a number of counters are devoted to tracking this activity. Reassembly can fail due to errors or time-outs.

The Transmission Control Protocol (TCP) supplies end-to-end connections using IP and assures all packets are delivered. If they are not, retransmission is invoked. This object provides a simple high-level view of the number of packets sent and received.

The User Datagram Protocol (UDP) provides a direct, rapid interface to IP without the need to first establish a connection with the recipient. However, the delivery of packets can be out of sequence or duplicated, or packets can be dropped. Usually a given application will use either TCP or UDP to communicate with IP. So these counters were all zero in this test case.

The Internet Control Message Protocol (ICMP) is an ancillary protocol layer attached just above IP. It handles a number of special internet message tasks:

- Echoing messages to verify that communication is possible (used by the **ping** utility)
- Redirecting a node to use a preferred route
- Directing a node to lower the transmission rate to relieve network congestion (source quench)
- Sending Destination Unreachable messages if a datagram cannot be delivered as requested.

These counters are also all 0 in this case, so they are not shown.

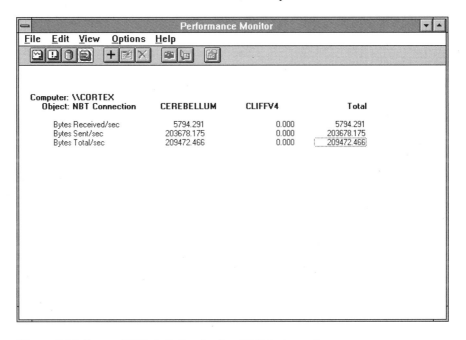

Figure 7.34 Server NBT statistics during 2048-byte reads

The NetBEUI TCP/IP Connection (NBT Connection) object individually records transmissions to all connection points and is an extremely useful item on congested servers. NBT Connection resides on top of the TCP layer in the protocol stack. NBT counts inbound and outbound byte rates, and has an instance for each open connection and a total for all connections. You can use it to determine which of several connections is sourcing a load, and in which direction. It's handy, handy, handy. We wish every protocol had it.

We generated a little UDP traffic so that it wouldn't be left out. UDP always gets a bum rap because its known in Internet circles as being unreliable. Imagine, value judgments on protocols. Anyway, the next few figures show some UDP action from the server's perspective. We are sending 1024-byte writes from a process on the client to a process on the server using Windows Sockets (WinSock) to connect to UDP. In this case WinSock provides the end-to-end packet integrity and so can use the "unreliable" UDP. This does not invoke the server process on the server at all, but acts more like an application such as SQL server might.

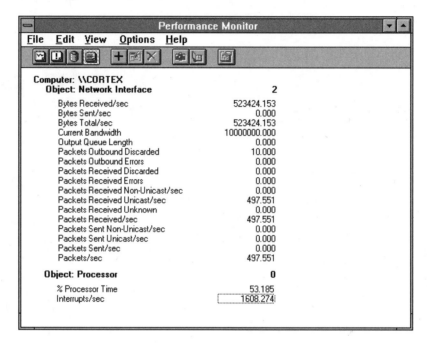

Figure 7.35 Server's Network Interface statistics during 1024-byte writes to the server

Now that's one cookin' protocol. That is as fast as we have seen bytes fly for this record size. And that's as high an interrupt rate as we have seen, too. It has resulted in a correspondingly high processor usage. All just as pretty as can be!

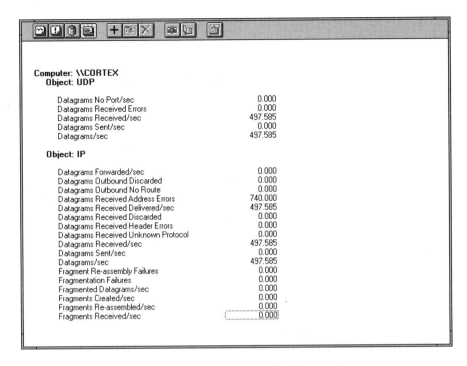

Figure 7.36 Server's UDP/IP statistics during 1024-byte writes to server

After all that blazing speed, the UDP counters are a little anti-climactic. Don't worry about those 740 IP: Datagrams Received Address Errors. They all occurred during the setup of the test. Since this is an instantaneous count of the current total number of such errors, we just have to chart it during the test. If it does not change while we are testing, then all the errors occurred before the test. We checked, and they did.

Anyway, there's a brief rundown of the TCP/IP counter set. You can get all the basic throughput information you need to determine your throughput ceilings. And you get that wonderful NBT Connection object thrown in, not to mention some pretty special performance from the WinSock/UDP/IP protocol stack.

Monitoring NWLink Performance

The NWLink protocol stack provides Windows NT with a method of communicating on Novell NetWare-compatible networks. Much like the NBT/TCP/UDP stack, NWLink provides analogous NWLink NetBIOS, NWLink IPX, and NWLink SPX services. The first figure shows our throughput test where the client is reading unbuffered data from the server's cache for a variety of record sizes, starting at 2048 bytes and then proceeding in 4096-byte page multiples.

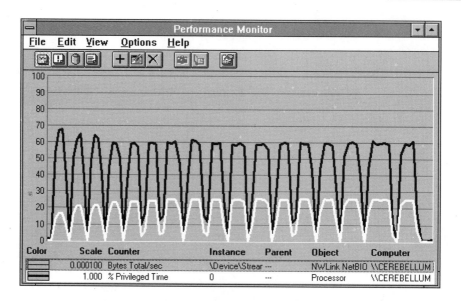

Figure 7.37 Client's throughput for unbuffered reading with NWLink NetBIOS

Once again we have a Streams implementation and we suffer some capacity loss as a result. Nonetheless, it is pretty handy to have this protocol available. It's actually quite good for a protocol implemented in just a few months. And it's worth mentioning again that it is common for Streams implementations to be replaced by higher-performance implementations as soon as they become available.

Let's take a look at the counters for NWLink NetBIOS. Here we have to make something of an apology, because the fact is we added these counters just a few weeks before shipping Windows NT, and the quick and reliable way to do that was to use the counters that were in use by the NetBIOS protocol. The minor crime we committed here is that if you are used to using the IPX/SPX protocol in another context, the labeling of the counters will be quite strange to you. Cut us a little slack on this one. We figured providing the data was more important than getting the nomenclature just so. We realize this is irritating to some people, but compared to not having the data it looked like no contest. Your patience is appreciated.

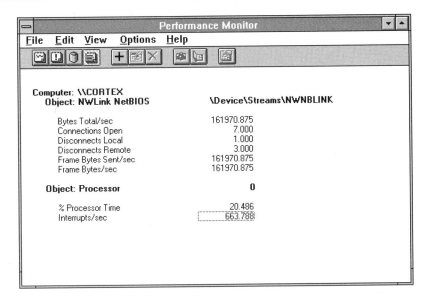

Figure 7.38 Server's NWLink NetBIOS statistics for 2048-byte reads

Here we have the most important measure of network throughput, the total number of bytes transferred per second. This is accompanied by a few connection statistics that can aid you during capacity planning (discussed in the next chapter). Processor usage is indeed higher than for a single NetBEUI client, and the interrupt rate is higher as well, being in part responsible for the increased processor overhead.

Let's generate some random NWLink IPX activity. We have a test program that uses multiple threads communicating with another computer in which a receiving process resides. These threads send and receive data simultaneously and also connect and disconnect from the other computer. This tweaks just about all the counters active from IPX, which gives the data you see in Figure 7.39.

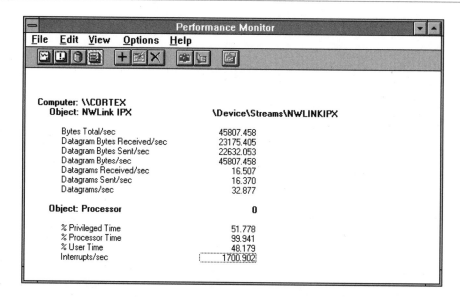

Figure 7.39 General IPX activity as seen by Performance Monitor

So far this is the award-winning interrupt rate, and the processor is saturated. Since the IPX exerciser had multiple threads, sequencing has disappeared. They're sure talking a lot, although they're not moving a lot of data. Sounds like some people we know!

We can generate some similar NWLink SPX traffic with a WinSock utility. This is a program that rapidly connects and disconnects from the server. Not a lot of bytes flow here since most of the activity relates to connecting up the two computers.

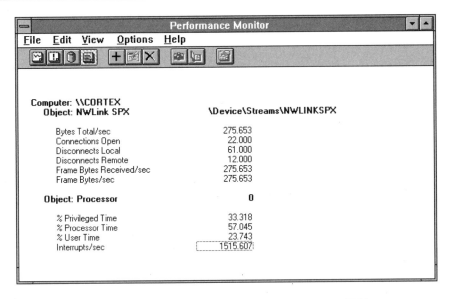

Figure 7.40 Connection and disconnection between NWLink SPX partners

But wait a second. Look at that processor usage and that interrupt rate. Does it really take all that horsepower to transfer 276 bytes per second? What's going on here? If we could see the packet rates, that would help us understand that there is a lot flowing here besides the data bytes. We have so much connection activity that we are swamped by it. This is indicated by the increasing disconnect rates in the next figure.

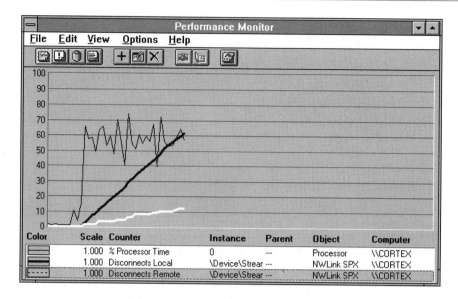

Figure 7.41 SPX connect/disconnect activity swamps server

So don't pass over those other innocuous counters hanging around. Look at everything; ignore nothing. Only you can determine what is important for your application environment. Just try to imagine what those programmers have done to your system! That ought to scare you. No counter is irrelevant when hunting bottlenecks. The fact that a counter is not changing can be just as important as the fact that it is. In the past few chapters we have focused on a few of the critical issues surrounding the hunting of bottlenecks. If you deal with this issue in the real world you know we have but scratched the surface. Don't oversimplify. Be patient. Be suspicious. Be fearless. Be relentless. And happy hunting!

C H A P T E R 8

Capacity Planning

You might think that capacity planning is something that only large Information Systems organizations need to do, but actually all of us change our work habits over time as we acquire new software. It can be fascinating to watch the computer system become taxed over time. But this fascination has its practical side—if we watch closely enough, we'll know exactly what to do to improve the performance of the system as the demand for it increases.

In this chapter, we'll give you some tips on how to stay one step ahead of the demand for your system, whether its a network server or a desktop computer. Capacity planning begins with keeping records of the performance of your system over time. These records can become so huge as to be practically useless if you're not careful, so a significant part of capacity planning is thoughtful and organized record keeping. Once you have good records to sift through, you can get to the analysis of those records.

The analysis is really just the application of the concepts of bottleneck detection we have explained in Chapters 3 through 7, from the perspective of watching how your computer usage habits have changed in the past, and where they are heading. Mercifully, we will not repeat those chapters here.

As a fringe benefit, the whole task of bottleneck detection is greatly simplified with even a little capacity planning. It's easier to see what's changed than to start from scratch to determine what's wrong. That Memory: Non-Paged Pool Bytes, didn't that used to be lower? Was it that new application we got, or was it adding TCP/IP to the network protocols? Just a little history is worth its weight in charts here.

Monitoring Multiple Servers

First, let's take a look at a few ways to monitor multiple servers. This is a common need for keeping records of performance on computer networks. (In "Monitoring Desktop Computers," later in this chapter, we'll discuss what you should do differently when you monitor workstations.)

It's usually easier to log the servers' performance data. If you don't log, you have to be pretty quick on the PRINT SCREEN key. You can log from multiple servers into a single log file. How many servers? That depends on how much data you collect from each one and how often you collect it.

Typically, you'll be doing bottleneck detection on your servers on a daily basis anyway. It's actually quite easy to take the information you're gathering for bottleneck detection and use it later for capacity planning.

Let's talk about what data you want to collect from your servers for bottleneck detection. At first, you might want to log just the following objects: Processor, System, Memory, Cache, Logical Disk, and the protocol at the adapter card level if possible. This is quite economical, and it is very easy to see exactly how much disk space this costs you. Switch Performance Monitor to Log view, set up to log these objects, and set logging to manual update mode. Then click the camera icon a few times. Note the file size. Click again. Note the new size. The difference is the cost of logging this data on that system. On a typical system, this is under 7K. If you have 10 such systems you have 70K, and if you have 100 systems, you have 700K (ouch).

Now, how often should you collect data? Let's suppose we have 25 servers so we are collecting 175K with each snapshot of the data, and that we collect data every minute. At the end of an eight-hour shift we'll have about 84 MB of data. As long as you reduce the data as described below so you don't have to save this much after each day's activity, it might not be considered prohibitive. But we aren't the ones buying the disks, so you might want to collect a little bit less. If you know how much disk space you can use for this each day, you can use the procedures we've just outlined to determine which objects to monitor, and at what time interval.

If you have an application server, you might want to collect some additional objects such as processes or even threads (so you can see the critical System: Processor Queue Length counter). The application itself might provide some extended object counters for Performance Monitor. If so, these might be worth keeping an eye on.

Another way to watch lots of systems is to use the Alert view. We've said little about alerts so far in this book, but nothing handles the monitoring of lots of systems (without taking up lots of disk space) quite as well. And your own creativity is the limit. That's because you can use Microsoft Test or a similar product to change Performance Monitor's settings in response to an alert. (Microsoft Test for Windows NT will ship in the Windows NT SDK until it is included in the product release for the next version of MS Test.) You can reduce the time interval, add objects, and start or stop logging, all in response to alerts.

You can have the alert messages sent to you anywhere on the network just by adding a special name to the system you are using. For example, typing **net name wizard /add** adds the name "wizard" to the system you are on. If you then direct the alert to send a message to "wizard," it will find you no matter where you are—even out on a RAS client laptop somewhere over the South Pole.

One thing you will surely want to do is set an alert on the % Free Space on your file server logical drives. You do not have to enable DISKPERF.SYS to see the free space on your logical drives, but you already have DISKPERF.SYS enabled on all your servers because you ran some experiments after reading the previous chapters (right?), so this is not an issue. The next figure shows how you can set an alert on several drives at once. After setting this alert, we will get an alert as soon as the free space on any of the logical disk drives falls below five percent.

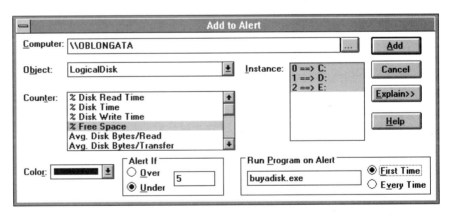

Figure 8.1 Setting alerts on disk free space for multiple drives

Archiving and Storing Performance Data

Let's continue with the example we started in the previous section. We collected data on 25 servers using a one-minute time interval. Most server bottlenecks can be found at this resolution. After all, if the server is slow only for a minute or less, it's not that inconvenient for the server's users.

Once the day is over, or perhaps the week, we no longer need that much detail. Now it's time to relog the data to a Performance Monitor archive. An archive is just a log file with data from multiple days that we'd like to keep around for a while. Internally it has the same format as the original log file.

Suppose we use Performance Monitor to open the first daily log file. The sensible thing to do here is to set the time window on a couple of busy periods of the day, such as mid-morning and mid-afternoon. (Alternatively, you might want to chart a key value such as System: Total Interrupts/sec to find where to set the time window.) If you are collecting from multiple servers, it is usually better to collect the data from them all at the same time of day.

After you've set the time window, open the log settings file with which you created the original log (here's where you're glad you saved that settings file). The settings file selects all the computers and objects you logged the first time. An alternative is to have a separate settings file for archiving the logged data, in which only a subset of the original objects are logged. For example, you probably don't need the Cache object in the archive, and you might not need all levels of the TCP/IP protocol if you logged them originally.

Having selected the objects to archive, use the Log Options dialog box to name the archive file. In this file you are building up a history of network activity during peak hours. Each day's peak activity is appended to the end of this file when you relog it, as shown in Figure 8.2.

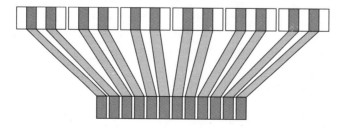

Figure 8.2 Creating an archive log file from daily logs

Before you append today's data to the archive, change the time interval to something like 600 seconds or whatever suits you. This reduces the data to one-tenth its original size (assuming the original log was made with a one-minute time interval). If you also archive only half of your workday (such as two hours of peak activity in the morning and two more in the afternoon), the size of the data is reduced to 4.2 MB from your original 84 MB, assuming we keep all those original objects in the archive. This is not an outrageous amount of data for a daily record of 25 systems. This is about 20 MB per work week, or one gigabyte for the year.

One gigabyte is not to be sneezed at, and Performance Monitor would be slow (to say the least) to process such a large file. So once a month we should engage in some further data reduction. You will want to browse through the counters to determine the ones you think best indicate system usage growth. System: % Total Processor Time, System: Total Interrupts/sec, Total Bytes/sec of the protocol, % Disk Time, and % Disk Free Space suggest themselves immediately. Number of connections and files open might also be interesting. To monitor system memory, you'll want to watch Pages/sec, but also keep an eye on Page Faults/sec and Cache Faults/sec so you can determine whether your paging is due to disk file activity or too many large processes.

You then chart the counters you selected over the month's time. At this point, we have 4 hours per day times 6 observations per hour, or 24 data points per day. With 22 working days in a month, this gives 528 data points for the month for each chart line. Of course, on a Performance Monitor chart you will see only 100 points, but as they say Down Under, no worries.

Analyzing Trends

Continuing our example, the next thing you'll do is export the chart. Now you have all 528 data points in a format suitable for a spreadsheet or database application. It's trend analysis time! Once you import this file into your application, you will get another huge reduction in data storage requirements. You are now in a position to plot 3-D charts, annotate them with sound and videos of your network humming along, and so on.

The next figure is an example showing the growth in processor utilization and interrupt rate on a server over a period of several months. The processor usage has climbed to near 75% at the right of the chart, and the interrupt rate is 1,180 per second. Time to order that second processor!

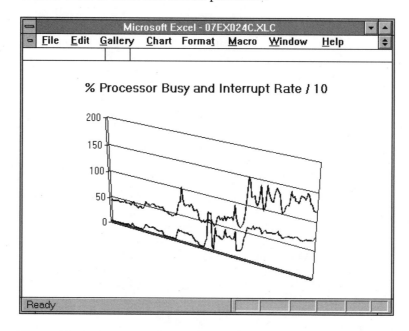

Figure 8.3 Processor-usage growth on a server over several months

You can automate a lot of this using Microsoft Test for Windows NT or a similar tool. If you do this by recording your actions, then wherever you can, use keystrokes instead of mouse movements to navigate. This makes the MS Test script more readily portable to different display resolutions.

Monitoring Desktop Computers

On clients, we recommend collecting less data. The same objects could be collected, but an hour's activity each day should be enough. Use the **at** command to schedule the MS Test script to log the data each day. You can skip a step by recording at 6-minute intervals initially. This gives ten data points, or 70K, per day. Append these directly to your archive. This will grow to 1.5 MB in a month, which could be compressed and placed on a floppy disk after it is exported, so it can be used by a spreadsheet or database application. (Utilities to compress and expand files are shipped on the Windows NT SDK.) Log files compress to about 30–40% of their original size. Again, all of this can be automated with MS Test with a little effort.

Once you have all this data, the chances that you will be able to get that next piece of equipment when you need it are greatly improved. Bosses are easily swayed by 3-D charts. If that doesn't work, add music, or a full-motion video of you working in slow motion. On second thought, maybe that last idea wasn't so great.

C H A P T E R   9

Writing High-Performance Windows NT Applications

It's time to talk about how to avoid lots of problems. An ounce of prevention is worth a pound of cure. (Catchy phrase, isn't it?)

In this chapter, we go over some guidelines and hints to help you write high-performance Windows NT applications. For years, a body of lore has accumulated surrounding the creation of high-performance and well-behaved 16-bit Windows applications. However, Windows NT is a completely new operating system, and the rules have changed. (For example, the constraints of a 16-bit address space have been removed within the operating system, so there are fewer limits on internally stored objects.)

The sophisticated virtual memory manager in Windows NT permits applications to have direct access to very large data structures. Increased protection permits applications to be less concerned about cooperating with other applications, and more focused on being responsive to the user. But costs associated with increased protection and with portability to multiple processors necessitate a rejection of some coding styles of the past.

If you think this chapter is only for programmers, think again. There is nothing more satisfying than going to your lead programmer and pointing out a more efficient way to do something. So if you're a programmer you'd better read this in self defense, and if you're not, this is your chance to get even.

Managing Memory

You have at your disposal a large virtual address space and probably more physical memory than in the old days, too. With 32 bits of address space, you can address 4 gigabytes. Each application program on Windows NT has the lower 2 gigabytes of linear virtual address space at its disposal. You don't get quite all of it, of course. If you have a console application, the system will use 5.5 MB of that lower 2 gigabytes to permit you to view portions of the system that reside elsewhere. If you have a Windows application, that number rises to 9 MB. But these are small potatoes compared to 2 gigabytes, so think of yourself as owning it all.

If your application is being ported from another operating system or from an earlier version of Windows, you might have developed a special virtual memory scheme for your own private use. Get rid of it. Otherwise you will be paying the price of having two virtual memory systems operating at one time, and believe me, one is enough.

You should consider using memory mapped files under certain conditions. Do this if you are going to randomly access the file read-only or read-share write-exclusive. Shared writing to memory-mapped files from multiple processes requires quite a bit of internal system structure and does not work well if the file is remote, because you will have to manage your own remote synchronization. There are better ways to spend your time, because this problem is automatically solved by facilities in each of the various file systems.

For sequential file access, memory-mapped access is a bit faster but uses more memory than does access through the file system cache. And if you are going to access a file sequentially, be certain to tell that to the file system in the CreateFile call by setting FILE_FLAG_SEQUENTIAL_SCAN. (In general, use CreateFile instead of the obsolete OpenFile call.) This increases the size of the read-ahead by the cache manager. If, however, you are going to access the file randomly and sparsely, you definitely should use file mapping. You do this by first calling CreateFile to open the file, and then CreateFileMapping to place it directly into your address space. This is what Performance Monitor does when reading in log files, because sparse random access to a log file is common.

You should also get rid of your temporary files if you know their maximum size. You can map a large temporary space which is backed by the system paging files instead of by a pre-existing file. Simply pass 0xffffffff as the file handle to CreateFileMapping, and specify the size you need.

You can also create large tracts of space to play in with the VirtualAlloc call. This is space backed by the paging file(s), but because it has no name it is not sharable with another process, so it's a little different from CreateFileMapping. You can form some really large private data spaces backed by the paging file with this much address space, but it may not be wise to reserve disk space for all that area. You may need your application to run on machines that are short on disk space. There's no point in taking more than you need.

What you can do is tell the system how much you might need in the worst case, and have it reserve that amount of linear address space. Then you can commit only those pages which you actually need to use as you go along. The reserved virtual space will be contiguous, but disk space will only be obtained in the paging file for the committed bytes. To reserve memory, call VirtualAlloc specifying the MEM_RESERVE flag, and later you can commit the memory with another call to VirtualAlloc, specifying MEM_COMMIT.

One useful thing about the CreateFileMapping call that we alluded to above is you can share the memory section you create or map with other processes on the same computer. All they need to do is a CreateFileMapping on the same filename. This is a much faster way to share information between multiple processes than named pipes, RPC, or shared file access. For example, it is how Performance Monitor would prefer to get its data from extended objects. You might need a mutex to protect access to the shared section, but hey, we got those too, and they're priced at a bargain.

Using the Kernel Wisely

If you decide to use the file system to access your file data, get a reasonable chunk of data at a time. If you are processing a file sequentially, get 4K or 8K at a time to reduce the number of calls you have to make to the file system. There is no point in crossing the boundary between user mode and privileged mode and going through a slew of protection and security checks unnecessarily. Of course, if you randomly access small amounts of data, you are probably better off not reading or writing large numbers of bytes you don't need. In that case try to map the file.

Think about using multiple threads to improve your performance on multiple processor computers. Just because you have a desktop application does not mean you cannot take advantage of multiple threads. First, you can use multiple threads as a technique to get back to the user quickly when the user has requested a task that takes a little time. Second, the day is not far off when we will see multiple processors on the desktop.

If you are working on a server application, you certainly want to use multiple threads, because multiprocessor servers will soon be commonplace.

Note It may not be wise to use multiple threads to get lots of concurrency in your file access. Be aware that Windows NT supports asynchronous file access. This means you can fire off many file requests, and the system will notify you when they complete. This is much more efficient than having a separate thread for each concurrent file request that you might have outstanding.

In MS-DOS systems, there was a limit on the number of files the system could have open at one time. This led to a coding style of opening and closing files frequently. Because of the additional protection and security in Windows NT, the action of opening a file uses more resources, and we don't encourage this coding style. Open files and leave them open for access. There is no limit on how many can be opened at one time, other than the size of non-paged pool; it cannot be allocated so large as to take all of physical memory. But we are talking many thousands of files before this is a consideration. So don't be afraid to leave your files open.

In Windows there was a distinction between memory obtained using LocalAlloc versus memory obtained with GlobalAlloc. Windows NT supports both allocation calls to make porting to Windows NT easier, but for 32-bit applications they execute the identical underlying code. The memory allocated is local to your process, and will be deleted by the system when your process dies. You cannot share it with another process; that's what CreateFileMapping is for. The one place where this is not true is when the memory is flagged as GMEM_DDESHARE, which Windows NT handles differently. Only applications using dynamic data exchange (DDE) or the clipboard will specify this flag. For 16-bit applications the calls appear to work as they did on 16-bit Windows, because these all execute in the NTVDM process.

If you're looking for the acme of performance on short bursts of activity, use the Real-Time Priority class. It's most useful for an application which is processing data in real time or doing time-sensitive communication with an external device. Your application must run in short bursts and not keep the processor for very long before waiting for the device to deliver more data. This is because you will be preempting all activity on the system, including the work of Windows NT system processes.

Another useful facility for development of real-time applications is the VirtualLock call. This permits you to identify a small number of pages to retain in memory so you will not have to wait for pages to come in from the disk when attempting to respond to a real-time device. You should implement a design that minimizes the amount of code that executes in the Real-Time Priority class with locked pages. You can use Event objects and shared named memory to exchange information with processes running at normal priority and thus minimize the real-time code.

One way to improve your performance when storing and retrieving data from the Configuration Registry is to use the new data type MULTI_SZ. This data type permits you to store a set of data values under the name of a single value by concatenating the strings into a single "multistring." A multistring has multiple individual strings separated by TEXT('/0'), with the last one followed by an additional TEXT('/0'). One call to the registry will retrieve all the strings. This is very efficient, especially if the value is accessed remotely. Performance Monitor counter names and Explain text are stored in two giant MULTI_SZ multistrings. Performance Monitor retrieves them all with just two RPC calls to the remote registry during remote monitoring.

This touches on another point. Internally, Windows NT uses Unicode. (Unicode is a 16-bit character-coding standard which includes symbols for all international languages.) When an application passes ASCII text strings to the system (to be stored in the Configuration Registry for example), they are translated to Unicode right off the bat. They must be translated in the reverse direction if the application is coded to deal with ASCII. So the obvious right thing to do, at least from a performance viewpoint, is to write the application to work with Unicode. This will avoid some unnecessary overhead and make the application easier to port to foreign languages, especially in the Far East. So if you want those trips to the Far East to work on the Asian versions of your application, use Unicode.

Grappling with Graphics

In Chapter 3 we discussed the graphics architecture of Windows NT. The illustration is reproduced here to jog your memory. When an application wants to write to the display it must send its request to the Client Server Runtime System (CSRSS). (This is called a client-server architecture because it mimics the network client-server model we covered in detail in Chapter 7. However, the client and the server for graphics in Windows NT must be on the same computer because, as we shall see, they share common data.) This provides a high degree of portable protection to the windowing and graphics managers, but there is a cost of about a thousand instructions for each call. This fact dominates life in graphics land on Windows NT and has important implications for how you code your application.

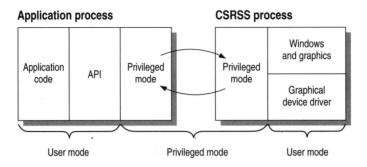

Figure 9.1 Windows NT client-server graphics architecture

You might wonder why we did not just use another protection ring and place the windowing system there. This would have kept it out of privileged mode and still protected it from the applications. The reason is that many machines only have the two protection levels: user and privileged modes. If we had tried to use a third level, Windows NT would not have been portable.

One way the system improves on the effective per-call cost of the client-server transition is to batch up calls and send them together. This gets them over to CSRSS at a "bulk rate." Several events can trigger the release of a batch of calls to CSRSS. If too much time passes between calls, the current batch is released. If too many calls pile up, the batch is released (ten is the default batch limit). And certain calls (those that require the graphics display to be updated in order to return their values) will "flush the batch." We'll discuss these in a moment.

In order to minimize the number of transitions to the CSRSS process, the system caches quite a bit of information in the application process. For example, the first time the application requests font metrics much of the information for responding to questions about the metrics on the font is copied to the application process for further reference. Another thing that applications do a lot is compute transforms between the logical and physical display coordinates, so the information for these transforms is cached in the application. Basically, anything frequently used that can be changed only by the application is cached. Anything that other applications using the windows and graphics subsystems can change cannot be cached in the application, but must be retained in CSRSS.

Another thing Windows NT does to minimize the need to cross over to CSRSS is to share, as read-only, some of the CSRSS address space with the application. This permits windows calls which need to read information in CSRSS data structures to do so without having to transfer to the CSRSS process to look at the data. An example here is the application's message queue. By mapping it to the address space of the application, the system can avoid a transition to CSRSS to determine if a message is waiting in the queue, as is done in a PeekMessage call. The system also maps data about such commonly-referenced items as existing windows, menus, and system colors.

Batch Processing for Graphics

You can see why effective Windows NT programming largely is about managing the batch of calls routed to CSRSS. Making sure this batch is as large as possible, when appropriate, is the goal.

When is it not appropriate? When you need the display to immediately reflect the drawing you do, you want to flush the batch explicitly no matter how large or small it is. Performance Monitor does this as soon as it has updated the display with a new chart data point. Failing to do this causes the data to be updated with noticeably odd timing. Also, you want to minimize the batch when you are debugging your application. Otherwise, an error returned to an application programming interface (API) call in the middle of a batch may not be returned until some other call flushes the batch; it will appear then that the wrong call failed. This seems pretty serious until you learn that debugged applications cannot get failures on API calls which can be batched. This is one of the criteria the system designers used for determining if an API can be batched. Finally, if you are doing certain performance measurements on your application, you will want to set the batch to one. We'll discuss this in the next chapter.

In general, you can batch graphical output functions that return a Boolean value indicating success or failure. A few frequently used APIs that return non-Boolean results which were seldom used have new replacement calls that just return Boolean results. SetPixelV and MoveToEx are the new calls in two important cases. (Remember this: there will be a test later.)

Three new API calls help you manage the batch. They are all optional; the default works fine except in rather odd cases, such as Performance Monitor updating a display in real time. GdiSetBatchLimit allows you to raise and lower the batch limit which, as we mentioned, defaults to ten. For best performance, you should set the limit as high as possible while avoiding jerky drawing on the display. You will want to test any changes to the batch limit on a very slow machine and a very fast one to be sure you have not introduced a problem which will only appear in one environment or the other. You can call GdiGetBatchLimit to determine the current limit. And you can call GdiFlush to flush the batch to CSRSS at the end of an operation you would like to see displayed immediately.

Most calls that manipulate the window system flush the batch. One reason is that much of the window system is visible to all processes on the desktop and so the central data repository for the common information is within CSRSS. We mentioned that PeekMessage does not flush the batch, but GetMessage does. So do graphics calls that return a handle or a number. An important exception to this is the group of calls for selecting fonts, brushes, and pens. These are batched. But selecting bitmaps and regions flush the batch. So do SetWorldTransform and SetMapMode. We are telling you all this so that (when possible) you will try to organize your code to group graphical calls together, and then make the calls that flush the batch.

Another way to reduce the overhead for the client-server architecture is to write your application to take advantage of the several calls beginning with "Poly." These exploit the fact that many drawing calls use identical attributes, and so multiple items can be drawn in a single call once the brushes, pens, colors, and fonts have been selected. Whenever possible be sure to use PolyTextOut, PolyPolyline, PolylineTo, PolyDraw, PolyBezier and PolyBezierTo. The Windows NT console window uses PolyTextOut. This change reduced scrolling time in a console window by 30% when it was implemented during the development of Windows NT.

Managing the Device Context

Windows NT provides a veritable sea of memory. Boy, this feels different compared to 16-bit Windows. Not only can our applications stretch their legs, the system itself no longer has to fit inside 16-bit-addressable blocks, and we have room for lots and lots of pens and brushes and fonts. In the 16-bit Windows programming environment, it was important to conserve the use of drawing objects. In the 32-bit world we have to have richer data structures to hold this new wealth of data. And that means it takes longer to look things up.

The old limitations gave rise to a coding style which created, selected, used, and destroyed objects (like pens and brushes) constantly. Create, select, use, destroy; create, select, use, destroy. This limited the number of objects in the system and kept the application from bouncing into the address space walls, or worse, forcing another application into them. Because of the client-server transition, object creation and destruction are much more expensive on Windows NT. Because of the new capacity for large numbers of objects, selecting objects is a bit slower too. So create all your objects when you first need them. Then try to get into the pattern of select, use, use, use; select, use, use, use. Don't destroy them at all until you really are done with them.

Let's take an example from real life. We had someone porting to Windows NT complaining that their graphics were slower than before. We had them use the API logger (which we'll cover in the next chapter) to see what was wrong. We found them using the following pattern: select(grey); patblt(...); select(black); patblt(...); select(grey); patblt(...); select(black); patblt(...).

We had them change this to select(grey); patblt(...); patblt(...); patblt(...); select(black); patblt(...); patblt(...); patblt(...). This solved the problem because it avoids the repeated lookups in the new data structures. This technique is applicable to pens, fonts, colors, palettes, and brushes.

While we're on the topic of graphical device contents (DCs), into which we've been selecting these objects, let's blow away another piece of lore. If you were a 16-bit Windows programmer, you were told to avoid the use of your own DC's because the system could only support a few. This is not true on Windows NT. Use the creation style CS_OWNDC as much as you can in your RegisterClass API call. This avoids repeated use of the relatively expensive GetDC and ReleaseDC calls every time you have to draw. It also preserves the selected objects in your own DC in between calls, eliminating the need to select them again after each call to GetDC.

Asynchronous Input and the Window Manager

The elimination of address space constraints permeates many aspects of the windows environment as well. For example, timers are no longer precious objects. Feel free to create and use as many as you like (but be aware that they are a poor man's substitute for threads in certain cases).

Arguably the biggest difference between the 16-bit and 32-bit window manager is the asynchronous input model. On 16-bit Windows you have a synchronous input model, sometimes called "cooperative multitasking." In this model, each application must always process its messages because every application saw every message and if you did not process each one and yield to another program quickly, you would hold up all the other programs on the system. This necessitated a coding style where the most frequently called API was PeekMessage, because every application constantly had to check the message queue for messages and pass them on. If they did not, the system would appear to hang. (This also gave rise to a generation of applications that, by default, loop in the processor checking for messages with PeekMessage instead of calling GetMessage which will return control to the window system until a message arrives. This does not really hurt anything, but as a coding style we find it offensive. We'll have no more of that, thank you.)

On Windows NT, messages are sent only to the processes that need to see them. If one process ceases to deal with its messages it may become unresponsive and may cease to update its display area, but the rest of the system will carry on just fine. This means PeekMessage no longer has to be the most popular API in the system. You still want to remain responsive to the user, of course, so you should still call it, but maybe not so often.

For the window manager, it is more important than ever that you write your application using Unicode. Having to translate everything that goes onto the display from ASCII to Unicode slows the important path from your application to the user's vision. Unicode, Unicode, Unicode. We love Unicode.

Considerations for RISC Computers

One thing that surprises designers porting applications to, or writing applications for, Windows NT is how easy it is to get their application to run on RISC processors. There are virtually no processor dependencies in the Win32™ API layer.

However, you can give up a lot of performance in your applications if your data is not properly aligned. The right way to handle this problem is to align the data in your source for both RISC and non-RISC machines. You want to assure that you have DWORDs on DWORD boundaries, and LARGE_INTEGERS on 8-byte boundaries. Normally the compiler makes this happen, but there are cases when you need to force unalignment, such as data coming in from a file or from over a network. Such structures may not follow these alignment rules.

In this case, you will want to use the pragmas PACK and UNPACK to define the structures, and the modifier UNALIGNED to declare pointers to them. This will get the compiler to generate the appropriate code. If you do not do this you will get alignment faults. On some systems these will simply trap and you can fix your program. We are more concerned about the systems that handle your unaligned references with a trap handler. This will slow your application down in a way that is not very obvious.

Choosing Between API Sets

The number of Win32 implementations the application designer might be considering is growing. At present these consist of Windows NT and Win32s™. As you certainly know by now, Win32s is implemented on top of 16-bit Windows so that Win32s applications can gain the benefits of a 32-bit address space, but still execute on existing 16-bit Windows systems. The existence of these two flavors of the Win32 API complicates the design decisions for the application programmer primarily in the performance arena. This is because Win32s offers the application the advantages of the 32-bit address space, but continues to be subject to the internal restrictions of 16-bit Windows (and to some extent, MS-DOS).

Therefore optimizations made for Windows NT will not always port to Win32s, and vice versa. Here we'll summarize which optimizations apply to which Win32 implementations.

The following table lists the various optimizations and tools presented in this chapter, and indicates where they apply. (Many of the tools listed at the end of the table are discussed in Chapter 10, "Tuning Windows NT Applications," and Chapter 11, "Tuning the Working Set of Your Application.") The abbreviations used in the table are:

Yes	OK to use in this implementation
N/A	Not applicable, does not apply to Win32s
No-op	You can do this without effect on Win32s
No	No, don't do this on Win32s

Optimization	Windows NT	Win32s
Kernel optimizations:		
Large address space	Yes	Yes
Discard old custom virtual memory schemes	Yes	Yes
Use memory-mapped files for file access	Yes	1
Reserve large data address spaces, but commit only what you need	Yes	Yes
Use named shared virtual memory	Yes	1
For sequential I/O, use 4K or 8K blocks	Yes	Yes

Optimization	Windows NT	Win32s
Kernel optimizations (*continued*):		
Use threads to enhance concurrency	Yes	No
Keep files open	Yes	No
Global and Local allocation are the same	Yes	No
Real-time priority for data communications	Yes	No
Page-Locking API is provided	Yes	Yes
Use new data type MULTI_SZ in Registry	Yes	No
Write the application using Unicode	Yes	No
No disk cache tuning required	Yes	No
Graphics:		
Client-server protection dominates	Yes	N/A
Batching of calls amortizes cost	Yes	N/A
Caching of values on client side reduces cost	Yes	N/A
Mapping of server data read-only to client	Yes	N/A
Batch output functions that return a Boolean result	Yes	N/A
SetPixelV and MoveToEx are batched	Yes	No-op
New APIs Gdi{Get|Set}BatchLimit, GdiFlush help	Yes	No-op
Set batch limit as high as possible while avoiding jerky display	Yes	No-op
Most "user" (that is, Windows management) calls flush the batch	Yes	No-op
GDI calls that return a number or a handle flush the batch	Yes	No-op
Selecting fonts, brushes, and pens do not flush the batch	Yes	No-op
Selecting bitmaps and regions flush the batch	Yes	No-op
SetWorldTransform and SetMapMode flush the batch	Yes	No-op
GdiSetBatchLimit(1) only to see errors, or	Yes	No-op
GdiSetBatchLimit(1) only to profile API calls	Yes	No-op
Use new Poly calls as much as possible	Yes	Yes
Avoid Create, Select, Use, Select former, Destroy	Yes	No
Create, Create, Create; Select and Use, Use, Use...	Yes	No
Richer structures to hold unlimited objects	Yes	N/A
Group attribute usage: gray, gray, gray, red, red	Yes	Yes

Optimization	Windows NT	Win32s
Graphics (*continued*):		
Grouping avoids cache lookup for pens, fonts, colors, palettes, brushes	Yes	Yes
Use CS_OWNDC in RegisterClass	Yes	No
CreateWindow, Get(Own)DC set DC attributes only once	Yes	No
Timers are no longer precious	Yes	No
Less need to use PeekMessage frequently	Yes	No
Write to Unicode	Yes	No
RISC:		
Be sure to align data	Yes	No
Compiler pragma for handling file/net data	Yes	Yes
Exception handling for data alignment not supported	varies	N/A
Tools:		
Win32 API Profiler	Yes	Yes[2]
Win32 Call/Attributed Profiler	Yes	No
Working Set Tuner	Yes	[3]
VADump	Yes	[3]
PView	Yes	No
Debugger **wt** command	Yes	No
Performance Monitor	Yes	No

1 This feature is targeted for Win32s release 1.1.

2 There are two Win32 API Profilers: one for Windows NT, and another for Win32s.

3 Working set tuning done on Windows NT will apply without further effort to the same application running on Win32s.

C H A P T E R   1 0

Tuning Windows NT Applications

If you've done everything we mentioned in the last chapter and you're as good a programmer as you claim, you can, of course, skip this chapter. If instead you are mortal like the rest of us, you may discover that your application's performance could use a bit of improvement.

When you set out to make that improvement, having the perfect knowledge of the static structure of your program is not enough to lead you down the right path. No one is surprised more often by the dynamic behavior of a program than its author.

You need tools for performance tuning. In this chapter we discuss the tools you can use to help you find performance problems in your application. The tools we discuss here are flexible and can address a wide variety of tuning issues. To cover them all completely would give us yet another volume. So instead, we'll show you how to use each tool and what it can tell you, and refer you to the documentation supplied with each one for the gory details.

Run Performance Monitor First

Usually you can tell you have a performance problem because someone is beating down your door complaining about it. (And that someone may well be yourself.) What to do then?

Your first reaction should always be to run Performance Monitor. The objective of Performance Monitor is not to solve all performance problems, but rather to make sure no one wastes any time barking up the wrong tree. The Windows NT SDK provides a number of tools you can use to tune your application, and running Performance Monitor before tuning helps you make sure you pick up the right tools to use next.

Let's take an example from the early days of the development of Windows NT. We ported the Solitaire program to Windows NT from 16-bit Windows. Initial users of the game complained about its performance when the cards cascade at the end of a winning game. You've never seen this because you've never beaten Solitaire? Well, on Windows NT we have built this in as a graphics demo. To see it, start Solitaire from the Games group and press SHIFT+ALT+2. That's the number 2, not the F2 key. We hope you're not disappointed with the speed, because the tuning work we are about to demonstrate has already been done on the copy of Solitaire you are running.

When we heard complaints about Solitaire, our first step was to run Performance Monitor. Because we didn't think Solitaire used the network, we logged the data across the LAN so we didn't interfere with any possible disk activity. We set the time interval to five seconds because the operation we wanted to time takes about 90 seconds. This gave us only 18 data points, which we figured was probably enough. If it wasn't, we could have built a version of Solitaire that performs the cascade operation repeatedly. You can't get too far exploring application performance problems unless you can isolate the problem.

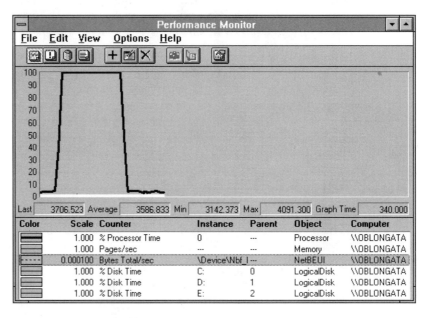

Figure 10.1 Overview of the Solitaire cascade

The overview from our log file of Solitaire is plotted in Figure 10.1. It's pretty clear that we have a processor bottleneck. All the other chart lines are flat, except for the LAN activity generated by Performance Monitor. How can we be sure this activity is caused by Performance Monitor? The average NetBEUI: Bytes Total/sec (3587) times the length of the run in seconds (340) is just about the size of the Performance Monitor log file (1120260 bytes; we learned this from the **dir** command).

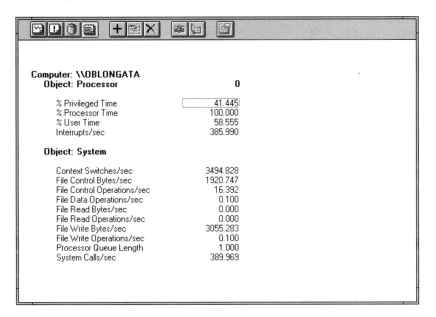

Figure 10.2 Processor and system statistics during the Solitaire cascade

We're spending 41.445% of the time in privileged mode, and we see a pretty high context switch rate for this computer, a 486/33. Because the value of File Write Bytes/sec is close to the NetBEUI: Bytes Total/sec we saw in Figure 10.1, we can tell that the File Write Bytes/sec rate was caused by the redirector when it wrote Performance Monitor data. The interrupt rate is consistent with a system connected to a busy network, but not too active on it. We followed our own advice from Chapter 3, and looked at which processes were eating up the processor.

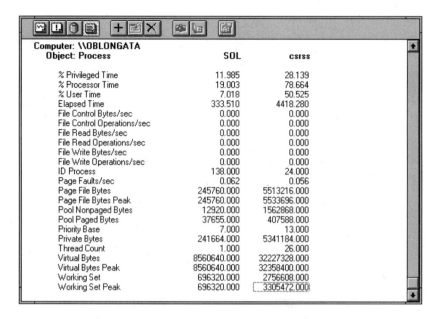

Figure 10.3 Process activity during the Solitaire cascade

Looks like CSRSS was doing all the work. Between Sol and CSRSS, the processor was maxed out. We decided to see if looking at the threads could give us any more information about what was going on here.

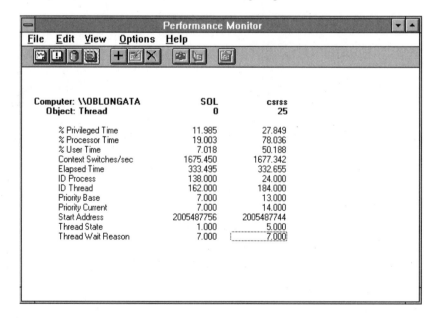

Figure 10.4 Thread statistics during the Solitaire cascade

Now we can see where all those context switches were going. Solitaire is calling CSRSS constantly, and most of the time is spent in CSRSS in a single thread. (For clarity, we omitted the 25 idle or near-idle CSRSS threads from the report shown here.)

We're not spending a great deal of time in the Solitaire program. So it must be Windows NT that has the problem, right? Let's make sure that's true by using the next indicated tool, the Windows API Profiler.

The Windows API Profiler

The Windows API Profiler, affectionately known as WAP, is useful for determining which Windows 32-bit API calls are taking up time. WAP can effectively profile any number of processes and threads concurrently. You can run it on a program without having to recompile the program, and it runs on both the Intel and MIPS processor families. WAP intercepts the calls from the application to the system and counts and times them. WAP is available in the Windows NT SDK.

WAP modifies the executable image to point to a set of measurement DLLs that sandwich themselves between the application and the system DLLs. See Figure 10.5. If your application performs a checksum on its executable, you must disable the checksum to run WAP.

Application process before API profiler is started

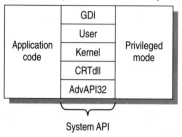

System API

Application process while API profiler is running

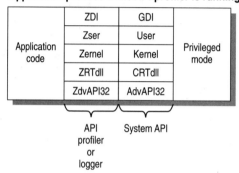

API   System API
profiler
or
logger

Figure 10.5 Application interface to the system before and after running apf32cvt

WAP sets the client-server batch size to one before taking any measurements. This assures that the proper API call gets billed for its time. If WAP did not do this, the time for all the API calls in the batch would be counted against the last one in the batch, totally confusing the data (not to mention confusing you). Setting the batch limit to one is a good idea, but you may notice a slowdown in the operation of the application because there are many more client-server transitions. Set another plate: Heisenberg invited himself to the party again.

If you are concerned about the impact of setting the batch level to one for your application, you can get an idea of the cost of a client-server transition on your computer by looking in the WAP data for a call to SetWindowLong. It's a pretty common call. If you don't see a SetWindowLong call, use WAP to find such a call in another application, such as WinHlp32.

The Win32 APIs are contained in the following dynamic link libraries: KERNEL32.DLL, ADVAPI32.DLL, GDI32.DLL, USER32.DLL, and CRTDLL.DLL. The profiler is in the form of five DLL files, one for each DLL to be profiled. As shown in Figure 10.5, these DLLs sit between an application and the Win32 DLL to be profiled, intercept API calls to them, and then make and time a call to the Win32 API. The profiling DLL records the following information for each API:

- The number of times the API is called

- The total time spent executing the API during those calls

- The average time per call, computed by dividing the total time spent in the API by the number of times the API is called

- The time of the first call to the API

- After the first call, the maximum time spent in the API on any one call

- After the first call, the minimum time spent in the API on any one call

- The number of calls that were not timed, due to a timer overflow (timer overflows should not happen)

All result times are in microseconds.

The profiler determines overhead by reading the timer 2000 times upon initialization of the profiling DLL. The minimum time of these calls obtained during this process is subtracted from the time for each API call, thus eliminating the majority of timer overhead from the final results. For accurate timing, it is important that the system be inactive during the calibration process.

Setting Up the Profiling Environment

There are a few utilities that assist the profiler. You must place APF32CVT.EXE and APF32DMP.EXE in the path of the measurement computer. You use **apf32cvt** to prepare the application for profiling. You also use **apf32cvt** again after profiling, to restore the application to its original state.

The **apf32dmp** utility is used to collect the profiling data during and after the profiling run.

The following DLLs are required and must also be placed somewhere on the operating system's path:

- ZDVAPI32.DLL, the profiling DLL for ADVAPI32.DLL

- ZERNAL.DLL, the profiling DLL for KERNAL32.DLL

- ZDI32.DLL, the profiling DLL for GDI32.DLL

- ZSER32.DLL, the profiling DLL for USER32.DLL

- ZRTDLL.DLL, the profiling DLL for CRTDLL.DLL

- FASTIMER.DLL, the timing DLL

Profiling an Application

The **apf32cvt** utility prepares an application for a profiling run. It does this by modifying the application to load the profiling DLLs instead of the system DLLs. It displays a list of all the DLLs loaded by an application as well as any changes to this list.

To prepare a group of applications for the profiling of all system DLLs with WAP, type:

apf32cvt win32 *<app list>*

where *<app list>* is a list of one or more names of the executable applications or DLLs to be profiled during the profiling run. The argument *<app list>* must be the last argument to **apf32cvt**. You must include the file extensions in the application list; for example, to prepare the Solitaire program for profiling, type:

apf32cvt win32 sol.exe

Listing an Application's DLLs

You can also use the **apf32cvt** utility to simply display the DLLs that an application loads. To display the DLL list of an application or applications, type:

apf32cvt *<app list>*

Collecting WAP Data

If you want to collect profile data while an application is running, you must start **apf32dmp** before you start the application, and it must remain running throughout the execution of the application. The **apf32dmp** utility also provides a means to collect data during selected phases of the profiling run (see below). The application may now be executed normally. Profiling will begin as soon as the application is started.

When you stop **apf32dmp**, it writes the profiling data to ASCII files. The data is written to *DLLNAME*.END, where *DLLNAME* is the name of the system DLL that is being profiled. For example, KERNEL32.END would contain data from the last profiling run of KERNEL32.DLL. After each run, you should rename the .END data files so that they aren't overwritten with the data from the next run.

Data from concurrent processes and threads is written to the same data file, and there is no method for separating that data. If you need separate data on different processes, profile them individually in separate runs. If you need separate data on different threads, use the CAP tool discussed later in this chapter.

The program **apf32dmp** also allows data to be dumped to a file or cleared from memory at any time during the profiling run. By default, the data is dumped to a file but not cleared from memory. If you choose both options, the data is first dumped and then cleared. If you clear any data without first dumping it to a file, the data will be lost. Then you'll get to do the experiment again. Some fun, huh?

To specify whether data is dumped to a file or cleared, choose the option you want in the **apf32dmp** dialog box.

The utility data dumps to a file *DLLNAME.EXT*, where *DLLNAME* is the name of the system DLL being profiled, and *.EXT* is a file extension you define. By default, this extension is .WAP, but you may change it if you want. (Do not use the extension .END, as the profiler uses this extension.) *DLLNAME.EXT* is placed in the working directory of **apf32dmp**.

Excluding Some APIs from Analysis with WAP

When you use WAP, you should exclude certain APIs from analysis because they either make callbacks into the application or wait for some event to take place. You shouldn't concern yourself with time spent in these APIs.

Certain parent APIs call back into the application to complete their task. It may so happen that, in this process, the application might make certain other child API calls. The times for executing the child APIs are included in the time for the parent API in addition to being reported for the child API.

There are other APIs that wait on events; for example, user input. An example of this is DialogBox, which waits for the user to respond. Another example is WaitMessage, where the application is suspended and control is yielded to other applications until a message is placed in the queue of the application under consideration.

Representative APIs in these categories include the following:

- DispatchMessage
- WaitMessage
- GetMessage
- SendMessage
- DialogBox
- WaitEvent
- CallWindowProc
- DefWindowProc
- DefFrameProc
- Escape
- UpdateWindow
- CreateWindow
- ShowWindow
- DestroyWindow
- MoveWindow
- EnableWindow

Running WAP on Solitaire

In Figure 10.6, we show the essential data we found when we ran WAP on the Solitaire cascade. We start **apf32cvt**, and then SOL.EXE. We clear the counters first with **apf32dmp** because we don't want to see all those API calls that occur during the initialization of Solitaire (that's another performance problem to deal with separately). Then we press SHIFT+ALT+2 to start the cascade. When the cascade is complete, we dump the data.

```
┌─────────────────────────────────────────────────────────────┐
│ ─            Notepad - GDI32.SLO                      ▼ ▲   │
├─────────────────────────────────────────────────────────────┤
│ File  Edit  Search  Help                                     │
├─────────────────────────────────────────────────────────────┤
│ gdi32.wap:  Api profile of gdi32.                        ▲  │
│ All times are in microseconds (us)                          │
│ Excess Timer Overhead = 1 us                                │
│ First Time is not included in Max/Min computation           │
│                                                              │
│                                                              │
│ API Name               Num Calls  Total Time  Time/Call     │
│                                                              │
│ BitBlt                      4127    19482143       4720      │
│ CreateCompatibleBitmap        19      155764       8198      │
│ CreateCompatibleDC          4146     3132590        755      │
│ CreateSolidBrush               2         583        291      │
│ DeleteDC                    4146     2669705        643      │
│ DeleteObject                  21        7275        346      │
│ GetPixel                   49296    24762415        502      │
│ GetTextExtentPointA           93        6969         74      │
│ PatBlt                      3676     1960444        533      │
│ SelectObject                8314     3152617        379      │
│ SetBrushOrgEx                  9       16212       1801      │
│ SetPixel                   52928    20594375        389      │
│ SetTextColor                  62        5222         84      │
│ TextOutA                       2        2288       1144   ▼  │
│ ◄                                                        ► │
└─────────────────────────────────────────────────────────────┘
```

Figure 10.6 GDI32.DLL activity during the Solitaire cascade

Very interesting. We would have guessed that the program was spending a lot of time in the BitBlt routine putting the card images on the display, and it is. But what about all that time in GetPixel and SetPixel? There were almost 12 calls to each routine for every BitBlt call! Most of the time was spent there. And by the rules outlined in the last chapter, both of these calls cross the client-server boundary so they will be flushing the batch in the bargain.

It's time to take a step back and think about what we've discovered. We have card images flowing all over the screen, and on top of that we set individual pixels. No way could a user see those individual pixels, so this definitely seems an excessive refinement. We want to want to find out why Solitaire is making so many of these calls during the cascade. To do that we have to move on to another tool called CAP. But first, we clean up the WAP conversion.

Ending WAP

You use **apf32cvt** to restore the application executables to their original state after you are done profiling. To remove all profiling DLLs from a list of applications, type:

apf32cvt undo *<app list>*

where *<app list>* is the list of applications to be restored. In our example, we typed:

apf32cvt undo sol.exe

The Call Attributed Profiler

The Call Attributed Profiler, or CAP, details the internal function calls within an application. You use it to see how much time is spent in each function and in the functions called by that function. You can also use it to see how much time is spent in the function itself, ignoring the functions that it calls. This gives a complete picture of how time is spent throughout the application.

Many older-generation application profilers were sampling profilers. They would interrupt the processor at high frequency and take a snapshot of the instruction pointer. The areas in the program most heavily hit during sampling were the program's "hot spots." Tuning the application consisted of recoding its hot spots. This approach is very successful in programs that are computationally rich. Modern applications tend to be highly structured, having thousands of functions—none of which are computationally intensive. Such programs yield a flat sampled profile and thus do not lend themselves to tuning with such profilers.

A different approach was needed to help resolve this issue, and this led to the evolution of CAP. In CAP, each function call is timed. The start time is stored in a data structure allocated to the function when it is called (suppose it's named "foo"), and attached to the calling function's structure (call this one "sweet"). A count is incremented so we'll know how many times the function foo was called by the function sweet, as well as total time in the function. When another function, say "bar," is first called, a new data structure is allocated. (Now you know what we do with all that memory.) The result is a dynamic call tree showing the sequence sweet->foo->bar with counts and times at each level. This permits the entire structure and not just the individual functions to be tuned.

Initial proposals for call attributed profiling on Windows NT involved using the debugging APIs to intercept the function calls. This design would have had the advantage of not requiring you to recompile the application to measure it with the profiler. While older systems with simple debuggers could probably get away with this, the extra protection and security features of Windows NT made the debugging APIs, well, rich. Using them would have used all the space in the processor's cache and thus greatly distorted the execution time of the functions. Cousin Heisenberg again. Initial estimates indicated this would severely degrade the accuracy of the results. So instead, the module is recompiled with the **-Gh** compiler option, and a special call is inserted by the compiler at the start of every function. This invokes a measurement module called CAP.DLL which takes the measurement. It still interferes with the processor's caches, but nowhere near as much as using the debugging APIs would have.

CAP uses an elapsed time clock to measure time in functions. This has both benefits and liabilities. The benefit is that you see where time is spent during disk or LAN activity. The flip side is that if your thread gets switched out while the national debt is being computed by another application, it will appear as though the preempted function used all that time. So it is important to control the environment when using CAP. (Actually the principle is not unique to CAP: it applies equally to WAP.)

CAP can be used to measure the functions within one or more executable programs and/or dynamic-link libraries. The activity in each thread of each process is tracked in a separate call tree. It can also monitor the calls from one such module to another, just as WAP does. Unlike WAP, however, CAP is not restricted to measuring only the calls to system DLLs. Calls to any DLL can be monitored with CAP, whether the DLL belongs to the application or to Windows NT.

By default, CAP collects data only on functions written in Microsoft C or C++ or a compatible product from another vendor. Data is collected from assembly language procedures only if you provide some special support in those routines. And, CAP is only available on x86 processors at present (a shortage of resources prevented a wider implementation).

Using CAP

Windows NT does not ship with debugging symbols in its modules because it takes many megabytes of disk space to provide them. So, as discussed previously, you should run **apf32cvt** on your application with no action specified. This will give you a list of the system DLLs (modules) you need to have with symbols. You can get the versions with symbols from the SUPPORT\DEBUG directory in the Windows NT SDK. First you rename the current system module; for example, type **ren gdi32.dll gdi32.nsm**. Then copy the one from the SDK to GDI32.DLL. Once you have done this for all the DLLs you want to measure, you must shut down and restart Windows NT so the modules with symbols get loaded.

Next we need to set up an initialization file called CAP.INI in the root directory of the C drive. CAP.INI has four sections that control the set of .EXEs and DLLs profiled. Each .EXE or .DLL listed must be placed on a separate line. It is important that you get the format of this file right, because otherwise Windows NT might not start. The four sections of CAP.INI are as follows:

- [EXES] A list of applications to be profiled. When CAP.DLL initializes, it checks the current executable name against this list and will start profiling if the name is on the list. If the name is not on the list, CAP doesn't profile that process.

- [PATCH IMPORTS] A list of .DLLs and .EXEs to be profiled for imported entries. That is, listing a .DLL or .EXE here causes the profiling of all functions (located in other modules) called by the listed .DLLs and .EXEs.

- [PATCH CALLERS] A list of .DLLs to be profiled for exported entries. That is, .DLLs listed here are profiled when called by the applications listed in the [EXE] section, or by any of their .DLLs.

- [NAME LENGTH] The maximum length of a symbol. This number must be in the range from 20 to 2048. We recommend for C++ program this value be set to at least 128 due to the name elaboration that is performed by the linker. If a symbol is longer than this value, it is truncated. If the field is not specified or is 0, the value defaults to 40. This field is optional.

Headers for the first three sections ([EXES], [PATCH IMPORTS], and [PATCH CALLERS]) are required to be in the CAP.INI file, but the contents of any section may be left blank.

In our example we want to profile the Solitaire program, so our CAP.INI file looks like this:

```
[EXES]
sol.exe

[PATCH IMPORTS]
sol.exe

[PATCH CALLERS]
```

This profiles SOL.EXE and measures any calls it makes to functions in other modules, including the system DLLs. In our case, there is nothing after the [PATCH CALLERS] header. You'll want to use that section to profile particular DLLs that you've developed when you have listed in the [EXES] section the applications that call your DLLs.

We also want to measure the functions inside the Solitaire program, because we want to know where all those calls to GetPixel and SetPixel are coming from. And no, we can't just search the source for the calls, because they are called from many functions (nice try, though). So we'll recompile Solitaire specifying the **-Gh** and **-Zd** compiler options, and we'll link specifying the CAP.LIB library and using the **-debugtype:coff** and **-debug:partial** linker options.

Important   You must slip a call to GdiSetBatchLimit(1) into the initialization code for each thread before you recompile, or batching will really confuse the data. WAP does this for you but with CAP you're on your own.

It's measurement time! We provide a Capdump program allowing you to control which application activity you measure. First we start Capdump, and then we start the recompiled version of Solitaire. We'll tell Capdump to clear the counters because we are not concerned at present about the performance while Solitaire starts. Once Capdump clears the counters, we press CTRL+ALT+2 to activate the cascade. After the cascade is done, we shift to Capdump to dump the data. Data files with the default .CAP extension appear in the directory where each measured application resides.

A center section of the results from the SOL.CAP file produced by this run are shown in Figure 10.7 for function times including called functions, and in Figure 10.8 for function calls excluding called functions.

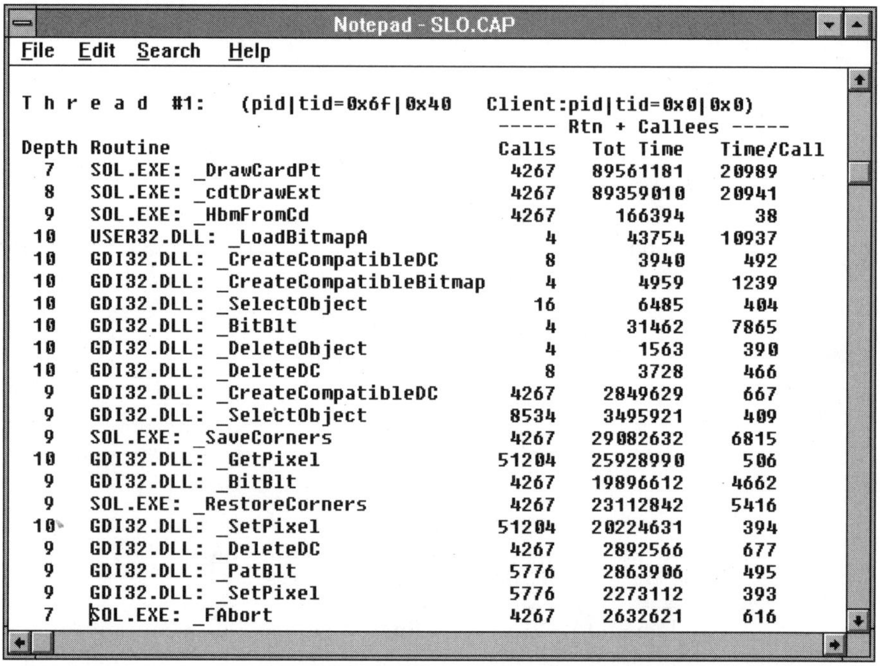

```
─                         Notepad - SLO.CAP                    ▼  ▲
 File   Edit   Search    Help

T h r e a d  #1:    (pid|tid=0x6f|0x40    Client:pid|tid=0x0|0x0)
                                     ----- Rtn + Callees -----
Depth Routine                          Calls    Tot Time   Time/Call
   7   SOL.EXE: _DrawCardPt            4267     89561181    20989
   8   SOL.EXE: _cdtDrawExt            4267     89359010    20941
   9   SOL.EXE: _HbmFromCd             4267       166394       38
  10   USER32.DLL: _LoadBitmapA           4        43754    10937
  10   GDI32.DLL: _CreateCompatibleDC      8         3940      492
  10   GDI32.DLL: _CreateCompatibleBitmap  4         4959     1239
  10   GDI32.DLL: _SelectObject           16         6485      404
  10   GDI32.DLL: _BitBlt                  4        31462     7865
  10   GDI32.DLL: _DeleteObject            4         1563      390
  10   GDI32.DLL: _DeleteDC                8         3728      466
   9   GDI32.DLL: _CreateCompatibleDC   4267      2849629      667
   9   GDI32.DLL: _SelectObject         8534      3495921      409
   9   SOL.EXE: _SaveCorners            4267     29082632     6815
  10   GDI32.DLL: _GetPixel            51204     25928990      506
   9   GDI32.DLL: _BitBlt               4267     19896612     4662
   9   SOL.EXE: _RestoreCorners         4267     23112842     5416
  10   GDI32.DLL: _SetPixel            51204     20224631      394
   9   GDI32.DLL: _DeleteDC             4267      2892566      677
   9   GDI32.DLL: _PatBlt               5776      2863906      495
   9   GDI32.DLL: _SetPixel             5776      2273112      393
   7   SOL.EXE: _FAbort                 4267      2632621      616
◄ ─────────────────────────────────────────────────────────── ►
```

Figure 10.7 Call/attributed profile of Solitaire cascade, called functions included

```
┌─────────────────────────────────────────────────────────────────────┐
│ ─                         Notepad - SLO2.CAP                  ▼  ▲   │
├─────────────────────────────────────────────────────────────────────┤
│ File   Edit   Search   Help                                         │
├─────────────────────────────────────────────────────────────────────┤
│ T h r e a d  #1:    (pid|tid=0x6f|0x40    Client:pid|tid=0x0|0x0)  ▲│
│                                         ----- Rtn - Callees ----    ░│
│ Depth Routine                           Tot Time    Time/Call       ░│
│    7   SOL.EXE: _DrawCardPt               202170          46        ░│
│    8   SOL.EXE: _cdtDrawExt              2725391         637        ░│
│    9   SOL.EXE: _HbmFromCd                 70500          15        ░│
│   10   USER32.DLL: _LoadBitmapA            43754       10937        ░│
│   10   GDI32.DLL: _CreateCompatibleDC       3940         492        ░│
│   10   GDI32.DLL: _CreateCompatibleBitmap   4959        1239        ░│
│   10   GDI32.DLL: _SelectObject             6485         404        ░│
│   10   GDI32.DLL: _BitBlt                  31462        7865        ░│
│   10   GDI32.DLL: _DeleteObject             1563         390        ░│
│   10   GDI32.DLL: _DeleteDC                 3728         466        ░│
│    9   GDI32.DLL: _CreateCompatibleDC    2849629         667        ░│
│    9   GDI32.DLL: _SelectObject          3495921         409        ░│
│    9   SOL.EXE: _SaveCorners             3153642         738        ░│
│   10   GDI32.DLL: _GetPixel             25928990         506        ░│
│    9   GDI32.DLL: _BitBlt               19896612        4662        ░│
│    9   SOL.EXE: _RestoreCorners          2888211         676        ░│
│   10   GDI32.DLL: _SetPixel             20224631         394        ░│
│    9   GDI32.DLL: _DeleteDC              2892566         677        ░│
│    9   GDI32.DLL: _PatBlt                2863906         495        ░│
│    9   GDI32.DLL: _SetPixel             2273112         393        ░│
│    7   SOL.EXE: _FAbort                   347749          81        ▼│
├─────────────────────────────────────────────────────────────────────┤
│ ◄  █                                                            ►   │
└─────────────────────────────────────────────────────────────────────┘
```

Figure 10.8 CAP of Solitaire cascade, excluding called functions

In the leftmost column is the function call nesting depth. This starts at zero with the first function call that CAP encounters. If a function is called but has not returned when the data is dumped, there will be an asterisk to the left of this number. Next we have a column with the module name followed by the function name. If the function is not known because the coff symbols with the function names in them are not contained in the module, **???: ???** will appear instead of *module: function.*

This section of the results, where SOL.EXE executed for 89 seconds, starts at call level 7 with _DrawCardPt, which was called 4267 times. It called _cdtDrawExt each time it was called, and that called _HbmFromCd. We didn't spend much time here: only 1.6 out of the 89 seconds. This called the USER32.DLL Win32 API call _LoadBitMapA four times. The final "A" in this function name means this is the ASCII form of the call, so right away we know that Solitaire is not a Unicode application (in which case it would have been a final "W"). But Solitaire does almost no text output, so maybe we can let that pass. The _HbmFromCd call used some graphics primitives in GDI32.DLL, but only a few times even though it was called 4267 times. So this is not the central cause of the poor performance.

The call level returns to 9 which means _cdtDrawExt at level 8 is back in control. We see from Figure 10.7 that even though we spent 89 seconds in this routine and the routines it called, we spent only 2.7 seconds in the routine itself. The other 86-plus seconds were in the functions it called.

Let's see where. It calls _CreateCompatibleDC each time it is called, and then _SelectObject twice on every call. We have over 6 seconds between them. Looks like we should investigate an own DC for Solitaire. Then there is a call to _SaveCorners, which takes 29 seconds. Looking at Figure 10.8 we see only 3.1 seconds in _SaveCorners itself, so the rest must be in GetPixel. A similar story applies to _RestoreCorners and _SetPixel right after the call to _BitBlt.

We went to the developer porting Solitaire at this point and asked what on earth _SaveCorner and _RestoreCorners were up to. It turned out that they modify three pixels on each corner of the bitmap of a card to make the corner look a little more rounded. We shared our observation that this was excessive refinement when cards were cascading on the screen, and how each call forced a client-server transition. We discussed using SetPixelV to remove one of the client-server transitions, but decided the real solution was to remove the calls altogether during a cascade. This was a very small change, just a few lines of code, but it made the Solitaire cascade twice as fast.

Capview: a Visual Form of CAP

Looking at Figures 10.7 and 10.8 is educational but a mite tedious if you have a large program with hundreds or thousands of functions. There is a great alternative: Capview. Figures 10.9 through 10.11 show some of the data from running the repaired Solitaire as it is seen by Capview.

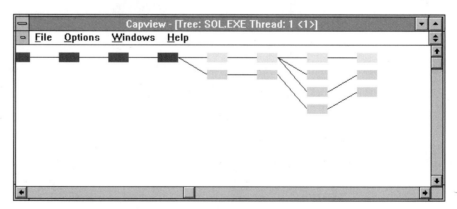

Figure 10.9 Capview tree profile of Solitaire cascade, zoomed out

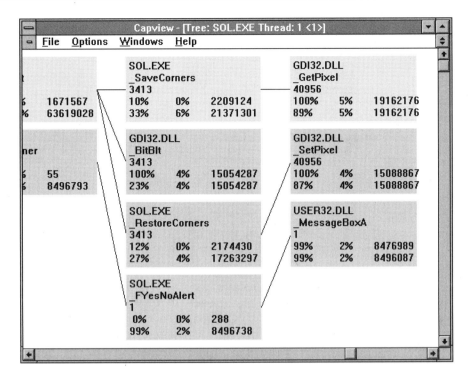

Figure 10.10 Capview tree profile of Solitaire cascade, zoomed in

Each box in the Capview tree represents a line in the SOL.CAP file. If you zoom out you get the overview, and if you zoom in you can see the details of each line.

The first figure in the box is the number of calls made to that routine.

The rightmost number in the next line of figures is the time spent in the function itself, expressed in microseconds. The left number is the *attributed time*. This is the time spent in the function expressed as a percentage of the time in the function plus the time in the functions it calls. The middle figure is time in the function as a percentage of time in the entire program.

In the last line, the rightmost number is the attributed time. The middle number is the attributed time in this function as a percentage of time in the program. And the leftmost number is the time in this function as a percentage of attributed time in the calling function.

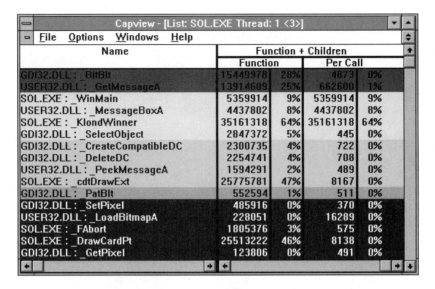

Figure 10.11 Capview list profile of Solitaire cascade

The List view of Capview is illustrated in Figure 10.11. The attributed columns are shown but the function-only columns are also available.

We think Capview is the cat's meow when it comes to viewing CAP data, but if you think it can be improved, give it a whirl: it's a sample application in the Windows NT SDK. Please feel free to send us your improved versions; we appreciate all the help we can get!

The FIOSAP Profiler

Let's take a look at another case. You know so much now, we can present Performance Monitor information without comment. Look this over and form your own conclusions, and then read on.

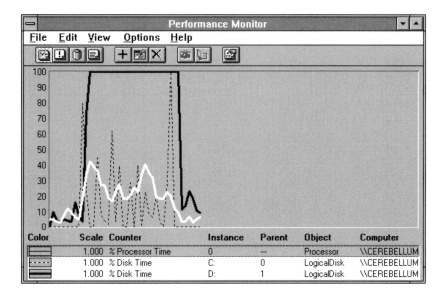

Figure 10.12 Overview of an application without a processor problem

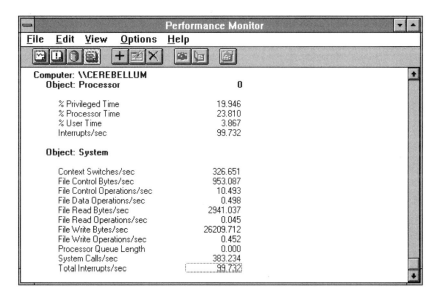

Figure 10.13 System and processor views of an application without a processor problem

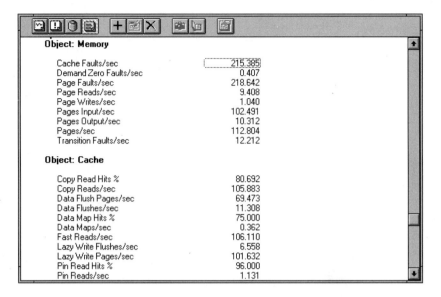

Figure 10.14 Memory and cache views of an application without a processor problem

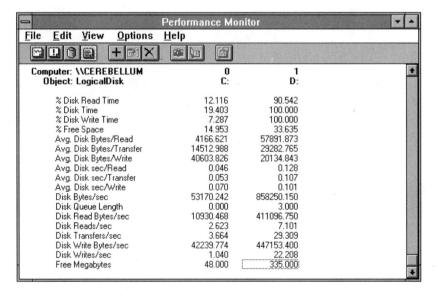

Figure 10.15 Logical disk view of an application without a processor problem

You've convinced me, the disk is the bottleneck here. Now what can we do about it? It's not going to do us a great deal of good to use the tools we've shown so far, although we might be able to deduce which files are in play by seeing which functions of the program are busy. (There's a bit of fun detective work to try.) We have an easier, softer way.

Using the I/O Profiler

The File I/O and Synchronization Win32 API Profiler (FIOSAP) is an outgrowth of WAP designed to profile applications that possibly have multiple concurrent threads. The Windows NT File I/O and Synchronization APIs are contained in the KERNEL32.DLL. The profiler is in the form of a single FERNEL32.DLL, corresponding to the KERNEL32 DLL. This DLL sits between an application and KERNEL32.DLL, intercepts file I/O and synchronization API calls to KERNEL32.DLL, and then makes and times a call to the actual API. It also collects various statistics useful in monitoring the overall file, event, mutex and semaphore activity of the application(s).

FERNEL32.DLL reports the number of operations, total time and average time in each operation, as well as the additional statistics for some of these operations. The following list shows exactly what additional operations are measured. Times are expressed in microseconds.

- Statistics summed over all operations on all files
- Open file operations
- Create file operations
- Write file operations
  - Total number of bytes written
  - Average number of bytes written per operation
  - Standard deviation of the number of bytes written per operation
- Read file operations
  - Total number of bytes read
  - Average number of bytes read per operation
  - Standard deviation of the number of bytes read per operation
- Flush file buffers operations
- Set file pointer operations
- Get file information operations
- Lock and unlock file operations
  - Total number of bytes locked
  - Average number of bytes locked
  - Standard deviation of the number of bytes locked
- Set end of file operations
- Close file operations

The profiling DLL also records the following information for each synchronization (event, mutex, or semaphore object) handle that the process uses:

- Statistics summed over all operations on all semaphores, all events, and all mutexes
- Open operations
- Create operations
- Release operations (only for mutex and semaphore objects)
- Set event operations (only for event objects)
- Reset event operations (only for event objects)
- Pulse event operations (only for event objects)
- Wait operations (the statistics are kept separately for Single, Multiple-All, and Multiple-Any Wait operations)
- Close file operations

To profile a list of applications with FIOSAP, type:

apf32cvt fernel32 *<app list>*

where *<app list>* is a list of one or more names of the executable applications or DLLs that are to be profiled during the profiling run. As with WAP, *<app list>* must be the last argument to **apf32cvt**. For the Zapdata application we are looking at in this example, we type:

apf32cvt fernel32 zapdata.exe

In the next two figures we show part of the results of the run of FIOSAP on Zapdata.

```
┌─────────────────────────────────────────────────────────────────────┬───┬───┐
│─                            Notepad - FERNEL32.001                    │ ▼ │ ▲ │
├─────────────────────────────────────────────────────────────────────┴───┴───┤
│ File   Edit   Search   Help                                                  │
├──────────────────────────────────────────────────────────────────────────┬──┤
│ File: E:\1993\wimblton.dat                                                 │▲ │
│ ----------+----------+----------+----------+----------+----------+--------- │  │
│ Operation |  Total   |Number of | Average  |  Total   |   Mean   | Std Dev │  │
│   Name    |  Time    |operations|  Time    |  Bytes   |  Bytes   |  Bytes  │  │
│ ----------+----------+----------+----------+----------+----------+--------- │  │
│ Overall   |   972726 |      21  |   46320  |        - |        - |         │  │
│ Create    |     1578 |       1  |    1578  |        - |        - |         │  │
│ Read      |   970334 |      18  |   53907  |  1170432 |    65024 |         │  │
│ Info      |      348 |       1  |     348  |        - |        - |         │  │
│ Close     |      466 |       1  |     466  |        - |        - |         │  │
│                                                                            │  │
│                                                                            │  │
│ -------------------------------------------------------------------------- │  │
│ Statistics for all file activity  (Number of files used: 6)                │  │
│ ----------+----------+----------+----------+----------+----------+--------- │  │
│ Operation |  Total   |Number of | Average  |  Total   |   Mean   | Std Dev │  │
│   Name    |  Time    |operations|  Time    |  Bytes   |  Bytes   |  Bytes  │  │
│ ----------+----------+----------+----------+----------+----------+--------- │  │
│ Overall   | 23965469 |     375  |   63907  |        - |        - |         │  │
│ Create    |    94046 |       6  |   15674  |        - |        - |         │  │
│ Read      | 17244253 |     180  |   95801  | 11704320 |    65024 |         │  │
│ Write     |  6432526 |     177  |   36341  | 11455298 |    64719 |  762713 │  │
│ Info      |   117536 |       6  |   19589  |        - |        - |         │  │
│ Close     |    77108 |       6  |   12851  |        - |        - |         │▼ │
├──┬─────────────────────────────────────────────────────────────────────┬──┴──┤
│←│└                                                                      │ → │  │
└──┴─────────────────────────────────────────────────────────────────────┴───┘
```

Figure 10.16 Partial FIOSAP file statistics on the Zapdata application

```
┌─────────────────────────────────────────────────────────────────────┬───┬───┐
│─                            Notepad - FERNEL32.002                    │ ▼ │ ▲ │
├─────────────────────────────────────────────────────────────────────┴───┴───┤
│ File   Edit   Search   Help                                                  │
├──────────────────────────────────────────────────────────────────────────┬──┤
│ -------------------------------------------------------------------------- │▲ │
│ Event:          Type: Auto Reset                                           │  │
│ ------------------+----------+----------+----------+----------+             │  │
│      Operation    |  Total   |Number of | Average  |Successful             │  │
│        Name       |  Time    |operations|  Time    |  Waits                │  │
│ ------------------+----------+----------+----------+----------+             │  │
│ Overall           |  9482271 |     231  |   41048  |     -                 │  │
│ Create            |      265 |       1  |     265  |     -                 │  │
│ Set               |   410876 |     129  |    3185  |     -                 │  │
│ Wait              |  9070985 |     100  |   90709  |    100                │  │
│    Single         |  9070985 |     100  |   90709  |    100                │  │
│ Close             |      145 |       1  |     145  |     -                 │  │
│                                                                            │  │
│                                                                            │  │
│ -------------------------------------------------------------------------- │  │
│ Semaphore: Duplicate Semaphore           Max Count: 0                       │  │
│ ------------------+----------+----------+----------+----------+             │  │
│      Operation    |  Total   |Number of | Average  |Successful             │  │
│        Name       |  Time    |operations|  Time    |  Waits                │  │
│ ------------------+----------+----------+----------+----------+             │  │
│ Overall           |    49972 |       2  |   24986  |     -                 │  │
│ Close             |    49972 |       2  |   24986  |     -                 │▼ │
├──┬─────────────────────────────────────────────────────────────────────┬──┴──┤
│←│└                                                                      │ → │  │
└──┴─────────────────────────────────────────────────────────────────────┴───┘
```

Figure 10.17 Partial FIOSAP event and semaphore statistics on the Zapdata application

Data from FIOSAP is written to FERNEL32.END, in the working directory of the application. FIOSAP will write data from concurrent multiple threads to the same data file, and there is no method for separating the data based upon threads. However, FIOSAP will write data from concurrent multiple processes to different data files, as long as the profiled concurrent processes have different working directories. If you have two concurrent processes with the same working directory, the data for one of them will be lost.

So now, if you have an application and you want to know what it is waiting for when it is not burning up the processor, you know just what to do.

The Win32 API Logger

We've all had those discouraging moments when summary statistics of API calls just won't solve our problems. We've got the solution for those darned old API summation blues. Just install the Windows NT 32-bit API logger and you can look at every single API call and the parameters that are passed to it. There's hardly a better way to spend a summer afternoon.

The Win32 API Logger comes on the Windows NT SDK but is not automatically installed by the SDK setup. To locate it, refer to the Readme document for the SDK.

Currently, the API Logger works only on Intel processors, and there is no logger DLL for CRTDLL.DLL. The WAP and logging measurement DLLs have the same names, so be sure not to get them mixed up.

Like FIOSAP, the Win32 API Logger is an outgrowth of the WAP technology. You use the same program, **apf32cvt**, to install the API profiler. The API logger also has the identical measurement DLL names for ZSER32.DLL, ZERNEL.DLL, and so on. But **apf32dmp** has no role to play here. The logger just spews out data about API calls as soon as your application starts. It can chew up disk space faster than Performance Monitor. So, API logging noticeably slows down the application.

The API Logger writes a line for every API call and every return. It logs this information to two files: OUTPUT.LOG and OUTPUT.DAT. These go into the working directory of the application. OUTPUT.LOG is an ASCII file with the log of the API calls, the parameters to each call, and the return values. If a parameter is a pointer to a structure defined in the API, the structure will be output, enclosed in braces. OUTPUT.DAT is a binary file containing any parameters that are more than 128 characters long. In this case, the parameter in OUTPUT.LOG is "DATAFILE *offset*" where *offset* is the parameter's offset into OUTPUT.DAT.

The next figure shows a fragment of an API log file of Performance Monitor drawing a chart legend.

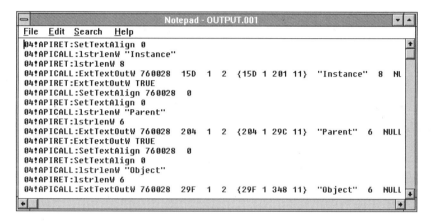

Figure 10.18 Log of API calls made by Performance Monitor when drawing a chart legend

Other Useful Tools

We have included on the floppy disk with this book a number of additional tools which you should find handy from time to time when you look at the performance of Windows NT systems and their applications. You'll want to refer to the documentation on the Windows SDK for the full details; here we'll just make sure you know they exist. They are:

- PView
- PMon
- WPerf
- **wt** command in the NTSD debugger

PView

PView is useful for getting a quick view of what programs are running in a system and how they are using their virtual memory space. You can see their priority, and the priority of their threads. You can look at the modules the application calls, and see how much virtual address space they have allocated. The next two figures show the PView display for File Manager.

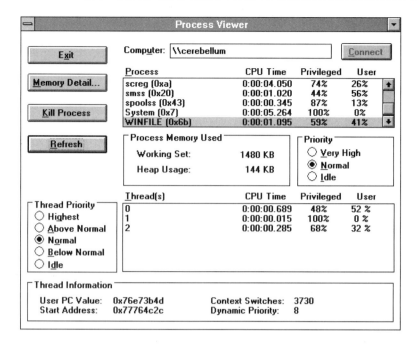

Figure 10.19 File Manager as seen by PView

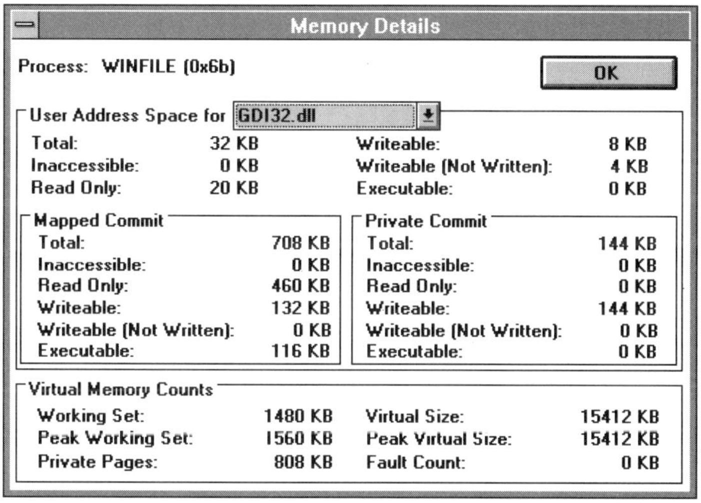

Figure 10.20 File Manager memory details as seen by PView

One thing to keep in mind is the Refresh button. PView shows the state of the system when PView starts. It won't change until you choose to Refresh, even if you start or stop applications in the meantime. So refresh, refresh, refresh.

PMon

PMon is another handy program. PMon shows in a console window the memory usage of each running process, and of the cache. PMon updates its statistics every five seconds. A sample of the display is in the next figure.

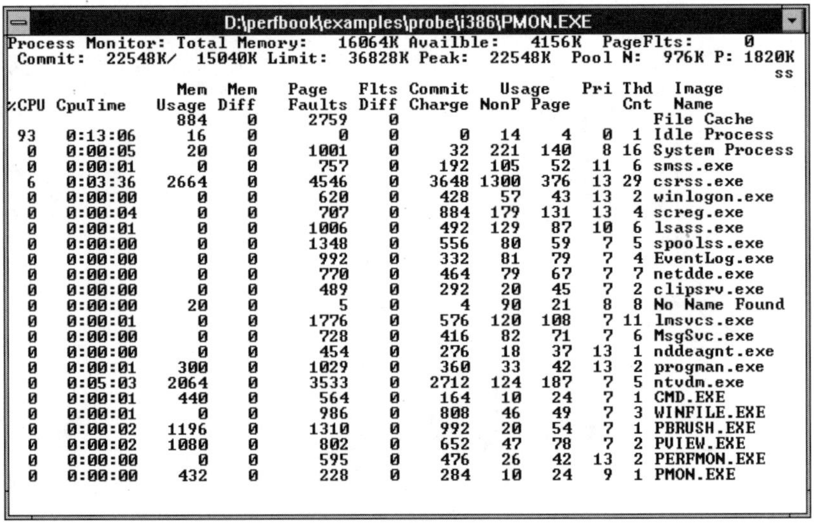

```
┌─────┬────────────────────────────────────────────────────────────────┬────┐
│ ─   │              D:\perfbook\examples\probe\i386\PMON.EXE            │ ▼  │
├─────┴────────────────────────────────────────────────────────────────┴────┤
│Process Monitor: Total Memory:    16064K Availble:    4156K  PageFlts:     0 │
│ Commit:   22548K/  15040K Limit:   36828K Peak:   22548K  Pool N:   976K P: 1820K │
│                                                                          ss │
│          Mem  Mem   Page  Flts Commit   Usage     Pri Thd  Image             │
│%CPU CpuTime Usage Diff  Faults Diff Charge NonP Page     Cnt  Name          │
│             884    0    2759    0                              File Cache    │
│ 93  0:13:06   16    0       0    0      0   14    4    0   1  Idle Process   │
│  0  0:00:05   20    0    1001    0     32  221  140    8  16  System Process │
│  0  0:00:01    0    0     757    0    192  105   52   11   6  smss.exe       │
│  6  0:03:36 2664    0    4546    0   3648 1300  376   13  29  csrss.exe      │
│  0  0:00:00    0    0     620    0    428   57   43   13   2  winlogon.exe   │
│  0  0:00:04    0    0     707    0    884  179  131   13   4  screg.exe      │
│  0  0:00:01    0    0    1006    0    492  129   87   10   6  lsass.exe      │
│  0  0:00:00    0    0    1348    0    556   80   59    7   5  spoolss.exe    │
│  0  0:00:00    0    0     992    0    332   81   79    7   4  EventLog.exe   │
│  0  0:00:00    0    0     770    0    464   79   67    7   7  netdde.exe     │
│  0  0:00:00    0    0     489    0    292   20   45    7   2  clipsrv.exe    │
│  0  0:00:00   20    0       5    0      4   90   21    8   8  No Name Found  │
│  0  0:00:01    0    0    1776    0    576  120  108    7  11  lmsvcs.exe     │
│  0  0:00:00    0    0     728    0    416   82   71    7   6  MsgSvc.exe     │
│  0  0:00:00    0    0     454    0    276   18   37   13   1  nddeagnt.exe   │
│  0  0:00:01  300    0    1029    0    360   33   42   13   2  progman.exe    │
│  0  0:05:03 2064    0    3533    0   2712  124  187    7   5  ntvdm.exe      │
│  0  0:00:01  440    0     564    0    164   10   24    7   1  CMD.EXE        │
│  0  0:00:01    0    0     986    0    808   46   49    7   3  WINFILE.EXE    │
│  0  0:00:02 1196    0    1310    0    992   20   54    7   1  PBRUSH.EXE     │
│  0  0:00:02 1080    0     802    0    652   47   78    7   2  PVIEW.EXE      │
│  0  0:00:00    0    0     595    0    476   26   42   13   2  PERFMON.EXE    │
│  0  0:00:00  432    0     228    0    284   10   24    9   1  PMON.EXE       │
│                                                                            │
└────────────────────────────────────────────────────────────────────────────┘
```

Figure 10.21 PMon view of the universe

At the top of the display you see some system global statistics: memory size and available bytes, the virtual memory commitment, and pool sizes.

Then, for each process, PMon shows processor usage during the last update interval. The next column is total processor time in the format hours:minutes:seconds. The third column is how many pages each process is using, and then the change since the last update. PMon also shows how many Page Faults have occurred in the process, and the change since the last update. Next is the virtual memory commitment charge, and then the pool usage estimates for the process. Finally you see process priority, and number of threads. There's nothing here that is not in Performance Monitor, but this is a pretty darn handy overview that requires no selections to be made.

WPerf

WPerf is another little performance monitor that presents data a little differently than Windows NT Performance Monitor. Be sure to grab a corner of the window when it comes up, and enlarge the window. Then double click on the window to get to the Select menu. This permits the selection of a variety of counters, including two counting TB fills that are not available in Performance Monitor because they are only relevant to certain RISC machines. The TB is the page translation buffer in the processor, which is used to translate virtual addresses to physical addresses without having to go to memory to do so. On some RISC machines resolving TB misses is a software operation, and its high frequency is a drain on system performance.

The Symbolic Debugger wt Command

Finally, we'd like to point out that there is a special cool performance feature in the Windows NT symbolic debugger. The **wt** command can be used to trace calls in a program and the number of instructions between them. Just type **wt** and watch those instructions fly!

```
━                     C:\MSTOOLS\bin\NTSD.EXE                   ▼ ▲
    1              gdi32!_CsrClientSendMessage                        ◆
   44             ntdll!_CsrClientSendMessage
   33            gdi32!_SelectObject
    4        sol!_cdtAnimate
    1          sol!_SelectObject
   96          gdi32!_SelectObject
    1              gdi32!_CsrClientSendMessage
   44             ntdll!_CsrClientSendMessage
   33            gdi32!_SelectObject
   13        sol!_cdtAnimate
    1          sol!_BitBlt
  148          gdi32!_BitBlt
    4        sol!_cdtAnimate
    1          sol!_SelectObject
   88          gdi32!_SelectObject
    1              gdi32!_CsrClientSendMessage
   44             ntdll!_CsrClientSendMessage
   33            gdi32!_SelectObject
    4        sol!_cdtAnimate
    1          sol!_SelectObject
   94          gdi32!_SelectObject
    1              gdi32!_CsrClientSendMessage
   44             ntdll!_CsrClientSendMessage                        ◆
◆                                                                    ◆
```

Figure 10.22 NTSD wt command of a portion of the Solitaire cascade

This is a tool that lets you get right down to the details of what is happening in your code without the burden of tracing every instruction. In a way it gives you the same information as CAP, though far less quickly. But it avoids the recompile that CAP requires, and sometimes you just want to take a quick look at a small issue. That's when **wt** is a diamond in the rough. It can help to have those same system DLLs with debugging symbols that CAP uses. Go get them and have at it.

CHAPTER 11

Tuning the Working Set of Your Application

Space: the final frontier. We're not quite sure whether we programmers get yelled at more because our programs are slow or because they take up too much space. We don't understand—hasn't the boss heard that memory is now cheap?

Apparently not. So in this chapter we'll discuss the Windows NT Working Set Tuner. It can help you reduce the amount of space your program takes in RAM. You should tune your application's working set even if you are perfectly happy with its speed. It's important to keep in mind that your program will probably have to coexist with other executing applications, so there's just no point in wasting space if you don't have to. The code in Windows NT itself has been tuned with the Working Set Tuner.

Even if you don't care about all the space you are taking away from other programs, you probably care about the time it takes to load your own program into RAM from disk. None of us is overjoyed about application load time. The Working Set Tuner can help with that too.

The Working Set Tuner can improve the speed of your program in another way you might not have thought of. We've discussed the processor caches, and in the last chapter we briefly mentioned the translation buffer, which is another processor cache used for page translation. Working set tuning can reduce the amount of space your program requires in both types of caches, in particular in the use of the translation buffer. Not only will your application code execute faster, it will interfere less with the code in Windows NT. To see why, we'll have to look under the covers and see how the Windows NT Working Set Tuner operates.

At the end of this chapter, we'll also describe how to use the **vadump** tool, which lets you look inside your application's working set.

How Working Set Tuning Can Help You

The counter Process: Working Set shows the number of pages in memory for the process, as we discussed at some length in Chapter 5. The working set includes both shared and private data. The shared data includes pages containing any instructions your application executes, including those in your own DLLs and those of the system. It is efficient that these pages are shared between processes, so that their working sets overlap to whatever extent sharing is possible. Still, it can amount to a whole slew of pages.

The Windows NT Working Set Tuner reduces the number of code pages that have to be in RAM for your program to execute. It reduces them by helping the linker put your executable together in a way that minimizes the number of pages you use.

Normally your executable image is put together in the order in which address references are resolved. This has nothing at all to do with the need for particular routines to reside together in memory, because lots of functions get called only under error conditions or other unusual situations. The references to these routines are, of course, right next to references to those routines which are used all the time. Consider the following example.

```
status = DoSomethingFirst(...);
while (status == WONDERFUL) {
    status = ProcessNormally(...);
} else {
    PressThePanicButton(...);
}
```

Assuming this is the first time the linker has seen these symbols, it would put DoSomethingFirst in the .EXE, followed by ProcessNormally, and then it would put in PressThePanicButton. But DoSomethingFirst is only used during initialization, and PressThePanicButton is only called when the sky is falling. It would be better if ProcessNormally were placed in the .EXE with other routines which are used frequently, DoSomethingFirst were placed with routines which were used to initialize the applications, and PressThePanicButton were placed somewhere else (and we really don't care where). If the linker sets them up that way, a page brought in when ProcessNormally is first executed would likely contain only routines which are used frequently. And the page containing DoSomethingFirst could be discarded after initialization, because it would likely be packed with initialization routines. And best of all, the page containing PressThePanicButton would come into memory only if the error condition arose.

The Working Set Tuner accomplishes precisely these objectives. It provides a packing list to the linker so the linker can place functions into the executable image in the order that most reduces paging. It does this by determining which functions are used together in time. The functions which are used most often are placed together in the .EXE image. This continues in order of usage until the never-referenced functions are reached. It places these at the end of the .EXE in "don't care" order.

In order to determine which functions are used together in time, the Working Set Tuner starts with a measurement of your application. For this utility to do a good job, you must define your scenario to include all the commonly used functions in your application. Your scenario should spend the most time on the most commonly used function, fading to those less frequently used. For example, when we performed working set tuning on Performance Monitor, our scenario included the following:

- Logging all objects at 3-second intervals.
- Charting Processor, Memory, and System counters at 5-second intervals.
- Reporting on the same objects at 10-second intervals.
- Alerting on the same objects at 15-second intervals.

The tuned working set that resulted from this set of tasks was smallest for logging, which we wanted because it is the most serious use of the tool, when we want Heisenberg in the trunk. For charting, which is quite common, we let Heisenberg sit in the back seat. And so on.

How good a job does the Working Set Tuner do? The results for Performance Monitor executing the scenario described above are in the next table.

Table 11.1   Code Working Set Tuning of Performance Monitor

Executable image pages	RAM pages before tuning	RAM pages after tuning
41	30	11

That's a pretty dramatic saving. Typically we see between 25% and 50% savings on code space used. You can normally expect a 30% reduction in your code space for the scenario that you measure. But the operational results of your efforts depend almost entirely on how good a job you did at devising your scenario. A quick "let's just run something" without preparation won't help. So think carefully about that test scenario.

How the Working Set Tuner Works

Here's how it works. Like CAP, the Working Set Tuner gets called every time a function in your application is called. It assigns each function in your application a bit. This bit is set when the function is called. Periodically, the Working Set Tuner takes a snapshot of all the bits, and then clears them. The default time interval is 1000 milliseconds, but you can adjust this. We find the results are not too sensitive to this parameter, and we rarely change it. If anything, we tend to make it longer if the scenario is very long, to reduce the time spent in the analysis phase by the Working Set Tuner.

The snapshot of the bits tells the Working Set Tuner which functions executed during the last time interval. In sequence, the snapshots give a history of function references over time. Because the bits are cleared after every snapshot, a function with all its bits set is referenced on every snapshot. A function with no bits set was never called during the scenario. Pretty clever, huh?

In the next table we show how this looks. We ran the Working Set Tuner on the Solitaire cascade of cards we discussed in the last chapter. If we were really trying to optimize Solitaire, this is not the scenario we would use: playing a game would have been a much better choice. But playing a game of Solitaire is a tough thing to automate with MS Test, so we chose this simple case instead. For the purposes of this illustration it doesn't matter what we do, because we won't relink Solitaire based on these results. We just want to clarify how the Working Set Tuner operates.

In the next table, each line corresponds to a function. Each function has a row (left-to-right) and each column of 1s and 0s represents a snapshot of each function's activity at that moment.

In the first image, the functions are ordered in the way that they appear in the executable after a normal compile and link of the application. Not all the functions in the program are shown, just the ones at the start of the executable image. Each 0 or 1 corresponds to a Time Interval. The bit is 0 if the function was not referenced during that particular time interval during the cascade, and 1 if it was.

Table 11.2   Function Reference Patterns Before and After Working Set Tuning

Before tuning	After tuning
00000000000000000000000000000000	11111111111111111111111111100000
00000000000000000000000000000000	11111111111111111111111111100000
00100000000000000000000000000000	11111111111111111111111111100000
11111110111011110000100000000000	00001111111111111111111111100000
00101000000000000000000000000000	00001111111111111111111111100000
00001000000000000000000000000000	00001111111111111111111111100000
00000000000000000000000000000000	00001111111111111111111111100000
11111111111111111111111111100000	00001111111111111111111111100000
00000000000000000000000000000000	00001111111111111111111111100000
00000000000000000000000000000000	11111110111011110000100000000000
00000000000000000000000000000000	00101000000000000000000000000000
00000000000000000000000000000000	00101000000000000000000000000000
00000000000000000000000000000000	00100000000000000000000000000000
00000000000000000000000000000000	00001000000000000000000000000000
00000000000000000000000000000000	00001000000000000000000000000000
00000000000000000000000000000000	00001000000000000000000000000000
00000000000000000000000000000000	00001000000000000000000000000000
00000000000000000000000000000000	00001000000000000000000000000000
00000000000000000000000000000000	00001000000000000000000000000000
00000000000000000000000000000000	00001000000000000000000000000000
00000000000000000000000000000000	00001000000000000000000000000000
00001111111111111111111111100000	00001000000000000000000000000000
00000000000000000000000000000000	00001000000000000000000000000000
00000000000000000000000000000000	00100000000000000000000000000000
00000000000000000000000000000000	00001000000000000000000000000000
00000000000000000000000000000000	00001000000000000000000000000000
00000000000000000000000000000000	00001000000000000000000000000000
00000000000000000000000000000000	00001000000000000000000000000000
00000000000000000000000000000000	00100000000000000000000000000000
00000000000000000000000000000000	00001000000000000000000000000000
00000000000000000000000000000000	00001000000000000000000000000000
00000000000000000000000000000000	00001000000000000000000000000000
00001000000000000000000000000000	00001000000000000000000000000000
00001000000000000000000000000000	00001000000000000000000000000000

In the second column, we show the routines that are at the start of the packing list after tuning the working set. These are all the routines which have 1 bits set anytime during the test. All the rest of the routines in the image were not used during cascade. Notice the string of routines towards the bottom which had only one bit set. These occurred because we moved the mouse across the cascade while it was running. If we had not done this, these routines would have remained scattered throughout the image. If you automate your scenario with MS Test (which you really must do unless you plan to do it by hand every time your application changes), this is one time when some use of the mouse is a good idea. For most applications, you can just pick a screen resolution for the scenario and stick with it. If the screen resolution affects the operation of your application, you can take the time to make your script independent of screen resolution with some clever MS Test programming.

You can see how this works, and that the Working Set tuner does a pretty good job of ordering routines in a rational way, although it is not perfect. The routines at the sixth and the eleventh lines from the bottom should probably have been placed together at the bottom of the list. (If you like, you can fuss with the packing list after running the Working Set Tuner and before linking. It's probably not worth the trouble, but suit yourself.) But using the Working Set Tuner beats the heck out of trying to do it all by hand.

Using the Working Set Tuner

Using the Working Set Tuner is similar to using CAP, from which it is derived. You must first recompile your application with the **-Gh** and **-Zd** switches. Then, you link it using the WST.LIB and the linker options **debugtype:coff** and **debug:partial**. This prepares your executable's C routines to be prepped for the working set tuner.

To run the Working Set Tuner, you first create a WST directory in the root of your C drive. Into C:\WST you place a WST.INI file. This file contains three required section headers:

- [EXES] Names of applications to be tuned, each on a separate line.
- [PATCH IMPORTS] This section must be here but must be blank.
- [TIME INTERVAL] The snapshot time interval in milliseconds. If left blank, 1000 is used.

In our case WST.INI looked like this:

```
[EXES]
sol.exe
[PATCH IMPORTS]
[TIME INTERVAL]
```

Before you take a measurement you must place the WST.DLL measurement library on your path.

You use the **wstdump** utility to specify which portion of your application's operation is tuned. As with the other measurement control utilities, you can clear and dump the counters at any time. When the application ends, these data files are dumped automatically. Dumping the data always places it into the C:\WST directory in files with names of the form *modulename*.WSP and *modulename*.TMI. If you dump data multiple times, the file extensions from each dump will be modified to .W*??* and .T*??*, where *??* is a hexadecimal number between 0x01 and 0xFF inclusive.

You can concatenate the data from multiple scenarios using the **wtscat** utility. It produces composite .WSP and .TMI files after renaming the original ones to .WXX and .TXX. The weight of the files in the concatenated result depends on the length of each experiment, or more accurately—because you might have varied the time interval—on the number of snapshots in each. The bits for each function from the multiple files are concatenated, not or'd together.

When you are done with the measurement, you produce the packing list with the **wstune** utility:

wstune /o *modulename*.**wsp**

The principal result of **wstune** is a *modulename*.PRF file, which you use when you recompile your application. You will link with the **order:***modulename*.**prf** directive. The **wstune** utility also produces a .DT file showing the tuned order of functions with the bitstrings, and a .DN file showing the unordered functions and, at the bottom, a count of how many pages were touched in the unordered case.

To implement the working set improvements, recompile your application using the **-Gy** compiler option. This option assures the linker knows the location of the start and end of each function. Then you can link the application using the linker option by typing:

-order@*modulename*.**prf**

That's all there is to it. Next to Performance Monitor, the Working Set Tuner is our favorite tool.

Looking Inside Your Working Set

You may want to get a better understanding of the pieces inside the working set of your application. For example, you may save a lot of code space with the Working Set Tuner only to discover that the code space is only a small portion of your overall working set. In fact, this might even be something you want to do before you go to all the trouble to tune your code space. Aren't you glad you read this far?

We put this section here at the end anyway because you have to fuss around a bit to do the next set of measurements. You probably want to do these on a test computer, one you don't use for production activity. That's because we are going to ask you to replace the Windows NT kernel with a special kernel for measurement. Of course you can easily set everything straight again afterwards, but why take chances?

Since we only had room on the floppy disk for one kernel, you'll have to run this experiment on an x86 processor. And you'll want to run it on a machine which is large enough to hold your entire working-set tuning test scenario in memory. (You may need to discover this size through the trial and error process we describe in this section.)

The tool we use for this is called Virtual Address Dump, or **vadump**. The **vadump** tool looks inside the working set of a process and determines the nature of each page. You need a number of tools from the floppy disk provided with this book in order to run a controlled experiment with **vadump**.

First you will need a special kernel which enables **vadump** to take measurements. We provide this x86 kernel on the diskette. Before you use the special kernel, you must rename your original NTOSKRNL.EXE, which you will find in the SYSTEM32 directory of your %SystemRoot%. You can rename NTOSKRNL.EXE while the system is running without any difficulty. In our example, we'll type:

ren ntoskernl.exe ntoskrnl.31

After you rename your original kernel, copy the NTOSKRNL.EXE provided on the floppy disk included with this book to the %SystemRoot%\SYSTEM32 directory. Then shut down and restart Windows NT.

Note Don't copy NTOSKRNL.EXE straight from the floppy disk; it's been compressed. Use the disk's Setup to install the tools first, then do the copy.

So far so good. Now you start your application. Then you start PView, which you will also find on the floppy disk provided with this book. Use PView to note the Process ID of your application. You'll need to supply this to **vadump**.

Get your application to the point just prior to the scenario whose working set you want to measure. Run Performance Monitor to discover it's ID Process (PID). Leave Performance Monitor running, and get a command window set up so you can run **vadump**. Type the following in the command window, but don't press ENTER yet.

vadump -wo -p *PID* **>app.vad**

Here **-wo** tells **vadump** that this is the original type working set measurement, and **-p** indicates the next number (*PID*) is the Process ID of the process to measure. In our example command line the output is directed to the file APP.VAD.

But you haven't pressed ENTER yet, right?

In another window, set up **clearmem**, a utility that flushes everything from memory and the disk cache. (It is provided on the floppy disk you got with this book.) It will drive your application out of memory.

To be sure this happens, use Performance Monitor to chart the working set of your application. Also chart your application's Page Faults/sec.

Now switch to **clearmem**. Run it repeatedly (while keeping an eye on Performance Monitor) until your application has no pages in memory. Running **clearmem** once or twice typically does the trick. If your application is the type that wakes up periodically to do some housekeeping chores, it will always have some pages in memory. In this case, run **clearmem** a few times until Performance Monitor shows your application has reached as low a working set as it will attain.

Now switch to your application and execute the test scenario you devised earlier in this chapter for working set tuning.

Use Performance Monitor to note the size of your application's working set. Do this by selecting the Working Set line in the legend and reading the Last value.

Now switch to the **vadump** window and execute the **vadump** command set up above by pressing the ENTER key. The results will be put in APP.VAD if you use the command line we showed above.

Take a look at Performance Monitor again and get the new size for your application's working set. This is likely to be a bit larger now than before, because **vadump** itself must bring some pages into the working set in order to scan all the page tables and working set entries for your application.

Run the scenario in your application again. Performance Monitor should get no page faults in your application during this run. If it does, you may not have enough memory on the system to hold your application's working set (we know, it's hard to believe, isn't it?) Add physical memory to the computer and try again.

The output from **vadump** shows the nature of each page in the working set of
your process. See Figure 11.1. The System pages are those allocated for the page
tables and for the working set list itself. As indicated above, this might be larger
than your application actually needs because **vadump** needs to scan them. So use
Performance Monitor as described to determine the difference. For the example in
Figure 11.1, where we looked at the working set of Performance Monitor while
charting, running **vadump** added 5 pages to the working set. Your mileage may
vary.

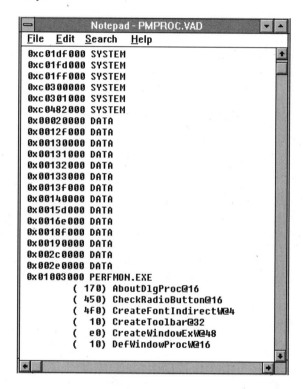

Figure 11.1 Partial vadump results of Performance Monitor charting

The DATA pages are dynamically allocated "heap" data or data allocated
for .DLLs called by the application. It can be difficult to determine who is
using this space, and you may need to look at pointers within your application
using the debugger to be sure.

Other pages that belong to specific modules are indicated by listing which public
symbols occur within the page. This helps you to understand why a particular
page has been brought into memory. If the module was compiled without
symbols, the message "NO SYMBOL FOUND!" is displayed for the page.

Any pages listed as belonging to the module "ERROR" are pages that did not resolve to a particular module. Frankly, we don't know to whom these belong. When you find out, please let us know.

You will also find some DATA pages at the upper end of the application's address space. These are for such system-related items as the Process Environment Block, the Thread Environment Blocks, the Per-Thread Data Area, and so on and so forth.

Finally, there is a summary of SYSTEM, DATA, and ERROR pages. These just summarize the pages already listed, so take care not to count them again.

Remember that all the code pages in your working set may be shared with other processes, and will appear in their working sets as well, even though a shared code page takes up only one page frame in RAM.

When you've finished your experiment, be kind to your coworkers. Change to the %SystemRoot%\SYSTEM32 directory, type the following to restore the original kernel, and shut down and restart Windows NT.

copy ntoskrnl.31 ntoskrnl.exe

CHAPTER 12

Writing a Custom Windows NT Performance Monitor

Windows NT Performance Monitor is one fine tool, but nothing is perfect. You may find yourself needing to look at performance information not provided in Performance Monitor. Or maybe you just think you can do better. Go for it!

Of course your plans may be a little different. You might just need to look closely at your own application's behavior in ways our program doesn't. A few API calls are provided to let you easily measure what is happening inside your application. The section "Monitoring Within an Application" at the end of this chapter covers those API calls.

Even if you do not plan to write your own performance monitor, this chapter might help you understand the tool better. Not to mention, we have first-hand knowledge that the information in this chapter makes great party conversation.

Performance Monitor Source Code

If you do plan to write your own performance monitor, you may want to know that the source code for the Windows NT Performance Monitor is included as sample code in the Windows NT SDK. If you have the Windows NT SDK, cut and paste to suit. This, of course, will void any warranties on the resulting code either expressed or implied or alluded to in private.

There are also examples in the *Win32 API Reference*. See Chapter 66, "Performance Monitoring," in Volume 2 of the Overviews. If you have the Windows NT SDK, you can cut and paste from these to your favorite editor. To do so, first type:

win32hlp api32wh.hlp

Then choose Functions and Overviews: Performance Monitoring, and choose the Overview button.

Design Philosophy

Performance Monitor itself is not the be-all end-all system administration tool. We had hoped to provide a tool that is to bottleneck detection and capacity planning what NotePad is to word processing. To us this meant a basic ability to view system information using real-time charts, logs, reports, and alerts. It also meant providing concurrent monitoring of multiple remote systems. Beyond these basic facilities, we felt it would be better to expose the interfaces we describe in this chapter than to try to solve everyone's problems in one fell swoop.

The structure of Performance Monitor is a trifle involved, and it won't make any sense to you why we did all this unless you have a grasp of what we had hoped to accomplish. We had some rather lofty goals at the start of this project, and these greatly influenced the data structures and mechanisms we chose to use.

A key objective was to not tie Performance Monitor to the counter set in any one system. It was clear that there would be multiple Win32 system implementations, and they might support completely different sets of counters. This consideration permits us to port Performance Monitor to those systems easily, and also lets Performance Monitor collect and display data from non-Windows systems such as Novell NetWare servers or UNIX® systems.

It seemed to be a good idea to allow device drivers, network protocols, and server applications to add their own objects and counters to Performance Monitor. This was not a difficult addition to the plan, because the Performance Monitor itself was already designed to be independent of the counters in the system. This led to the facility to add extended objects, which is covered in detail in Chapter 13, "Adding Application Performance Counters."

We wanted the overhead of Performance Monitor to be low, and its level to be controlled by the user. This led to letting the user select the time interval for sampling. As the project evolved, we discovered that to really control overhead, we had to let the user select objects as well. A finer level of selection did not seem to buy much.

We wanted monitoring of remote systems to be just as easy as monitoring local systems. Through the magic of remote procedure call (RPC), this was an easy goal to achieve.

We also wanted it to be relatively easy to write performance monitors. This led to a certain amount of redundancy in the data. Structures we had dealt with in prototype monitors were more efficient, but required lots of logic in Performance Monitor and the system in order to achieve what appeared to be somewhat trivial savings. For example, the name of a process is returned with each block of data collected for the process, so the monitor does not have to keep separate track of object instance names and somehow tie them to their collected data. This makes operations like appending log files and relogging at longer time intervals much easier. It also makes it simple to construct performance monitors that limit log file space and reuse space when it becomes full; although ours does not work that way, yours could.

Finally, we wanted Performance Monitor to be language-independent. All strings displayed to the user are in resources that can be edited separately from the program. Because Performance Monitor is independent of the system, the names of the counters are not in the monitor's resources. We nonetheless needed to be able to translate the counters and Explain text into other languages. This text is instead stored in the Registry in the languages supported on the system.

Retrieving Performance Data

Performance counters in Windows NT always increment and are never cleared. The basic mission of a performance monitor in Windows NT is to take a snapshot of the performance counters at the beginning of a time interval, and then take another snapshot at the end of the interval. Find the difference between the values in the first and second snapshots for each counter, and voilà, performance data!

When your custom monitor application is ready to retrieve some performance data, how it does so depends on whether you are monitoring the local computer or a remote computer.

Your first call will open the key for you. To obtain performance data from the local system, use the RegQueryValueEx function, with the HKEY_PERFORMANCE_DATA key. You don't need to open the HKEY_PERFORMANCE_DATA handle or use the RegOpenKey function, but be sure to use RegCloseKey to close the handle when it has finished running. By closing the key when you are finished, you allow the software being monitored to be installed or removed. A software component cannot be installed or removed while it is being monitored. Figure 12.1 shows how Performance Monitor obtains data from the local computer.

System under measurement

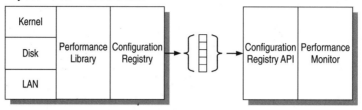

Figure 12.1 How Performance Monitor collects performance data

To obtain performance information from a remote system, your monitor should first use the RegConnectRegistry function with the computer name of the remote system and the HKEY_PERFORMANCE_DATA key. This function retrieves a key representing the performance data for the remote system. Then, to retrieve the data, you call RegQueryValueEx using the key you obtained in the RegConnectRegistry call, rather than the HKEY_PERFORMANCE_DATA key.

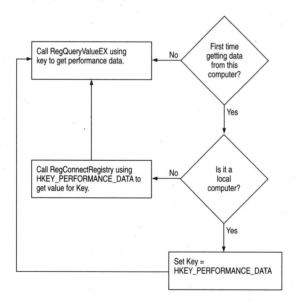

Figure 12.2 How to obtain performance data

Although you use the register-querying function RegQueryValueEx to collect performance data, the performance data does not come from the Registry database. Instead, calling this function with the appropriate key causes the system to collect the data from the appropriate system object managers. The Registry knows that delegating work to others is a useful skill.

When using the RegQueryValueEx function, your monitor must use the *lpcbData* parameter to specify a byte count of the amount of data to retrieve. Estimating this amount can be tricky. The amount of data varies between systems because of different configurations, and even different requests on the same system will vary because of differing amounts of system activity (such as the number of current threads).

If a RegQueryValueEx call does not provide enough space, the return value will be ERROR_MORE_DATA. To solve this, your application should include a retry loop in which it passes increasing amounts of buffer space until it no longer gets the error. Then, the application should use the successful buffer size as the starting point for subsequent calls to RegQueryValueEx.

How the Performance Data Is Structured

By now you must be wondering how the data is structured. We have a nifty table at the end of this section detailing the contents of each of the performance data structures, and the structures are defined in excruciating detail in the WINPERF.H header file supplied with the Windows NT SDK.

The structure of the data retrieved by RegQueryValueEx begins with a single header structure, PERF_DATA_BLOCK. The PERF_DATA_BLOCK structure is followed by the data for the various object types returning data. For each object type defined on the system there is a PERF_OBJECT_TYPE structure and the accompanying data for that object.

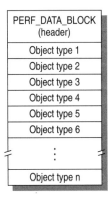

Figure 12.3 Basic structure of performance data

The PERF_DATA_BLOCK structure describes the system and the performance data. Each PERF_OBJECT_TYPE structure describes the performance data for one type of object.

Following the PERF_OBJECT_TYPE structure for each object is a list of PERF_COUNTER_DEFINITION structures, one for each counter defined for the object.

How the performance data for each object is structured depends on whether the object has instances. You'll remember from earlier in this book that some objects, such as memory, do not have instances. Objects such as thread, disk, and processor do have one or more instances. For example, each thread in the system is an instance of the thread object type.

For an object with no instances, the data following the PERF_COUNTER_DEFINITION structures consists of a single PERF_COUNTER_BLOCK structure, followed by the data for each counter.

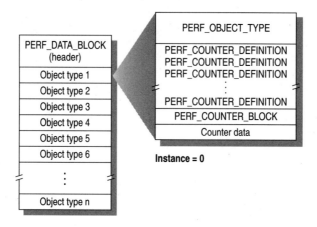

Figure 12.4 Performance data structure of an object with no instances

For an object type with one or more instances, the list of counter definitions is followed by a PERF_INSTANCE_DEFINITION structure and a PERF_COUNTER_BLOCK structure for each instance.

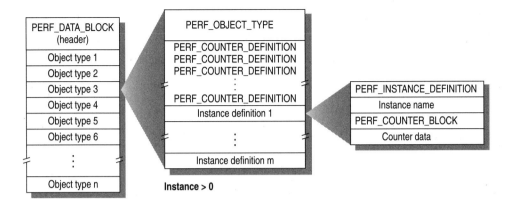

Figure 12.5 Performance data structure of an object with one or more instances

Table 12.1   Performance Data Structures

Data structure	Contents
PERF_DATA_BLOCK	Length of the entire data block, including all objects and their counters.
	Offset to the Unicode system name and its length.
	Time stamp.
	Size of entire data structure.
	Number of object type definitions contained in this data.
	Offset of the first object type definition.
PERF_OBJECT_TYPE	Size of the structure and the accompanying data for this object type.
	Number of counters defined for the object type.
	Number of instances of this object type.
	Parent of this object (if any).
	Level of expertise required by the user to understand this object's data.
	Offsets to the first definition counter under this object, and to the next PERF_OBJECT_TYPE structure.
	Indexes to the object name and Explain text in the title database.

Table 12.1   Performance Data Structures (*continued*)

Data structure	Contents
PERF_COUNTER_DEFINITION	Type of counter.
	Offset to the counter and its size.
	The level of expertise required by the user to understand this counter.
	Indexes to counter name and Explain text.
PERF_COUNTER_BLOCK	Length of the PERF_COUNTER_BLOCK structure and the data that follows it.
PERF_INSTANCE_DEFINITION	Offset to instance name, and its length.
	Index to parent instance (if any).
	Unique identifier (if any).

Navigating Through the Performance Data Structures

As you can see from the previous table, offsets are used frequently in the performance data.

The data structures use offsets because the number of object types, instances, and counters may vary from one RegQueryValueEx call to another. Therefore, the number and size of structures included in the performance data as well as the size of the data that follows each structure may vary. To ensure that your application receives the appropriate performance information, it must use the offsets included in the performance structures to navigate through the data. Every offset is a count of bytes relative to the structure containing it.

Retrieving Counter Names and Explanations

Object type names, counter names and Explain text are not returned in the data structures described in the previous section. Instead, those structures contain indices to a structure in the Registry where the Unicode names and descriptions for each object and counter are stored, possibly in multiple languages.

To access object type and counter names and Explain text, an application must open the following Registry node:

```
\SOFTWARE\Microsoft\Windows NT\CurrentVersion\Perflib\<langid>
```

The *langid* is the ASCII representation of the 3-digit hexadecimal language identifier. For example, the U.S. English *langid* is 009. Language Identifiers are defined in the *winnt.h* header file distributed in the Windows NT SDK. On a non-English version of Windows NT, counters are stored in both the native language of the system and in English. When a user first adds to a chart or a log, for example, Performance Monitor tries to find the above Registry node for the user's language. If it is not there, the *langid* 009 is used and the counters appear in English.

Once your application opens this node, it can query the node for the values of either 'Counters' or 'Help' (Explain text). The 'Counters' and 'Help' data are stored in MULTI_SZ strings, each terminated with UNICODE_NULL. The last string is followed by an additional UNICODE_NULL.

The MULTI_SZ strings are listed in pairs. The first string of each pair is the Unicode string of the index, and the second string is the actual name of the index.

The 'Counters' data contains only indexes with even numbers, while the 'Help' data has odd-numbered indexes.

The following serves as an example of the 'Counters' list, with object and counter name strings:

```
2        System
4        Memory
6        % Processor Time
```

The next example is from the 'Help' data. To save space in this example, each set of Explain text is truncated. By convention, we generally alternated counter and Explain text to aid in checking for any problems.

```
3        The System object type includes those counters that...
5        The Memory object type includes those counters that...
7        Processor Time is expressed as a percentage of the...
```

If your custom monitor is independent of the system counters (as Performance Monitor is), it should do the following to retrieve a name or Explain text for an object type or counter:

1. If the system is remote, use RegConnectRegistry.

2. Use RegOpenKeyEx, specifying

    \SOFTWARE\Microsoft\Windows NT\CurrentVersion\Perflib*langid*,
    where *langid* is the appropriate language identifier.

3. Use RegQueryValueEx, specifying either 'Counters' or 'Help' as the name of
    the value to query. This provides MULTI_SZ data containing either the names
    of all the objects and counters, or Explain text for all objects and counters.

4. Convert the appropriate index
    (PERF_OBJECT_TYPE.ObjectNameTitleIndex,
    PERF_OBJECT_TYPE.ObjectHelpTitleIndex,
    PERF_COUNTER_DEFINITION.CounterNameTitleIndex, or
    PERF_COUNTER_DEFINITION.CounterHelpTitleIndex) into Unicode
    or ASCII, depending on whether the application is Unicode or ASCII.

5. Search the MULTI_SZ data for the appropriate index.

6. Retrieve the string following the matching index. The string contains the
    object or counter name or Explain text.

But we know that not all of you want to write a full-blown monitor that is
independent of the system counters. We know that some of you just may not be
able to resist writing tools specifically for Windows NT. For example, you might
want to write a tool that quickly displays the most active processors. In that case,
the program should look up the object name in English (*langid* 009), and match
by name the one you want to monitor; "Processor" in this example. The previous
string is then the object title index for the Processor object type. Now you can
convert this from Unicode or ASCII to an integer, and scan the returned data for
an object type with this title index. You can do the same for specific counters.
Each counter name is unique even if it appears in multiple objects.

We strongly discourage you from discovering the object title index for your
object, and then embedding it in your program, attempting to bypass the above
lookup. These might change in some future release, and we don't want your
efforts to break. That's why there is no header file defining these for the system.
So do the lookup. The sample code has several variants that you can use.

Retrieving Selected Data

Retrieving the performance data is not without cost to the system, especially in
terms of processor and memory requirements. In cases where your application
does not need all the performance data, you can use the *lpszValueName* parameter
of **RegQueryValueEx** to indicate the amount of information to retrieve. The
following table lists the values you can specify for *lpszValueName*. Note that the
value strings are case-sensitive, and if a string includes more than one word, your
words must be separated by a space.

Table 12.2   Possible Values for *lpszValueName*

String	Meaning
Global	The function returns all data for counters on the local computer except those included in the **Costly** category, described later in this table.
nnn xx yyy	Each of these is a Unicode string representing the decimal value for a PERF_OBJECT_TYPE.ObjectNameTitleIndex. The function only returns data about the specified object types on the local computer. [1]
	Using the example above, if your program were to pass "2 4" as the *lpszValueName* the System and Memory objects would be retrieved.
Foreign *ssss*	The string *ssss* is the name of a foreign computer, such as a Novell NetWare server or a UNIX system that does not support the Registry calls for returning data remotely. The function returns all data for counters on the foreign computer, if your system is capable of collecting data from a foreign computer. You may want to try this approach if RegConnectRegistry fails to connect to a foreign computer.
Foreign *ssss nnn xx yyy*	This format combines **Foreign *ssss*** and ***nnn xx yyy*** discussed above, and returns all data for the specified objects on the foreign computer, if your system is capable of collecting data from a foreign computer.
Costly	Data for object types whose data is expensive to collect (in terms of processor time or memory usage) is returned. If you want to respond to the user during data collection, you may want to start a secondary thread to access this data. PView does this. **Costly** data includes all the data normally returned by **Global**, and the expensive stuff too. For example, to return the current instruction pointer, the data collection code must map into every process's address space. This is too expensive for routine performance monitoring but may be useful in other situations.

1 If you request an object type that requires other object types, the required object types will also be returned. For example, processes are needed to identify threads, so if you request threads you will also receive data about processes.

Performance Counter Definitions

The performance counters returned by Windows NT each have a type definition that determines how a performance monitor is supposed to use the counter to display data to the user.

The Counter Type words are divided into a number of fields, each of which defines a particular attribute of the counter. Each field can contain one of several values. Most values are mutually exclusive in their fields, with the exception that the values for the Calculation Modifiers field can be combined. The fields are later or'd into several basic counter types currently in use in Windows NT.

First, we'll list the Fields and their possible values and definitions in Table 12.3. To do this clearly we need a little nomenclature. We assume data is available for two points in time, Time 0 (T0) and Time 1 (T1). Time 1 comes after Time 0. (Time units depend on the counter definition as described below.)

The counter value at T0 we'll call C0, and at T1 we call the value C1. Some counters are computed using the counter and the one that follows it in the counter block, which is usually a base of some kind. Call these values B0 and B1 respectively.

DeltaT = T1 - T0.

DeltaC = C1 - C0.

DeltaB = B1 - B0.

Table 12.3   Counter Type Field Definitions

Field name	Value name	Definition
Size	PERF_SIZE_DWORD	4 bytes long.
Size	PERF_SIZE_LARGE	8 bytes long.
Size	PERF_SIZE_ZERO	Size is in CounterLength field of COUNTER_DEFINITION structure.
Size	PERF_SIZE_VARIABLE_LEN	Size is in first DWORD of data.
Type	PERF_TYPE_NUMBER	A number (not a counter).
Type	PERF_TYPE_COUNTER	An increasing numeric value.
Type	PERF_TYPE_TEXT	A text field.
Type	PERF_TYPE_ZERO	Display a zero always.
SubType of Type PERF_TYPE_NUMBER	PERF_NUMBER_HEX	Display as hexadecimal number.
SubType of Type PERF_TYPE_NUMBER	PERF_NUMBER_DECIMAL	Display as decimal number.
SubType of Type PERF_TYPE_NUMBER	PERF_NUMBER_DEC_1000	Display as decimal number/1000.
SubType of Type PERF_TYPE_COUNTER	PERF_COUNTER_VALUE	Display DeltaC.

Table 12.3   Counter Type Field Definitions (*continued*)

Field name	Value name	Definition
SubType of Type PERF_TYPE_COUNTER	PERF_COUNTER_RATE	Display DeltaC/DeltaT.
SubType of Type PERF_TYPE_COUNTER	PERF_COUNTER_FRACTION	Display DeltaC/DeltaB.
SubType of Type PERF_TYPE_COUNTER	PERF_COUNTER_BASE	Don't display, just use in calculating other counter.
SubType of Type PERF_TYPE_COUNTER	PERF_COUNTER_ELAPSED	Display T1 - C1, meaning subtract counter from current time.
SubType of Type PERF_TYPE_COUNTER	PERF_COUNTER_QUEUELEN	Space-Time product of queue length. (C1 + (T1 * B1))/DeltaT
SubType of Type PERF_TYPE_COUNTER	PERF_COUNTER_HISTOGRAM	Counter begins or ends a histogram.
SubType of Type PERF_TYPE_TEXT	PERF_TEXT_UNICODE	Text is Unicode.
SubType of Type PERF_TYPE_TEXT	PERF_TEXT_ASCII	ASCII using CodePage as defined by PERF_OBJECT_TYPE.CodePage.
Timer Subtype	PERF_TIMER_TICK	Uses frequency in PERF_DATA_BLOCK.PerfFreq.
Timer Subtype	PERF_TIMER_100NS	Time is in units of 100 nanoseconds.
Timer Subtype	PERF_OBJECT_TIMER	Time is in units defined in PERF_OBJECT_TYPE.PerfFreq.
Calculation Modifiers	PERF_DELTA_COUNTER	Compute difference first: DeltaC.
Calculation Modifiers	PERF_DELTA_BASE	Compute the base difference: DeltaB.
Calculation Modifiers	PERF_INVERSE_COUNTER	After computing, subtract resulting fraction from 1.
Calculation Modifiers	PERF_MULTI_COUNTER	Sum of multiple instances. Divide by number of instances (in B1) after computing to get average.
Display	PERF_DISPLAY_NO_SUFFIX	No suffix.
Display	PERF_DISPLAY_PER_SEC	"/second"
Display	PERF_DISPLAY_PERCENT	"%"
Display	PERF_DISPLAY_SECONDS	"seconds"
Display	PERF_DISPLAY_NOSHOW	Don't display the value at all.

In the next table we define a number of pre-existing counter types used in counter definitions. These are combinations of the above flags. Currently, Performance Monitor supports only the counter types defined in Table 12.4, except for PERF_COUNTER_TEXT and PERF_COUNTER_QUEUELEN_TYPE.

Table 12.4   Predefined Counter Types and How to Display Them

Counter type name	Composition	Definition/computation
PERF_COUNTER_COUNTER	PERF_SIZE_DWORD | PERF_TYPE_COUNTER | PERF_COUNTER_RATE | PERF_TIMER_TICK | PERF_DELTA_COUNTER | PERF_DISPLAY_PER_SEC	32-bit rate of counts. DeltaC / DeltaT The most common sort of counter.
PERF_COUNTER_TIMER	PERF_SIZE_LARGE | PERF_TYPE_COUNTER | PERF_COUNTER_RATE | PERF_TIMER_TICK | PERF_DELTA_COUNTER | PERF_DISPLAY_PERCENT	64-bit Timer. (DeltaC / DeltaT) * 100 The most common sort of timer.
PERF_COUNTER_QUEUELEN_TYPE	PERF_SIZE_DWORD | PERF_TYPE_COUNTER | PERF_COUNTER_QUEUELEN | PERF_TIMER_TICK | PERF_DELTA_COUNTER | PERF_DISPLAY_NO_SUFFIX	Space-Time product of queue length. (C1 + (T1 * B1))/DeltaT Not used in the current release of Windows NT.
PERF_COUNTER_BULK_COUNT	PERF_SIZE_LARGE | PERF_TYPE_COUNTER | PERF_COUNTER_RATE | PERF_TIMER_TICK | PERF_DELTA_COUNTER | PERF_DISPLAY_PER_SEC	64-bit rate of count. Used to count byte transmission rates. DeltaC / DeltaT
PERF_COUNTER_TEXT	PERF_SIZE_VARIABLE_LEN | PERF_TYPE_TEXT | PERF_TEXT_UNICODE | PERF_DISPLAY_NO_SUFFIX	Indicates the counter is not a counter but rather Unicode text. Display as text.
PERF_COUNTER_RAWCOUNT	PERF_SIZE_DWORD | PERF_TYPE_NUMBER | PERF_NUMBER_DECIMAL | PERF_DISPLAY_NO_SUFFIX	A raw count that should not be averaged. Used for instantaneous counts. Display B1.

Table 12.4   Predefined Counter Types and How to Display Them (*continued*)

Counter type name	Composition	Definition/computation
PERF_SAMPLE_FRACTION	PERF_SIZE_DWORD | PERF_TYPE_COUNTER | PERF_COUNTER_FRACTION | PERF_DELTA_COUNTER | PERF_DELTA_BASE | PERF_DISPLAY_PERCENT	A count that is either 1 or 0 on each sampling interrupt. Display as percentage. (DeltaC / DeltaB) * 100
PERF_SAMPLE_COUNTER	PERF_SIZE_DWORD | PERF_TYPE_COUNTER | PERF_COUNTER_RATE | PERF_TIMER_TICK | PERF_DELTA_COUNTER | PERF_DISPLAY_NO_SUFFIX	A count that is sampled on each sampling interrupt. Display without a suffix. DeltaC/DeltaT
PERF_COUNTER_NODATA	PERF_SIZE_ZERO | PERF_DISPLAY_NOSHOW	This is not to be displayed.
PERF_COUNTER_TIMER_INV	PERF_SIZE_LARGE | PERF_TYPE_COUNTER | PERF_COUNTER_RATE | PERF_TIMER_TICK | PERF_DELTA_COUNTER | PERF_INVERSE_COUNTER | PERF_DISPLAY_PERCENT	This is used to show how busy the processor is, but it is really time in the idle process. (1 - (DeltaC/DeltaT)) * 100
PERF_SAMPLE_BASE	PERF_SIZE_DWORD | PERF_TYPE_COUNTER | PERF_COUNTER_BASE | PERF_DISPLAY_NOSHOW	The divisor for a sample (previous counter). Check that this is > 0 before dividing! Don't display.
PERF_AVERAGE_TIMER	PERF_SIZE_LARGE | PERF_TYPE_COUNTER | PERF_COUNTER_FRACTION | PERF_DISPLAY_SECONDS	A timer which, when divided by a base, yields a time per operation. DeltaC / DeltaB
PERF_AVERAGE_BASE	PERF_SIZE_DWORD | PERF_TYPE_COUNTER | PERF_COUNTER_BASE | PERF_DISPLAY_NOSHOW	Used as the denominator in the computation of time or count averages. Do not display.
PERF_AVERAGE_BULK	PERF_SIZE_LARGE | PERF_TYPE_COUNTER | PERF_COUNTER_FRACTION | PERF_DISPLAY_NO_SUFFIX	A 64-bit count which when divided (typically) by the number of operations gives (typically) the bytes/operation. DeltaC / DeltaB

Table 12.4   Predefined Counter Types and How to Display Them (*continued*)

Counter type name	Composition	Definition/computation
PERF_100NSEC_TIMER	PERF_SIZE_LARGE | PERF_TYPE_COUNTER | PERF_COUNTER_RATE | PERF_TIMER_100NS | PERF_DELTA_COUNTER | PERF_DISPLAY_PERCENT	64-bit timer in 100 nanosecond units. (DeltaC / DeltaT) * 100
PERF_100NSEC_TIMER_INV	PERF_SIZE_LARGE | PERF_TYPE_COUNTER | PERF_COUNTER_RATE | PERF_TIMER_100NS | PERF_DELTA_COUNTER | PERF_INVERSE_COUNTER | PERF_DISPLAY_PERCENT	64-bit timer inverse, that is, we measure idle time, then display (1-(idle time)) (1 - (DeltaC / DeltaT)) * 100
PERF_COUNTER_MULTI_TIMER	PERF_SIZE_LARGE | PERF_TYPE_COUNTER | PERF_COUNTER_RATE | PERF_DELTA_COUNTER | PERF_TIMER_TICK | PERF_MULTI_COUNTER | PERF_DISPLAY_PERCENT	Timer for multiple instances, so sum of result can exceed 100%. Number of instances is in the next counter. 100 * (DeltaC / DeltaT) / B1 Display as percentage.
PERF_COUNTER_MULTI_TIMER_INV	PERF_SIZE_LARGE | PERF_TYPE_COUNTER | PERF_COUNTER_RATE | PERF_DELTA_COUNTER | PERF_MULTI_COUNTER | PERF_TIMER_TICK | PERF_INVERSE_COUNTER | PERF_DISPLAY_PERCENT	Display inverse of timer for multiple instances. 100 * (1 - ((DeltaC / DeltaT) / B1))
PERF_COUNTER_MULTI_BASE	PERF_SIZE_LARGE | PERF_TYPE_COUNTER | PERF_COUNTER_BASE | PERF_MULTI_COUNTER | PERF_DISPLAY_NOSHOW	Base for _MULTI_ counters. Do not display.
PERF_100NSEC_MULTI_TIMER	PERF_SIZE_LARGE | PERF_TYPE_COUNTER | PERF_DELTA_COUNTER | PERF_COUNTER_RATE | PERF_TIMER_100NS | PERF_MULTI_COUNTER | PERF_DISPLAY_PERCENT	Timer for multiple instances, so sum of result can exceed 100%. Number of instances is in the next counter. 100 * (DeltaC / DeltaT) / B1 Display as percentage.

Table 12.4   Predefined Counter Types and How to Display Them (*continued*)

Counter type name	Composition	Definition/computation
PERF_100NSEC_MULTI_TIMER_INV	PERF_SIZE_LARGE | PERF_TYPE_COUNTER | PERF_DELTA_COUNTER | PERF_COUNTER_RATE | PERF_TIMER_100NS | PERF_MULTI_COUNTER | PERF_INVERSE_COUNTER | PERF_DISPLAY_PERCENT	Display inverse of timer for multiple instances. $100 * (1 - ((DeltaC / DeltaT) / B1))$
PERF_RAW_FRACTION	PERF_SIZE_DWORD | PERF_TYPE_COUNTER | PERF_COUNTER_FRACTION | PERF_DISPLAY_PERCENT	Fraction of next counter, display as a percentage. $(DeltaC / DeltaB) * 100$
PERF_RAW_BASE	PERF_SIZE_DWORD | PERF_TYPE_COUNTER | PERF_COUNTER_BASE | PERF_DISPLAY_NOSHOW	Used as a base for the preceding counter. Do not display.
PERF_ELAPSED_TIME	PERF_SIZE_LARGE | PERF_TYPE_COUNTER | PERF_COUNTER_ELAPSED | PERF_OBJECT_TIMER | PERF_DISPLAY_SECONDS ·	The data collected in this counter is actually the start time of the item being measured. For display, this data is subtracted from the snapshot time to yield the elapsed time (the difference between the two). In the definition to the left, the PerfTime field of the PERF_OBJECT_TYPE contains the sample time as indicated by the PERF_OBJECT_TIMER bit and the difference is scaled by the PerfFreq of the PERF_OBJECT_TYPE to convert the time units into seconds.

Whew! Okay, now you know how to compute and display all the different types of counters that come back from the call to the Configuration Registry when you specify HKEY_PERFORMANCE_DATA as the key. Hey, we said you'd be stimulating at parties, didn't we? Now get to work on that monitor!

Monitoring Within an Application

Now that you know what is involved in writing a performance monitor, you may want to measure your own application to get some understanding of how it is operating. You can display the data when your application quits.

One thing you can do is simply run the **ntimer** command included on the floppy disk provided with this book. Typing the following will start the application you want to time, and then when the application ends, it prints basic execution statistics of elapsed, user, and kernel time in the application process.

ntimer *application*

For looking inside your application, the high resolution performance timer on the system is read using the QueryPerformanceCounter API call. This returns a 64-bit counter that contains the current count. The resolution of this counter varies from one system to the next. You can use the QueryPerformanceFrequency call to get this frequency on the system you are running on. Peruse the API documentation for the details. There is some sample code in the Windows NT SDK which provides 64-bit arithmetic routines. Look for MSTOOLS\SAMPLES\LARGEINT.

A couple of other calls may also be handy for you. These are GetProcessTimes and GetThreadTimes. These return the same information printed by the **ntimer** utility. Realize that these timers are all subject to the granularity of the system clock. Even though the values returned are in 100-nanosecond units, the system clocks on the 486 tick at 15-millisecond intervals, and on the MIPS at 10-millisecond intervals. So calling these more frequently within a program will not yield accurate results. Beware misleading advertising!

CHAPTER 13

Adding Application Performance Counters

Windows NT provides a mechanism for developers to add performance objects and counters for their applications and other software components, including non-Windows NT computers. These objects and counters can provide performance data to Windows NT Performance Monitor or to your customized performance monitoring programs.

Performance counters specific to your application can help you tune performance while you develop and debug the application. After your application is complete and installed on target systems, the counters can help system administrators adjust your application's configurable settings.

Adding Performance Counters: the Big Picture

Performance Monitor was designed so that developers could add performance counters for their own applications to the system. To add performance counters to the system, you must create an extended object. Your extended object is called when Performance Monitor collects data, as shown in Figure 13.1. The Configuration Registry is handled by ADVAPI32.DLL in the Performance Monitor process on the local computer, and by SCREG.EXE on remotely monitored computers.

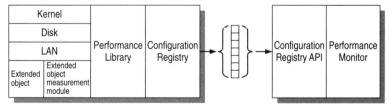

Figure 13.1 How Performance Monitor collects data from an extended object

To add performance objects and counters for your application, follow the basic steps in the list below. Each of these steps is discussed in detail in following sections of this chapter.

1. Design the object types and counters for the application.
2. Set up the necessary performance monitoring entries in the Registry. This includes the following steps:
   a. Create a Performance key in the application's Services node in the Registry. If you don't have such a node you must create one. Create it under HKEY_LOCAL_MACHINE\SYSTEM\CurrentControlSet\Services.
   b. Create an .INI file containing the names and descriptions of the counter objects and counters.
   c. Create an .H file containing the relative offsets at which the counter objects and counters will be installed in the Registry.
   d. Use the **lodctr** utility with the .INI and .H files to install the information in the Registry. **Lodctr** succeeds only if a Performance key exists in the application's Services node.
   e. Add Library, Open, Collect, and Close value entries to the application's Services node in the Registry. These entries specify the name of the application's performance DLL, and the names of the DLLs required functions. The Open and Close entries are optional.
3. To your application, add functions and data structures for collecting and storing performance data, and a mechanism for communicating the data to the performance DLL.
4. Create a performance DLL containing a set of exported functions that provide the link between the application and a performance monitoring application (such as Windows NT Performance Monitor).
5. Modify the application's OEMSETUP.INF file to automate the Registry setup described in step 2.

Object and Counter Design

A performance counter object is an entity for which performance data is available. A performance counter defines the type of data that is available for a particular type of counter object. An application can provide information for multiple counter objects, each with more than one counter.

Using the Windows NT system to illustrate the relationship between objects and counters, objects include memory, disk, and cache. Each of these objects has multiple counters relating to that object: the Memory object includes the counters Available Bytes and Page Faults/sec, for example.

An application can also define objects that have multiple instances. For example, a SCSI® application could use a single set of counter definitions to define a drive object with two counters, such as Bytes Read and Bytes Written. Using this object, the application's performance DLL could report performance data for multiple instances of the drive object (for example, for each drive controlled by the application).

Performance Monitor always shows counters denoting raw counts as rates, such as Page Faults/sec. This gives context to the viewer, who doesn't have to do in-the-head calculations to compare data from different time intervals. However, you don't have to worry about this when you design a counter. Just let the counter count incrementally, and let the monitor application do the work of converting raw counts to a rate.

Setting Up the Registry

To enable performance counters for your application, there are two ways you must modify the Registry.

- Create a Performance key in the application's Services node, and add value entries under it specifying the name of the application's performance DLL and the names of the DLL functions.

- Use the **lodctr** utility to install counter names and descriptions into the Registry.

The following sections explain how you can manually enable performance counters for use as you develop and tune your application.

If you include performance counters with your finished product, you'll want to include enough information in your application's OEMSETUP.INF file so that the necessary modifications to the Registry are made automatically when the application is installed. For more information about this process, see "Installing Your Application," later in this chapter.

Creating the Application's Performance Key

An application that supports performance counters must have a Performance subkey in a Services node. For development, an application writer can use Regedt32 to manually create the Performance key and the **Library**, **Open**, **Collect**, and **Close** values.

The following code shows the values under this key:

```
\HKEY_LOCAL_MACHINE
    \SYSTEM
        \CurrentControlSet
            \Services
                \ApplicationName
                    \Performance
                        Library = DLL_Name
                        Open = Open_Function_Name
                        Collect = Collect_Function_Name
                        Close = Close_Function_Name
                        First Counter =
                        First Help =
                        Last Counter =
                        Last Help =
```

The **Library**, **Open**, **Collect**, and **Close** values provide the name of the application's performance DLL and the names of the exported functions in the DLL. When a performance monitoring application requests performance data, the Registry controller uses these values to determine the performance DLLs to load and the DLL functions to call. The Open and Close entries are optional.

You do not need to add manually the **First Counter**, **First Help**, **Last Counter**, and **Last Help** values. These are created automatically by the **lodctr** utility when you add counter names and descriptions to the Registry. These entries are explained in the following section.

Adding Counter Names and Descriptions to the Registry

The names and Explain text of objects and counters are stored in the Registry. You must add this information to the Registry for any objects and counters you add to the system.

The following diagram shows the Registry location where performance counter names and descriptions are stored.

```
\HKEY_LOCAL_MACHINE
    \SOFTWARE
        \Microsoft
            \Windows NT
                \CurrentVersion
                    \Perflib
                        Last Counter =
                        Last Help =
                        \009
                            Counters = 2 System 4 Memory
                            Help = 3 The System object type includes...
                        \other supported languages
                            Counters =
                            Help =
```

The Perflib key has one or more subkeys, representing each language supported on the computer. The name in each subkey is the language ID: for example, 009 is the language ID for U.S. English.

Under each language subkey are Counters and Explain text entries that store multiple Unicode strings containing information about all registered objects and counters. In the Registry example above, part of the Counters and Help entries for U.S. English are shown.

As described in the last chapter, for each counter or counter object the Counters value stores an index and a name that identifies the counter or counter object. Similarly, the Help value stores an index and a string that describes the counter or counter object. (The strings in the Help value are shown when you choose the Explain button in Performance Monitor.)

The Counters index for each counter is always an even number, and the Help index is usually one greater than the Counters index for that counter. This convention makes it easy to associate the help text with its counter during debugging. The following table shows a fragment from typical Counters and Help values:

Table 13.1   Performance Counters and Help Values

Counters		Help	
Index	**Name**	**Index+1**	**Description**
820	VGA	821	The VGA Object Type handles the VGA device on your system.
822	BitBlts/sec	823	BitBlts/sec is the rate at which your system sends blocks of pixels to the display.
824	TextOuts/sec	825	TextOuts/sec is the rate at which your system sends lines of text to the display.

Performance monitoring applications and performance DLLs use the Counters index to identify the counter or counter object. A performance monitoring application uses the Counters name and the Help description to display information about a counter.

Also under the Perflib key are the Last Counter and Last Help values. These values are set to the highest index numbers used in the Counters and Help values.

To add names and descriptions of the objects and counters for your application, use the **lodctr** utility included on the diskette provided with this book (it's also in the Windows NT DDK). The **lodctr** utility takes strings from an .INI file and adds them to the Counters and Help values under the appropriate language subkeys under the Perflib key. It also updates the Last Counter and Last Help values under PerfLib.

You should add all your counters at one time. Running **lodctr** twice to add more counters without running **unlodctr** in between will not work. Avoid this scurrilous practice.

The .INI file can include strings for any number of languages, but **lodctr** only installs the strings for languages that have existing subkeys under PerfLib. You should set up your .INI file to install strings for all languages you might ever want to see your objects and counters in. If you have not yet translated them, consider installing the English strings as placeholders until you have time to translate. It's not perfect, but it's better than nothing.

While it modifies the values in the PerfLib node, **lodctr** creates a value called 'Updating' in the Perflib node to act as a semaphore to synchronize PerfLib modifications. Before it stops, **lodctr** deletes the Updating value.

In addition to making the additions under PerfLib, the **lodctr** utility also adds the following value entries to the Performance subkey in the application's **Services** node:

```
\HKEY_LOCAL_MACHINE
    \SYSTEM
        \CurrentControlSet
            \Services
                \ApplicationName
                    \Performance
                        First Counter =
                        First Help =
                        Last Counter =
                        Last Help =
```

The following table explains these values.

Table 13.2   LodCtr-Added Value Names and Descriptions

Value name	Description
First Counter	Counter index of the first counter or counter object that LodCtr installed for this application.
First Help	Help index of the first counter or counter object that LodCtr installed for this application.
Last Counter	Counter index of the last counter or counter object that LodCtr installed for this application.
Last Help	Help index of the last counter or counter object that LodCtr installed for this application.

The command-line syntax for **lodctr** is:

lodctr *MyApplication***.ini**

The .INI file used by **lodctr** has the following format:

```
[info]
applicationname=ApplicationName
symbolfile=SymbolFile

[languages] // one key (value optional) for each language supported
langid=
    .
    .
    .


[text]  // name and description for each counter or counter object
offset_langid_NAME=Name        // "Counters" name string
offset_langid_HELP=Description  // "Help" description string
    .
    .
    .
```

The .INI file entries are variables with the following meanings:

Table 13.3   LodCtr Variables

Variable	Description
ApplicationName	The name of the application found under the CurrentControlSet\Services key.
SymbolFile	An .H file containing symbolic offsets of counters. The performance DLL also uses the offsets in this file along with the First Counter and First Help Registry values to determine the indexes of the various counters and counter objects.
langid	An ID corresponding to the language subkey in the Registry (for example, 009 for U.S. English).
offset	A symbolic constant defined in *SymbolFile*. Offsets must be consecutive, even numbers beginning with zero. These offsets determine the order in which the counters are installed in the Counters and Help values in the Registry.

The following listings show examples of a *SymbolFile* and an .INI file:

```
// begin symfile.h example

#define OBJECT_1        0
#define DEVICE_COUNTER_1    2
#define DEVICE_COUNTER_2    4

// end symfile.h example

-----------------------------------------------------
// begin .INI file example
[info]
applicationname=ApplicationName
symbolfile=symfile.h

[languages]
009=English
011=OtherLanguage

[text]
OBJECT_1_009_NAME=Device Name
OBJECT_1_009_HELP=Displays performance statistics on Device Name
OBJECT_1_011_NAME=Device Name in other language
OBJECT_1_011_HELP=Displays performance of Device Name in other language

DEVICE_COUNTER_1_009_NAME=Counter A
DEVICE_COUNTER_1_009_HELP=Displays the current value of Counter A
DEVICE_COUNTER_1_011_NAME=Counter A in other language
DEVICE_COUNTER_1_011_HELP=Displays the value of Counter A in other
language

DEVICE_COUNTER_2_009_NAME=Counter B
DEVICE_COUNTER_2_009_HELP=Displays the current rate of Device B
DEVICE_COUNTER_2_011_NAME=Counter B in other language
DEVICE_COUNTER_2_011_HELP=Displays the rate of Device B in other
language

// end .INI file
```

If you run **lodctr** to add counters for an application and the application does not have a Performance subkey, **lodctr** returns without modifying the PerfLib values.

Removing Counter Names and Descriptions from the Registry

If you need to remove counter names and Explain text from the Registry, use the **unlodctr** utility. This removes the Registry entries made by **lodctr**. The command-line syntax for **unlodctr** is:

unlodctr *ApplicationName*

The **unlodctr** utility looks up the First Counter and Last Counter values in the application's **Performance** key to determine the indexes of the counter objects to remove. Using these indexes, it makes the following changes to the Last Counter, Last Help, Counters, and Help values under the **Perflib** node:

```
\HKEY_LOCAL_MACHINE
   \SOFTWARE
      \Microsoft
         \Windows NT
            \CurrentVersion
               \Perflib
                  Last Counter = (updated if changed)
                  Last Help =    (updated if changed)
                  \009
                     Counters (application's text removed)
                     Help     (application's text removed)
                  \other supported languages
                     Counters (application's text removed)
                     Help     (application's text removed)
```

Then, **unlodctr** removes the First Counter, First Help, Last Counter, and Last Help value entries from the application's **Performance** key.

Other Registry Entries

In some cases, additional Registry entries are required.

To obtain the performance data for some applications (those that return counters via the DeviceIOControlFile call), it is necessary to use the CreateFile function to open the device associated with the application. In this case, the name specified in CreateFile must also be installed in the DOS Devices node of the Registry:

```
\HKEY_LOCAL_MACHINE
    \SYSTEM
        \CurrentControlSet
            \Control
                \Session Manager
                    \DOS Devices
```

For applications that manage multiple device instances with performance data for each device, the application's Services node must have a Linkage key containing an Export value whose data is a list of the device names. For example, a system with two Etherlink cards could have the following Registry entries:

```
\HKEY_LOCAL_MACHINE
    \SYSTEM\CurrentControlSet\Services
        \Elnkii
            \Linkage
                Export = "\Device\Elnk01" "\Device\Elnk02"
            \Performance
                Library = "ElnkStat.dll"
                Open = "OpenElnkStats"
                Collect = "GetElnkStats"
                Close = "CloseElnkStats"
        \Elnk01
            Parameters
            Linkage
        \Elnk02
            Parameters
            Linkage
```

When the Registry controller calls the Open function in an application's performance DLL, the function's argument is a string containing the list of device names from the application's Export value (if present). The Open function can then use these names to determine the devices for which to collect performance data.

Collecting Performance Data

The next steps are to build functions and data structures into your application to collect and store performance data, and to provide a mechanism for making the data available to the performance DLL.

The method you use to collect the data can be as simple as incrementing a counter each time a particular routine in the application is called, or it can involve time-consuming calculations. Counters and timers should increment and never be cleared. It's all right for a counter to wrap as long as it does not wrap twice between two Performance Monitor snapshots. If it might, use a 64-bit counter instead of a 32-bit counter. Counter types are defined in Table 12.4 in Chapter 12. Your program can collect and store data during the normal course of application operations, though you should do it so it doesn't affect the application's performance. The sample performance code at the end of this chapter shows a performance counter in a VGA application that uses this method.

For some types of data, it may be more efficient or appropriate to collect the data on demand. In this situation, the performance DLL must communicate to the application that the data has been requested. For data that is expensive to collect (in terms of processor time or memory usage), consider collecting data only when the performance monitoring program requests **Costly** data. This allows a custom performance monitoring program to routinely request data for all counters that are not costly. The data can be requested only when needed. Windows NT Performance Monitor does not collect **Costly** data.

Communication between an application and its performance DLL differ for user-mode and privileged-mode applications. The application's performance DLL executes in user mode. Because of this, user-mode applications, such as print and display applications, can use any of the Win32 techniques for interprocess communication, such as named file mapping or RPC. For example, the DDK's sample performance counter code shows a user-mode VGA application that uses a file mapping object to create shared memory mapped into the address space of both the application and the performance DLL. The shared memory provides both storage and interprocess communication. If you use shared memory, consider using a named mutex object so you don't change the data while it is being collected.

Privileged-mode applications must provide an IOCTL interface that returns the performance data to the performance DLL.

Creating the Performance DLL

An application's performance DLL defines the counter and object data structures that it uses to pass performance data to the performance monitor application. The DLL also provides up to three exported functions—Open, Collect, and Close—that are called by the Registry controller in response to requests from a performance monitoring program. The Collect function is required, while Open and Close are optional. Whichever ones you provide, be sure to export them in your .DEF file.

The prototypes for these functions, and the structures and constants used to define counters and counter objects, are defined in the WINPERF.H file distributed with the Windows NT Software Development Kit (SDK). For more information about using the structures and constants to define counters and counter objects, refer to Chapter 13 of this book, the comments in the WINPERF.H file, and to the SDK documentation on performance monitoring.

Table 13.4   Performance DLL Functions

Function	Description
Open	Initializes performance monitoring for the application
Collect	Reports performance data when requested
Close	Closes performance monitoring

When it is necessary to recompile the DLL during development, stop DLL performance monitoring between DLL changes. This is necessary because ADVAPI32.DLL and SCREG.EXE keep the old version open as long as you are monitoring.

How the DLL Interfaces with a Performance Monitor Application

As discussed in Chapter 12 of this book, a performance monitor program retrieves performance data by specifying the HKEY_PERFORMANCE_DATA special handle in a call to the RegQueryValueEx function. If successful, RegQueryValueEx fills a buffer of the application with the requested performance data.

The first time an application calls RegQueryValueEx, or if the application uses the RegOpenKey function to open HKEY_PERFORMANCE_DATA, the Registry controller calls the Open function for all applications with the necessary Performance key entries. This gives each performance DLL an opportunity to initialize its performance data structures. Then, for performance DLLs whose Open function returned successfully, or for those with a Collect function but no Open function, the Registry controller calls the performance DLL's Collect function.

After the initial Open function calls, subsequent application calls to RegQueryValueEx only cause the Registry controller to call the Collect functions.

When the application has finished collecting performance data, it specifies HKEY_PERFORMANCE_DATA in a call to the RegCloseKey function. This causes the Registry controller to call the Close function for all applications. The performance DLLs will then be unloaded.

Note that it is possible for multiple programs to collect performance data at the same time. The Registry controller calls a performance DLL's Open and Close functions only once for each performance monitoring process. For remote measurement, the Registry controller limits access to these routines to only one thread at a time, so synchronization (for example, re-entrancy) is not a problem.

Important For local measurement, because multiple processes may be making simultaneous calls, the program must prevent any conflicts from multiple concurrent requests for data.

The Open Function

The Registry controller calls the Open function, if one is provided, whenever a performance monitor application first connects to the Registry to collect performance data. This function performs whatever initialization is required for the application to provide performance data. Use the PM_OPEN_PROC function prototype defined in WINPERF.H:

```
PM_OPEN_PROC OpenPerformanceData;
DWORD OpenPerformanceData(LPWSTR lpDeviceNames);
```

The *lpDeviceNames* argument points to a buffer containing the REG_MULTI_SZ strings stored in the Export value at the ...\Services*ApplicationName*\Linkage key in the Registry. If this entry does not exist, *lpDeviceNames* is NULL. The strings are Unicode, separated by a UNICODE_NULL, and terminated by two UNICODE_NULL characters. The strings are the names of the devices managed by this application, and the Open function should call CreateFile to open a handle to each device named. If a CreateFile call fails, the Open function should return the error code returned by the GetLastError function; otherwise, it should return ERROR_SUCCESS.

The Open function initializes the data structures it returns to the performance monitor application. In particular, it examines the Registry to get the Counters and Help indexes of the objects and counters supported by the application. These indexes are then stored in the appropriate members of the PERF_OBJECT_TYPE and PERF_COUNTER_DEFINITION structures, which define the application's counter objects and counters. The example code at the end of this chapter shows the technique for using the First Counter and First Help values that the **lodctr** utility creates in the program's Performance key to determine the Counters and Help indexes of the program's counter objects and counters.

Other initialization tasks that might be performed by the Open function include the following:

- Open and map a file mapping object used by the program to store performance data.

- Initialize event logging, if the DLL uses event logging to report errors (it should, but not on every Collect function call).

- Open an internal table of handles to each device instance, to be used by the Collect function to obtain statistics.

- Perform other initialization tasks necessary for the Collect function to collect performance data efficiently.

The Collect Function

The Registry controller calls each application's Collect function whenever a performance monitor program calls the RegQueryValueEx function to collect performance data. This function returns the application's performance data in the format described in Chapter 12, "Writing a Custom Windows NT Performance Monitor." Use the PM_COLLECT_PROC function prototype defined in WINPERF.H:

```
PM_COLLECT_PROC CollectPerformanceData;
DWORD CollectPerformanceData(LPWSTR lpwszValue, LPVOID *lppData,
          LPDWORD lpcbBytes, LPDWORD lpcObjectTypes);
```

Table 13.5   Collect Function Arguments and Descriptions

Argument	Description
lpwszValue	Points to a string specified by the performance monitor program in the RegQueryValueEx call. For an example of code that parses this string, see the example at the end of this chapter. The string uses one of the following case-sensitive formats to identify the type of data being requested:

Global

Requests data for all counters on the local machine except those included in the **Costly** category.

index1 index2 ...

Requests data for the specified objects, where *index 1, index2*, and so forth, are whitespace-separated Unicode strings representing the decimal value of an object's Counters index. The Collect function needs to convert the strings to integers and then compare them to the Counters indexes of the application's counter objects. The Collect function returns data for all counters associated with the specified counter objects.

Foreign *ComputerName*

Requests data for all counters on a computer that does not support the Windows NT Registry calls for returning data remotely. *ComputerName* identifies the computer. If this application is a provider of foreign remote statistics, it should keep a handle that enables access to the foreign system. This avoids reconnection for each data collection. The Collect function should use the handle to get the data.

Foreign *ComputerName index1 index2 ...*

Requests data for the specified objects on a foreign computer.

Costly

Requests data for all counters whose data is expensive to collect. It is up to the application writer to determine whether any of the application's counter objects are in this category. Windows NT Performance Monitor does not use this category.

Table 13.5   Collect Function Arguments and Descriptions (*continued*)

Argument	Description
lppData	On input, points to a pointer to the location where the data is to be placed. On successful exit, set **lppData* to the next byte in the buffer available for data, such as one byte past the last byte of your data. The data returned must be a multiple of a **DWORD** in length. It must conform to the PERF_OBJECT_TYPE data definition and its descendants as specified in WINPERF.H, unless this is a collection from a foreign computer. If foreign, any PERF_OBJECT_TYPE structures returned must be preceded by a PERF_DATA_BLOCK structure for the foreign computer. If the **Collect** function fails for any reason, leave **lppData* unchanged.
lpcbBytes	On input, points to a 32-bit value that specifies the size, in bytes, of the *lppData* buffer. On successful exit, set **lpcbBytes* to the size, in bytes, of the data written to the *lppData* buffer. This must be a multiple of sizeof(**DWORD**) (a multiple of 4). If the **Collect** function fails for any reason, set **lpcbBytes* to zero.
lpcObjectTypes	On successful exit, set **lpcObjectTypes* to the number of object type definitions being returned. If the **Collect** function fails for any reason, it should set **lpcObjectTypes* to zero.

If the requested data specified by *lpwszValue* does not correspond to any of the object indexes or foreign computers supported by your program, leave **lppData* unchanged, and set **lpcbBytes* and **lpcObjectTypes* both to zero. This indicates that no data is returned.

For foreign computer interfaces, the opening of a channel to the foreign computer must be done in the Collect function because the computer name is not provided to the Open function. The performance DLL should save a handle to the foreign computer to avoid reconnecting on each data collection call.

The Collect function must return one of the values shown in the following table.

Table 13.6   Collect Function Return Values and Descriptions

Return value	Description
ERROR_MORE_DATA	Indicates that the size of the *lppData* buffer as specified by **lpcbBytes* is not large enough to store the data to be returned. In this case, leave **lppData* unchanged, and set **lpcbBytes* and **lpcObjectTypes* to zero. No attempt is made to indicate the required buffer size, because this may change before the next call.
ERROR_SUCCESS	Return this value in all other cases, even if no data is returned or an error occurs. To report errors other than insufficient buffer size, use the system event log, but do not flood the event log with errors on every data collection operation.

The Close Function

The Registry controller calls each application's Close function when a performance monitor application calls the RegCloseKey function to close the HKEY_PERFORMANCE_DATA handle. This function performs any cleanup operations required by the application's performance data collection mechanism. For example, the function could close device handles opened by CreateFile, or close a handle to a file mapping object. Use the PM_CLOSE_PROC function prototype defined in WINPERF.H:

```
PM_CLOSE_PROC ClosePerformanceData;
DWORD ClosePerformanceData();
```

The function should return ERROR_SUCCESS.

Error Handling in the DLL

Use event logging to record errors that occur during any of the functions in the performance DLL. Logging error events aids in troubleshooting applications providing performance data during development and after installation. Be careful not to log error events on every Collect call, however, because data collection can be frequent. For information about using event logging in the performance DLL or in a user-mode application, refer to the Windows NT SDK documentation. For information about using event logging in a kernel-mode application, refer to the Windows NT Device Driver Kit documentation.

Measuring Foreign Computers

If you are providing an extended object that is returning data from a non-Windows NT computer (as shown in Figure 13.2), there are a few additional considerations.

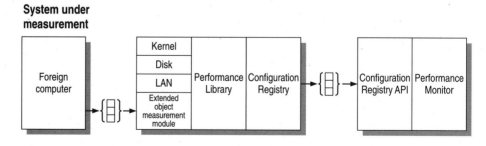

Figure 13.2 Collecting performance data from a non-Windows NT computer

Unlike other applications with extended object types, you will not know at Open time what computers you have been asked to monitor. This will only become known to you at Collection time when you extract the name of the computer following the keyword "Foreign" in the *lpwszValue* parameter. After you extract the computer name, you should look up in a table whether you have opened communication with that computer. Please do not reconnect to the computer on every data collection, or you will render Performance Monitor's speed glacial. If you have never connected with that computer and you need to before you request data, connect, and then store the computer's "handle" or id in your own system lookup table. Next time data is requested you'll find its handle in the table and shoot off the request for data straight away.

Once you get the data, you will have to construct a PERF_DATA_BLOCK as the first thing in *lppData. This is because you are the computer returning data in this case, and you must provide the required information such as the time at the system you are measuring, and so on. If the system you are measuring is not courteous enough to give it to you, you can fake this stuff out any way you like. You should use values from the local system for time and counter frequency if they are not provided remotely. You may need to use the PERF_OBJECT_TYPE.PerfTime and .PerfFreq for some counters as well. Do this if they use a different time base and if the remote system time is unknown so that you have to use the local times in the PERF_DATA_BLOCK. This may take a bit of thought, but usually something can be worked out. Hey, that's why they pay you the big bucks!

The remainder of your response to the Collect function is just like that for other applications. You may return multiple objects, of course.

There is nothing that exploits the real power of Windows NT Performance Monitor more than retrieving and displaying statistics from foreign computers. Your work will be richly rewarded. Well, we can hope.

Installing Your Application

If you want system administrators to be able to collect performance data from your finished application, you must use your application's SETUP.INF file. The script in this file can perform the following tasks:

- Create keys and values in the Registry. Use this to create the application's Performance key and the Library, Open, Collect, and Close values under this key.
- Copy the application's performance DLL file into the *NT_root* directory.
- Run the **lodctr** utility to install the application's counters and counter objects in the PerfLib node.

For more information about writing a SETUP.INF script, see the Windows NT Device Driver Kit documentation.

Sample Code

There are two parts to the instrumentation of an application. First, you need to count the activity the application wants to track. Then you need to provide the measurement DLL which will collect the data for the performance monitor.

In this sample we will place a couple of counters in the VGA driver. This is a pretty simple case, with one counter that counts BitBlts, and another for counting TextOut calls. So we can focus on the instrumentation and ignore lots of application issues.

The source for the VGA driver is included in the Windows NT DDK, and the following sample code is also provided there. So if you want, this code can be a starting place for your own instrumentation efforts.

Instrumenting the VGA Driver

In the VGA driver source module ENABLE.C we allocate the data segment into which the counters will be placed, and from which the VGACTRS.DLL will read the counters.

First, add the following #include to ENABLE.C:

```
#include "winperf.h"        // for Performance API structure definitions
```

Now add the following global variables to ENABLE.C:

```
HMODULE ghmodDrv = (HMODULE) 0;
PPERF_COUNTER_BLOCK  pCounterBlock;  // data structure for counter values
```

Now add the following .DLL initialization routine to ENABLE.C:

```
/*********************************************************************\
* BOOL bInitProc(HMODULE hmod)
*
* DLL initialization procedure.  Save the module handle and exit.
*
*    This routine creates a named mapped memory section that is used
*    to communicate the driver's performance data to the extensible counter
*    DLL. This method will only work with "user" mode driver DLL's.
*    Kernel or privileged drivers need to provide an IOCTL interface that
*    will communicate the performance data to the extensible counter DLL.
*
\*********************************************************************/

BOOL bInitProc(HMODULE hmod, ULONG Reason, LPVOID Reserved)
{
    HANDLE hMappedObject;
    TCHAR  szMappedObjectName[] = TEXT("VGA_COUNTER_BLOCK");

    if (Reason == DLL_PROCESS_ATTACH) {
    //
    //  create named section for the performance data
    //
    hMappedObject = CreateFileMapping((HANDLE)0xFFFFFFFF,
                    NULL,
                    PAGE_READWRITE,
                    0,
                    4096,
                    szMappedObjectName);
        if (hMappedObject == NULL) {
            // Should put out an EventLog error message here
            DISPDBG((0, "VGA: Could not Create Mapped Object for Counters %x",
                GetLastError()));
            pCounterBlock = NULL;
            } else {
            // Mapped object created okay
            //
            // map the section and assign the counter block pointer
            // to this section of memory
            //
            pCounterBlock = (PPERF_COUNTER_BLOCK)
                    MapViewOfFile(hMappedObject,
                            FILE_MAP_ALL_ACCESS,
                            0,
                            0,
                            0);
            if (pCounterBlock == NULL) {
                // Failed to Map View of file
                DISPDBG((0, "VGA: Failed to Map View of File %x",
                    GetLastError()));
```

```
            }
        }

    ghmodDrv = hmod;
    }

    return(TRUE);

    Reserved=Reserved;
}
```

To the BITBLT.C module, add the following #include:

```
#include <winperf.h>      // include performance API definitions
```

Add the following external declaration to BITBLT.C:

```
// Global counter block for performance data
extern PPERF_COUNTER_BLOCK pCounterBlock;
```

In the DrvBitBlt routine in BITBLT.C, add the following declaration:

```
    PDWORD    pdwCounter;     // Pointer to counter to increment
```

Add the following code as the first thing the DrvBitBlt routine does:

```
// Increment BitBlt counter
    pdwCounter = (PDWORD) pCounterBlock;
    (*pdwCounter)++;
```

To the TEXTOUT.C csource module, add the following #include:

```
#include "winperf.h"              // performance API definitions
```

Add the external declaration to TEXTOUT.C:

```
// definition of counter data area for performance counters
extern PPERF_COUNTER_BLOCK pCounterBlock;
```

Add the following as the last declaration and first code to execute in the DrvTextOut routine in TEXTOUT.C:

```
  PDWORD  pdwCounter;                        // Pointer to counter to increment

// Increment TextOut counter
  pdwCounter = ( (PDWORD) pCounterBlock  ) + 1;
  (*pdwCounter)++;
```

That's all there is to it. The VGA driver is now instrumented for its two most important calls. These account for about 80% for display driver activity in the general case. So to heck with the other operations!

Data Collection DLL

The data collection DLL, called VGACTRS.DLL, is included here in the next few sections. First, lets start with the input to the **lodctr** utility.

The first file we need is the one giving offsets to the counters, called here VGACTRNM.H:

```
//
//  vgactrnm.h
//
//  Offset definition file for extensible counter objects and counters
//
//  These "relative" offsets must start at 0 and be multiples of 2 (i.e.
//  even numbers). In the Open Procedure, they will be added to the
//  "First Counter" and "First Help" values for the device they belong to,
//  in order to determine the absolute location of the counter and
//  object names and corresponding Explain text in the registry.
//
//  This file is used by the extensible counter DLL code as well as the
//  counter name and Explain text definition file (.INI) file that is used
//  by LODCTR to load the names into the registry.
//
#define VGAOBJ 0
#define BITBLTS 2
#define TEXTOUTS 4
```

Next we have the file defining the object name and the counter names, and the Explain text. Each Explain text line must actually be one (possibly long) line of text.

```
[info]
drivername=VGA
symbolfile=vgactrnm.h

[languages]
009=English

[text]
VGAOBJ_009_NAME=VGA
VGAOBJ_009_HELP=The VGA Object Type handles the VGA device on your system.
BITBLTS_009_NAME=BitBlts/sec
BITBLTS_009_HELP=BitBlts/sec is the rate your system is sending blocks of pixels to the
display.
TEXTOUTS_009_NAME=TextOuts/sec
TEXTOUTS_009_HELP=TextOuts/sec is the rate your system is sending lines of text to the
display.
```

The next file defines the data structures that will be returned to the performance monitor.

```
/*++ BUILD Version: 0001     // Increment this if a change has global effects

Copyright (c) 1992 Microsoft Corporation

Module Name:

    datavga.h

Abstract:

    Header file for the VGA Extensible Object data definitions

    This file contains definitions to construct the dynamic data
    which is returned by the Configuration Registry.  Data from
    various driver API calls is placed into the structures shown
    here.

--*/

#ifndef _DATAVGA_H_
#define _DATAVGA_H_

//
//  The routines that load these structures assume that all fields
//  are packed and aligned on DWORD boundaries. Alpha support may
//  change this assumption so the pack pragma is used here to insure
//  the DWORD packing assumption remains valid.
//
#pragma pack (4)

//
//  Extensible Object definitions
//

//  Update the following sort of define when adding an object type.

#define VGA_NUM_PERF_OBJECT_TYPES 1

//-----------------------------------------------------------------

//
//  VGA Resource object type counter definitions.
//
//  These are used in the counter definitions to describe the relative
//  position of each counter in the returned data.
//
```

```
#define NUM_BITBLTS_OFFSET      sizeof(DWORD)
#define NUM_TEXTOUTS_OFFSET     NUM_BITBLTS_OFFSET + sizeof(DWORD)
#define SIZE_OF_VGA_PERFORMANCE_DATA \
                NUM_TEXTOUTS_OFFSET + sizeof(DWORD)


//
//  This is the counter structure presently returned by VGA.
//

typedef struct _VGA_DATA_DEFINITION {
    PERF_OBJECT_TYPE        VgaObjectType;
    PERF_COUNTER_DEFINITION NumBitBlts;
    PERF_COUNTER_DEFINITION NumTextOuts;
} VGA_DATA_DEFINITION;

#pragma pack ()

#endif //_DATAVGA_H_
```

In the next file we have the initialization of the object and counter definition structures with constant data. To understand this file, you will have to dust off your copy of the WINPERF.H header file where the structures are defined.

```
/*++ BUILD Version: 0001     // Increment this if a change has global effects

Copyright (c) 1992  Microsoft Corporation

Module Name:

    datavga.c

Abstract:

    A file containing the constant data structures used by the Performance
    Monitor data for the VGA Extensible Objects.

    This file contains a set of constant data structures which are
    currently defined for the VGA Extensible Objects.  This is an
    example of how other such objects could be defined.

Revision History:

    None.

--*/
//
//  Include Files
//

#include <windows.h>
#include <winperf.h>
#include "vgactrnm.h"
#include "datavga.h"

//
//  Constant structure initializations
//      defined in datavga.h
//

VGA_DATA_DEFINITION VgaDataDefinition = {

    {   sizeof(VGA_DATA_DEFINITION) ı SIZE_OF_VGA_PERFORMANCE_DATA,
        sizeof(VGA_DATA_DEFINITION),
        sizeof(PERF_OBJECT_TYPE),
        VGAOBJ,
        0,
        VGAOBJ,
        0,
        PERF_DETAIL_NOVICE,
        (sizeof(VGA_DATA_DEFINITION)-sizeof(PERF_OBJECT_TYPE))/
            sizeof(PERF_COUNTER_DEFINITION),
```

```
0,
0,
0
},
{    sizeof(PERF_COUNTER_DEFINITION),
BITBLTS,
0,
BITBLTS,
0,
0,
PERF_DETAIL_NOVICE,
PERF_COUNTER_COUNTER,
    sizeof(DWORD),
NUM_BITBLTS_OFFSET
},
{    sizeof(PERF_COUNTER_DEFINITION),
TEXTOUTS,
0,
TEXTOUTS,
0,
0,
PERF_DETAIL_NOVICE,
PERF_COUNTER_COUNTER,
    sizeof(DWORD),
NUM_TEXTOUTS_OFFSET
}
};
```

In the next file, PERFUTIL.H, are some useful declarations we have found handy for performance data collection DLLs:

```
/*++ BUILD Version: 0001     // Increment this if a change has global effects

Copyright (c) 1992 Microsoft Corporation

Module Name:

    perfutil.h

Abstract:

    This file supports routines used to parse and create Performance Monitor Data
    Structures. It actually supports Performance Object types with multiple instances

Revision History:

--*/
#ifndef _PERFUTIL_H_
#define _PERFUTIL_H_

// enable this define to log process heap data to the event log
#ifdef PROBE_HEAP_USAGE
#undef PROBE_HEAP_USAGE
#endif
//
// Utility macro.  This is used to reserve a DWORD multiple of bytes for Unicode strings
// embedded in the definitional data, viz., object instance names.
//
#define DWORD_MULTIPLE(x) (((x+sizeof(DWORD)-1)/sizeof(DWORD))*sizeof(DWORD))

//    (assumes dword is 4 bytes long and pointer is a dword in size)
#define ALIGN_ON_DWORD(x) ((VOID *)( ((DWORD) x & 0x00000003) ? ( ((DWORD) x & 0xFFFFFFFC)
+ 4 ) : ( (DWORD) x ) ))

extern WCHAR   GLOBAL_STRING[];     // Global command (get all local ctrs)
extern WCHAR   FOREIGN_STRING[];         // get data from foreign computers
extern WCHAR   COSTLY_STRING[];
extern WCHAR   NULL_STRING[];

#define QUERY_GLOBAL    1
#define QUERY_ITEMS     2
#define QUERY_FOREIGN   3
#define QUERY_COSTLY    4

//
// The definition of the only routine of perfutil.c, It builds part of a performance data
// instance (PERF_INSTANCE_DEFINITION) as described in winperf.h
//
```

```
HANDLE MonOpenEventLog ();
VOID MonCloseEventLog ();
DWORD GetQueryType (IN LPWSTR);
BOOL IsNumberInUnicodeList (DWORD, LPWSTR);

typedef struct _LOCAL_HEAP_INFO_BLOCK {
    DWORD    AllocatedEntries;
    DWORD    AllocatedBytes;
    DWORD    FreeEntries;
    DWORD    FreeBytes;
} LOCAL_HEAP_INFO, *PLOCAL_HEAP_INFO;


//
//  Memory Probe macro
//
#ifdef PROBE_HEAP_USAGE

#define HEAP_PROBE()    { \
    DWORD    dwHeapStatus[5]; \
    NTSTATUS CallStatus; \
    dwHeapStatus[4] = __LINE__; \
    if (!(CallStatus = memprobe (dwHeapStatus, 16L, NULL))) { \
        REPORT_INFORMATION_DATA (VGA_HEAP_STATUS, LOG_DEBUG,    \
            &dwHeapStatus, sizeof(dwHeapStatus));  \
    } else {  \
        REPORT_ERROR_DATA (VGA_HEAP_STATUS_ERROR, LOG_DEBUG, \
            &CallStatus, sizeof (DWORD)); \
    } \
}

#else

#define HEAP_PROBE()    ;

#endif

#endif  //_PERFUTIL_H_
```

Similarly, the next file holds functions generally useful to performance data collection DLLs. These handle two routine chores: handling of the Event Log, and parsing of the Unicode Value string which tells your DLL what objects are being collected by the performance monitor. We wanted to be sure to include it, just for you.

```
/*++ BUILD Version: 0001     // Increment this if a change has global effects

Copyright (c) 1992  Microsoft Corporation

Module Name:

    perfutil.c

Abstract:

    This file implements the utility routines used to construct the
     common parts of a PERF_INSTANCE_DEFINITION (see winperf.h) and
    perform event logging functions.


Revision History:

--*/
//
//  include files
//
#include <windows.h>
#include <string.h>
#include <winperf.h>
#include "vgactrs.h"      // error message definition
#include "perfmsg.h"
#include "perfutil.h"

#define INITIAL_SIZE     1024L
#define EXTEND_SIZE      1024L

//
// Global data definitions.
//

ULONG                ulInfoBufferSize = 0;

HANDLE hEventLog = NULL;        // event log handle for reporting events
                                // initialized in Open... routines
DWORD   dwLogUsers = 0;         // count of functions using event log

DWORD MESSAGE_LEVEL = 0;

WCHAR GLOBAL_STRING[] = L"Global";
WCHAR FOREIGN_STRING[] = L"Foreign";
WCHAR COSTLY_STRING[] = L"Costly";

WCHAR NULL_STRING[] = L"\0";     // pointer to null string
```

```
// test for delimiter, end of line and non-digit characters
// used by IsNumberInUnicodeList routine
//
#define DIGIT        1
#define DELIMITER    2
#define INVALID      3

#define EvalThisChar(c,d) ( \
     (c == d) ? DELIMITER : \
     (c == 0) ? DELIMITER : \
     (c < (WCHAR)'0') ? INVALID : \
     (c > (WCHAR)'9') ? INVALID : \
     DIGIT)


HANDLE
MonOpenEventLog (
)
/*++

Routine Description:

    Reads the level of event logging from the registry and opens the
        channel to the event logger for subsequent event log entries.

Arguments:

        None

Return Value:

    Handle to the event log for reporting events.
    NULL if open not successful.

--*/
{
    HKEY hAppKey;
    TCHAR LogLevelKeyName[] = "SOFTWARE\\Microsoft\\Windows NT\\CurrentVersion\\Perflib";
    TCHAR LogLevelValueName[] = "EventLogLevel";

    LONG lStatus;

    DWORD dwLogLevel;
    DWORD dwValueType;
    DWORD dwValueSize;

    // if global value of the logging level not initialized or is disabled,
    //  check the registry to see if it should be updated.

    if (!MESSAGE_LEVEL) {
```

```
        lStatus = RegOpenKeyEx (HKEY_LOCAL_MACHINE,
                                LogLevelKeyName,
                                0,
                                KEY_READ,
                                &hAppKey);

    dwValueSize = sizeof (dwLogLevel);

    if (lStatus == ERROR_SUCCESS) {
        lStatus = RegQueryValueEx (hAppKey,
                                   LogLevelValueName,
                                   (LPDWORD)NULL,
                                   &dwValueType,
                                   (LPBYTE)&dwLogLevel,
                                   &dwValueSize);

        if (lStatus == ERROR_SUCCESS) {
           MESSAGE_LEVEL = dwLogLevel;
        } else {
           MESSAGE_LEVEL = MESSAGE_LEVEL_DEFAULT;
        }
        RegCloseKey (hAppKey);
    } else {
      MESSAGE_LEVEL = MESSAGE_LEVEL_DEFAULT;
    }
}

if (hEventLog == NULL){
    hEventLog = RegisterEventSource (
        (LPTSTR)NULL,              // Use Local Machine
        APP_NAME);                // event log app name to find in registry

    if (hEventLog != NULL) {
        REPORT_INFORMATION (UTIL_LOG_OPEN, LOG_DEBUG);
    }
}

if (hEventLog != NULL) {
    dwLogUsers++;              // increment count of perfctr log users
}
return (hEventLog);
}
```

```
VOID
MonCloseEventLog (
)
/*++

Routine Description:

    Closes the handle to the event logger if this is the last caller

Arguments:

    None

Return Value:

    None

--*/
{
    if (hEventLog != NULL) {
        dwLogUsers--;            // decrement usage
        if (dwLogUsers <= 0) {     // and if we're the last, then close up log
            REPORT_INFORMATION (UTIL_CLOSING_LOG, LOG_DEBUG);
            DeregisterEventSource (hEventLog);
        }
    }
}
```

```
DWORD
GetQueryType (
    IN LPWSTR lpValue
)
/*++

GetQueryType

    returns the type of query described in the lpValue string so that
    the appropriate processing method may be used

Arguments

    IN lpValue
        string passed to PerfRegQuery Value for processing

Return Value

    QUERY_GLOBAL
        if lpValue == 0 (null pointer)
            lpValue == pointer to Null string
            lpValue == pointer to "Global" string

    QUERY_FOREIGN
        if lpValue == pointer to "Foreign" string

    QUERY_COSTLY
        if lpValue == pointer to "Costly" string

    otherwise:

    QUERY_ITEMS

--*/
{
    WCHAR    *pwcArgChar, *pwcTypeChar;
    BOOL     bFound;

    if (lpValue == 0) {
        return QUERY_GLOBAL;
    } else if (*lpValue == 0) {
        return QUERY_GLOBAL;
    }

    // check for "Global" request

    pwcArgChar = lpValue;
    pwcTypeChar = GLOBAL_STRING;
    bFound = TRUE;  // assume found until contradicted
```

```
// check to the length of the shortest string

while ((*pwcArgChar != 0) && (*pwcTypeChar != 0)) {
    if (*pwcArgChar++ != *pwcTypeChar++) {
        bFound = FALSE; // no match
        break;          // bail out now
    }
}

if (bFound) return QUERY_GLOBAL;

// check for "Foreign" request

pwcArgChar = lpValue;
pwcTypeChar = FOREIGN_STRING;
bFound = TRUE;  // assume found until contradicted

// check to the length of the shortest string

while ((*pwcArgChar != 0) && (*pwcTypeChar != 0)) {
    if (*pwcArgChar++ != *pwcTypeChar++) {
        bFound = FALSE; // no match
        break;          // bail out now
    }
}

if (bFound) return QUERY_FOREIGN;

// check for "Costly" request

pwcArgChar = lpValue;
pwcTypeChar = COSTLY_STRING;
bFound = TRUE;  // assume found until contradicted

// check to the length of the shortest string

while ((*pwcArgChar != 0) && (*pwcTypeChar != 0)) {
    if (*pwcArgChar++ != *pwcTypeChar++) {
        bFound = FALSE; // no match
        break;          // bail out now
    }
}

if (bFound) return QUERY_COSTLY;

// if not Global and not Foreign and not Costly,
// then it must be an item list

return QUERY_ITEMS;
```

```
}

BOOL
IsNumberInUnicodeList (
    IN DWORD   dwNumber,
    IN LPWSTR  lpwszUnicodeList
)
/*++

IsNumberInUnicodeList

Arguments:

    IN dwNumber
        DWORD number to find in list

    IN lpwszUnicodeList
        Null terminated, Space delimited list of decimal numbers

Return Value:

    TRUE:
            dwNumber was found in the list of unicode number strings

    FALSE:
            dwNumber was not found in the list.

--*/
{
    DWORD   dwThisNumber;
    WCHAR   *pwcThisChar;
    BOOL    bValidNumber;
    BOOL    bNewItem;
    BOOL    bReturnValue;
    WCHAR   wcDelimiter;    // could be an argument to be more flexible

    if (lpwszUnicodeList == 0) return FALSE;    // null pointer, # not found

    pwcThisChar = lpwszUnicodeList;
    dwThisNumber = 0;
    wcDelimiter = (WCHAR)' ';
    bValidNumber = FALSE;
    bNewItem = TRUE;
```

```
    while (TRUE) {
        switch (EvalThisChar (*pwcThisChar, wcDelimiter)) {
            case DIGIT:
                // if this is the first digit after a delimiter, then
                // set flags to start computing the new number
                if (bNewItem) {
                    bNewItem = FALSE;
                    bValidNumber = TRUE;
                }
                if (bValidNumber) {
                    dwThisNumber *= 10;
                    dwThisNumber += (*pwcThisChar - (WCHAR)'0');
                }
                break;

            case DELIMITER:
                // a delimiter is either the delimiter character or the
              , // end of the string ('\0') if when the delimiter has been
                // reached a valid number was found, then compare it to the
                // number from the argument list. if this is the end of the
                // string and no match was found, then return.
                //
                if (bValidNumber) {
                    if (dwThisNumber == dwNumber) return TRUE;
                    bValidNumber = FALSE;
                }
                if (*pwcThisChar == 0) {
                    return FALSE;
                } else {
                    bNewItem = TRUE;
                    dwThisNumber = 0;
                }
                break;

            case INVALID:
                // if an invalid character was encountered, ignore all
                // characters up to the next delimiter and then start fresh.
                // the invalid number is not compared.
                bValidNumber = FALSE;
                break;

            default:
                break;

        }
        pwcThisChar++;
    }

}   // IsNumberInUnicodeList
```

The next file is the one that has all the active code for opening data collection, collecting data, and closing the DLL. We had to get here eventually. We call the heart of the matter PERFVGA.C. Creative, huh?

```
/*++ BUILD Version: 0001     // Increment this if a change has global effects

Copyright (c) 1992  Microsoft Corporation

Module Name:

    perfvga.c

Abstract:

    This file implements the Extensible Objects for the Vga object type

Revision History


--*/

//
//   Include Files
//

#include <windows.h>
#include <string.h>
#include <wcstr.h>
#include <winperf.h>
#include "vgactrs.h" // error message definition
#include "perfmsg.h"
#include "perfutil.h"
#include "datavga.h"

//
//   References to constants which initialize the Object type definitions
//

extern VGA_DATA_DEFINITION VgaDataDefinition;

DWORD    dwOpenCount = 0;       // count of "Open" threads
BOOL     bInitOK = FALSE;       // true = DLL initialized OK

//
// Vga data structures
//

HANDLE hVgaSharedMemory;            // Handle of Vga Shared Memory
PPERF_COUNTER_BLOCK pCounterBlock;
```

```
//
//   Function Prototypes
//
//        these are used to insure that the data collection functions
//        accessed by Perflib will have the correct calling format.
//

PM_OPEN_PROC    OpenVgaPerformanceData;
PM_COLLECT_PROC    CollectVgaPerformanceData;
PM_CLOSE_PROC   CloseVgaPerformanceData;

DWORD
OpenVgaPerformanceData(
    LPWSTR lpDeviceNames
    )

/*++

Routine Description:

    This routine will open and map the memory used by the VGA driver to
    pass performance data in. This routine also initializes the data
    structures used to pass data back to the registry

Arguments:

    Pointer to object ID of each device to be opened (VGA)


Return Value:

    None.

--*/

{
    LONG status;
    TCHAR szMappedObject[] = TEXT("VGA_COUNTER_BLOCK");
    HKEY hKeyDriverPerf;
    DWORD size;
    DWORD type;
    DWORD dwFirstCounter;
    DWORD dwFirstHelp;
```

```
//
//   Since SCREG is multi-threaded and will call this routine in
//   order to service remote performance queries, this library
//   must keep track of how many times it has been opened (i.e.
//   how many threads have accessed it). the registry routines will
//   limit access to the initialization routine to only one thread
//   at a time so synchronization (i.e. reentrancy) should not be
//   a problem
//

if (!dwOpenCount) {
    // open Eventlog interface

    hEventLog = MonOpenEventLog();

    // open shared memory used by device driver to pass performance values

    hVgaSharedMemory = OpenFileMapping(FILE_MAP_READ,
                    FALSE,
                    szMappedObject);
    pCounterBlock = NULL;   // initialize pointer to memory

    // log error if unsuccessful

    if (hVgaSharedMemory == NULL) {
        REPORT_ERROR (VGAPERF_OPEN_FILE_MAPPING_ERROR, LOG_USER);
        // this is fatal, if we can't get data then there's no
        // point in continuing.
        status = GetLastError(); // return error
        goto OpenExitPoint;
    } else {
        // if opened ok, then map pointer to memory
        pCounterBlock = (PPERF_COUNTER_BLOCK)
                MapViewOfFile(hVgaSharedMemory,
                    FILE_MAP_READ,
                    0,
                    0,
                    0);
        if (pCounterBlock == NULL) {
            REPORT_ERROR (VGAPERF_UNABLE_MAP_VIEW_OF_FILE, LOG_USER);
            // this is fatal, if we can't get data then there's no
            // point in continuing.
            status = GetLastError(); // return error
        }
    }
}
```

```
// get counter and help index base values from registry
//      Open key to registry entry
//      read First Counter and First Help values
//      update static data structures by adding base to
//          offset value in structure.

status = RegOpenKeyEx (
    HKEY_LOCAL_MACHINE,
    "SYSTEM\\CurrentControlSet\\Services\\Vga\\Performance",
    0L,
    KEY_ALL_ACCESS,
    &hKeyDriverPerf);

if (status != ERROR_SUCCESS) {
    REPORT_ERROR_DATA (VGAPERF_UNABLE_OPEN_DRIVER_KEY, LOG_USER,
        &status, sizeof(status));
    // this is fatal, if we can't get the base values of the
    // counter or help names, then the names won't be available
    // to the requesting application  so there's not much
    // point in continuing.
    goto OpenExitPoint;
}


size = sizeof (DWORD);
status = RegQueryValueEx(
        hKeyDriverPerf,
        "First Counter",
        0L,
        &type,
        (LPBYTE)&dwFirstCounter,
        &size);

if (status != ERROR_SUCCESS) {
    REPORT_ERROR_DATA (VGAPERF_UNABLE_READ_FIRST_COUNTER, LOG_USER,
        &status, sizeof(status));
    // this is fatal, if we can't get the base values of the
    // counter or help names, then the names won't be available
    // to the requesting application  so there's not much
    // point in continuing.
    goto OpenExitPoint;
}

size = sizeof (DWORD);
status = RegQueryValueEx(
        hKeyDriverPerf,
        "First Help",
        0L,
        &type,
        (LPBYTE)&dwFirstHelp,
    &size);
```

```
    if (status != ERROR_SUCCESS) {
        REPORT_ERROR_DATA (VGAPERF_UNABLE_READ_FIRST_HELP, LOG_USER,
            &status, sizeof(status));
        // this is fatal, if we can't get the base values of the
        // counter or help names, then the names won't be available
        // to the requesting application  so there's not much
        // point in continuing.
        goto OpenExitPoint;
    }


    //
    //  NOTE: the initialization program could also retrieve
    //        LastCounter and LastHelp if they wanted to do
    //        bounds checking on the new number. e.g.
    //
    //        counter->CounterNameTitleIndex += dwFirstCounter;
    //        if (counter->CounterNameTitleIndex > dwLastCounter) {
    //            LogErrorToEventLog (INDEX_OUT_OF_BOUNDS);
    //        }

    VgaDataDefinition.VgaObjectType.ObjectNameTitleIndex += dwFirstCounter;
    VgaDataDefinition.VgaObjectType.ObjectHelpTitleIndex += dwFirstHelp;

    VgaDataDefinition.NumBitBlts.CounterNameTitleIndex += dwFirstCounter;
    VgaDataDefinition.NumBitBlts.CounterHelpTitleIndex += dwFirstHelp;

    VgaDataDefinition.NumTextOuts.CounterNameTitleIndex += dwFirstCounter;
    VgaDataDefinition.NumTextOuts.CounterHelpTitleIndex += dwFirstHelp;

    RegCloseKey (hKeyDriverPerf); // close key to registry

    bInitOK = TRUE; // ok to use this function
    }

    dwOpenCount++;  // increment OPEN counter

    status = ERROR_SUCCESS; // for successful exit

OpenExitPoint:

    return status;
}
```

```
DWORD
CollectVgaPerformanceData(
    IN      LPWSTR  lpValueName,
    IN OUT  LPVOID  *lppData,
    IN OUT  LPDWORD lpcbTotalBytes,
    IN OUT  LPDWORD lpNumObjectTypes
)
/*++
```

Routine Description:

    This routine will return the data for the VGA counters.

Arguments:

    IN   LPWSTR   lpValueName
            pointer to a wide character string passed by registry.

    IN OUT LPVOID   *lppData
            IN: pointer to the address of the buffer to receive the completed
            PerfDataBlock and subordinate structures. This routine will
            append its data to the buffer starting at the point referenced
            by *lppData.
            OUT: points to the first byte after the data structure added by this
            routine. This routine updated the value at lppdata after appending
            its data.

    IN OUT LPDWORD lpcbTotalBytes
            IN: the address of the DWORD that tells the size in bytes of the
            buffer referenced by the lppData argument
            OUT: the number of bytes added by this routine is written to the
            DWORD pointed to by this argument

    IN OUT LPDWORD NumObjectTypes
            IN: the address of the DWORD to receive the number of objects added
            by this routine
            OUT: the number of objects added by this routine is written to the
            DWORD pointed to by this argument

Return Value:

        ERROR_MORE_DATA if buffer passed is too small to hold data
            any error conditions encountered are reported to the event log if
            event logging is enabled.

        ERROR_SUCCESS if success or any other error. Errors, however are
            also reported to the event log.
```
```

```
--*/
{
    //   Variables for reformatting the data

    ULONG SpaceNeeded;
    PDWORD pdwCounter;
    PERF_COUNTER_BLOCK *pPerfCounterBlock;
    VGA_DATA_DEFINITION *pVgaDataDefinition;

    //   Variables for collecting data about Vga Resouces

    LPWSTR                          lpFromString;
    LPWSTR                          lpToString;
    INT                             iStringLength;

    //   variables used for error logging

    DWORD                           dwDataReturn[2];
    DWORD                           dwQueryType;

    //
    // before doing anything else, see if Open went OK
    //
    if (!bInitOK) {
        // unable to continue because open failed.
        *lpcbTotalBytes = (DWORD) 0;
        *lpNumObjectTypes = (DWORD) 0;
        return ERROR_SUCCESS; // yes, this is a successful exit
    }

    // see if this is a foreign (i.e. non-NT) computer data request
    //
    dwQueryType = GetQueryType (lpValueName);

    if (dwQueryType == QUERY_FOREIGN) {
        // this routine does not service requests for data from
        // Non-NT computers
        *lpcbTotalBytes = (DWORD) 0;
        *lpNumObjectTypes = (DWORD) 0;
        return ERROR_SUCCESS;
    }
```

```
    if (dwQueryType == QUERY_ITEMS){
    if ( !(IsNumberInUnicodeList (VgaDataDefinition.VgaObjectType.ObjectNameTitleIndex,
lpValueName))) {

        // request received for data object not provided by this routine
        *lpcbTotalBytes = (DWORD) 0;
        *lpNumObjectTypes = (DWORD) 0;
        return ERROR_SUCCESS;
    }
}

pVgaDataDefinition = (VGA_DATA_DEFINITION *) *lppData;

SpaceNeeded = sizeof(VGA_DATA_DEFINITION) +
    SIZE_OF_VGA_PERFORMANCE_DATA;

if ( *lpcbTotalBytes < SpaceNeeded ) {
    *lpcbTotalBytes = (DWORD) 0;
    *lpNumObjectTypes = (DWORD) 0;
    return ERROR_MORE_DATA;
}

//
// Copy the (constant, initialized) Object Type and counter definitions
//  to the caller's data buffer
//

memmove(pVgaDataDefinition,
    &VgaDataDefinition,
    sizeof(VGA_DATA_DEFINITION));

//
//  Format and collect VGA data from shared memory
//

pPerfCounterBlock = (PERF_COUNTER_BLOCK *) &pVgaDataDefinition[1];

pPerfCounterBlock->ByteLength = SIZE_OF_VGA_PERFORMANCE_DATA;

pdwCounter = (PDWORD) (&pPerfCounterBlock[1]);

*pdwCounter = *((PDWORD) pCounterBlock);
*++pdwCounter = ((PDWORD) pCounterBlock)[1];

*lppData = (PVOID) ++pdwCounter;

// update arguments fore return

*lpNumObjectTypes = 1;
```

```
    *lpcbTotalBytes = (PBYTE) pdwCounter - (PBYTE) pVgaDataDefinition;

    return ERROR_SUCCESS;
}


DWORD
CloseVgaPerformanceData(
)

/*++

Routine Description:

    This routine closes the open handles to VGA device performance counters

Arguments:

    None.


Return Value:

    ERROR_SUCCESS

--*/

{
    if (!(--dwOpenCount)) { // when this is the last thread...

        CloseHandle(hVgaSharedMemory);

        pCounterBlock = NULL;

        MonCloseEventLog();
    }

    return ERROR_SUCCESS;

}
```

The next two counters handle declarations for the messages used in the Event Log.

```
/*++ BUILD Version: 0001     // Increment this if a change has global effects

Copyright (c) 1992 Microsoft Corporation

Module Name:

    perfmsg.h

Abstract:

    This file provides the macros and definitions used by the extensible
    counters for reporting events to the event logging facility


Revision History:


--*/
#ifndef _PERFMSG_H_
#define _PERFMSG_H_
//
// Report error message ID's for Counters
//

#define APP_NAME  "vgactrs"

//
// The constant below defines how many (if any) messages will be reported
// to the event logger. As the number goes up in value more and more events
// will be reported. The purpose of this is to allow lots of messages during
// development and debugging (e.g. a message level of 3) to a minimum of
// messages (e.g. operational messages with a level of 1) or no messages if
// message logging inflicts too much of a performance penalty. Right now
// this is a compile time constant, but could later become a registry entry.
//
//     Levels:  LOG_NONE = No event log messages ever
//              LOG_USER = User event log messages (e.g. errors)
//              LOG_DEBUG = Minimum Debugging
//              LOG_VERBOSE = Maximum Debugging
//

#define  LOG_NONE     0
#define  LOG_USER     1
#define  LOG_DEBUG    2
#define  LOG_VERBOSE  3

#define  MESSAGE_LEVEL_DEFAULT  LOG_USER

// define macros
```

```
//
// Format for event log calls without corresponding insertion strings is:
//    REPORT_xxx (message_value, message_level)
//       where:
//          xxx is the severity to be displayed in the event log
//          message_value is the numeric ID from above
//          message_level is the "filtering" level of error reporting
//              using the error levels above.
//
// if the message has a corresponding insertion string whose symbol conforms
// to the format CONSTANT = numeric value and CONSTANT_S = string constant for
// that message, then the
//
//    REPORT_xxx_STRING (message_value, message_level)
//
// macro may be used.
//


//
// REPORT_SUCCESS was intended to show Success in the error log, rather it
// shows "N/A" so for now it's the same as information, though it could
// (should) be changed  in the future
//


#define REPORT_SUCCESS(i,l) (MESSAGE_LEVEL >= l ? ReportEvent (hEventLog,
EVENTLOG_INFORMATION_TYPE, \
   0, i, (PSID)NULL, 0, 0, NULL, (PVOID)NULL) : FALSE)

#define REPORT_INFORMATION(i,l) (MESSAGE_LEVEL >= l ? ReportEvent (hEventLog,
EVENTLOG_INFORMATION_TYPE, \
   0, i, (PSID)NULL, 0, 0, NULL, (PVOID)NULL) : FALSE)

#define REPORT_WARNING(i,l) (MESSAGE_LEVEL >= l ? ReportEvent (hEventLog,
EVENTLOG_WARNING_TYPE, \
   0, i, (PSID)NULL, 0, 0, NULL, (PVOID)NULL) : FALSE)

#define REPORT_ERROR(i,l) (MESSAGE_LEVEL >= l ? ReportEvent (hEventLog,
EVENTLOG_ERROR_TYPE, \
   0, i, (PSID)NULL, 0, 0, NULL, (PVOID)NULL) : FALSE)

#define REPORT_INFORMATION_DATA(i,l,d,s) (MESSAGE_LEVEL >= l ? ReportEvent (hEventLog,
EVENTLOG_INFORMATION_TYPE, \
   0, i, (PSID)NULL, 0, s, NULL, (PVOID)(d)) : FALSE)

#define REPORT_WARNING_DATA(i,l,d,s) (MESSAGE_LEVEL >= l ? ReportEvent (hEventLog,
EVENTLOG_WARNING_TYPE, \
   0, i, (PSID)NULL, 0, s, NULL, (PVOID)(d)) : FALSE)
```

```
#define REPORT_ERROR_DATA(i,l,d,s) (MESSAGE_LEVEL >= 1 ? ReportEvent (hEventLog,
EVENTLOG_ERROR_TYPE, \
    0, i, (PSID)NULL, 0, s, NULL, (PVOID)(d)) : FALSE)

// External Variables

extern HANDLE hEventLog;    // handle to event log
extern DWORD  dwLogUsers;   // counter of event log using routines
extern DWORD  MESSAGE_LEVEL; // event logging detail level

#endif //_PERFMSG_H_
```

Here's some more message stuff:

```
;
;Copyright (c) 1992  Microsoft Corporation
;
;Module Name:
;
;    vgactrs.h
;        (derived from vgactrs.mc by the message compiler  )
;
;Abstract:
;
;    Event message definitions used by routines in VGACTRS.DLL
;
;Revision History:
;
;--*/
;//
;#ifndef _VGACTRS_H_
;#define _VGACTRS_H_
;//
MessageIdTypedef=DWORD
;//
;//      Perfutil messages
;//
MessageId=1900
Severity=Informational
Facility=Application
SymbolicName=UTIL_LOG_OPEN
Language=English
An extensible counter has opened the Event Log for VGACTRS.DLL
.
;//
MessageId=1999
Severity=Informational
Facility=Application
SymbolicName=UTIL_CLOSING_LOG
Language=English
An extensible counter has closed the Event Log for VGACTRS.DLL
.
;//
MessageId=2000
Severity=Error
Facility=Application
SymbolicName=VGAPERF_OPEN_FILE_MAPPING_ERROR
Language=English
Unable to open mapped file containing VGA driver performance data.
.
```

```
;//
MessageId=+1
Severity=Error
Facility=Application
SymbolicName=VGAPERF_UNABLE_MAP_VIEW_OF_FILE
Language=English
Unable to map to shared memory file containing VGA driver performance data.
.
;//
MessageId=+1
Severity=Error
Facility=Application
SymbolicName=VGAPERF_UNABLE_OPEN_DRIVER_KEY
Language=English
Unable open "Performance" key of VGA driver in registry. Status code is returned in data.
.
;//
MessageId=+1
Severity=Error
Facility=Application
SymbolicName=VGAPERF_UNABLE_READ_FIRST_COUNTER
Language=English
Unable to read the "First Counter" value under the Vga\Performance Key. Status codes
returned in data.
.
;//
MessageId=+1
Severity=Error
Facility=Application
SymbolicName=VGAPERF_UNABLE_READ_FIRST_HELP
Language=English
Unable to read the "First Help" value under the Vga\Performance Key. Status codes returned
in data.
.
;//
;#endif // _VGACTRS_H_
```

The remaining files are used in the process of building the measurement DLL.
First we have **VGACTRS.EF**.

```
LIBRARY vgactrs

DESCRIPTION 'Performance Monitor Counter'

EXPORTS
    OpenVgaPerformanceData    @1
    CollectVgaPerformanceData    @2
    CloseVgaPerformanceData  @3
```

The MAKFILE is crucial to the build process, as you might already suspect:

```
#
# DO NOT EDIT THIS FILE!!!  Edit .\sources. if you want to add a new source
# file to this component.  This file merely indirects to the real make file
# that is shared by all the driver components of the Windows NT DDK
#

!INCLUDE $(NTMAKEENV)\makefile.def
```

Next is MAKEFILE.INC:

```
.\msg00001.bin : vgactrs.mc
    erase .\vgactrs.h
    erase .\msg00001.bin
    erase .\vgactrs.rc
    mc -v -s vgactrs.mc

.\vgactrs.rc : vgactrs.mc
    erase .\vgactrs.h
    erase .\msg00001.bin
    erase .\vgactrs.rc
    mc -v -s vgactrs.mc

.\vgactrs.h: vgactrs.mc
    erase .\vgactrs.h
    erase .\msg00001.bin
    erase .\vgactrs.rc
    mc -v -s vgactrs.mc
```

Finally, the glue that binds it all together, the SOURCES file that describes the build procedure to the **build** utility:

```
TARGETNAME=vgactrs
TARGETPATH=$(BASEDIR)\lib
TARGETTYPE=DYNLINK

TARGETLIBS=$(BASEDIR)\lib\*\$(DDKBUILDENV)\kernel32.lib      \
        $(BASEDIR)\lib\*\$(DDKBUILDENV)\advapi32.lib

DLLBASE=0x7500000

USE_CRTDLL=1

SOURCES=perfutil.c      \
    perfvga.c       \
    datavga.c       \
    vgactrs.rc

C_DEFINES= -DWIN32 -DSTRICT

NTTARGETFILE0=vgactrs.h vgactrs.rc msg00001.bin
```

Okay, now it's your turn.

APPENDIX A

Windows NT Performance Counters

This appendix lists the Windows NT object types, performance counters, and explain text.

The section headings show where each object type begins. Within each section, the object type's counters are listed in alphabetical order. The object types are also listed in alphabetical order.

For the listing of each counter, the following format is used:

Counter Name   *Complexity*

   Explain text.

   Index: *Index*   Default Scale: *Scale Factor*

   Counter Type: *Type*   Counter Size: S*ize*

The following table explains the values in the counter listings.

Table A.1   Performance Counter Reference Information

Field	Explanation
Counter name	Name of the counter.
Complexity	Level of Windows NT expertise recommended to effectively use the counter. Ranges from Novice, for the simplest counters, to Wizard, for the counters of interest only to serious Windows NT programmers.
Explain text	Description of the counter.

Table A.1   Performance Counter Reference Information *(continued)*

Field	Explanation
Index	Index of the counter in the "Counters" list in the Registry. Note that the index of the explain text is not shown.
Scale factor	Number which Performance Monitor multiplies.
Type	The type of this counter. For more information on counter types, see Chapter 12 of this book, "Writing a Custom Windows NT Performance Monitor."
Size	Size of the counter.

Cache Object

Object: Cache   Index: 086   *Advanced*

The Cache object type manages memory for rapid access to files. Files on Windows NT are cached in main memory in units of pages. Main memory not being used in the working sets of processes is available to the Cache for this purpose. The Cache preserves file pages in memory for as long as possible to permit access to the data through the file system without having to access the disk.

Async Copy Reads/sec   *Wizard*

Async Copy Reads/sec is the frequency of reads from Cache pages that involve a memory copy of the data from the Cache to the application's buffer. The application will regain control immediately even if the disk must be accessed to retrieve the page.

Index: 110   Default Scale: 1

Counter Type: PERF_COUNTER_COUNTER   Counter Size: 4 bytes

Async Data Maps/sec   *Wizard*

Async Data Maps/sec is the frequency that an application using a file system such as NTFS or HPFS to map a page of a file into the Cache to read the page, and does not wish to wait for the Cache to retrieve the page if it is not in main memory.

Index: 092   Default Scale: 1

Counter Type: PERF_COUNTER_COUNTER   Counter Size: 4 bytes

Async Fast Reads/sec   *Wizard*

Async Fast Reads/sec is the frequency of reads from Cache pages that bypass the installed file system and retrieve the data directly from the Cache. Normally, file I/O requests will invoke the appropriate file system to retrieve data from a file, but this path permits direct retrieval of Cache data without file system involvement if the data is in the Cache. Even if the data is not in the Cache, one invocation of the file system is avoided. If the data is not in the Cache, the request (application program call) will not wait until the data has been retrieved from disk, but will get control immediately.

Index: 128   Default Scale: 0.1

Counter Type: PERF_COUNTER_COUNTER   Counter Size: 4 bytes

Async MDL Reads/sec   *Wizard*

Async MDL Reads/sec is the frequency of reads from Cache pages using a Memory Descriptor List (MDL) to access the pages. The MDL contains the physical address of each page in the transfer, thus permitting Direct Memory Access (DMA) of the pages. If the accessed page(s) are not in main memory, the calling application program will not wait for the pages to fault in from disk.

Index: 118   Default Scale: 1

Counter Type: PERF_COUNTER_COUNTER   Counter Size: 4 bytes

Async Pin Reads/sec   *Wizard*

Async Pin Reads/sec is the frequency of reading data into the Cache preparatory to writing the data back to disk. Pages read in this fashion are pinned in memory at the completion of the read. The file system will regain control immediately even if the disk must be accessed to retrieve the page. While pinned, a page's physical address will not be altered.

Index: 102   Default Scale: 1

Counter Type: PERF_COUNTER_COUNTER   Counter Size: 4 bytes

Copy Read Hits %   *Expert*

Copy Read Hits is the percentage of Cache Copy Read requests that hit the Cache, that is, did not require a disk read in order to provide access to the page in the Cache. A Copy Read is a file read operation that is satisfied by a memory copy from a Cache page to the application's buffer. The LAN Redirector uses this method for retrieving Cache information, as does the LAN Server for small transfers. This is a method used by the disk file systems as well.

Index: 112   Default Scale: 1

Counter Type: PERF_SAMPLE_FRACTION   Counter Size: 4 bytes

Copy Reads/sec   *Expert*

Copy Reads/sec is the frequency of reads from Cache pages that involve a memory copy of the data from the Cache to the application's buffer. The LAN Redirector uses this method for retrieving Cache information, as does the LAN Server for small transfers. This is a method used by the disk file systems as well.

Index: 106   Default Scale: 1

Counter Type: PERF_COUNTER_COUNTER   Counter Size: 4 bytes

Data Flush Pages/sec   *Advanced*

Data Flush Pages/sec is the number of pages the Cache has flushed to disk as a result of a request to flush or to satisfy a write-through file write request. More than one page can be transferred on each flush operation.

Index: 140   Default Scale: 1

Counter Type: PERF_COUNTER_COUNTER   Counter Size: 4 bytes

Data Flushes/sec   *Wizard*

Data Flushes/sec is the frequency the Cache has flushed its contents to disk as the result of a request to flush or to satisfy a write-through file write request. More than one page can be transferred on each flush operation.

Index: 138   Default Scale: 1

Counter Type: PERF_COUNTER_COUNTER   Counter Size: 4 bytes

Data Map Hits %   *Wizard*

Data Map Hits is the percentage of Data Maps in the Cache that could be resolved without having to retrieve a page from the disk, that is the page was already in physical memory.

Index: 094   Default Scale: 1

Counter Type: PERF_SAMPLE_BASE   Counter Size: 4 bytes

Data Map Pins/sec   *Wizard*

Data Map Pins/sec is the frequency of Data Maps in the Cache that resulted in pinning a page in main memory, an action usually preparatory to writing to the file on disk. While pinned, a page's physical address in main memory and virtual address in the Cache will not be altered.

Index: 096   Default Scale: 1

Counter Type: PERF_SAMPLE_FRACTION   Counter Size: 4 bytes

Data Maps/sec   *Expert*

Data Maps/sec is the frequency that a file system such as NTFS or HPFS maps a page of a file into the Cache to read the page.

Index: 088   Default Scale: 1

Counter Type: PERF_COUNTER_COUNTER   Counter Size: 4 bytes

Fast Read Not Possibles/sec   *Wizard*

Fast Read Not Possibles/sec is the frequency of attempts by an application program interface (API) function call to bypass the file system to get at Cache data, that could not be honored without invoking the file system after all.

Index: 132   Default Scale: 1

Counter Type: PERF_COUNTER_COUNTER   Counter Size: 4 bytes

Fast Read Resource Misses/sec   *Wizard*

Fast Read Resource Misses/sec is the frequency of Cache misses necessitated by the lack of available resources to satisfy the request.

Index: 130   Default Scale: 1

Counter Type: PERF_COUNTER_COUNTER   Counter Size: 4 bytes

Fast Reads/sec   *Expert*

Fast Reads/sec is the frequency of reads from Cache pages that bypass the installed file system and retrieve the data directly from the Cache. Normally, file I/O requests invoke the appropriate file system to retrieve data from a file, but this path permits direct retrieval of Cache data without file system involvement if the data is in the Cache. Even if the data is not in the Cache, one invocation of the file system is avoided.

Index: 124   Default Scale: 0.1

Counter Type: PERF_COUNTER_COUNTER   Counter Size: 4 bytes

Lazy Write Flushes/sec   *Wizard*

Lazy Write Flushes/sec is the frequency the Cache's Lazy Write thread has written to disk. Lazy Writing is the process of updating the disk after the page has been changed in memory, so the application making the change to the file does not have to wait for the disk write to complete before proceeding. More than one page can be transferred on each write operation.

Index: 134   Default Scale: 1

Counter Type: PERF_COUNTER_COUNTER   Counter Size: 4 bytes

Lazy Write Pages/sec   *Advanced*

Lazy Write Pages/sec is the frequency the Cache's Lazy Write thread has written to disk. Lazy Writing is the process of updating the disk after the page has been changed in memory, so the application making the change to the file does not have to wait for the disk write to complete before proceeding. More than one page can be transferred on a single disk write operation.

Index: 136   Default Scale: 1

Counter Type: PERF_COUNTER_COUNTER   Counter Size: 4 bytes

MDL Read Hits %   *Expert*

MDL Read Hits is the percentage of Cache Memory Descriptor List (MDL) Read requests that hit the Cache, that is, did not require disk accesses in order to provide memory access to the page(s) in the Cache.

Index: 120   Default Scale: 1

Counter Type: PERF_SAMPLE_BASE   Counter Size: 4 bytes

MDL Reads/sec   *Expert*

MDL Reads/sec is the frequency of reads from Cache pages that use a Memory Descriptor List (MDL) to access the data. The MDL contains the physical address of each page involved in the transfer, and thus can employ a hardware Direct Memory Access (DMA) device to effect the copy. The LAN Server uses this method for large transfers out of the server.

Index: 114   Default Scale: 1

Counter Type: PERF_COUNTER_COUNTER   Counter Size: 4 bytes

Pin Read Hits %   *Expert*

Pin Read Hits is the percentage of Cache Pin Read requests that hit the Cache, that is, did not require a disk read in order to provide access to the page in the Cache. While pinned, a page's physical address in the Cache will not be altered. The LAN Redirector uses this method for retrieving Cache information, as does the LAN Server for small transfers. This is usually the method used by the disk file systems as well.

Index: 104   Default Scale: 1

Counter Type: PERF_SAMPLE_BASE   Counter Size: 4 bytes

Pin Reads/sec   *Expert*

Pin Reads/sec is the frequency of reading data into the Cache preparatory to writing the data back to disk. Pages read in this fashion are pinned in memory at the completion of the read. While pinned, a page's physical address in the Cache will not be altered.

Index: 098   Default Scale: 1

Counter Type: PERF_COUNTER_COUNTER   Counter Size: 4 bytes

Read Aheads/sec   *Advanced*

Read Aheads/sec is the frequency of Cache reads where the Cache detects sequential access to a file. The read aheads permit the data to be transferred in larger blocks than those being requested by the application, reducing the overhead per access.

Index: 122   Default Scale: 1

Counter Type: PERF_SAMPLE_BASE   Counter Size: 4 bytes

Sync Copy Reads/sec   *Wizard*

Sync Copy Reads/sec is the frequency of reads from Cache pages that involve a memory copy of the data from the Cache to the application's buffer. The file system will not regain control until the copy operation is complete, even if the disk must be accessed to retrieve the page.

Index: 108   Default Scale: 1

Counter Type: PERF_COUNTER_COUNTER   Counter Size: 4 bytes

Sync Data Maps/sec   *Wizard*

Sync Data Maps/sec counts the frequency that a file system such as NTFS or HPFS maps a page of a file into the Cache to read the page, and wishes to wait for the Cache to retrieve the page if it is not in main memory.

Index: 090   Default Scale: 1

Counter Type: PERF_COUNTER_COUNTER   Counter Size: 4 bytes

Sync Fast Reads/sec   *Wizard*

Sync Fast Reads/sec is the frequency of reads from Cache pages that bypass the installed file system and retrieve the data directly from the Cache. Normally, file I/O requests invoke the appropriate file system to retrieve data from a file, but this path permits direct retrieval of Cache data without file system involvement if the data is in the Cache. Even if the data is not in the Cache, one invocation of the file system is avoided. If the data is not in the Cache, the request (application program call) will wait until the data has been retrieved from disk.

Index: 126   Default Scale: 0.1

Counter Type: PERF_COUNTER_COUNTER   Counter Size: 4 bytes

Sync MDL Reads/sec   *Wizard*

Sync MDL Reads/sec is the frequency of reads from Cache pages that use a Memory Descriptor List (MDL) to access the pages. The MDL contains the physical address of each page in the transfer, thus permitting Direct Memory Access (DMA) of the pages. If the accessed page(s) are not in main memory, the caller will wait for the pages to fault in from the disk.

Index: 116   Default Scale: 1

Counter Type: PERF_COUNTER_COUNTER   Counter Size: 4 bytes

Sync Pin Reads/sec   *Wizard*

Sync Pin Reads/sec is the frequency of reading data into the Cache preparatory to writing the data back to disk. Pages read in this fashion are pinned in memory at the completion of the read. The file system will not regain control until the page is pinned in the Cache, in particular if the disk must be accessed to retrieve the page. While pinned, a page's physical address in the Cache will not be altered.

Index: 100   Default Scale: 1

Counter Type: PERF_COUNTER_COUNTER   Counter Size: 4 bytes

ICMP Object

Object: ICMP   Index: 582   *Advanced*

The ICMP Object Type includes those counters that describe the rates that ICMP Messages are received and sent by a certain entity using the ICMP protocol. It also describes various error counts for the ICMP protocol.

Messages Outbound Errors   *Advanced*

Messages Outbound Errors is the number of ICMP messages that this entity did not send due to problems discovered within ICMP such as lack of buffers. This value should not include errors discovered outside the ICMP layer such as the inability of IP to route the resultant datagram. In some implementations there may be no types of error that contribute to this counter's value.

Index: 614   Default Scale: 1

Counter Type: PERF_COUNTER_RAWCOUNT   Counter Size: 4 bytes

Messages Received Errors   *Advanced*

Messages Received Errors is the number of ICMP messages that the entity received but determined as having errors (bad ICMP checksums, bad length, and so on).

Index: 588   Default Scale: 1

Counter Type: PERF_COUNTER_RAWCOUNT   Counter Size: 4 bytes

Messages Received/sec   *Advanced*

Messages Received/sec is the rate that ICMP messages are received by the entity. The rate includes those messages received in error.

Index: 586   Default Scale: 0.1

Counter Type: PERF_COUNTER_COUNTER   Counter Size: 4 bytes

Messages Sent/sec   *Advanced*

Messages Sent/sec is the rate that ICMP messages are attempted to be sent by the entity. The rate includes those messages sent in error.

Index: 612   Default Scale: 0.1

Counter Type: PERF_COUNTER_COUNTER   Counter Size: 4 bytes

Messages/sec   *Advanced*

Messages/sec is the total rate that ICMP messages are received and sent by the entity. The rate includes those messages received or sent in error.

Index: 584   Default Scale: 0.1

Counter Type: PERF_COUNTER_COUNTER   Counter Size: 4 bytes

Received Address Mask   *Expert*

Received Address Mask is the number of ICMP Address Mask Request messages received.

Index: 608   Default Scale: 1

Counter Type: PERF_COUNTER_RAWCOUNT   Counter Size: 4 bytes

Received Address Mask Reply   *Expert*

Received Address Mask Reply is the number of ICMP Address Mask Reply messages received.

Index: 610   Default Scale: 1

Counter Type: PERF_COUNTER_RAWCOUNT   Counter Size: 4 bytes

Received Dest. Unreachable   *Advanced*

Received Destination Unreachable is the number of ICMP Destination Unreachable messages received.

Index: 590   Default Scale: 1

Counter Type: PERF_COUNTER_RAWCOUNT   Counter Size: 4 bytes

Received Echo Reply/sec   *Expert*

Received Echo Reply/sec is the rate of ICMP Echo Reply messages received.

Index: 602   Default Scale: 0.1

Counter Type: PERF_COUNTER_COUNTER   Counter Size: 4 bytes

Received Echo/sec   *Expert*

Received Echo/sec is the rate of ICMP Echo messages received.

Index: 600   Default Scale: 0.1

Counter Type: PERF_COUNTER_COUNTER   Counter Size: 4 bytes

Received Parameter Problem *Expert*

Received Parameter Problem is the number of ICMP Parameter Problem messages received.

Index: 594   Default Scale: 1

Counter Type: PERF_COUNTER_RAWCOUNT   Counter Size: 4 bytes

Received Redirect/sec *Advanced*

Received Redirect/sec is the rate of ICMP Redirect messages received.

Index: 598   Default Scale: 0.1

Counter Type: PERF_COUNTER_COUNTER   Counter Size: 4 bytes

Received Source Quench *Wizard*

Received Source Quench is the number of ICMP Source Quench messages received.

Index: 596   Default Scale: 1

Counter Type: PERF_COUNTER_RAWCOUNT   Counter Size: 4 bytes

Received Time Exceeded *Advanced*

Received Time Exceeded is the number of ICMP Time Exceeded messages received.

Index: 592   Default Scale: 1

Counter Type: PERF_COUNTER_RAWCOUNT   Counter Size: 4 bytes

Received Timestamp Reply/sec *Expert*

Received Timestamp Reply/sec is the rate of ICMP Timestamp Reply messages received.

Index: 606   Default Scale: 0.1

Counter Type: PERF_COUNTER_COUNTER   Counter Size: 4 bytes

Received Timestamp/sec *Expert*

Received Timestamp/sec is the rate of ICMP Timestamp (request) messages received.

Index: 604   Default Scale: 0.1

Counter Type: PERF_COUNTER_COUNTER   Counter Size: 4 bytes

Sent Address Mask   *Expert*

Sent Address Mask is the number of ICMP Address Mask Request messages sent.

Index: 634   Default Scale: 1

Counter Type: PERF_COUNTER_RAWCOUNT   Counter Size: 4 bytes

Sent Address Mask Reply   *Expert*

Sent Address Mask Reply is the number of ICMP Address Mask Reply messages sent.

Index: 636   Default Scale: 1

Counter Type: PERF_COUNTER_RAWCOUNT   Counter Size: 4 bytes

Sent Destination Unreachable   *Advanced*

Sent Destination Unreachable is the number of ICMP Destination Unreachable messages sent.

Index: 616   Default Scale: 1

Counter Type: PERF_COUNTER_RAWCOUNT   Counter Size: 4 bytes

Sent Echo Reply/sec   *Expert*

Sent Echo Reply/sec is the rate of ICMP Echo Reply messages sent.

Index: 628   Default Scale: 0.1

Counter Type: PERF_COUNTER_COUNTER   Counter Size: 4 bytes

Sent Echo/sec   *Expert*

Sent Echo/sec is the rate of ICMP Echo messages sent.

Index: 626   Default Scale: 0.1

Counter Type: PERF_COUNTER_COUNTER   Counter Size: 4 bytes

Sent Parameter Problem   *Expert*

Sent Parameter Problem is the number of ICMP Parameter Problem messages sent.

Index: 620   Default Scale: 1

Counter Type: PERF_COUNTER_RAWCOUNT   Counter Size: 4 bytes

Sent Redirect/sec   *Advanced*

Sent Redirect/sec is the rate of ICMP Redirect messages sent.

Index: 624   Default Scale: 0.1

Counter Type: PERF_COUNTER_COUNTER   Counter Size: 4 bytes

Sent Source Quench   *Wizard*

Sent Source Quench is the number of ICMP Source Quench messages sent.

Index: 622   Default Scale: 1

Counter Type: PERF_COUNTER_RAWCOUNT   Counter Size: 4 bytes

Sent Time Exceeded   *Advanced*

Sent Time Exceeded is the number of ICMP Time Exceeded messages sent.

Index: 618   Default Scale: 1

Counter Type: PERF_COUNTER_RAWCOUNT   Counter Size: 4 bytes

Sent Timestamp/sec   *Expert*

Sent Timestamp/sec is the rate of ICMP Timestamp (request) messages sent.

Index: 630   Default Scale: 0.1

Counter Type: PERF_COUNTER_COUNTER   Counter Size: 4 bytes

Sent Timestamp Reply/sec   *Expert*

Sent Timestamp Reply/sec is the rate of ICMP Timestamp Reply messages sent.

Index: 632   Default Scale: 0.1

Counter Type: PERF_COUNTER_COUNTER   Counter Size: 4 bytes

Image Object

Object: Image   Index: 740   *Wizard*

The Image object type displays information about the virtual address usage of the images being executed by a process on the computer.

Executable   *Wizard*

Image Space is the virtual address space in use by the selected image with this protection. Executable memory is memory that can be executed by programs, but may not be read or written. This type of protection is not supported by all processor types.

Index: 796   Default Scale: 1

Counter Type: PERF_COUNTER_RAWCOUNT   Counter Size: 4 bytes

Exec Read Only   *Wizard*

Image Space is the virtual address space in use by the selected image with this protection. Execute/Read Only memory is memory that can be executed as well as read.

Index: 798   Default Scale: 1

Counter Type: PERF_COUNTER_RAWCOUNT   Counter Size: 4 bytes

Exec Read/Write   *Wizard*

Image Space is the virtual address space in use by the selected image with this protection. Execute/Read/Write memory is memory that can be executed by programs as well as read and written.

Index: 800   Default Scale: 1

Counter Type: PERF_COUNTER_RAWCOUNT   Counter Size: 4 bytes

Exec Write Copy   *Wizard*

Image Space is the virtual address space in use by the selected image with this protection. Execute Write Copy is memory that can be executed by programs as well as read and written. This type of protection is used when memory needs to be shared between processes. If the sharing processes only read the memory, then they will all use the same memory. If a sharing process desires write access, then a copy of this memory will be made for that process.

Index: 802   Default Scale: 1

Counter Type: PERF_COUNTER_RAWCOUNT   Counter Size: 4 bytes

No Access *Wizard*

Image Space is the virtual address space in use by the selected image with this protection. No Access protection prevents a process from writing or reading these pages and will generate an access violation if either is attempted.

Index: 788   Default Scale: 1

Counter Type: PERF_COUNTER_RAWCOUNT   Counter Size: 4 bytes

Read Only *Wizard*

Image Space is the virtual address space in use by the selected image with this protection. Read Only protection prevents the contents of these pages from being modified. Any attempts to write or modify these pages will generate an access violation.

Index: 790   Default Scale: 1

Counter Type: PERF_COUNTER_RAWCOUNT   Counter Size: 4 bytes

Read/Write *Wizard*

Image Space is the virtual address space in use by the selected image with this protection. Read/Write protection allows a process to read, modify and write to these pages.

Index: 792   Default Scale: 1

Counter Type: PERF_COUNTER_RAWCOUNT   Counter Size: 4 bytes

Write Copy *Wizard*

Image Space is the virtual address space in use by the selected image with this protection. Write Copy protection is used when memory is shared for reading but not for writing. When processes are reading this memory, they can share the same memory, however, when a sharing process wants to have read/write access to this shared memory, a copy of that memory is made for writing to.

Index: 794   Default Scale: 1

Counter Type: PERF_COUNTER_RAWCOUNT   Counter Size: 4 bytes

IP Object

Object: IP   Index: 546   *Advanced*

The IP Object Type includes those counters that describe the rates that IP datagrams are received and sent by a certain computer using the IP protocol. It also describes various error counts for the IP protocol.

Datagrams Forwarded/sec   *Advanced*

Datagrams Forwarded/sec is the rate of input datagrams for that this entity was not their final IP destination, as a result of which an attempt was made to find a route to forward them to that final destination. In entities that do not act as IP Gateways, this rate will include only those packets that were Source-Routed via this entity, and the Source-Route option processing was successful.

Index: 556   Default Scale: 0.1

Counter Type: PERF_COUNTER_COUNTER   Counter Size: 4 bytes

Datagrams Outbound Discarded   *Advanced*

Datagrams Outbound Discarded is the number of output IP datagrams for which no problems were encountered to prevent their transmission to their destination, but which were discarded (for example, for lack of buffer space.) This counter would include datagrams counted in Datagrams Forwarded if any such packets met this (discretionary) discard criterion.

Index: 566   Default Scale: 1

Counter Type: PERF_COUNTER_RAWCOUNT   Counter Size: 4 bytes

Datagrams Outbound No Route   *Advanced*

Datagrams Outbound No Route is the number of IP datagrams discarded because no route could be found to transmit them to their destination. This counter includes any packets counted in Datagrams Forwarded that meet this 'no route' criterion.

Index: 568   Default Scale: 1

Counter Type: PERF_COUNTER_RAWCOUNT   Counter Size: 4 bytes

Datagrams Received Header Errors   *Advanced*

Datagrams Received Header Errors is the number of input datagrams discarded due to errors in their IP headers, including bad checksums, version number mismatch, other format errors, time-to-live exceeded, errors discovered in processing their IP options, and so on.

Index: 552   Default Scale: 1

Counter Type: PERF_COUNTER_RAWCOUNT   Counter Size: 4 bytes

Datagrams Received Address Errors   *Advanced*

Datagrams Received Address Errors is the number of input datagrams discarded because the IP address in their IP header's destination field was not a valid address to be received at this entity. This count includes invalid addresses (for example, 0.0. 0.0) and addresses of unsupported Classes (for example, Class E). For entities that are not IP Gateways and therefore do not forward datagrams, this counter includes datagrams discarded because the destination address was not a local address.

Index: 554   Default Scale: 1

Counter Type: PERF_COUNTER_RAWCOUNT   Counter Size: 4 bytes

Datagrams Received Delivered/sec   *Advanced*

Datagrams Received Delivered/sec is the rate that input datagrams are successfully delivered to IP user-protocols (including ICMP).

Index: 562   Default Scale: 0.1

Counter Type: PERF_COUNTER_COUNTER   Counter Size: 4 bytes

Datagrams Received Discarded   *Advanced*

Datagrams Received Discarded is the number of input IP datagrams for which no problems were encountered to prevent their continued processing, but which were discarded (for example, for lack of buffer space). This counter does not include any datagrams discarded while awaiting re-assembly.

Index: 560   Default Scale: 1

Counter Type: PERF_COUNTER_RAWCOUNT   Counter Size: 4 bytes

Datagrams Received Unknown Protocol   *Advanced*

Datagrams Received Unknown Protocol is the number of locally-addressed datagrams received successfully but discarded because of an unknown or unsupported protocol.

Index: 558   Default Scale: 1

Counter Type: PERF_COUNTER_RAWCOUNT   Counter Size: 4 bytes

Datagrams Received/sec   *Advanced*

Datagrams Received/sec is the rate that IP datagrams are received from the interfaces, including those in error.

Index: 446   Default Scale: 0.1

Counter Type: PERF_COUNTER_COUNTER   Counter Size: 4 bytes

Datagrams Sent/sec   *Advanced*

Datagrams Sent/sec is the rate that IP datagrams are supplied to IP for transmission by local IP user-protocols (including ICMP). That this counter does not include any datagrams counted in Datagrams Forwarded.

Index: 442   Default Scale: 0.1

Counter Type: PERF_COUNTER_COUNTER   Counter Size: 4 bytes

Datagrams/sec   *Advanced*

Datagrams/sec is the rate that IP datagrams are received from or sent to the interfaces, including those in error. Any forwarded datagrams are not included in this rate.

Index: 438   Default Scale: 0.1

Counter Type: PERF_COUNTER_COUNTER   Counter Size: 4 bytes

Fragmentation Failures   *Advanced*

Fragmentation Failures is the number of IP datagrams that have been discarded because they needed to be fragmented at this entity but could not be, for example, because their 'Don't Fragment' flag was set.

Index: 578   Default Scale: 1

Counter Type: PERF_COUNTER_RAWCOUNT   Counter Size: 4 bytes

Fragments Received/sec   *Advanced*

Fragments Received/sec is the rate that IP fragments that need to be re-assembled at this entity are received.

Index: 570   Default Scale: 0.1

Counter Type: PERF_COUNTER_COUNTER   Counter Size: 4 bytes

Fragments Re-assembled/sec   *Advanced*

Fragments Re-assembled/sec is the rate that IP fragments are successfully re-assembled.

Index: 572   Default Scale: 0.1

Counter Type: PERF_COUNTER_COUNTER   Counter Size: 4 bytes

Fragment Re-assembly Failures   *Advanced*

Fragment Re-assembly Failures is the number of failures detected by the IP re-assembly algorithm (for whatever reason: timed out, errors, and so on.). This is not necessarily a count of discarded IP fragments since some algorithms (notably RFC 815) can lose track of the number of fragments by combining them as they are received.

Index: 574   Default Scale: 1

Counter Type: PERF_COUNTER_RAWCOUNT   Counter Size: 4 bytes

Fragmented Datagrams/sec   *Advanced*

Fragmented Datagrams/sec is the rate that datagrams are successfully fragmented at this entity.

Index: 576   Default Scale: 0.1

Counter Type: PERF_COUNTER_COUNTER   Counter Size: 4 bytes

Fragments Created/sec   *Advanced*

Fragments Created/sec is the rate that IP datagram fragments have been generated as a result of fragmentation at this entity.

Index: 580   Default Scale: 0.1

Counter Type: PERF_COUNTER_COUNTER   Counter Size: 4 bytes

LogicalDisk Object

Object: LogicalDisk   Index:236   *Novice*

A Logical Disk object type is a partition on a hard or fixed disk drive and assigned a drive letter, such as C. Disks can be partitioned into distinct sections where they can store file, program, and page data. The disk is read to retrieve these items, and written to record changes to them.

% Disk Read Time   *Novice*

Disk Read Time is the percentage of elapsed time that the selected disk drive is busy servicing read requests.

Index: 202   Default Scale: 1

Counter Type: PERF_COUNTER_TIMER   Counter Size: 8 bytes

% Disk Time   *Novice*

Disk Time is the percentage of elapsed time that the selected disk drive is busy servicing read or write requests.

Index: 200   Default Scale: 1

Counter Type: PERF_COUNTER_TIMER   Counter Size: 8 bytes

% Disk Write Time   *Novice*

Disk Write Time is the percentage of elapsed time that the selected disk drive is busy servicing write requests.

Index: 204   Default Scale: 1

Counter Type: PERF_COUNTER_TIMER   Counter Size: 8 bytes

% Free Space   *Novice*

Percent Free Space is the ratio of the free space available on the logical disk unit to the total usable space provided by the selected logical disk drive.

Index: 408   Default Scale: 1

Counter Type: PERF_RAW_BASE   Counter Size: 4 bytes

Avg. Disk Bytes/Read   *Expert*

Avg. Disk Bytes/Read is the average number of bytes transferred from the disk during read operations.

Index: 226   Default Scale: 1

Counter Type: PERF_AVERAGE_BASE   Counter Size: 4 bytes

Avg. Disk Bytes/Transfer   *Expert*

Avg. Disk Bytes/Transfer is the average number of bytes transferred to or from the disk during write or read operations.

Index: 224   Default Scale: 1

Counter Type: PERF_AVERAGE_BASE   Counter Size: 4 bytes

Avg. Disk Bytes/Write   *Expert*

Avg. Disk Bytes/Write is the average number of bytes transferred to the disk during write operations.

Index: 228   Default Scale: 1

Counter Type: PERF_AVERAGE_BASE   Counter Size: 4 bytes

Avg. Disk sec/Read   *Advanced*

Avg. Disk sec/Read is the average time in seconds of a read of data from the disk.

Index: 208   Default Scale: 1000

Counter Type: PERF_AVERAGE_TIMER   Counter Size: 8 bytes

Avg. Disk sec/Transfer   *Advanced*

Avg. Disk sec/Transfer is the time in seconds of the average disk transfer.

Index: 206   Default Scale: 1

Counter Type: PERF_AVERAGE_BASE   Counter Size: 4 bytes

Avg. Disk sec/Write   *Advanced*

Avg. Disk sec/Write is the average time in seconds of a write of data to the disk.

Index: 210   Default Scale: 1

Counter Type: PERF_AVERAGE_BASE   Counter Size: 4 bytes

Disk Bytes/sec   *Advanced*

Disk Bytes/sec is the rate bytes are transferred to or from the disk during write or read operations.

Index: 218   Default Scale: 0.0001

Counter Type: PERF_COUNTER_BULK_COUNT   Counter Size: 8 bytes

Disk Queue Length   *Novice*

Disk Queue Length is the number of requests outstanding on the disk at the time the performance data is collected. It includes requests in service at the time of the snapshot. This is an instantaneous length, not an average over the time interval. Multi-spindle disk devices can have multiple requests active at one time, but other concurrent requests are awaiting service. This counter may reflect a transitory high or low queue length, but if there is a sustained load on the disk drive, it is likely that this will be consistently high. Requests are experiencing delays proportional to the length of this queue minus the number of spindles on the disks. This difference should average less than 2 for good performance.

Index: 198   Default Scale: 10

Counter Type: PERF_COUNTER_RAWCOUNT   Counter Size: 4 bytes

Disk Read Bytes/sec   *Advanced*

Disk Read Bytes/sec is the rate bytes are transferred from the disk during read operations.

Index: 220   Default Scale: 0.0001

Counter Type: PERF_COUNTER_BULK_COUNT   Counter Size: 8 bytes

Disk Reads/sec   *Novice*

Disk Reads/sec is the rate of read operations on the disk.

Index: 214   Default Scale: 1

Counter Type: PERF_COUNTER_COUNTER   Counter Size: 4 bytes

Disk Transfers/sec   *Novice*

Disk Transfers/sec is the rate of read and write operations on the disk.

Index: 212   Default Scale: 1

Counter Type: PERF_COUNTER_COUNTER   Counter Size: 4 bytes

Disk Writes/sec   *Novice*

Disk Writes/sec is the rate of write operations on the disk.

Index: 216   Default Scale: 1

Counter Type: PERF_COUNTER_COUNTER   Counter Size: 4 bytes

Disk Write Bytes/sec   *Advanced*

Disk Write Bytes is rate bytes are transferred to the disk during write operations.

Index: 222   Default Scale: 0.0001

Counter Type: PERF_COUNTER_BULK_COUNT   Counter Size: 8 bytes

Free Megabytes   *Novice*

Free Megabytes displays the unallocated space on the disk drive in megabytes. One megabyte = 1,048,576 bytes.

Index: 410   Default Scale: 1

Counter Type: PERF_COUNTER_RAWCOUNT   Counter Size: 4 bytes

Memory Object

Object: Memory   Index:004   *Novice*

The Memory object type includes those counters that describe the behavior of both real and virtual memory on the computer. Real memory is allocated in units of pages. Virtual memory may exceed real memory in size, causing page traffic as virtual pages are moved between disk and real memory.

Available Bytes   *Expert*

Available Bytes displays the size of the virtual memory currently on the Zeroed, Free, and Standby lists. Zeroed and Free memory is ready for use, with Zeroed memory cleared to zeros. Standby memory is memory removed from a process's Working Set but still available. Notice that this is an instantaneous count, not an average over the time interval.

Index: 024   Default Scale: 0.00001

Counter Type: PERF_COUNTER_RAWCOUNT   Counter Size: 4 bytes

Cache Bytes   *Advanced*

Cache Bytes measures the number of bytes currently in use by the system Cache. The system Cache is used to buffer data retrieved from disk or LAN. The system Cache uses memory not in use by active processes in the computer.

Index: 818   Default Scale: 0.00001

Counter Type: PERF_COUNTER_RAWCOUNT   Counter Size: 4 bytes

Cache Bytes Peak   *Advanced*

Cache Bytes Peak measures the maximum number of bytes used by the system Cache. The system Cache is used to buffer data retrieved from disk or LAN. The system Cache uses memory not in use by active processes in the computer.

Index: 820   Default Scale: 0.00001

Counter Type: PERF_COUNTER_RAWCOUNT   Counter Size: 4 bytes

Cache Faults/sec   *Wizard*

Cache Faults occur whenever the Cache manager does not find a file's page in the immediate Cache and must ask the memory manager to locate the page elsewhere in memory or on the disk so that it can be loaded into the immediate Cache.

Index: 036   Default Scale: 0.1

Counter Type: PERF_COUNTER_COUNTER   Counter Size: 4 bytes

Commit Limit   *Wizard*

Commit Limit is the size (in bytes) of virtual memory that can be committed without having to extend the paging file(s). If the paging file(s) can be extended, this is a soft limit.

Index: 030   Default Scale: 0.000001

Counter Type: PERF_COUNTER_RAWCOUNT   Counter Size: 4 bytes

Committed Bytes   *Expert*

Committed Bytes displays the size of virtual memory (in bytes) that has been Committed (as opposed to simply reserved). Committed memory must have backing (that is, disk) storage available, or must be assured never to need disk storage (because main memory is large enough to hold it). Notice that this is an instantaneous count, not an average over the time interval.

Index: 026   Default Scale: 0.000001

Counter Type: PERF_COUNTER_RAWCOUNT   Counter Size: 4 bytes

Demand Zero Faults/sec   *Wizard*

Demand Zero Faults are the number of page faults for pages that must be filled with zeros before the fault is satisfied. If the Zeroed list is not empty, the fault can be resolved by removing a page from the Zeroed list.

Index: 038   Default Scale: 0.1

Counter Type: PERF_COUNTER_COUNTER   Counter Size: 4 bytes

Free System Page Table Entries   *Wizard*

The number of Page Table Entries not currently in use by the system.

Index: 678   Default Scale: 0.01

Counter Type: PERF_COUNTER_RAWCOUNT   Counter Size: 4 bytes

Page Faults/sec   *Novice*

Page Faults/sec is a count of the Page Faults in the processor. A page fault occurs when a process refers to a virtual memory page that is not in its Working Set in main memory. A Page Fault will not cause the page to be fetched from disk if that page is on the standby list, and hence already in main memory, or if it is in use by another process with whom the page is shared.

Index: 028   Default Scale: 0.1

Counter Type: PERF_COUNTER_COUNTER   Counter Size: 4 bytes

Page Reads/sec   *Expert*

Page Reads/sec is the number of times the disk was read to retrieve pages of virtual memory necessary to resolve page faults. Multiple pages can be read during a disk read operation.

Index: 042   Default Scale: 1

Counter Type: PERF_COUNTER_COUNTER   Counter Size: 4 bytes

Page Writes/sec   *Expert*

Page Writes/sec is a count of the number of times pages have been written to the disk because they were changed since last retrieved. Each such write operation may transfer a number of pages.

Index: 050   Default Scale: 1

Counter Type: PERF_COUNTER_COUNTER   Counter Size: 4 bytes

Pages Input/sec   *Novice*

Pages Input/sec is the number of pages read from the disk to resolve memory references to pages that were not in memory at the time of the reference. This counter includes paging traffic on behalf of the system Cache to access file data for applications. This is an important counter to observe if you are concerned about excessive memory pressure (that is, thrashing), and the excessive paging that may result.

Index: 822   Default Scale: 1

Counter Type: PERF_COUNTER_COUNTER   Counter Size: 4 bytes

Pages Output/sec   *Advanced*

Pages Output/sec is a count of the number of pages that are written to disk because the pages have been modified in main memory.

Index: 048   Default Scale: 1

Counter Type: PERF_COUNTER_COUNTER   Counter Size: 4 bytes

Pages/sec   *Novice*

Pages/sec is the number of pages read from the disk or written to the disk to resolve memory references to pages that were not in memory at the time of the reference. This is the sum of Pages Input/sec and Pages Output/sec. This counter includes paging traffic on behalf of the system Cache to access file data for applications. This is the primary counter to observe if you are concerned about excessive memory pressure (that is, thrashing), and the excessive paging that may result.

Index: 040   Default Scale: 1

Counter Type: PERF_COUNTER_COUNTER   Counter Size: 4 bytes

Pool Paged Allocs   *Wizard*

Pool Paged Allocs is the number of calls to allocate space in the system Paged Pool. Paged Pool is a system memory area where space is acquired by operating system components as they accomplish their appointed tasks. Paged Pool pages can be paged out to the paging file when not accessed by the system for sustained periods of time.

Index: 060   Default Scale: 0.01

Counter Type: PERF_COUNTER_RAWCOUNT   Counter Size: 4 bytes

Pool Paged Bytes   *Advanced*

Pool Paged Bytes is the number of bytes in the Paged Pool, a system memory area where space is acquired by operating system components as they accomplish their appointed tasks. Paged Pool pages can be paged out to the paging file when not accessed by the system for sustained periods of time.

Index: 056   Default Scale: 0.00001

Counter Type: PERF_COUNTER_RAWCOUNT   Counter Size: 4 bytes

Pool Nonpaged Allocs   *Wizard*

Pool Nonpaged Allocs is the number of calls to allocate space in the system Nonpaged Pool. Nonpaged Pool is a system memory area where space is acquired by operating system components as they accomplish their appointed tasks. Nonpaged Pool pages cannot be paged out to the paging file, but instead remain in main memory as long as they are allocated.

Index: 064   Default Scale: 0.01

Counter Type: PERF_COUNTER_RAWCOUNT   Counter Size: 4 bytes

Pool Nonpaged Bytes   *Advanced*

Pool Nonpaged Bytes is the number of bytes in the Nonpaged Pool, a system memory area where space is acquired by operating system components as they accomplish their appointed tasks. Nonpaged Pool pages cannot be paged out to the paging file, but instead remain in main memory as long as they are allocated.

Index: 058   Default Scale: 0.00001

Counter Type: PERF_COUNTER_RAWCOUNT   Counter Size: 4 bytes

Transition Faults/sec   *Wizard*

Transition Faults/sec is the number of page faults resolved by recovering pages that were in transition, that is, being written to disk at the time of the page fault. The pages were recovered without additional disk activity.

Index: 034   Default Scale: 0.1

Counter Type: PERF_COUNTER_COUNTER   Counter Size: 4 bytes

Write Copies/sec   *Wizard*

Write Copies/sec is the number of page faults that have been satisfied by making a copy of a page when an attempt to write to the page is made. This is an economical way of sharing data since the copy of the page is only made on an attempt to write to the page; otherwise, the page is shared.

Index: 032   Default Scale: 1

Counter Type: PERF_COUNTER_COUNTER   Counter Size: 4 bytes

NBT Connection Object

Object: NBT Connection   Index: 502   *Advanced*

The NBT Connection Object Type includes those counters that describe the rates that bytes are received and sent over a single NBT connection connecting the local computer with some remote computer. The connection is identified by the name of the remote computer.

Bytes Received/sec   *Advanced*

Bytes Received/sec is the rate that bytes are received by the local computer over an NBT connection to some remote computer. All the bytes received by the local computer over the particular NBT connection are counted.

Index: 264   Default Scale: 0.0001

Counter Type: PERF_COUNTER_COUNTER   Counter Size: 4 bytes

Bytes Sent/sec   *Advanced*

Bytes Sent/sec is the rate that bytes are sent by the local computer over an NBT connection to some remote computer. All the bytes sent by the local computer over the particular NBT connection are counted.

Index: 506   Default Scale: 0.0001

Counter Type: PERF_COUNTER_COUNTER   Counter Size: 4 bytes

Bytes Total/sec   *Advanced*

Bytes Total/sec is the rate that bytes are sent or received by the local computer over an NBT connection to some remote computer. All the bytes sent or received by the local computer over the particular NBT connection are counted.

Index: 388   Default Scale: 0.0001

Counter Type: PERF_COUNTER_COUNTER   Counter Size: 4 bytes

NetBEUI Object

Object: NetBEUI   Index: 492   *Advanced*

The NetBEUI protocol handles data transmission for that network activity which follows the NetBIOS End User Interface standard.

Bytes Total/sec   *Advanced*

Bytes Total/sec is the sum of Frame Bytes/sec and Datagram Bytes/sec. This is the total rate of bytes sent to or received from the network by the protocol, but only counts the bytes in frames (that is, packets) which carry data.

Index: 388   Default Scale: 0.0001

Counter Type: PERF_COUNTER_BULK_COUNT   Counter Size: 8 bytes

Connection Session Timeouts   *Advanced*

Connection Session Timeouts is the number of connections that were dropped due to a session timeout. This number is an accumulator and shows a running total.

Index: 426   Default Scale: 1

Counter Type: PERF_COUNTER_RAWCOUNT   Counter Size: 4 bytes

Connections Canceled   *Advanced*

Connections Canceled is the number of connections that were canceled. This number is an accumulator and shows a running total.

Index: 428   Default Scale: 1

Counter Type: PERF_COUNTER_RAWCOUNT   Counter Size: 4 bytes

Connections No Retries   *Advanced*

Connections No Retries is the total count of connections that were successfully made on the first try. This number is an accumulator and shows a running total.

Index: 414   Default Scale: 1

Counter Type: PERF_COUNTER_RAWCOUNT   Counter Size: 4 bytes

Connections Open   *Advanced*

Connections Open is the number of connections currently open for this protocol. This counter shows the current count only and does not accumulate over time.

Index: 412   Default Scale: 1

Counter Type: PERF_COUNTER_RAWCOUNT   Counter Size: 4 bytes

Connections With Retries   *Advanced*

Connections With Retries is the total count of connections that were made after retrying the attempt. A retry occurs when the first connection attempt failed. This number is an accumulator and shows a running total.

Index: 416   Default Scale: 1

Counter Type: PERF_COUNTER_RAWCOUNT   Counter Size: 4 bytes

Datagram Bytes Received/sec   *Advanced*

Datagram Bytes Received/sec is the rate that datagram bytes are received by the computer. A datagram is a connectionless packet whose delivery to a remote computer is not guaranteed.

Index: 448   Default Scale: 0.0001

Counter Type: PERF_COUNTER_BULK_COUNT   Counter Size: 8 bytes

Datagram Bytes Sent/sec   *Advanced*

Datagram Bytes Sent/sec is the rate that datagram bytes are sent from the computer. A datagram is a connectionless packet whose delivery to a remote computer is not guaranteed.

Index: 444   Default Scale: 0.0001

Counter Type: PERF_COUNTER_BULK_COUNT   Counter Size: 8 bytes

Datagram Bytes/sec   *Advanced*

Datagram Bytes/sec is the rate that datagram bytes are processed by the computer. This counter is the sum of datagram bytes that are sent as well as received. A datagram is a connectionless packet whose delivery to a remote is not guaranteed.

Index: 440   Default Scale: 0.0001

Counter Type: PERF_COUNTER_BULK_COUNT   Counter Size: 8 bytes

Datagrams Received/sec   *Advanced*

Datagrams Received/sec is the rate that datagrams are received by the computer. A datagram is a connectionless packet whose delivery to a remote computer is not guaranteed.

Index: 446   Default Scale: 0.1

Counter Type: PERF_COUNTER_COUNTER   Counter Size: 4 bytes

Datagrams Sent/sec   *Advanced*

Datagrams Sent/sec is the rate that datagrams are sent from the computer. A datagram is a connectionless packet whose delivery to a remote computer is not guaranteed.

Index: 442   Default Scale: 0.1

Counter Type: PERF_COUNTER_COUNTER   Counter Size: 4 bytes

Datagrams/sec   *Advanced*

Datagrams/sec is the rate that datagrams are processed by the computer. This counter displays the sum of datagrams sent and datagrams received. A datagram is a connectionless packet whose delivery to a remote is not guaranteed.

Index: 438   Default Scale: 0.1

Counter Type: PERF_COUNTER_COUNTER   Counter Size: 4 bytes

Disconnects Local   *Advanced*

Disconnects Local is the number of session disconnections that were initiated by the local computer. This number is an accumulator and shows a running total.

Index: 418   Default Scale: 1

Counter Type: PERF_COUNTER_RAWCOUNT   Counter Size: 4 bytes

Disconnects Remote   *Advanced*

Disconnects Remote is the number of session disconnections that were initiated by the remote computer. This number is an accumulator and shows a running total.

Index: 420   Default Scale: 1

Counter Type: PERF_COUNTER_RAWCOUNT   Counter Size: 4 bytes

Expirations Ack   *Advanced*

Expirations Ack is the count of T2 timer expirations

Index: 478   Default Scale: 1

Counter Type: PERF_COUNTER_RAWCOUNT   Counter Size: 4 bytes

Expirations Response   *Wizard*

Expirations Response is the count of T1 timer expirations.

Index: 476   Default Scale: 1

Counter Type: PERF_COUNTER_RAWCOUNT   Counter Size: 4 bytes

Failures Adapter   *Advanced*

Failures Adapter is the number of connections that were dropped due to an adapter failure. This number is an accumulator and shows a running total.

Index: 424   Default Scale: 1

Counter Type: PERF_COUNTER_RAWCOUNT   Counter Size: 4 bytes

Failures Link   *Advanced*

Failures Link is the number of connections that were dropped due to a link failure. This number is an accumulator and shows a running total.

Index: 422   Default Scale: 1

Counter Type: PERF_COUNTER_RAWCOUNT   Counter Size: 4 bytes

Failures No Listen   *Advanced*

Failures No Listen is the number of connections that were rejected because the remote computer was not listening for connection requests.

Index: 436   Default Scale: 1

Counter Type: PERF_COUNTER_RAWCOUNT   Counter Size: 4 bytes

Failures Not Found   *Advanced*

Failures Not Found is the number of connection attempts that failed because the remote computer could not be found. This number is an accumulator and shows a running total.

Index: 434   Default Scale: 1

Counter Type: PERF_COUNTER_RAWCOUNT   Counter Size: 4 bytes

Failures Resource Local   *Advanced*

Failures Resource Local is the number of connections that failed because of resource problems or shortages on the local computer. This number is an accumulator and shows a running total.

Index: 432   Default Scale: 1

Counter Type: PERF_COUNTER_RAWCOUNT   Counter Size: 4 bytes

Failures Resource Remote *Advanced*

Failures Resource Remote is the number of connections that failed because of resource problems or shortages on the remote computer. This number is an accumulator and shows a running total.

Index: 430   Default Scale: 1

Counter Type: PERF_COUNTER_RAWCOUNT   Counter Size: 4 bytes

Frame Bytes Received/sec *Advanced*

Frame Bytes Received/sec is the rate that data bytes are received by the computer. This counter only counts the frames (packets) that carry data.

Index: 466   Default Scale: 0.0001

Counter Type: PERF_COUNTER_BULK_COUNT   Counter Size: 8 bytes

Frame Bytes Rejected/sec *Expert*

Frame Bytes Rejected/sec is the rate that data bytes are rejected. This counter only counts the bytes in data frames (packets) that carry data.

Index: 474   Default Scale: 0.0001

Counter Type: PERF_COUNTER_BULK_COUNT   Counter Size: 8 bytes

Frame Bytes Re-Sent/sec *Wizard*

Frame Bytes Re-Sent/sec is the rate that data bytes are re-sent by the computer. This counter only counts the bytes in frames that carry data.

Index: 470   Default Scale: 0.0001

Counter Type: PERF_COUNTER_BULK_COUNT   Counter Size: 8 bytes

Frame Bytes Sent/sec *Advanced*

Frame Bytes Sent/sec is the rate that data bytes are sent by the computer. This counter only counts the bytes in frames (packets) that carry data.

Index: 462   Default Scale: 0.0001

Counter Type: PERF_COUNTER_BULK_COUNT   Counter Size: 8 bytes

Frame Bytes/sec *Advanced*

Frame Bytes/sec is the rate that data bytes are processed by the computer. This counter is the sum of data frame bytes sent and received. This counter only counts the byte in frames (packets) that carry data.

Index: 458   Default Scale: 0.0001

Counter Type: PERF_COUNTER_BULK_COUNT   Counter Size: 8 bytes

Frames Received/sec   *Advanced*

Frames Received/sec is the rate that data frames are received by the computer. This counter only counts the frames (packets) that carry data.

Index: 464   Default Scale: 0.1

Counter Type: PERF_COUNTER_COUNTER   Counter Size: 4 bytes

Frames Rejected/sec   *Expert*

Frames Rejected/sec is the rate that data frames are rejected. This counter only counts the frames (packets) that carry data.

Index: 472   Default Scale: 0.1

Counter Type: PERF_COUNTER_COUNTER   Counter Size: 4 bytes

Frames Re-Sent/sec   *Expert*

Frames Re-Sent/sec is the rate that data frames (packets) are re-sent by the computer. This counter only counts the frames or packets that carry data.

Index: 468   Default Scale: 0.1

Counter Type: PERF_COUNTER_COUNTER   Counter Size: 4 bytes

Frames Sent/sec   *Advanced*

Frames Sent/sec is the rate that data frames are sent by the computer. This counter only counts the frames (packets) that carry data.

Index: 460   Default Scale: 0.1

Counter Type: PERF_COUNTER_COUNTER   Counter Size: 4 bytes

Frames/sec   *Advanced*

Frames/sec is the rate that data frames (or packets) are processed by the computer. This counter is the sum of data frames sent and data frames received. This counter only counts those frames (packets) that carry data.

Index: 456   Default Scale: 0.1

Counter Type: PERF_COUNTER_COUNTER   Counter Size: 4 bytes

Packets Received/sec   *Expert*

Packets Received/sec is the rate that packets are received by the computer. This counter counts all packets processed: control as well as data packets.

Index: 266   Default Scale: 0.1

Counter Type: PERF_COUNTER_COUNTER   Counter Size: 4 bytes

Packets Sent/sec *Advanced*

Packets Sent/sec is the rate that packets are sent by the computer. This counter counts all packets sent by the computer, control as well as data packets.

Index: 452   Default Scale: 0.1

Counter Type: PERF_COUNTER_COUNTER   Counter Size: 4 bytes

Packets/sec *Advanced*

Packets/sec is the rate that packets are processed by the computer. This count is the sum of Packets Sent and Packets Received per second. This counter includes all packets processed: control as well as data packets.

Index: 400   Default Scale: 0.1

Counter Type: PERF_COUNTER_COUNTER   Counter Size: 4 bytes

Piggyback Ack Queued/sec *Advanced*

Piggyback Ack Queued/sec is the rate that piggybacked acknowledgments are queued. Piggyback acknowledgments are acknowledgments to received packets that are to be included in the next outgoing packet to the remote computer.

Index: 484   Default Scale: 0.1

Counter Type: PERF_COUNTER_COUNTER   Counter Size: 4 bytes

Piggyback Ack Timeouts *Advanced*

Piggyback Ack Timeouts is the number of times that a piggyback acknowledgment could not be sent because there was no outgoing packet to the remote on which to piggyback. A piggyback ack is an acknowledgment to a received packet that is sent along in an outgoing data packet to the remote computer. If no outgoing packet is sent within the timeout period, then an ack packet is sent and this counter is incremented.

Index: 486   Default Scale: 0.1

Counter Type: PERF_COUNTER_RAWCOUNT   Counter Size: 4 bytes

Window Send Average *Advanced*

Window Send Average is the running average number of data bytes that were sent before waiting for an acknowledgment from the remote computer.

Index: 482   Default Scale: 1

Counter Type: PERF_COUNTER_RAWCOUNT   Counter Size: 4 bytes

Window Send Maximum   *Advanced*

Window Send Maximum is the maximum number of bytes of data that will be sent before waiting for an acknowledgment from the remote computer.

Index: 480   Default Scale: 1

Counter Type: PERF_COUNTER_RAWCOUNT   Counter Size: 4 bytes

NetBEUI Resource Object

Object: NetBEUI Resource   Index: 494   *Advanced*

The NetBEUI Resource object tracks the use of resources (that is, buffers) by the NetBEUI protocol.

Times Exhausted   *Advanced*

Times Exhausted is the number of times all the resources (buffers) were in use. The number in parentheses following the resource name is used to identify the resource in Event Log messages.

Index: 500   Default Scale: 1

Counter Type: PERF_COUNTER_RAWCOUNT   Counter Size: 4 bytes

Used Average   *Advanced*

Used Average is the current number of resources (buffers) in use at this time. The number in parentheses following the resource name is used to identify the resource in Event Log messages.

Index: 498   Default Scale: 1

Counter Type: PERF_COUNTER_RAWCOUNT   Counter Size: 4 bytes

Used Maximum   *Advanced*

Used Maximum is the maximum number of NetBEUI resources (buffers) in use at any point in time. This value is useful in sizing the maximum resources provided. The number in parentheses following the resource name is used to identify the resource in Event Log messages.

Index: 496   Default Scale: 1

Counter Type: PERF_COUNTER_RAWCOUNT   Counter Size: 4 bytes

Network Interface Object

Object: Network Interface   Index: 510   *Advanced*

The Network Interface Object Type includes those counters that describe the rates that bytes and packets are received and sent over a Network TCP/IP connection. It also describes various error counts for the same connection.

Bytes Received/sec   *Advanced*

Bytes Received/sec is the rate that bytes are received on the interface, including framing characters.

Index: 264   Default Scale: 0.0001

Counter Type: PERF_COUNTER_COUNTER   Counter Size: 4 bytes

Bytes Sent/sec   *Advanced*

Bytes Sent/sec is the rate that bytes are sent on the interface, including framing characters.

Index: 506   Default Scale: 0.0001

Counter Type: PERF_COUNTER_COUNTER   Counter Size: 4 bytes

Bytes Total/sec   *Advanced*

Bytes Total/sec is the rate that bytes are sent and received on the interface, including framing characters.

Index: 388   Default Scale: 0.0001

Counter Type: PERF_COUNTER_COUNTER   Counter Size: 4 bytes

Current Bandwidth   *Advanced*

Current Bandwidth is an estimate of the interface's current bandwidth in bits per second (bps). For interfaces that do not vary in bandwidth or for those where no accurate estimation can be made, this value is the nominal bandwidth.

Index: 520   Default Scale: 0.000001

Counter Type: PERF_COUNTER_RAWCOUNT   Counter Size: 4 bytes

Output Queue Length   *Advanced*

Output Queue Length is the length of the output packet queue (in packets.) If this is longer than 2, delays are being experienced and the bottleneck should be found and eliminated if possible. Since the requests are queued by NDIS in this implementation, this will always be 0.

Index: 544   Default Scale: 1

Counter Type: PERF_COUNTER_RAWCOUNT   Counter Size: 4 bytes

Packets Outbound Discarded   *Advanced*

Packets Outbound Discarded is the number of outbound packets that were chosen to be discarded even though no errors had been detected to prevent their being transmitted. One possible reason for discarding such a packet could be to free up buffer space.

Index: 540   Default Scale: 1

Counter Type: PERF_COUNTER_RAWCOUNT   Counter Size: 4 bytes

Packets Outbound Errors   *Advanced*

Packets Outbound Errors is the number of outbound packets that could not be transmitted because of errors.

Index: 542   Default Scale: 1

Counter Type: PERF_COUNTER_RAWCOUNT   Counter Size: 4 bytes

Packets Received Discarded   *Advanced*

Packets Received Discarded is the number of inbound packets that were chosen to be discarded even though no errors had been detected to prevent their being deliverable to a higher-layer protocol. One possible reason for discarding such a packet could be to free up buffer space.

Index: 528   Default Scale: 1

Counter Type: PERF_COUNTER_RAWCOUNT   Counter Size: 4 bytes

Packets Received Errors   *Advanced*

Packets Received Errors is the number of inbound packets that contained errors preventing them from being deliverable to a higher-layer protocol.

Index: 530   Default Scale: 1

Counter Type: PERF_COUNTER_RAWCOUNT   Counter Size: 4 bytes

Packets Received Non-Unicast/sec   *Expert*

Packets Received Non-Unicast/sec is the rate that non-unicast (that is, subnet broadcast or subnet multicast) packets are delivered to a higher-layer protocol.

Index: 526   Default Scale: 0.1

Counter Type: PERF_COUNTER_COUNTER   Counter Size: 4 bytes

Packets Received Unicast/sec   *Expert*

Packets Received Unicast/sec is the rate that (subnet) unicast packets are delivered to a higher-layer protocol.

Index: 524   Default Scale: 0.1

Counter Type: PERF_COUNTER_COUNTER   Counter Size: 4 bytes

Packets Received Unknown   *Advanced*

Packets Received Unknown is the number of packets received via the interface that were discarded because of an unknown or unsupported protocol.

Index: 532   Default Scale: 1

Counter Type: PERF_COUNTER_RAWCOUNT   Counter Size: 4 bytes

Packets Received/sec   *Advanced*

Packets Received/sec is the rate that packets are received on the network interface.

Index: 266   Default Scale: 0.1

Counter Type: PERF_COUNTER_COUNTER   Counter Size: 4 bytes

Packets Sent/sec   *Advanced*

Packets Sent/sec is the rate that packets are sent on the network interface.

Index: 452   Default Scale: 0.1

Counter Type: PERF_COUNTER_COUNTER   Counter Size: 4 bytes

Packets Sent Non-Unicast/sec   *Expert*

Packets Sent Non-Unicast/sec is the rate that packets are requested to be transmitted to non-unicast (that is, subnet broadcast or subnet multicast) addresses by higher-level protocols. The rate includes the packets that were discarded or not sent.

Index: 538   Default Scale: 0.1

Counter Type: PERF_COUNTER_COUNTER   Counter Size: 4 bytes

Packets Sent Unicast/sec   *Expert*

Packets Sent Unicast/sec is the rate that packets are requested to be transmitted to subnet-unicast addresses by higher-level protocols. The rate includes the packets that were discarded or not sent.

Index: 536   Default Scale: 0.1

Counter Type: PERF_COUNTER_COUNTER   Counter Size: 4 bytes

Packets/sec   *Advanced*

Packets/sec is the rate that packets are sent and received on the network interface.

Index: 400   Default Scale: 0.1

Counter Type: PERF_COUNTER_COUNTER   Counter Size: 4 bytes

NWLink IPX Object

Object: NWLink IPX   Index: 488   *Advanced*

The NWLink IPX transport handles datagram transmission to and from computers using the IPX protocol.

Bytes Total/sec   *Advanced*

Bytes Total/sec is the sum of Frame Bytes/sec and Datagram Bytes/sec. This is the total rate of bytes sent to or received from the network by the protocol, but only counts the bytes in frames (that is, packets) which carry data.

Index: 388   Default Scale: 0.0001

Counter Type: PERF_COUNTER_BULK_COUNT   Counter Size: 8 bytes

Connection Session Timeouts   *Advanced*

Connection Session Timeouts is the number of connections that were dropped due to a session timeout. This number is an accumulator and shows a running total.

Index: 426   Default Scale: 1

Counter Type: PERF_COUNTER_RAWCOUNT   Counter Size: 4 bytes

Connections Canceled   *Advanced*

Connections Canceled is the number of connections that were canceled. This number is an accumulator and shows a running total.

Index: 428   Default Scale: 1

Counter Type: PERF_COUNTER_RAWCOUNT   Counter Size: 4 bytes

Connections No Retries   *Advanced*

Connections No Retries is the total count of connections that were successfully made on the first try. This number is an accumulator and shows a running total.

Index: 414   Default Scale: 1

Counter Type: PERF_COUNTER_RAWCOUNT   Counter Size: 4 bytes

Connections Open   *Advanced*

Connections Open is the number of connections currently open for this protocol. This counter shows the current count only and does not accumulate over time.

Index: 412   Default Scale: 1

Counter Type: PERF_COUNTER_RAWCOUNT   Counter Size: 4 bytes

Connections With Retries   *Advanced*

Connections With Retries is the total count of connections that were made after retrying the attempt. A retry occurs when the first connection attempt failed. This number is an accumulator and shows a running total.

Index: 416   Default Scale: 1

Counter Type: PERF_COUNTER_RAWCOUNT   Counter Size: 4 bytes

Datagram Bytes Received/sec   *Advanced*

Datagram Bytes Received/sec is the rate that datagram bytes are received by the computer. A datagram is a connectionless packet whose delivery to a remote computer is not guaranteed.

Index: 448   Default Scale: 0.0001

Counter Type: PERF_COUNTER_BULK_COUNT   Counter Size: 8 bytes

Datagram Bytes Sent/sec   *Advanced*

Datagram Bytes Sent/sec is the rate that datagram bytes are sent from the computer. A datagram is a connectionless packet whose delivery to a remote computer is not guaranteed.

Index: 444   Default Scale: 0.0001

Counter Type: PERF_COUNTER_BULK_COUNT   Counter Size: 8 bytes

Datagram Bytes/sec   *Advanced*

Datagram Bytes/sec is the rate that datagram bytes are processed by the computer. This counter is the sum of datagram bytes that are sent as well as received. A datagram is a connectionless packet whose delivery to a remote is not guaranteed.

Index: 440   Default Scale: 0.0001

Counter Type: PERF_COUNTER_BULK_COUNT   Counter Size: 8 bytes

Datagrams Received/sec   *Advanced*

Datagrams Received/sec is the rate that datagrams are received by the computer. A datagram is a connectionless packet whose delivery to a remote computer is not guaranteed.

Index: 446   Default Scale: 0.1

Counter Type: PERF_COUNTER_COUNTER   Counter Size: 4 bytes

Datagrams Sent/sec   *Advanced*

Datagrams Sent/sec is the rate that datagrams are sent from the computer. A datagram is a connectionless packet whose delivery to a remote computer is not guaranteed.

Index: 442   Default Scale: 0.1

Counter Type: PERF_COUNTER_COUNTER   Counter Size: 4 bytes

Datagrams/sec   *Advanced*

Datagrams/sec is the rate that datagrams are processed by the computer. This counter displays the sum of datagrams sent and datagrams received. A datagram is a connectionless packet whose delivery to a remote is not guaranteed.

Index: 438   Default Scale: 0.1

Counter Type: PERF_COUNTER_COUNTER   Counter Size: 4 bytes

Disconnects Local   *Advanced*

Disconnects Local is the number of session disconnections that were initiated by the local computer. This number is an accumulator and shows a running total.

Index: 418   Default Scale: 1

Counter Type: PERF_COUNTER_RAWCOUNT   Counter Size: 4 bytes

Disconnects Remote   *Advanced*

Disconnects Remote is the number of session disconnections that were initiated by the remote computer. This number is an accumulator and shows a running total.

Index: 420   Default Scale: 1

Counter Type: PERF_COUNTER_RAWCOUNT   Counter Size: 4 bytes

Expirations Ack   *Advanced*

Expirations Ack is the count of T2 timer expirations

Index: 478   Default Scale: 1

Counter Type: PERF_COUNTER_RAWCOUNT   Counter Size: 4 bytes

Expirations Response   *Wizard*

Expirations Response is the count of T1 timer expirations.

Index: 476   Default Scale: 1

Counter Type: PERF_COUNTER_RAWCOUNT   Counter Size: 4 bytes

Failures Adapter   *Advanced*

Failures Adapter is the number of connections that were dropped due to an adapter failure. This number is an accumulator and shows a running total.

Index: 424   Default Scale: 1

Counter Type: PERF_COUNTER_RAWCOUNT   Counter Size: 4 bytes

Failures Link   *Advanced*

Failures Link is the number of connections that were dropped due to a link failure. This number is an accumulator and shows a running total.

Index: 422   Default Scale: 1

Counter Type: PERF_COUNTER_RAWCOUNT   Counter Size: 4 bytes

Failures No Listen   *Advanced*

Failures No Listen is the number of connections that were rejected because the remote computer was not listening for connection requests.

Index: 436   Default Scale: 1

Counter Type: PERF_COUNTER_RAWCOUNT   Counter Size: 4 bytes

Failures Not Found   *Advanced*

Failures Not Found is the number of connection attempts that failed because the remote computer could not be found. This number is an accumulator and shows a running total.

Index: 434   Default Scale: 1

Counter Type: PERF_COUNTER_RAWCOUNT   Counter Size: 4 bytes

Failures Resource Local   *Advanced*

Failures Resource Local is the number of connections that failed because of resource problems or shortages on the local computer. This number is an accumulator and shows a running total.

Index: 432   Default Scale: 1

Counter Type: PERF_COUNTER_RAWCOUNT   Counter Size: 4 bytes

Failures Resource Remote   *Advanced*

Failures Resource Remote is the number of connections that failed because of resource problems or shortages on the remote computer. This number is an accumulator and shows a running total.

Index: 430   Default Scale: 1

Counter Type: PERF_COUNTER_RAWCOUNT   Counter Size: 4 bytes

Frame Bytes Received/sec   *Advanced*

Frame Bytes Received/sec is the rate that data bytes are received by the computer. This counter only counts the frames (packets) that carry data.

Index: 466   Default Scale: 0.0001

Counter Type: PERF_COUNTER_BULK_COUNT   Counter Size: 8 bytes

Frame Bytes Rejected/sec   *Expert*

Frame Bytes Rejected/sec is the rate that data bytes are rejected. This counter only counts the bytes in data frames (packets) that carry data.

Index: 474   Default Scale: 0.0001

Counter Type: PERF_COUNTER_BULK_COUNT   Counter Size: 8 bytes

Frame Bytes Re-Sent/sec   *Wizard*

Frame Bytes Re-Sent/sec is the rate that data bytes are re-sent by the computer. This counter only counts the bytes in frames that carry data.

Index: 470   Default Scale: 0.0001

Counter Type: PERF_COUNTER_BULK_COUNT   Counter Size: 8 bytes

Frame Bytes Sent/sec *Advanced*

Frame Bytes Sent/sec is the rate that data bytes are sent by the computer. This counter only counts the bytes in frames (packets) that carry data.

Index: 462   Default Scale: 0.0001

Counter Type: PERF_COUNTER_BULK_COUNT   Counter Size: 8 bytes

Frame Bytes/sec *Advanced*

Frame Bytes/sec is the rate that data bytes are processed by the computer. This counter is the sum of data frame bytes sent and received. This counter only counts the byte in frames (packets) that carry data.

Index: 458   Default Scale: 0.0001

Counter Type: PERF_COUNTER_BULK_COUNT   Counter Size: 8 bytes

Frames Received/sec *Advanced*

Frames Received/sec is the rate that data frames are received by the computer. This counter only counts the frames (packets) that carry data.

Index: 464   Default Scale: 0.1

Counter Type: PERF_COUNTER_COUNTER   Counter Size: 4 bytes

Frames Rejected/sec *Expert*

Frames Rejected/sec is the rate that data frames are rejected. This counter only counts the frames (packets) that carry data.

Index: 472   Default Scale: 0.1

Counter Type: PERF_COUNTER_COUNTER   Counter Size: 4 bytes

Frames Re-Sent/sec *Expert*

Frames Re-Sent/sec is the rate that data frames (packets) are re-sent by the computer. This counter only counts the frames or packets that carry data.

Index: 468   Default Scale: 0.1

Counter Type: PERF_COUNTER_COUNTER   Counter Size: 4 bytes

Frames Sent/sec *Advanced*

Frames Sent/sec is the rate that data frames are sent by the computer. This counter only counts the frames (packets) that carry data.

Index: 460   Default Scale: 0.1

Counter Type: PERF_COUNTER_COUNTER   Counter Size: 4 bytes

Frames/sec   *Advanced*

Frames/sec is the rate that data frames (or packets) are processed by the computer. This counter is the sum of data frames sent and data frames received. This counter only counts those frames (packets) that carry data.

Index: 456   Default Scale: 0.1

Counter Type: PERF_COUNTER_COUNTER   Counter Size: 4 bytes

Packets Received/sec   *Expert*

Packets Received/sec is the rate that packets are received by the computer. This counter counts all packets processed: control as well as data packets.

Index: 266   Default Scale: 0.1

Counter Type: PERF_COUNTER_COUNTER   Counter Size: 4 bytes

Packets Sent/sec   *Advanced*

Packets Sent/sec is the rate that packets are sent by the computer. This counter counts all packets sent by the computer, control as well as data packets.

Index: 452   Default Scale: 0.1

Counter Type: PERF_COUNTER_COUNTER   Counter Size: 4 bytes

Packets/sec   *Advanced*

Packets/sec is the rate that packets are processed by the computer. This count is the sum of Packets Sent and Packets Received per second. This counter includes all packets processed: control as well as data packets.

Index: 400   Default Scale: 0.1

Counter Type: PERF_COUNTER_COUNTER   Counter Size: 4 bytes

Piggyback Ack Queued/sec   *Advanced*

Piggyback Ack Queued/sec is the rate that piggybacked acknowledgments are queued. Piggyback acknowledgments are acknowledgments to received packets that are to be included in the next outgoing packet to the remote computer.

Index: 484   Default Scale: 0.1

Counter Type: PERF_COUNTER_COUNTER   Counter Size: 4 bytes

Piggyback Ack Timeouts   *Advanced*

Piggyback Ack Timeouts is the number of times that a piggyback acknowledgment could not be sent because there was no outgoing packet to the remote on which to piggyback. A piggyback ack is an acknowledgment to a received packet that is sent along in an outgoing data packet to the remote computer. If no outgoing packet is sent within the timeout period, then an ack packet is sent and this counter is incremented.

Index: 486   Default Scale: 0.1

Counter Type: PERF_COUNTER_RAWCOUNT   Counter Size: 4 bytes

Window Send Average   *Advanced*

Window Send Average is the running average number of data bytes that were sent before waiting for an acknowledgment from the remote computer.

Index: 482   Default Scale: 1

Counter Type: PERF_COUNTER_RAWCOUNT   Counter Size: 4 bytes

Window Send Maximum   *Advanced*

Window Send Maximum is the maximum number of bytes of data that will be sent before waiting for an acknowledgment from the remote computer.

Index: 480   Default Scale: 1

Counter Type: PERF_COUNTER_RAWCOUNT   Counter Size: 4 bytes

NWLink NetBIOS Object

Object: NWLink NetBIOS   Index: 398   *Advanced*

The NWLink NetBIOS protocol layer handles the interface to applications communicating over the IPX transport.

Bytes Total/sec   *Advanced*

Bytes Total/sec is the sum of Frame Bytes/sec and Datagram Bytes/sec. This is the total rate of bytes sent to or received from the network by the protocol, but only counts the bytes in frames (that is, packets) which carry data.

Index: 388   Default Scale: 0.0001

Counter Type: PERF_COUNTER_BULK_COUNT   Counter Size: 8 bytes

Connection Session Timeouts   *Advanced*

Connection Session Timeouts is the number of connections that were dropped due to a session timeout. This number is an accumulator and shows a running total.

Index: 426   Default Scale: 1

Counter Type: PERF_COUNTER_RAWCOUNT   Counter Size: 4 bytes

Connections Canceled   *Advanced*

Connections Canceled is the number of connections that were canceled. This number is an accumulator and shows a running total.

Index: 428   Default Scale: 1

Counter Type: PERF_COUNTER_RAWCOUNT   Counter Size: 4 bytes

Connections No Retries   *Advanced*

Connections No Retries is the total count of connections that were successfully made on the first try. This number is an accumulator and shows a running total.

Index: 414   Default Scale: 1

Counter Type: PERF_COUNTER_RAWCOUNT   Counter Size: 4 bytes

Connections Open   *Advanced*

Connections Open is the number of connections currently open for this protocol. This counter shows the current count only and does not accumulate over time.

Index: 412   Default Scale: 1

Counter Type: PERF_COUNTER_RAWCOUNT   Counter Size: 4 bytes

Connections With Retries   *Advanced*

Connections With Retries is the total count of connections that were made after retrying the attempt. A retry occurs when the first connection attempt failed. This number is an accumulator and shows a running total.

Index: 416   Default Scale: 1

Counter Type: PERF_COUNTER_RAWCOUNT   Counter Size: 4 bytes

Datagram Bytes Received/sec   *Advanced*

Datagram Bytes Received/sec is the rate that datagram bytes are received by the computer. A datagram is a connectionless packet whose delivery to a remote computer is not guaranteed.

Index: 448   Default Scale: 0.0001

Counter Type: PERF_COUNTER_BULK_COUNT   Counter Size: 8 bytes

Datagram Bytes Sent/sec   *Advanced*

Datagram Bytes Sent/sec is the rate that datagram bytes are sent from the computer. A datagram is a connectionless packet whose delivery to a remote computer is not guaranteed.

Index: 444   Default Scale: 0.0001

Counter Type: PERF_COUNTER_BULK_COUNT   Counter Size: 8 bytes

Datagram Bytes/sec   *Advanced*

Datagram Bytes/sec is the rate that datagram bytes are processed by the computer. This counter is the sum of datagram bytes that are sent as well as received. A datagram is a connectionless packet whose delivery to a remote is not guaranteed.

Index: 440   Default Scale: 0.0001

Counter Type: PERF_COUNTER_BULK_COUNT   Counter Size: 8 bytes

Datagrams Received/sec   *Advanced*

Datagrams Received/sec is the rate that datagrams are received by the computer. A datagram is a connectionless packet whose delivery to a remote computer is not guaranteed.

Index: 446   Default Scale: 0.1

Counter Type: PERF_COUNTER_COUNTER   Counter Size: 4 bytes

Datagrams Sent/sec   *Advanced*

Datagrams Sent/sec is the rate that datagrams are sent from the computer. A datagram is a connectionless packet whose delivery to a remote computer is not guaranteed.

Index: 442   Default Scale: 0.1

Counter Type: PERF_COUNTER_COUNTER   Counter Size: 4 bytes

Datagrams/sec   *Advanced*

Datagrams/sec is the rate that datagrams are processed by the computer. This counter displays the sum of datagrams sent and datagrams received. A datagram is a connectionless packet whose delivery to a remote is not guaranteed.

Index: 438   Default Scale: 0.1

Counter Type: PERF_COUNTER_COUNTER   Counter Size: 4 bytes

Disconnects Local   *Advanced*

Disconnects Local is the number of session disconnections that were initiated by the local computer. This number is an accumulator and shows a running total.

Index: 418   Default Scale: 1

Counter Type: PERF_COUNTER_RAWCOUNT   Counter Size: 4 bytes

Disconnects Remote   *Advanced*

Disconnects Remote is the number of session disconnections that were initiated by the remote computer. This number is an accumulator and shows a running total.

Index: 420   Default Scale: 1

Counter Type: PERF_COUNTER_RAWCOUNT   Counter Size: 4 bytes

Expirations Ack   *Advanced*

Expirations Ack is the count of T2 timer expirations

Index: 478   Default Scale: 1

Counter Type: PERF_COUNTER_RAWCOUNT   Counter Size: 4 bytes

Expirations Response   *Wizard*

Expirations Response is the count of T1 timer expirations.

Index: 476   Default Scale: 1

Counter Type: PERF_COUNTER_RAWCOUNT   Counter Size: 4 bytes

Failures Adapter   *Advanced*

Failures Adapter is the number of connections that were dropped due to an adapter failure. This number is an accumulator and shows a running total.

Index: 424   Default Scale: 1

Counter Type: PERF_COUNTER_RAWCOUNT   Counter Size: 4 bytes

Failures Link   *Advanced*

Failures Link is the number of connections that were dropped due to a link failure. This number is an accumulator and shows a running total.

Index: 422   Default Scale: 1

Counter Type: PERF_COUNTER_RAWCOUNT   Counter Size: 4 bytes

Failures No Listen   *Advanced*

Failures No Listen is the number of connections that were rejected because the remote computer was not listening for connection requests.

Index: 436   Default Scale: 1

Counter Type: PERF_COUNTER_RAWCOUNT   Counter Size: 4 bytes

Failures Not Found   *Advanced*

Failures Not Found is the number of connection attempts that failed because the remote computer could not be found. This number is an accumulator and shows a running total.

Index: 434   Default Scale: 1

Counter Type: PERF_COUNTER_RAWCOUNT   Counter Size: 4 bytes

Failures Resource Local   *Advanced*

Failures Resource Local is the number of connections that failed because of resource problems or shortages on the local computer. This number is an accumulator and shows a running total.

Index: 432   Default Scale: 1

Counter Type: PERF_COUNTER_RAWCOUNT   Counter Size: 4 bytes

Failures Resource Remote   *Advanced*

Failures Resource Remote is the number of connections that failed because of resource problems or shortages on the remote computer. This number is an accumulator and shows a running total.

Index: 430   Default Scale: 1

Counter Type: PERF_COUNTER_RAWCOUNT   Counter Size: 4 bytes

Frame Bytes Received/sec   *Advanced*

Frame Bytes Received/sec is the rate that data bytes are received by the computer. This counter only counts the frames (packets) that carry data.

Index: 466   Default Scale: 0.0001

Counter Type: PERF_COUNTER_BULK_COUNT   Counter Size: 8 bytes

Frame Bytes Rejected/sec   *Expert*

Frame Bytes Rejected/sec is the rate that data bytes are rejected. This counter only counts the bytes in data frames (packets) that carry data.

Index: 474   Default Scale: 0.0001

Counter Type: PERF_COUNTER_BULK_COUNT   Counter Size: 8 bytes

Frame Bytes Re-Sent/sec   *Wizard*

Frame Bytes Re-Sent/sec is the rate that data bytes are re-sent by the computer. This counter only counts the bytes in frames that carry data.

Index: 470   Default Scale: 0.0001

Counter Type: PERF_COUNTER_BULK_COUNT   Counter Size: 8 bytes

Frame Bytes Sent/sec   *Advanced*

Frame Bytes Sent/sec is the rate that data bytes are sent by the computer. This counter only counts the bytes in frames (packets) that carry data.

Index: 462   Default Scale: 0.0001

Counter Type: PERF_COUNTER_BULK_COUNT   Counter Size: 8 bytes

Frame Bytes/sec   *Advanced*

Frame Bytes/sec is the rate that data bytes are processed by the computer. This counter is the sum of data frame bytes sent and received. This counter only counts the byte in frames (packets) that carry data.

Index: 458   Default Scale: 0.0001

Counter Type: PERF_COUNTER_BULK_COUNT   Counter Size: 8 bytes

Frames Received/sec   *Advanced*

Frames Received/sec is the rate that data frames are received by the computer. This counter only counts the frames (packets) that carry data.

Index: 464   Default Scale: 0.1

Counter Type: PERF_COUNTER_COUNTER   Counter Size: 4 bytes

Frames Rejected/sec   *Expert*

Frames Rejected/sec is the rate that data frames are rejected. This counter only counts the frames (packets) that carry data.

Index: 472   Default Scale: 0.1

Counter Type: PERF_COUNTER_COUNTER   Counter Size: 4 bytes

Frames Re-Sent/sec   *Expert*

Frames Re-Sent/sec is the rate that data frames (packets) are re-sent by the computer. This counter only counts the frames or packets that carry data.

Index: 468   Default Scale: 0.1

Counter Type: PERF_COUNTER_COUNTER   Counter Size: 4 bytes

Frames Sent/sec   *Advanced*

Frames Sent/sec is the rate that data frames are sent by the computer. This counter only counts the frames (packets) that carry data.

Index: 460   Default Scale: 0.1

Counter Type: PERF_COUNTER_COUNTER   Counter Size: 4 bytes

Frames/sec   *Advanced*

Frames/sec is the rate that data frames (or packets) are processed by the computer. This counter is the sum of data frames sent and data frames received. This counter only counts those frames (packets) that carry data.

Index: 456   Default Scale: 0.1

Counter Type: PERF_COUNTER_COUNTER   Counter Size: 4 bytes

Packets Received/sec   *Expert*

Packets Received/sec is the rate that packets are received by the computer. This counter counts all packets processed: control as well as data packets.

Index: 266   Default Scale: 0.1

Counter Type: PERF_COUNTER_COUNTER   Counter Size: 4 bytes

Packets Sent/sec   *Advanced*

Packets Sent/sec is the rate that packets are sent by the computer. This counter counts all packets sent by the computer, control as well as data packets.

Index: 452   Default Scale: 0.1

Counter Type: PERF_COUNTER_COUNTER   Counter Size: 4 bytes

Packets/sec   *Advanced*

Packets/sec is the rate that packets are processed by the computer. This count is the sum of Packets Sent and Packets Received per second. This counter includes all packets processed: control as well as data packets.

Index: 400   Default Scale: 0.1

Counter Type: PERF_COUNTER_COUNTER   Counter Size: 4 bytes

Piggyback Ack Queued/sec   *Advanced*

Piggyback Ack Queued/sec is the rate that piggybacked acknowledgments are queued. Piggyback acknowledgments are acknowledgments to received packets that are to be included in the next outgoing packet to the remote computer.

Index: 484   Default Scale: 0.1

Counter Type: PERF_COUNTER_COUNTER   Counter Size: 4 bytes

Piggyback Ack Timeouts   *Advanced*

Piggyback Ack Timeouts is the number of times that a piggyback acknowledgment could not be sent because there was no outgoing packet to the remote on which to piggyback. A piggyback ack is an acknowledgment to a received packet that is sent along in an outgoing data packet to the remote computer. If no outgoing packet is sent within the timeout period, then an ack packet is sent and this counter is incremented.

Index: 486   Default Scale: 0.1

Counter Type: PERF_COUNTER_RAWCOUNT   Counter Size: 4 bytes

Window Send Average   *Advanced*

Window Send Average is the running average number of data bytes that were sent before waiting for an acknowledgment from the remote computer.

Index: 482   Default Scale: 1

Counter Type: PERF_COUNTER_RAWCOUNT   Counter Size: 4 bytes

Window Send Maximum   *Advanced*

Window Send Maximum is the maximum number of bytes of data that will be sent before waiting for an acknowledgment from the remote computer.

Index: 480   Default Scale: 1

Counter Type: PERF_COUNTER_RAWCOUNT   Counter Size: 4 bytes

NWLink SPX Object

Object: NWLink SPX   Index: 490   *Advanced*

The NWLink SPX transport handles data transmission and session connections for computers using the SPX protocol.

Bytes Total/sec   *Advanced*

Bytes Total/sec is the sum of Frame Bytes/sec and Datagram Bytes/sec. This is the total rate of bytes sent to or received from the network by the protocol, but only counts the bytes in frames (that is, packets) which carry data.

Index: 388   Default Scale: 0.0001

Counter Type: PERF_COUNTER_BULK_COUNT   Counter Size: 8 bytes

Connection Session Timeouts   *Advanced*

Connection Session Timeouts is the number of connections that were dropped due to a session timeout. This number is an accumulator and shows a running total.

Index: 426   Default Scale: 1

Counter Type: PERF_COUNTER_RAWCOUNT   Counter Size: 4 bytes

Connections Canceled   *Advanced*

Connections Canceled is the number of connections that were canceled. This number is an accumulator and shows a running total.

Index: 428   Default Scale: 1

Counter Type: PERF_COUNTER_RAWCOUNT   Counter Size: 4 bytes

Connections No Retries   *Advanced*

Connections No Retries is the total count of connections that were successfully made on the first try. This number is an accumulator and shows a running total.

Index: 414   Default Scale: 1

Counter Type: PERF_COUNTER_RAWCOUNT   Counter Size: 4 bytes

Connections Open   *Advanced*

Connections Open is the number of connections currently open for this protocol. This counter shows the current count only and does not accumulate over time.

Index: 412   Default Scale: 1

Counter Type: PERF_COUNTER_RAWCOUNT   Counter Size: 4 bytes

Connections With Retries   *Advanced*

Connections With Retries is the total count of connections that were made after retrying the attempt. A retry occurs when the first connection attempt failed. This number is an accumulator and shows a running total.

Index: 416   Default Scale: 1

Counter Type: PERF_COUNTER_RAWCOUNT   Counter Size: 4 bytes

Datagram Bytes Received/sec   *Advanced*

Datagram Bytes Received/sec is the rate that datagram bytes are received by the computer. A datagram is a connectionless packet whose delivery to a remote computer is not guaranteed.

Index: 448   Default Scale: 0.0001

Counter Type: PERF_COUNTER_BULK_COUNT   Counter Size: 8 bytes

Datagram Bytes Sent/sec   *Advanced*

Datagram Bytes Sent/sec is the rate that datagram bytes are sent from the computer. A datagram is a connectionless packet whose delivery to a remote computer is not guaranteed.

Index: 444   Default Scale: 0.0001

Counter Type: PERF_COUNTER_BULK_COUNT   Counter Size: 8 bytes

Datagram Bytes/sec   *Advanced*

Datagram Bytes/sec is the rate that datagram bytes are processed by the computer. This counter is the sum of datagram bytes that are sent as well as received. A datagram is a connectionless packet whose delivery to a remote is not guaranteed.

Index: 440   Default Scale: 0.0001

Counter Type: PERF_COUNTER_BULK_COUNT   Counter Size: 8 bytes

Datagrams Received/sec   *Advanced*

Datagrams Received/sec is the rate that datagrams are received by the computer. A datagram is a connectionless packet whose delivery to a remote computer is not guaranteed.

Index: 446   Default Scale: 0.1

Counter Type: PERF_COUNTER_COUNTER   Counter Size: 4 bytes

Datagrams Sent/sec   *Advanced*

Datagrams Sent/sec is the rate that datagrams are sent from the computer. A datagram is a connectionless packet whose delivery to a remote computer is not guaranteed.

Index: 442   Default Scale: 0.1

Counter Type: PERF_COUNTER_COUNTER   Counter Size: 4 bytes

Datagrams/sec   *Advanced*

Datagrams/sec is the rate that datagrams are processed by the computer. This counter displays the sum of datagrams sent and datagrams received. A datagram is a connectionless packet whose delivery to a remote is not guaranteed.

Index: 438   Default Scale: 0.1

Counter Type: PERF_COUNTER_COUNTER   Counter Size: 4 bytes

Disconnects Local   *Advanced*

Disconnects Local is the number of session disconnections that were initiated by the local computer. This number is an accumulator and shows a running total.

Index: 418   Default Scale: 1

Counter Type: PERF_COUNTER_RAWCOUNT   Counter Size: 4 bytes

Disconnects Remote   *Advanced*

Disconnects Remote is the number of session disconnections that were initiated by the remote computer. This number is an accumulator and shows a running total.

Index: 420   Default Scale: 1

Counter Type: PERF_COUNTER_RAWCOUNT   Counter Size: 4 bytes

Expirations Ack   *Advanced*

Expirations Ack is the count of T2 timer expirations

Index: 478   Default Scale: 1

Counter Type: PERF_COUNTER_RAWCOUNT   Counter Size: 4 bytes

Expirations Response   *Wizard*

Expirations Response is the count of T1 timer expirations.

Index: 476   Default Scale: 1

Counter Type: PERF_COUNTER_RAWCOUNT   Counter Size: 4 bytes

Failures Adapter   *Advanced*

Failures Adapter is the number of connections that were dropped due to an adapter failure. This number is an accumulator and shows a running total.

Index: 424   Default Scale: 1

Counter Type: PERF_COUNTER_RAWCOUNT   Counter Size: 4 bytes

Failures Link   *Advanced*

Failures Link is the number of connections that were dropped due to a link failure. This number is an accumulator and shows a running total.

Index: 422   Default Scale: 1

Counter Type: PERF_COUNTER_RAWCOUNT   Counter Size: 4 bytes

Failures No Listen   *Advanced*

Failures No Listen is the number of connections that were rejected because the remote computer was not listening for connection requests.

Index: 436   Default Scale: 1

Counter Type: PERF_COUNTER_RAWCOUNT   Counter Size: 4 bytes

Failures Not Found   *Advanced*

Failures Not Found is the number of connection attempts that failed because the remote computer could not be found. This number is an accumulator and shows a running total.

Index: 434   Default Scale: 1

Counter Type: PERF_COUNTER_RAWCOUNT   Counter Size: 4 bytes

Failures Resource Local   *Advanced*

Failures Resource Local is the number of connections that failed because of resource problems or shortages on the local computer. This number is an accumulator and shows a running total.

Index: 432   Default Scale: 1

Counter Type: PERF_COUNTER_RAWCOUNT   Counter Size: 4 bytes

Failures Resource Remote   *Advanced*

Failures Resource Remote is the number of connections that failed because of resource problems or shortages on the remote computer. This number is an accumulator and shows a running total.

Index: 430   Default Scale: 1

Counter Type: PERF_COUNTER_RAWCOUNT   Counter Size: 4 bytes

Frame Bytes Received/sec   *Advanced*

Frame Bytes Received/sec is the rate that data bytes are received by the computer. This counter only counts the frames (packets) that carry data.

Index: 466   Default Scale: 0.0001

Counter Type: PERF_COUNTER_BULK_COUNT   Counter Size: 8 bytes

Frame Bytes Rejected/sec   *Expert*

Frame Bytes Rejected/sec is the rate that data bytes are rejected. This counter only counts the bytes in data frames (packets) that carry data.

Index: 474   Default Scale: 0.0001

Counter Type: PERF_COUNTER_BULK_COUNT   Counter Size: 8 bytes

Frame Bytes Re-Sent/sec   *Wizard*

Frame Bytes Re-Sent/sec is the rate that data bytes are re-sent by the computer. This counter only counts the bytes in frames that carry data.

Index: 470   Default Scale: 0.0001

Counter Type: PERF_COUNTER_BULK_COUNT   Counter Size: 8 bytes

Frame Bytes Sent/sec   *Advanced*

Frame Bytes Sent/sec is the rate that data bytes are sent by the computer. This counter only counts the bytes in frames (packets) that carry data.

Index: 462   Default Scale: 0.0001

Counter Type: PERF_COUNTER_BULK_COUNT   Counter Size: 8 bytes

Frame Bytes/sec   *Advanced*

Frame Bytes/sec is the rate that data bytes are processed by the computer. This counter is the sum of data frame bytes sent and received. This counter only counts the byte in frames (packets) that carry data.

Index: 458   Default Scale: 0.0001

Counter Type: PERF_COUNTER_BULK_COUNT   Counter Size: 8 bytes

Frames Received/sec   *Advanced*

Frames Received/sec is the rate that data frames are received by the computer. This counter only counts the frames (packets) that carry data.

Index: 464   Default Scale: 0.1

Counter Type: PERF_COUNTER_COUNTER   Counter Size: 4 bytes

Frames Rejected/sec   *Expert*

Frames Rejected/sec is the rate that data frames are rejected. This counter only counts the frames (packets) that carry data.

Index: 472   Default Scale: 0.1

Counter Type: PERF_COUNTER_COUNTER   Counter Size: 4 bytes

Frames Re-Sent/sec   *Expert*

Frames Re-Sent/sec is the rate that data frames (packets) are re-sent by the computer. This counter only counts the frames or packets that carry data.

Index: 468   Default Scale: 0.1

Counter Type: PERF_COUNTER_COUNTER   Counter Size: 4 bytes

Frames Sent/sec   *Advanced*

Frames Sent/sec is the rate that data frames are sent by the computer. This counter only counts the frames (packets) that carry data.

Index: 460   Default Scale: 0.1

Counter Type: PERF_COUNTER_COUNTER   Counter Size: 4 bytes

Frames/sec   *Advanced*

Frames/sec is the rate that data frames (or packets) are processed by the computer. This counter is the sum of data frames sent and data frames received. This counter only counts those frames (packets) that carry data.

Index: 456   Default Scale: 0.1

Counter Type: PERF_COUNTER_COUNTER   Counter Size: 4 bytes

Packets Received/sec   *Expert*

Packets Received/sec is the rate that packets are received by the computer. This counter counts all packets processed: control as well as data packets.

Index: 266   Default Scale: 0.1

Counter Type: PERF_COUNTER_COUNTER   Counter Size: 4 bytes

Packets Sent/sec   *Advanced*

Packets Sent/sec is the rate that packets are sent by the computer. This counter counts all packets sent by the computer, control as well as data packets.

Index: 452   Default Scale: 0.1

Counter Type: PERF_COUNTER_COUNTER   Counter Size: 4 bytes

Packets/sec   *Advanced*

Packets/sec is the rate that packets are processed by the computer. This count is the sum of Packets Sent and Packets Received per second. This counter includes all packets processed: control as well as data packets.

Index: 400   Default Scale: 0.1

Counter Type: PERF_COUNTER_COUNTER   Counter Size: 4 bytes

Piggyback Ack Queued/sec   *Advanced*

Piggyback Ack Queued/sec is the rate that piggybacked acknowledgments are queued. Piggyback acknowledgments are acknowledgments to received packets that are to be included in the next outgoing packet to the remote computer.

Index: 484   Default Scale: 0.1

Counter Type: PERF_COUNTER_COUNTER   Counter Size: 4 bytes

Piggyback Ack Timeouts   *Advanced*

Piggyback Ack Timeouts is the number of times that a piggyback acknowledgment could not be sent because there was no outgoing packet to the remote on which to piggyback. A piggyback ack is an acknowledgment to a received packet that is sent along in an outgoing data packet to the remote computer. If no outgoing packet is sent within the timeout period, then an ack packet is sent and this counter is incremented.

Index: 486   Default Scale: 0.1

Counter Type: PERF_COUNTER_RAWCOUNT   Counter Size: 4 bytes

Window Send Average   *Advanced*

Window Send Average is the running average number of data bytes that were sent before waiting for an acknowledgment from the remote computer.

Index: 482   Default Scale: 1

Counter Type: PERF_COUNTER_RAWCOUNT   Counter Size: 4 bytes

Window Send Maximum   *Advanced*

Window Send Maximum is the maximum number of bytes of data that will be sent before waiting for an acknowledgment from the remote computer.

Index: 480   Default Scale: 1

Counter Type: PERF_COUNTER_RAWCOUNT   Counter Size: 4 bytes

Objects Object

Object: Objects   Index: 260   *Novice*

The Objects object type is a meta-object that contains information about the objects in existence on the computer. This information can be used to detect the unnecessary consumption of computer resources. Each object requires memory to store basic information about the object.

Events   *Expert*

Events is the number of events in the computer at the time of data collection. Notice that this is an instantaneous count, not an average over the time interval. An event is used when two or more threads wish to synchronize execution.

Index: 252   Default Scale: 0.1

Counter Type: PERF_COUNTER_RAWCOUNT   Counter Size: 4 bytes

Mutexes   *Expert*

Mutexes counts the number of mutexes in the computer at the time of data collection. This is an instantaneous count, not an average over the time interval. Mutexes are used by threads to assure only one thread is executing some section of code.

Index: 256   Default Scale: 1

Counter Type: PERF_COUNTER_RAWCOUNT   Counter Size: 4 bytes

Processes   *Novice*

Processes is the number of processes in the computer at the time of data collection. Notice that this is an instantaneous count, not an average over the time interval. Each process represents the running of a program.

Index: 248   Default Scale: 1

Counter Type: PERF_COUNTER_RAWCOUNT   Counter Size: 4 bytes

Sections   *Expert*

Sections is the number of sections in the computer at the time of data collection. Notice that this is an instantaneous count, not an average over the time interval. A section is a portion of virtual memory created by a process for a storing data. A process may share sections with other processes.

Index: 258   Default Scale: 0.1

Counter Type: PERF_COUNTER_RAWCOUNT   Counter Size: 4 bytes

Semaphores   *Expert*

Semaphores is the number of semaphores in the computer at the time of data collection. Notice that this is an instantaneous count, not an average over the time interval. Threads use semaphores to obtain exclusive access to data structures that they share with other threads.

Index: 254   Default Scale: 0.1

Counter Type: PERF_COUNTER_RAWCOUNT   Counter Size: 4 bytes

Threads   *Novice*

Threads is the number of threads in the computer at the time of data collection. Notice that this is an instantaneous count, not an average over the time interval. A thread is the basic executable entity that can execute instructions in a processor.

Index: 250   Default Scale: 0.1

Counter Type: PERF_COUNTER_RAWCOUNT   Counter Size: 4 bytes

Paging File Object

Object: Paging File   Index: 700   *Advanced*

Displays information about the system's Page File(s).

% Usage   *Advanced*

The amount of the Page File instance in use in percent. See also Process:Page File Bytes.

Index: 702   Default Scale: 1

Counter Type: PERF_RAW_FRACTION   Counter Size: 4 bytes

% Usage Peak   *Advanced*

The peak usage of the Page File instance in percent. See also Process:Page File Bytes Peak.

Index: 704   Default Scale: 1

Counter Type: PERF_RAW_BASE   Counter Size: 4 bytes

PhysicalDisk Object

Object: PhysicalDisk   Index: 234   *Novice*

A Physical Disk object type is a hard or fixed disk drive. It will contain 1 or more logical partitions. Disks are used to store file, program, and paging data. The disk is read to retrieve these items, and written to record changes to them.

% Disk Read Time   *Novice*

Disk Read Time is the percentage of elapsed time that the selected disk drive is busy servicing read requests.

Index: 202   Default Scale: 1

Counter Type: PERF_COUNTER_TIMER   Counter Size: 8 bytes

% Disk Time   *Novice*

Disk Time is the percentage of elapsed time that the selected disk drive is busy servicing read or write requests.

Index: 200   Default Scale: 1

Counter Type: PERF_COUNTER_TIMER   Counter Size: 8 bytes

% Disk Write Time   *Novice*

Disk Write Time is the percentage of elapsed time that the selected disk drive is busy servicing write requests.

Index: 204   Default Scale: 1

Counter Type: PERF_COUNTER_TIMER   Counter Size: 8 bytes

Avg. Disk Bytes/Read   *Expert*

Avg. Disk Bytes/Read is the average number of bytes transferred from the disk during read operations.

Index: 226   Default Scale: 0.01

Counter Type: PERF_AVERAGE_BULK   Counter Size: 8 bytes

Avg. Disk Bytes/Transfer   *Expert*

Avg. Disk Bytes/Transfer is the average number of bytes transferred to or from the disk during write or read operations.

Index: 224   Default Scale: 1

Counter Type: PERF_AVERAGE_BASE   Counter Size: 4 bytes

Avg. Disk Bytes/Write   *Expert*

Avg. Disk Bytes/Write is the average number of bytes transferred to the disk during write operations.

Index: 228   Default Scale: 1

Counter Type: PERF_AVERAGE_BASE   Counter Size: 4 bytes

Avg. Disk sec/Read   *Advanced*

Avg. Disk sec/Read is the average time in seconds of a read of data from the disk.

Index: 208   Default Scale: 1

Counter Type: PERF_AVERAGE_BASE   Counter Size: 4 bytes

Avg. Disk sec/Transfer   *Advanced*

Avg. Disk sec/Transfer is the time in seconds of the average disk transfer.

Index: 206   Default Scale: 1

Counter Type: PERF_AVERAGE_BASE   Counter Size: 4 bytes

Avg. Disk sec/Write   *Advanced*

Avg. Disk sec/Write is the average time in seconds of a write of data to the disk.

Index: 210   Default Scale: 1

Counter Type: PERF_AVERAGE_BASE   Counter Size: 4 bytes

Disk Bytes/sec   *Advanced*

Disk Bytes/sec is the rate bytes are transferred to or from the disk during write or read operations.

Index: 218   Default Scale: 0.0001

Counter Type: PERF_COUNTER_BULK_COUNT   Counter Size: 8 bytes

Disk Queue Length   *Novice*

Disk Queue Length is the number of requests outstanding on the disk at the time the performance data is collected. It includes requests in service at the time of the snapshot. This is an instantaneous length, not an average over the time interval. Multi-spindle disk devices can have multiple requests active at one time, but other concurrent requests are awaiting service. This counter may reflect a transitory high or low queue length, but if there is a sustained load on the disk drive, it is likely that this will be consistently high. Requests are experiencing delays proportional to the length of this queue minus the number of spindles on the disks. This difference should average less than 2 for good performance.

Index: 198   Default Scale: 10

Counter Type: PERF_COUNTER_RAWCOUNT   Counter Size: 4 bytes

Disk Read Bytes/sec   *Advanced*

Disk Read Bytes/sec is the rate bytes are transferred from the disk during read operations.

Index: 220   Default Scale: 0.0001

Counter Type: PERF_COUNTER_BULK_COUNT   Counter Size: 8 bytes

Disk Reads/sec   *Novice*

Disk Reads/sec is the rate of read operations on the disk.

Index: 214   Default Scale: 1

Counter Type: PERF_COUNTER_COUNTER   Counter Size: 4 bytes

Disk Transfers/sec   *Novice*

Disk Transfers/sec is the rate of read and write operations on the disk.

Index: 212   Default Scale: 1

Counter Type: PERF_COUNTER_COUNTER   Counter Size: 4 bytes

Disk Writes/sec   *Novice*

Disk Writes/sec is the rate of write operations on the disk.

Index: 216   Default Scale: 1

Counter Type: PERF_COUNTER_COUNTER   Counter Size: 4 bytes

Disk Write Bytes/sec   *Advanced*

Disk Write Bytes is rate bytes are transferred to the disk during write operations.

Index: 222   Default Scale: 0.0001

Counter Type: PERF_COUNTER_BULK_COUNT   Counter Size: 8 bytes

Process Object

Object: Process   Index: 230   *Novice*

The Process object type is created when a program is run. All the threads in a process share the same address space and have access to the same data.

% Privileged Time   *Advanced*

Privileged Time is the percentage of elapsed time that this process's threads have spent executing code in Privileged Mode. When a Windows NT system service is called, the service will often run in Privileged Mode to gain access to system-private data. Such data is protected from access by threads executing in User Mode. Calls to the system may be explicit, or they may be implicit such as when a page fault or an interrupt occurs. Unlike some early operating systems, Windows NT uses process boundaries for subsystem protection in addition to the traditional protection of User and Privileged modes. These subsystem processes provide additional protection. Therefore, some work done by Windows NT on behalf of your application may appear in other subsystem processes in addition to the Privileged Time in your process.

Index: 144   Default Scale: 1

Counter Type: PERF_100NSEC_TIMER   Counter Size: 8 bytes

% **Processor Time**   *Novice*

Processor Time is the percentage of elapsed time that all of the threads of this process used the processor to execute instructions. An instruction is the basic unit of execution in a computer, a thread is the object that executes instructions, and a process is the object created when a program is run. Code executed to handle certain hardware interrupts or trap conditions may be counted for this process.

Index: 006   Default Scale: 1

Counter Type: PERF_100NSEC_TIMER   Counter Size: 8 bytes

% **User Time**   *Advanced*

User Time is the percentage of elapsed time that this process's threads have spent executing code in User Mode. Applications execute in User Mode, as do subsystems like the window manager and the graphics engine. Code executing in User Mode cannot damage the integrity of the Windows NT Executive, Kernel, and device drivers. Unlike some early operating systems, Windows NT uses process boundaries for subsystem protection in addition to the traditional protection of User and Privileged modes. These subsystem processes provide additional protection. Therefore, some work done by Windows NT on behalf of your application may appear in other subsystem processes in addition to the Privileged Time in your process.

Index: 142   Default Scale: 1

Counter Type: PERF_100NSEC_TIMER   Counter Size: 8 bytes

Elapsed Time   *Advanced*

The total elapsed time (in seconds) this process has been running.

Index: 684   Default Scale: 0.0001

Counter Type: PERF_ELAPSED_TIME   Counter Size: 8 bytes

File Control Bytes/sec   *Expert*

File Control Bytes/sec is the rate of bytes transferred by non-read and non-write operations issued by threads in this process to file system devices. File system control and status calls fall into this category.

Index: 020   Default Scale: 0.001

Counter Type: PERF_COUNTER_BULK_COUNT   Counter Size: 8 bytes

File Control Operations/sec   *Expert*

File Control Operations/sec is the rate of non-read and non-write operations on file system devices issued by threads in this process. File system control and status calls fall into this category.

Index: 014   Default Scale: 1

Counter Type: PERF_COUNTER_COUNTER   Counter Size: 4 bytes

File Read Bytes/sec   *Expert*

File Read Bytes/sec is the rate of bytes transferred by read operations issued by threads of this process on file system devices.

Index: 016   Default Scale: 0.0001

Counter Type: PERF_COUNTER_BULK_COUNT   Counter Size: 8 bytes

File Read Operations/sec   *Advanced*

File Read Operations/sec is the rate of read operations on file system devices issued by the threads in this process.

Index: 010   Default Scale: 1

Counter Type: PERF_COUNTER_COUNTER   Counter Size: 4 bytes

File Write Bytes/sec   *Expert*

File Write Bytes/sec is the rate of bytes transferred by write operations issued by threads in this process to file system devices.

Index: 018   Default Scale: 0.0001

Counter Type: PERF_COUNTER_BULK_COUNT   Counter Size: 8 bytes

File Write Operations/sec   *Advanced*

File Write Operations/sec is the rate of write operations on file system devices issued by threads in this process.

Index: 012   Default Scale: 1

Counter Type: PERF_COUNTER_COUNTER   Counter Size: 4 bytes

ID Process   *Novice*

ID Process is the unique identifier of this process. ID Process numbers are reused, so they only identify a process for the lifetime of that process.

Index: 784   Default Scale: 0.1

Counter Type: PERF_COUNTER_RAWCOUNT   Counter Size: 4 bytes

Page Faults/sec   *Novice*

Page Faults/sec is the rate of Page Faults by the threads executing in this process. A page fault occurs when a thread refers to a virtual memory page that is not in its working set in main memory. This will not cause the page to be fetched from disk if it is on the standby list and hence already in main memory, or if it is in use by another process with whom the page is shared.

Index: 028   Default Scale: 0.1

Counter Type: PERF_COUNTER_COUNTER   Counter Size: 4 bytes

Page File Bytes   *Advanced*

Page File Bytes is the current number of bytes this process has used in the paging file(s). Paging files are used to store pages of memory used by the process that are not contained in other files. Paging files are shared by all processes, and lack of space in paging files can prevent other processes from allocating memory.

Index: 184   Default Scale: 0.000001

Counter Type: PERF_COUNTER_RAWCOUNT   Counter Size: 4 bytes

Page File Bytes Peak   *Advanced*

Page File Bytes Peak is the maximum number of bytes this process has used in the paging file(s). Paging files are used to store pages of memory used by the process that are not contained in other files. Paging files are shared by all processes, and lack of space in paging files can prevent other processes from allocating memory.

Index: 182   Default Scale: 0.000001

Counter Type: PERF_COUNTER_RAWCOUNT   Counter Size: 4 bytes

Pool Nonpaged Bytes   *Advanced*

Pool Nonpaged Bytes is the number of bytes in the Nonpaged Pool, a system memory area where space is acquired by operating system components as they accomplish their appointed tasks. Nonpaged Pool pages cannot be paged out to the paging file, but instead remain in main memory as long as they are allocated.

Index: 058   Default Scale: 0.00001

Counter Type: PERF_COUNTER_RAWCOUNT   Counter Size: 4 bytes

Pool Paged Bytes   *Advanced*

Pool Paged Bytes is the number of bytes in the Paged Pool, a system memory area where space is acquired by operating system components as they accomplish their appointed tasks. Paged Pool pages can be paged out to the paging file when not accessed by the system for sustained periods of time.

Index: 056   Default Scale: 0.00001

Counter Type: PERF_COUNTER_RAWCOUNT   Counter Size: 4 bytes

Priority Base   *Advanced*

The current base priority of this process. Threads within a process can raise and lower their own base priority relative to the process's base priority.

Index: 682   Default Scale: 1

Counter Type: PERF_COUNTER_RAWCOUNT   Counter Size: 4 bytes

Private Bytes   *Advanced*

Private Bytes is the current number of bytes this process has allocated that cannot be shared with other processes.

Index: 186   Default Scale: 0.00001

Counter Type: PERF_COUNTER_RAWCOUNT   Counter Size: 4 bytes

Thread Count   *Advanced*

The number of threads currently active in this process. An instruction is the basic unit of execution in a processor, and a thread is the object that executes instructions. Every running process has at least one thread.

Index: 680   Default Scale: 1

Counter Type: PERF_COUNTER_RAWCOUNT   Counter Size: 4 bytes

Virtual Bytes   *Expert*

Virtual Bytes is the current size in bytes of the virtual address space the process is using. Use of virtual address space does not necessarily imply corresponding use of either disk or main memory pages. Virtual space is however finite, and by using too much, the process may limit its ability to load libraries.

Index: 174   Default Scale: 0.000001

Counter Type: PERF_COUNTER_RAWCOUNT   Counter Size: 4 bytes

Virtual Bytes Peak   *Expert*

Virtual Bytes Peak is the maximum number of bytes of virtual address space the process has used at any one time. Use of virtual address space does not necessarily imply corresponding use of either disk or main memory pages. Virtual space is however finite, and by using too much, the process may limit its ability to load libraries.

Index: 172   Default Scale: 0.000001

Counter Type: PERF_COUNTER_RAWCOUNT   Counter Size: 4 bytes

Working Set   *Novice*

Working Set is the current number of bytes in the Working Set of this process. The Working Set is the set of memory pages touched recently by the threads in the process. If free memory in the computer is above a threshold, pages are left in the Working Set of a process even if they are not in use. When free memory falls below a threshold, pages are trimmed from Working Sets. If they are needed they will then be soft-faulted back into the Working Set before they leave main memory.

Index: 180   Default Scale: 0.00001

Counter Type: PERF_COUNTER_RAWCOUNT   Counter Size: 4 bytes

Working Set Peak   *Advanced*

Working Set Peak is the maximum number of bytes in the Working Set of this process at any point in time. The Working Set is the set of memory pages touched recently by the threads in the process. If free memory in the computer is above a threshold, pages are left in the Working Set of a process even if they are not in use. When free memory falls below a threshold, pages are trimmed from Working Sets. If they are needed they will then be soft-faulted back into the Working Set before they leave main memory.

Index: 178   Default Scale: 0.00001

Counter Type: PERF_COUNTER_RAWCOUNT   Counter Size: 4 bytes

Process Address Space Object

Object: Process Address Space   Index: 786   *Wizard*

Process Address Space object type displays details about the virtual memory usage and allocation of the selected process.

Bytes Free   *Wizard*

Bytes Free is the total unused virtual address space of this process.

Index: 782   Default Scale: 0.0001

Counter Type: PERF_COUNTER_RAWCOUNT   Counter Size: 4 bytes

Bytes Image Free   *Wizard*

Bytes Image Free is the amount of virtual address space that is not in use or reserved by images within this process.

Index: 778   Default Scale: 0.0001

Counter Type: PERF_COUNTER_RAWCOUNT   Counter Size: 4 bytes

Bytes Image Reserved   *Wizard*

Bytes Image Reserved is the sum of all virtual memory reserved by images run within this process.

Index: 776   Default Scale: 0.0001

Counter Type: PERF_COUNTER_RAWCOUNT   Counter Size: 4 bytes

Bytes Reserved   *Wizard*

Bytes Reserved is the total amount of virtual memory reserved for future use by this process.

Index: 780   Default Scale: 0.0001

Counter Type: PERF_COUNTER_RAWCOUNT   Counter Size: 4 bytes

ID Process   *Wizard*

ID Process is the unique identifier of this process. ID Process numbers are reused, so they only identify a process for the lifetime of that process.

Index: 784   Default Scale: 1

Counter Type: PERF_COUNTER_RAWCOUNT   Counter Size: 4 bytes

Image Space Exec Read Only   *Wizard*

Image Space is the virtual address space in use by the images being executed by the process. This is the sum of all the address space with this protection allocated by images run by the selected process Execute/Read Only memory is memory that can be executed as well as read.

Index: 770   Default Scale: 0.00001

Counter Type: PERF_COUNTER_RAWCOUNT   Counter Size: 4 bytes

Image Space Exec Read/Write   *Wizard*

Image Space is the virtual address space in use by the images being executed by the process. This is the sum of all the address space with this protection allocated by images run by the selected process Execute/Read/Write memory is memory that can be executed by programs as well as read and written and modified.

Index: 772   Default Scale: 0.00001

Counter Type: PERF_COUNTER_RAWCOUNT   Counter Size: 4 bytes

Image Space Exec Write Copy   *Wizard*

Image Space is the virtual address space in use by the images being executed by the process. This is the sum of all the address space with this protection allocated by images run by the selected process Execute Write Copy is memory that can be executed by programs as well as read and written. This type of protection is used when memory needs to be shared between processes. If the sharing processes only read the memory, then they will all use the same memory. If a sharing process desires write access, then a copy of this memory will be made for that process.

Index: 774   Default Scale: 0.00001

Counter Type: PERF_COUNTER_RAWCOUNT   Counter Size: 4 bytes

Image Space Executable   *Wizard*

Image Space is the virtual address space in use by the images being executed by the process. This is the sum of all the address space with this protection allocated by images run by the selected process Executable memory is memory that can be executed by programs, but may not be read or written. This type of protection is not supported by all processor types.

Index: 768   Default Scale: 0.00001

Counter Type: PERF_COUNTER_RAWCOUNT   Counter Size: 4 bytes

Image Space No Access   *Wizard*

Image Space is the virtual address space in use by the images being executed by the process. This is the sum of all the address space with this protection allocated by images run by the selected process No Access protection prevents a process from writing to or reading from these pages and will generate an access violation if either is attempted.

Index: 760   Default Scale: 0.00001

Counter Type: PERF_COUNTER_RAWCOUNT   Counter Size: 4 bytes

Image Space Read Only   *Wizard*

Image Space is the virtual address space in use by the images being executed by the process. This is the sum of all the address space with this protection allocated by images run by the selected process Read Only protection prevents the contents of these pages from being modified. Any attempts to write or modify these pages will generate an access violation.

Index: 762   Default Scale: 0.00001

Counter Type: PERF_COUNTER_RAWCOUNT   Counter Size: 4 bytes

Image Space Read/Write   *Wizard*

Image Space is the virtual address space in use by the images being executed by the process. This is the sum of all the address space with this protection allocated by images run by the selected process Read/Write protection allows a process to read, modify and write to these pages.

Index: 764   Default Scale: 0.00001

Counter Type: PERF_COUNTER_RAWCOUNT   Counter Size: 4 bytes

Image Space Write Copy   *Wizard*

Image Space is the virtual address space in use by the images being executed by the process. This is the sum of all the address space with this protection allocated by images run by the selected process Write Copy protection is used when memory is shared for reading but not for writing. When processes are reading this memory, they can share the same memory, however, when a sharing process wants to have read/write access to this shared memory, a copy of that memory is made for writing to.

Index: 766   Default Scale: 0.00001

Counter Type: PERF_COUNTER_RAWCOUNT   Counter Size: 4 bytes

Mapped Space Exec Read Only   *Wizard*

Mapped Space is virtual memory that has been mapped to a specific virtual address (or range of virtual addresses) in the process's virtual address space. Execute/Read Only memory is memory that can be executed as well as read.

Index: 720   Default Scale: 0.00001

Counter Type: PERF_COUNTER_RAWCOUNT   Counter Size: 4 bytes

Mapped Space Exec Read/Write   *Wizard*

Mapped Space is virtual memory that has been mapped to a specific virtual address (or range of virtual addresses) in the process's virtual address space. Execute/Read/Write memory is memory that can be executed by programs as well as read and modified.

Index: 722   Default Scale: 0.00001

Counter Type: PERF_COUNTER_RAWCOUNT   Counter Size: 4 bytes

Mapped Space Exec Write Copy   *Wizard*

Mapped Space is virtual memory that has been mapped to a specific virtual address (or range of virtual addresses) in the process's virtual address space. Execute Write Copy is memory that can be executed by programs as well as read and written. This type of protection is used when memory needs to be shared between processes. If the sharing processes only read the memory, then they will all use the same memory. If a sharing process desires write access, then a copy of this memory will be made for that process.

Index: 724   Default Scale: 0.00001

Counter Type: PERF_COUNTER_RAWCOUNT   Counter Size: 4 bytes

Mapped Space Executable   *Wizard*

Mapped Space is virtual memory that has been mapped to a specific virtual address (or range of virtual addresses) in the process's virtual address space. Executable memory is memory that can be executed by programs, but may not be read or written. This type of protection is not supported by all processor types.

Index: 718   Default Scale: 0.00001

Counter Type: PERF_COUNTER_RAWCOUNT   Counter Size: 4 bytes

Mapped Space No Access   *Wizard*

Mapped Space is virtual memory that has been mapped to a specific virtual address (or range of virtual addresses) in the process's virtual address space. No Access protection prevents a process from writing to or reading from these pages and will generate an access violation if either is attempted.

Index: 710   Default Scale: 0.00001

Counter Type: PERF_COUNTER_RAWCOUNT   Counter Size: 4 bytes

Mapped Space Read Only   *Wizard*

Mapped Space is virtual memory that has been mapped to a specific virtual address (or range of virtual addresses) in the process's virtual address space. Read Only protection prevents the contents of these pages from being modified. Any attempts to write or modify these pages will generate an access violation.

Index: 712   Default Scale: 0.00001

Counter Type: PERF_COUNTER_RAWCOUNT   Counter Size: 4 bytes

Mapped Space Read/Write   *Wizard*

Mapped Space is virtual memory that has been mapped to a specific virtual address (or range of virtual addresses) in the process's virtual address space. Read/Write protection allows a process to read, modify and write to these pages.

Index: 714   Default Scale: 0.00001

Counter Type: PERF_COUNTER_RAWCOUNT   Counter Size: 4 bytes

Mapped Space Write Copy   *Wizard*

Mapped Space is virtual memory that has been mapped to a specific virtual address (or range of virtual addresses) in the process's virtual address space. Write Copy protection is used when memory is shared for reading but not for writing. When processes are reading this memory, they can share the same memory, however, when a sharing process wants to have write access to this shared memory, a copy of that memory is made.

Index: 716   Default Scale: 0.00001

Counter Type: PERF_COUNTER_RAWCOUNT   Counter Size: 4 bytes

Reserved Space Exec Read Only   *Wizard*

Reserved Space is virtual memory that has been reserved for future use by a process, but has not been mapped or committed. Execute/Read Only memory is memory that can be executed as well as read.

Index: 736   Default Scale: 0.00001

Counter Type: PERF_COUNTER_RAWCOUNT   Counter Size: 4 bytes

Reserved Space Exec Read/Write   *Wizard*

Reserved Space is virtual memory that has been reserved for future use by a process, but has not been mapped or committed. Execute/Read/Write memory is memory that can be executed by programs as well as read and modified.

Index: 738   Default Scale: 0.00001

Counter Type: PERF_COUNTER_RAWCOUNT   Counter Size: 4 bytes

Reserved Space Exec Write Copy   *Wizard*

Reserved Space is virtual memory that has been reserved for future use by a process, but has not been mapped or committed. Execute Write Copy is memory that can be executed by programs as well as read and written. This type of protection is used when memory needs to be shared between processes. If the sharing processes only read the memory, then they will all use the same memory. If a sharing process desires write access, then a copy of this memory will be made for that process.

Index: 742   Default Scale: 0.00001

Counter Type: PERF_COUNTER_RAWCOUNT   Counter Size: 4 bytes

Reserved Space Executable   *Wizard*

Reserved Space is virtual memory that has been reserved for future use by a process, but has not been mapped or committed. Executable memory is memory that can be executed by programs, but may not be read or written. This type of protection is not supported by all processor types.

Index: 734   Default Scale: 0.00001

Counter Type: PERF_COUNTER_RAWCOUNT   Counter Size: 4 bytes

Reserved Space No Access   *Wizard*

Reserved Space is virtual memory that has been reserved for future use by a process, but has not been mapped or committed. No Access protection prevents a process from writing to or reading from these pages and will generate an access violation if either is attempted.

Index: 726   Default Scale: 0.00001

Counter Type: PERF_COUNTER_RAWCOUNT   Counter Size: 4 bytes

Reserved Space Read Only   *Wizard*

Reserved Space is virtual memory that has been reserved for future use by a process, but has not been mapped or committed. Read Only protection prevents the contents of these pages from being modified. Any attempts to write or modify these pages will generate an access violation.

Index: 728   Default Scale: 0.00001

Counter Type: PERF_COUNTER_RAWCOUNT   Counter Size: 4 bytes

Reserved Space Read/Write   *Wizard*

Reserved Space is virtual memory that has been reserved for future use by a process, but has not been mapped or committed. Read/Write protection allows a process to read, modify and write to these pages.

Index: 730   Default Scale: 0.00001

Counter Type: PERF_COUNTER_RAWCOUNT   Counter Size: 4 bytes

Reserved Space Write Copy   *Wizard*

Reserved Space is virtual memory that has been reserved for future use by a process, but has not been mapped or committed. Write Copy protection is used when memory is shared for reading but not for writing. When processes are reading this memory, they can share the same memory, however, when a sharing process wants to have read/write access to this shared memory, a copy of that memory is made.

Index: 732   Default Scale: 0.00001

Counter Type: PERF_COUNTER_RAWCOUNT   Counter Size: 4 bytes

Unassigned Space Exec Read Only   *Wizard*

Unassigned Space is mapped and committed virtual memory in use by the process that is not attributable to any particular image being executed by that process. Execute/Read Only memory is memory that can be executed as well as read.

Index: 754   Default Scale: 0.00001

Counter Type: PERF_COUNTER_RAWCOUNT   Counter Size: 4 bytes

Unassigned Space Exec Read/Write   *Wizard*

Unassigned Space is mapped and committed virtual memory in use by the process that is not attributable to any particular image being executed by that process. Execute/Read/Write memory is memory that can be executed by programs as well as read and written.

Index: 756   Default Scale: 0.00001

Counter Type: PERF_COUNTER_RAWCOUNT   Counter Size: 4 bytes

Unassigned Space Exec Write Copy   *Wizard*

Unassigned Space is mapped and committed virtual memory in use by the process that is not attributable to any particular image being executed by that process. Execute Write Copy is memory that can be executed by programs as well as read and written. This type of protection is used when memory needs to be shared between processes. If the sharing processes only read the memory, then they will all use the same memory. If a sharing process desires write access, then a copy of this memory will be made for that process.

Index: 758   Default Scale: 0.00001

Counter Type: PERF_COUNTER_RAWCOUNT   Counter Size: 4 bytes

Unassigned Space Executable   *Wizard*

Unassigned Space is mapped and committed virtual memory in use by the process that is not attributable to any particular image being executed by that process. Executable memory is memory that can be executed by programs, but may not be read or written. This type of protection is not supported by all processor types.

Index: 752   Default Scale: 0.00001

Counter Type: PERF_COUNTER_RAWCOUNT   Counter Size: 4 bytes

Unassigned Space No Access   *Wizard*

Unassigned Space is mapped and committed virtual memory in use by the process that is not attributable to any particular image being executed by that process. No Access protection prevents a process from writing to or reading from these pages and will generate an access violation if either is attempted.

Index: 744   Default Scale: 0.00001

Counter Type: PERF_COUNTER_RAWCOUNT   Counter Size: 4 bytes

Unassigned Space Read Only   *Wizard*

Unassigned Space is mapped and committed virtual memory in use by the process that is not attributable to any particular image being executed by that process. Read Only protection prevents the contents of these pages from being modified. Any attempts to write or modify these pages will generate an access violation.

Index: 746   Default Scale: 0.00001

Counter Type: PERF_COUNTER_RAWCOUNT   Counter Size: 4 bytes

Unassigned Space Read/Write   *Wizard*

Unassigned Space is mapped and committed virtual memory in use by the process that is not attributable to any particular image being executed by that process. Read/Write protection allows a process to read, modify and write to these pages.

Index: 748   Default Scale: 0.00001

Counter Type: PERF_COUNTER_RAWCOUNT   Counter Size: 4 bytes

Unassigned Space Write Copy   *Wizard*

Unassigned Space is mapped and committed virtual memory in use by the process that is not attributable to any particular image being executed by that process. Write Copy protection is used when memory is shared for reading but not for writing. When processes are reading this memory, they can share the same memory, however, when a sharing process wants to have read/write access to this shared memory, a copy of that memory is made for writing to.

Index: 750   Default Scale: 0.00001

Counter Type: PERF_COUNTER_RAWCOUNT   Counter Size: 4 bytes

Processor Object

Object: "Processor" Index: 238   *Novice*

The Processor object type includes as instances all processors on the computer. A processor is the part in the computer that performs arithmetic and logical computations, and initiates operations on peripherals. It executes (runs) programs on the computer.

% **Privileged Time**   *Advanced*

Privileged Time is the percentage of processor time spent in Privileged Mode in non-Idle threads. The Windows NT service layer, the Executive routines, and the Windows NT Kernel execute in Privileged Mode. Device drivers for most devices other than graphics adapters and printers also execute in Privileged Mode. Unlike some early operating systems, Windows NT uses process boundaries for subsystem protection in addition to the traditional protection of User and Privileged modes. These subsystem processes provide additional protection. Therefore, some work done by Windows NT on behalf of your application may appear in other subsystem processes in addition to the Privileged Time in your process.

Index: 144   Default Scale: 1

Counter Type: PERF_100NSEC_TIMER   Counter Size: 8 bytes

% **Processor Time**   *Novice*

Processor Time is expressed as a percentage of the elapsed time that a processor is busy executing a non-Idle thread. It can be viewed as the fraction of the time spent doing useful work. Each processor is assigned an Idle thread in the Idle process which consumes those unproductive processor cycles not used by any other threads.

Index: 006   Default Scale: 1

Counter Type: PERF_100NSEC_TIMER_INV   Counter Size: 8 bytes

% User Time   *Advanced*

User Time is the percentage of processor time spent in User Mode in non-Idle threads. All application code and subsystem code execute in User Mode. The graphics engine, graphics device drivers, printer device drivers, and the window manager also execute in User Mode. Code executing in User Mode cannot damage the integrity of the Windows NT Executive, Kernel, and device drivers. Unlike some early operating systems, Windows NT uses process boundaries for subsystem protection in addition to the traditional protection of User and Privileged modes. These subsystem processes provide additional protection. Therefore, some work done by Windows NT on behalf of your application may appear in other subsystem processes in addition to the Privileged Time in your process.

Index: 142   Default Scale: 1

Counter Type: PERF_100NSEC_TIMER   Counter Size: 8 bytes

Interrupts/sec   *Novice*

Interrupts/sec is the number of device interrupts the processor is experiencing. A device interrupts the processor when it has completed a task or when it otherwise requires attention. Normal thread execution is suspended during interrupts. An interrupt may cause the processor to switch to another, higher priority thread. Clock interrupts are frequent and periodic and create a background of interrupt activity.

Index: 148   Default Scale: 0.01

Counter Type: PERF_COUNTER_COUNTER   Counter Size: 4 bytes

Redirector Object

Object: Redirector   Index: 262   *Novice*

The Redirector is the object that manages network connections to other computers that originate from your own computer.

Bytes Received/sec   *Advanced*

Bytes Received/sec is the rate of bytes coming in to the Redirector from the network. It includes all application data as well as network protocol information (such as packet headers).

Index: 264   Default Scale: 0.0001

Counter Type: PERF_COUNTER_BULK_COUNT   Counter Size: 8 bytes

Bytes Total/sec   *Novice*

Bytes Total/sec is the rate the Redirector is processing data bytes. This includes all application and file data in addition to protocol information such as packet headers.

Index: 388   Default Scale: 0.0001

Counter Type: PERF_COUNTER_BULK_COUNT   Counter Size: 8 bytes

Bytes Transmitted/sec   *Advanced*

Bytes Transmitted/sec is the rate that bytes are leaving the Redirector to the network. It includes all application data as well as network protocol information (such as packet headers and the like).

Index: 276   Default Scale: 0.0001

Counter Type: PERF_COUNTER_BULK_COUNT   Counter Size: 8 bytes

Connects Core   *Advanced*

Connects Core counts the number of connections you have to servers running the original MS-Net SMB protocol, including MS-Net itself and XENIX® and Vax's.

Index: 318   Default Scale: 1

Counter Type: PERF_COUNTER_RAWCOUNT   Counter Size: 4 bytes

Connects Lan Manager 2.0   *Advanced*

Connects LAN Manager 2.0 counts connections to LAN Manager 2.0 servers, including LMX servers.

Index: 320   Default Scale: 1

Counter Type: PERF_COUNTER_RAWCOUNT   Counter Size: 4 bytes

Connects Lan Manager 2.1   *Advanced*

Connects LAN Manager 2.1 counts connections to LAN Manager 2.1 servers, including LMX servers.

Index: 322   Default Scale: 1

Counter Type: PERF_COUNTER_RAWCOUNT   Counter Size: 4 bytes

Connects Windows NT   *Advanced*

Connects Windows NT counts the connections to Windows NT computers. Good choice!

Index: 324   Default Scale: 1

Counter Type: PERF_COUNTER_RAWCOUNT   Counter Size: 4 bytes

Current Commands   *Advanced*

Current Commands counts the number of requests to the Redirector that are currently queued for service. If this number is much larger than the number of network adapter cards installed in the computer, then the network(s) and/or the server(s) being accessed are seriously bottlenecked.

Index: 392   Default Scale: 1

Counter Type: PERF_COUNTER_RAWCOUNT   Counter Size: 4 bytes

File Data Operations/sec   *Novice*

File Data Operations/sec is the rate the Redirector is processing data operations. One operation includes (hopefully) many bytes. We say hopefully here because each operation has overhead. You can determine the efficiency of this path by dividing the Bytes/sec by this counter to determine the average number of bytes transferred/operation.

Index: 406   Default Scale: 1

Counter Type: PERF_COUNTER_COUNTER   Counter Size: 4 bytes

File Read Operations/sec   *Novice*

File Read Operations/sec is the rate that applications are asking the Redirector for data. Each call to a file system or similar application program interface (API) call counts as one operation.

Index: 010   Default Scale: 1

Counter Type: PERF_COUNTER_COUNTER   Counter Size: 4 bytes

File Write Operations/sec   *Novice*

File Write Operations/sec is the rate that applications are sending data to the Redirector. Each call to a file system or similar Application Program Interface (API) call counts as one operation.

Index: 012   Default Scale: 1

Counter Type: PERF_COUNTER_COUNTER   Counter Size: 4 bytes

Network Errors/sec   *Novice*

Network Errors/sec counts serious unexpected errors that generally indicate the Redirector and one or more Servers are having serious communication difficulties. For example an SMB (Server Message Block) protocol error will generate a Network Error. These result in an entry in the system Event Log, so look there for details.

Index: 312   Default Scale: 1

Counter Type: PERF_COUNTER_COUNTER   Counter Size: 4 bytes

Packets/sec   *Novice*

Packets/sec is the rate the Redirector is processing data packets. One packet includes (hopefully) many bytes. We say hopefully here because each packet has protocol overhead. You can determine the efficiency of this path by dividing the Bytes/sec by this counter to determine the average number of bytes transferred/packet. You can also divide this counter by Operations/sec to determine the average number of packets per operation, another measure of efficiency.

Index: 400   Default Scale: 0.1

Counter Type: PERF_COUNTER_BULK_COUNT   Counter Size: 8 bytes

Packets Received/sec   *Advanced*

Packets Received/sec is the rate that the Redirector is receiving packets (also called SMBs or Server Message Blocks). Network transmissions are divided into packets. The average number of bytes received in a packet can be obtained by dividing Bytes Received/sec by this counter. Some packets received may not contain incoming data, for example an acknowledgment to a write made by the Redirector would count as an incoming packet.

Index: 266   Default Scale: 0.1

Counter Type: PERF_COUNTER_BULK_COUNT   Counter Size: 8 bytes

Packets Transmitted/sec   *Advanced*

Packets Transmitted/sec is the rate that the Redirector is sending packets (also called SMBs or Server Message Blocks). Network transmissions are divided into packets. The average number of bytes transmitted in a packet can be obtained by dividing Bytes Transmitted/sec by this counter.

Index: 278   Default Scale: 0.1

Counter Type: PERF_COUNTER_BULK_COUNT   Counter Size: 8 bytes

Read Bytes Cache/sec   *Expert*

Read Bytes Cache/sec is the rate that applications on your computer are accessing the Cache using the Redirector. Some of these data requests may be satisfied by merely retrieving the data from the system Cache on your own computer if it happened to be used recently and there was room to keep it in the Cache. Requests that miss the Cache will cause a page fault (see Read Bytes Paging/sec).

Index: 272   Default Scale: 0.0001

Counter Type: PERF_COUNTER_BULK_COUNT   Counter Size: 8 bytes

Read Bytes Network/sec   *Novice*

Read Bytes Network/sec is the rate that applications are reading data across the network. For one reason or another the data was not in the system Cache, and these bytes actually came across the network. Dividing this number by Bytes Received/sec will indicate the 'efficiency' of data coming in from the network, since all of these bytes are real application data (see Bytes Received/sec).

Index: 274   Default Scale: 0.0001

Counter Type: PERF_COUNTER_BULK_COUNT   Counter Size: 8 bytes

Read Bytes Non-Paging/sec   *Expert*

Read Bytes Non-Paging/sec are those bytes read by the Redirector in response to normal file requests by an application when they are redirected to come from another computer. In addition to file requests, this counter includes other methods of reading across the network such as Named Pipes and Transactions. This counter does not count network protocol information, just application data.

Index: 270   Default Scale: 0.0001

Counter Type: PERF_COUNTER_BULK_COUNT   Counter Size: 8 bytes

Read Bytes Paging/sec   *Expert*

Read Bytes Paging/sec is the rate that the Redirector is attempting to read bytes in response to page faults. Page faults are caused by loading of modules (such as programs and libraries), by a miss in the Cache (see Read Bytes Cache/sec), or by files directly mapped into the address space of applications (a high-performance feature of Windows NT).

Index: 268   Default Scale: 0.0001

Counter Type: PERF_COUNTER_BULK_COUNT   Counter Size: 8 bytes

Read Operations Random/sec   *Advanced*

Read Operations Random/sec counts the rate that, on a file-by-file basis, reads are made that are not sequential. If a read is made using a particular file handle, and then is followed by another read that is not immediately the contiguous next byte, this counter is incremented by one.

Index: 290   Default Scale: 0.1

Counter Type: PERF_COUNTER_COUNTER   Counter Size: 4 bytes

Read Packets/sec   *Advanced*

Read Packets/sec is the rate that read packets are being placed on the network. Each time a single packet is sent with a request to read data remotely, this counter is incremented by one.

Index: 292   Default Scale: 0.1

Counter Type: PERF_COUNTER_COUNTER   Counter Size: 4 bytes

Read Packets Small/sec   *Expert*

Read Packets Small/sec is the rate that reads less than one-fourth of the server's negotiated buffer size are made by applications. Too many of these could indicate a waste of buffers on the server. This counter is incremented once for each read. It does not count packets.

Index: 296   Default Scale: 0.1

Counter Type: PERF_COUNTER_COUNTER   Counter Size: 4 bytes

Reads Denied/sec   *Advanced*

Reads Denied/sec is the rate that the server is unable to accommodate requests for Raw Reads. When a read is much larger than the server's negotiated buffer size, the Redirector requests a Raw Read which, if granted, would permit the transfer of the data without lots of protocol overhead on each packet. To accomplish this the server must lock out other requests, so the request is denied if the server is really busy.

Index: 308   Default Scale: 1

Counter Type: PERF_COUNTER_COUNTER   Counter Size: 4 bytes

Reads Large/sec   *Expert*

Reads Large/sec is the rate that reads over 2 times the server's negotiated buffer size are made by applications. Too many of these could place a strain on server resources. This counter is incremented once for each read. It does not count packets.

Index: 294   Default Scale: 1

Counter Type: PERF_COUNTER_COUNTER   Counter Size: 4 bytes

Server Disconnects   *Advanced*

Server Disconnects counts the number of times a Server has disconnected your Redirector. See also Server Reconnects.

Index: 326   Default Scale: 1

Counter Type: PERF_COUNTER_RAWCOUNT   Counter Size: 4 bytes

Server Reconnects   *Advanced*

Server Reconnects counts the number of times your Redirector has had to reconnect to a server in order to complete a new active request. You can be disconnected by the Server if you remain inactive for too long. Locally even if all your remote files are closed, the Redirector will keep your connections intact for (nominally) ten minutes. Such inactive connections are called Dormant Connections. Reconnecting is expensive in time.

Index: 316   Default Scale: 1

Counter Type: PERF_COUNTER_RAWCOUNT   Counter Size: 4 bytes

Server Sessions   *Novice*

Server Sessions counts the number of active security objects the Redirector is managing. For example, a Logon to a server followed by a network access to the same server will establish one connection, but two sessions.

Index: 314   Default Scale: 1

Counter Type: PERF_COUNTER_RAWCOUNT   Counter Size: 4 bytes

Server Sessions Hung   *Advanced*

Server Sessions Hung counts the number of active sessions that are timed out and unable to proceed due to a lack of response from the remote server.

Index: 328   Default Scale: 1

Counter Type: PERF_COUNTER_RAWCOUNT   Counter Size: 4 bytes

Write Bytes Cache/sec   *Expert*

Write Bytes Cache/sec is the rate that applications on your computer are writing to the Cache using the Redirector. The data may not leave your computer immediately, but may be retained in the Cache for further modification before being written to the network. This saves network traffic. Each write of a byte into the Cache is counted here.

Index: 284   Default Scale: 0.0001

Counter Type: PERF_COUNTER_BULK_COUNT   Counter Size: 8 bytes

Write Bytes Network/sec   *Novice*

Write Bytes Network/sec is the rate that your applications are writing data across the network. Either the system Cache was bypassed, as for Named Pipes or Transactions, or else the Cache wrote the bytes to make room for other data. Dividing this counter by Bytes Transmitted/sec will indicate the 'efficiency' of data written to the network, since all of these bytes are real application data (see Transmitted Bytes/sec).

Index: 286   Default Scale: 0.0001

Counter Type: PERF_COUNTER_BULK_COUNT   Counter Size: 8 bytes

Write Bytes Non-Paging/sec   *Expert*

Write Bytes Non-Paging/sec is the rate of the bytes that are written by the Redirector in response to normal file outputs by an application when they are redirected to go to another computer. In addition to file requests this counter includes other methods of writing across the network such as Named Pipes and Transactions. This counter does not count network protocol information, just application data.

Index: 282   Default Scale: 0.0001

Counter Type: PERF_COUNTER_BULK_COUNT   Counter Size: 8 bytes

Write Bytes Paging/sec   *Expert*

Write Bytes Paging/sec is the rate that the Redirector is attempting to write bytes changed in the pages being used by applications. The program data changed by modules (such as programs and libraries) that were loaded over the network are 'paged out' when no longer needed. Other output pages come from the Cache (see Write Bytes Cache/sec).

Index: 280   Default Scale: 0.0001

Counter Type: PERF_COUNTER_BULK_COUNT   Counter Size: 8 bytes

Write Operations Random/sec   *Advanced*

Write Operations Random/sec is the rate that, on a file-by-file basis, writes are made that are not sequential. If a write is made using a particular file handle, and then is followed by another write that is not immediately the next contiguous byte, this counter is incremented by one.

Index: 300   Default Scale: 0.1

Counter Type: PERF_COUNTER_COUNTER   Counter Size: 4 bytes

Write Packets Small/sec   *Expert*

Write Packets Small/sec is the rate that writes are made by applications that are less than one-fourth of the server's negotiated buffer size. Too many of these could indicate a waste of buffers on the server. This counter is incremented once for each write: it counts writes, not packets!

Index: 306   Default Scale: 0.1

Counter Type: PERF_COUNTER_COUNTER   Counter Size: 4 bytes

Write Packets/sec   *Advanced*

Write Packets/sec is the rate that writes are being sent to the network. Each time a single packet is sent with a request to write remote data, this counter is incremented by one.

Index: 302   Default Scale: 0.1

Counter Type: PERF_COUNTER_COUNTER   Counter Size: 4 bytes

Writes Denied/sec   *Advanced*

Writes Denied/sec is the rate that the server is unable to accommodate requests for Raw Writes. When a write is much larger than the server's negotiated buffer size, the Redirector requests a Raw Write which, if granted, would permit the transfer of the data without lots of protocol overhead on each packet. To accomplish this the server must lock out other requests, so the request is denied if the server is really busy.

Index: 310   Default Scale: 1

Counter Type: PERF_COUNTER_COUNTER   Counter Size: 4 bytes

Writes Large/sec   *Expert*

Writes Large/sec is the rate that writes are made by applications that are over 2 times the server's negotiated buffer size. Too many of these could place a strain on server resources. This counter is incremented once for each write: it counts writes, not packets.

Index: 304   Default Scale: 1

Counter Type: PERF_COUNTER_COUNTER   Counter Size: 4 bytes

Server Object

Object: Server   Index: 330   *Novice*

Server is the process that interfaces the services from the local computer to the network services.

Blocking Requests Rejected   *Advanced*

The number of times the server has rejected blocking SMBs due to insufficient count of free work items. Indicates whether the maxworkitem or minfreeworkitems server parameters may need tuning.

Index: 356   Default Scale: 1

Counter Type: PERF_COUNTER_COUNTER   Counter Size: 4 bytes

Bytes Received/sec   *Advanced*

The number of bytes the server has received from the network. Indicates how busy the server is.

Index: 264   Default Scale: 0.0001

Counter Type: PERF_COUNTER_BULK_COUNT   Counter Size: 8 bytes

Bytes Total/sec   *Novice*

The number of bytes the server has sent to and received from the network. This value provides an overall indication of how busy the server is.

Index: 388   Default Scale: 0.0001

Counter Type: PERF_COUNTER_BULK_COUNT   Counter Size: 8 bytes

Bytes Transmitted/sec   *Advanced*

The number of bytes the server has sent on the network. Indicates how busy the server is.

Index: 276   Default Scale: 0.0001

Counter Type: PERF_COUNTER_BULK_COUNT   Counter Size: 8 bytes

Context Block Queue Time   *Novice*

Context Block Queue Time is the average time, in milliseconds, a work context block sat on the server's FSP queue waiting for the server to act on the request.

Index: 402   Default Scale: 1

Counter Type: PERF_AVERAGE_BULK   Counter Size: 8 bytes

Context Blocks Queued/sec   *Novice*

Context Blocks Queued per second is the rate that work context blocks had to be placed on the server's FSP queue to await server action.

Index: 404   Default Scale: 0.1

Counter Type: PERF_COUNTER_COUNTER   Counter Size: 4 bytes

Errors Access Permissions   *Novice*

The number of times opens on behalf of clients have failed with STATUS_ACCESS_DENIED. Can indicate whether somebody is randomly attempting to access files in hopes of getting at something that was not properly protected.

Index: 350   Default Scale: 1

Counter Type: PERF_COUNTER_RAWCOUNT   Counter Size: 4 bytes

Errors Granted Access   *Advanced*

The number of times accesses to files opened successfully were denied. Can indicate attempts to access files without proper access authorization.

Index: 352   Default Scale: 1

Counter Type: PERF_COUNTER_RAWCOUNT   Counter Size: 4 bytes

Errors Logon   *Advanced*

The number of failed logon attempts to the server. Can indicate whether password guessing programs are being used to crack the security on the server.

Index: 348   Default Scale: 1

Counter Type: PERF_COUNTER_RAWCOUNT   Counter Size: 4 bytes

Errors System   *Expert*

The number of times an internal Server Error was detected. Unexpected errors usually indicate a problem with the Server.

Index: 354   Default Scale: 1

Counter Type: PERF_COUNTER_RAWCOUNT   Counter Size: 4 bytes

File Directory Searches   *Advanced*

The number of searches for files currently active in the server. Indicates current server activity.

Index: 366   Default Scale: 1

Counter Type: PERF_COUNTER_RAWCOUNT   Counter Size: 4 bytes

Files Open   *Novice*

The number of files currently opened in the server. Indicates current server activity.

Index: 362   Default Scale: 1

Counter Type: PERF_COUNTER_RAWCOUNT   Counter Size: 4 bytes

Files Opened Total   *Novice*

The number of successful open attempts performed by the server of behalf of clients. Useful in determining the amount of file I/O, determining overhead for path-based operations, determining the effectiveness of oplocks.

Index: 360   Default Scale: 0.001

Counter Type: PERF_COUNTER_RAWCOUNT   Counter Size: 4 bytes

Pool Nonpaged Bytes   *Expert*

The number of bytes of non-pageable computer memory the server is currently using. Can help in determining good values for the MaxNonpagedMemoryUsage parameter.

Index: 058   Default Scale: 0.0001

Counter Type: PERF_COUNTER_RAWCOUNT   Counter Size: 4 bytes

Pool Nonpaged Failures   *Wizard*

The number of times allocations from nonpaged pool have failed. Indicates that the computer's physical memory is too small.

Index: 370   Default Scale: 1

Counter Type: PERF_COUNTER_COUNTER   Counter Size: 4 bytes

Pool Nonpaged Peak   *Expert*

The maximum number of bytes of nonpaged pool the server has had in use at any one point. Indicates how much physical memory the computer should have.

Index: 372   Default Scale: 0.0001

Counter Type: PERF_COUNTER_RAWCOUNT   Counter Size: 4 bytes

Pool Paged Bytes   *Expert*

The number of bytes of pageable computer memory the server is currently using. Can help in determining good values for the MaxPagedMemoryUsage parameter.

Index: 056   Default Scale: 0.0001

Counter Type: PERF_COUNTER_RAWCOUNT   Counter Size: 4 bytes

Pool Paged Failures   *Wizard*

The number of times allocations from paged pool have failed. Indicates that the computer's physical memory of pagefile are too small.

Index: 376   Default Scale: 1

Counter Type: PERF_COUNTER_RAWCOUNT   Counter Size: 4 bytes

Pool Paged Peak   *Advanced*

The maximum number of bytes of paged pool the server has had allocated. Indicates the proper sizes of the Page File(s) and physical memory.

Index: 378   Default Scale: 0.0001

Counter Type: PERF_COUNTER_RAWCOUNT   Counter Size: 4 bytes

Server Sessions   *Novice*

The number of sessions currently active in the server. Indicates current server activity.

Index: 314   Default Scale: 1

Counter Type: PERF_COUNTER_RAWCOUNT   Counter Size: 4 bytes

Sessions Errored Out   *Advanced*

The number of sessions that have been closed due to unexpected error conditions. Indicates how frequently network problems are causing dropped sessions on the server.

Index: 342   Default Scale: 1

Counter Type: PERF_COUNTER_RAWCOUNT   Counter Size: 4 bytes

Sessions Forced Off   *Advanced*

The number of sessions that have been forced to log off. Can indicate how many sessions were forced to log off due to logon time constraints.

Index: 346   Default Scale: 1

Counter Type: PERF_COUNTER_RAWCOUNT   Counter Size: 4 bytes

Sessions Logged Off   *Advanced*

The number of sessions that have terminated normally. Useful in interpreting the Sessions Times Out and Sessions Errored Out statistics—allows percentage calculations.

Index: 344   Default Scale: 1

Counter Type: PERF_COUNTER_RAWCOUNT   Counter Size: 4 bytes

Sessions Timed Out   *Advanced*

The number of sessions that have been closed due to their idle time exceeding the autodisconnect parameter for the server. Shows whether the autodisconnect setting is helping to conserve resources.

Index: 340   Default Scale: 1

Counter Type: PERF_COUNTER_RAWCOUNT   Counter Size: 4 bytes

Work Item Shortages   *Advanced*

The number of times STATUS_DATA_NOT_ACCEPTED was returned at receive indication time. This occurs when no work item is available or can be allocated to service the incoming request. Indicates whether the InitWorkItems or MaxWorkItems parameters may need tuning.

Index: 358   Default Scale: 1

Counter Type: PERF_COUNTER_COUNTER   Counter Size: 4 bytes

System Object

Object: System   Index: 002   *Novice*

The System object type includes those counters that apply to all processors on the computer collectively. These counters represent the activity of all processors on the computer.

% Total Privileged Time   *Advanced*

The % Total Privileged Time is the average percentage of time spent in Privileged mode by all processors. On a multiprocessor system, if all processors are always in Privileged mode this is 100%, if all processors are 50% in Privileged mode this is 50% and if one-fourth of the processors are in Privileged mode this is 25%. When a Windows NT system service is called, the service will often run in Privileged Mode in order to gain access to system-private data. Such data is protected from access by threads executing in User Mode. Calls to the system may be explicit, or they may be implicit such as when a page fault or an interrupt occurs. Unlike some early operating systems, Windows NT uses process boundaries for subsystem protection in addition to the traditional protection of User and Privileged modes. These subsystem processes provide additional protection. Therefore, some work done by Windows NT on behalf of an application may appear in other subsystem processes in addition to the Privileged Time in the application process.

Index: 244   Default Scale: 1

Counter Type: PERF_100NSEC_TIMER   Counter Size: 8 bytes

% Total Processor Time   *Novice*

The % Total Processor Time is the average percentage of time that all the processors on the system are busy executing non-idle threads. On a multiprocessor system, if all processors are always busy this is 100%, if all processors are 50% busy this is 50% and if one-fourth of the processors are busy this is 25%. It can be viewed as the fraction of the time spent doing useful work. Each processor is assigned an Idle thread in the Idle process which consumes those unproductive processor cycles not used by any other threads.

Index: 240   Default Scale: 1

Counter Type: PERF_100NSEC_TIMER_INV   Counter Size: 8 bytes

% Total User Time   *Advanced*

The % Total User Time is the average percentage of time spent in User mode by all processors. On a multiprocessor system, if all processors are always in User mode this is 100%, if all processors are 50% in User mode this is 50% and if one-fourth of the processors are in User mode this is 25%. Applications execute in User Mode, as do subsystems like the window manager and the graphics engine. Code executing in User Mode cannot damage the integrity of the Windows NT Executive, Kernel, and device drivers. Unlike some early operating systems, Windows NT uses process boundaries for subsystem protection in addition to the traditional protection of User and Privileged modes. These subsystem processes provide additional protection. Therefore, some work done by Windows NT on behalf of an application may appear in other subsystem processes in addition to the Privileged Time in the application process.

Index: 242   Default Scale: 1

Counter Type: PERF_100NSEC_TIMER   Counter Size: 8 bytes

Context Switches/sec   *Advanced*

Context Switches/sec is the rate of switches from one thread to another. Thread switches can occur either inside of a single process or across processes. A thread switch may be caused either by one thread asking another for information, or by a thread being preempted by another, higher priority thread becoming ready to run. Unlike some early operating systems, Windows NT uses process boundaries for subsystem protection in addition to the traditional protection of User and Privileged modes. These subsystem processes provide additional protection. Therefore, some work done by Windows NT on behalf of an application may appear in other subsystem processes in addition to the Privileged Time in the application. Switching to the subsystem process causes one Context Switch in the application thread. Switching back causes another Context Switch in the subsystem thread.

Index: 146   Default Scale: 0.01

Counter Type: PERF_COUNTER_COUNTER   Counter Size: 4 bytes

File Control Bytes/sec   *Wizard*

File Control Bytes/sec is an aggregate of bytes transferred for all file system operations that are neither reads nor writes. These operations usually include file system control requests or requests for information about device characteristics or status.

Index: 020   Default Scale: 0.001

Counter Type: PERF_COUNTER_BULK_COUNT   Counter Size: 8 bytes

File Control Operations/sec   *Advanced*

File Control Operations/sec is an aggregate of all file system operations that are neither reads nor writes. These operations usually include file system control requests or requests for information about device characteristics or status.

Index: 014   Default Scale: 1

Type: PERF_COUNTER_COUNTER   Size: 4 bytes

File Data Operations/sec   *Novice*

File Data Operations per second is the rate that the computer is issuing Read and Write operations to file system devices. It does not include File Control Operations.

Index: 406   Default Scale: 1

Counter Type: PERF_COUNTER_COUNTER   Counter Size: 4 bytes

File Read Bytes/sec   *Expert* File Read Bytes/sec is an aggregate of the bytes transferred for all the file system read operations on the computer.

Index: 016   Default Scale: 0.0001

Type: PERF_COUNTER_BULK_COUNT   Size: 8 bytes

File Read Operations/sec   *Novice*

File Read Operations/sec is an aggregate of all the file system read operations on the computer.

Index: 010   Default Scale: 1

Type: PERF_COUNTER_COUNTER   Size: 4 bytes

File Write Bytes/sec   *Expert*

File Write Bytes/sec is an aggregate of the bytes transferred for all the file system write operations on the computer.

Index: 018   Default Scale: 0.0001

Type: PERF_COUNTER_BULK_COUNT   Size: 8 bytes

File Write Operations/sec   *Novice*

File Write Operations/sec is an aggregate of all the file system write operations on the computer.

Index: 012   Default Scale: 1

Type: PERF_COUNTER_COUNTER   Size: 4 bytes

Processor Queue Length   *Wizard*

Processor Queue Length is the instantaneous length of the processor queue in units of threads. This counter is always 0 unless you are also monitoring a thread counter. All processors use a single queue in which threads wait for processor cycles. This length does not include the threads that are currently executing. A sustained processor queue length greater than two generally indicates processor congestion. This is an instantaneous count, not an average over the time interval.

Index: 044   Default Scale: 10

Counter Type: PERF_COUNTER_RAWCOUNT   Counter Size: 4 bytes

System Calls/sec   *Advanced*

Systems Calls/sec is the frequency of calls to Windows NT system service routines. These routines perform all of the basic scheduling and synchronization of activities on the computer, and provide access to non-graphical devices, memory management, and name space management.

Index: 150   Default Scale: 0.1

Counter Type: PERF_COUNTER_COUNTER   Counter Size: 4 bytes

System Up Time   *Novice*

Total Time (in seconds) that the computer has been operational since it was last started.

Index: 674   Default Scale: 0.00001

Counter Type: PERF_ELAPSED_TIME   Counter Size: 8 bytes

Total Interrupts/sec   *Advanced*

Total Interrupts/sec is the rate the computer is receiving and servicing hardware interrupts. Some devices that may generate interrupts are the system timer, the mouse, data communication lines, network interface cards and other peripheral devices. This counter provides an indication of how busy these devices are on a computer-wide basis. See also Processor:Interrupts/sec.

Index: 246   Default Scale: 0.01

Counter Type: PERF_COUNTER_COUNTER   Counter Size: 4 bytes

TCP Object

Object: TCP   Index: 638   *Advanced*

The TCP Object Type includes those counters that describe the rates that TCP Segments are received and sent by a certain entity using the TCP protocol. In addition, it describes the number of TCP connections that are in each of the possible TCP connection states.

Connection Failures   *Advanced*

Connection Failures is the number of times TCP connections have made a direct transition to the CLOSED state from the SYN-SENT state or the SYN-RCVD state, plus the number of times TCP connections have made a direct transition to the LISTEN state from the SYN-RCVD state.

Index: 648   Default Scale: 1

Counter Type: PERF_COUNTER_RAWCOUNT   Counter Size: 4 bytes

Connections Active   *Advanced*

Connections Active is the number of times TCP connections have made a direct transition to the SYN-SENT state from the CLOSED state.

Index: 644   Default Scale: 1

Counter Type: PERF_COUNTER_RAWCOUNT   Counter Size: 4 bytes

Connections Established   *Advanced*

Connections Established is the number of TCP connections for which the current state is either ESTABLISHED or CLOSE-WAIT.

Index: 642   Default Scale: 1

Counter Type: PERF_COUNTER_RAWCOUNT   Counter Size: 4 bytes

Connections Passive   *Advanced*

Connections Passive is the number of times TCP connections have made a direct transition to the SYN-RCVD state from the LISTEN state.

Index: 646   Default Scale: 1

Counter Type: PERF_COUNTER_RAWCOUNT   Counter Size: 4 bytes

Connections Reset   *Advanced*

Connections Reset is the number of times TCP connections have made a direct transition to the CLOSED state from either the ESTABLISHED state or the CLOSE-WAIT state.

Index: 650   Default Scale: 1

Counter Type: PERF_COUNTER_RAWCOUNT   Counter Size: 4 bytes

Segments Received/sec   *Advanced*

Segments Received/sec is the rate that segments are received, including those received in error. This count includes segments received on currently established connections.

Index: 652   Default Scale: 0.1

Counter Type: PERF_COUNTER_COUNTER   Counter Size: 4 bytes

Segments Retransmitted/sec   *Advanced*

Segments Retransmitted/sec is the rate that segments are retransmitted, that is, segments transmitted containing one or more previously transmitted bytes.

Index: 656   Default Scale: 0.1

Counter Type: PERF_COUNTER_COUNTER   Counter Size: 4 bytes

Segments Sent/sec   *Advanced*

Segments Sent/sec is the rate that segments are sent, including those on current connections, but excluding those containing only retransmitted bytes.

Index: 654   Default Scale: 0.1

Counter Type: PERF_COUNTER_COUNTER   Counter Size: 4 bytes

Segments/sec   *Advanced*

Segments/sec is the rate that TCP segments are sent or received using the TCP protocol.

Index: 640   Default Scale: 0.1

Counter Type: PERF_COUNTER_COUNTER   Counter Size: 4 bytes

Thread Object

Object: Thread   Index: 232   *Novice*

The Thread object type is the basic object that executes instructions in a processor. Every running process has at least one thread.

% Privileged Time   *Advanced*

Privileged Time is the percentage of elapsed time that this thread has spent executing code in Privileged Mode. When a Windows NT system service is called, the service will often run in Privileged Mode in order to gain access to system-private data. Such data is protected from access by threads executing in User Mode. Calls to the system may be explicit, or they may be implicit such as when a page fault or an interrupt occurs. Unlike some early operating systems, Windows NT uses process boundaries for subsystem protection in addition to the traditional protection of User and Privileged modes. These subsystem processes provide additional protection. Therefore, some work done by Windows NT on behalf of your application may appear in other subsystem processes in addition to the Privileged Time in your process.

Index: 144   Default Scale: 1

Counter Type: PERF_100NSEC_TIMER   Counter Size: 8 bytes

% Processor Time   *Novice*

Processor Time is the percentage of elapsed time that this thread used the processor to execute instructions. An instruction is the basic unit of execution in a processor, and a thread is the object that executes instructions. Code executed to handle certain hardware interrupts or trap conditions may be counted for this thread.

Index: 006   Default Scale: 1

Counter Type: PERF_100NSEC_TIMER   Counter Size: 8 bytes

% User Time   *Advanced*

User Time is the percentage of elapsed time that this thread has spent executing code in User Mode. Applications execute in User Mode, as do subsystems like the window manager and the graphics engine. Code executing in User Mode cannot damage the integrity of the Windows NT Executive, Kernel, and device drivers. Unlike some early operating systems, Windows NT uses process boundaries for subsystem protection in addition to the traditional protection of User and Privileged modes. These subsystem processes provide additional protection. Therefore, some work done by Windows NT on behalf of your application may appear in other subsystem processes in addition to the Privileged Time in your process.

Index: 142   Default Scale: 1

Counter Type: PERF_100NSEC_TIMER   Counter Size: 8 bytes

Context Switches/sec   *Advanced*

Context Switches/sec is the rate of switches from one thread to another. Thread switches can occur either inside of a single process or across processes. A thread switch may be caused either by one thread asking another for information, or by a thread being preempted by another, higher priority thread becoming ready to run. Unlike some early operating systems, Windows NT uses process boundaries for subsystem protection in addition to the traditional protection of User and Privileged modes. These subsystem processes provide additional protection. Therefore, some work done by Windows NT on behalf of an application may appear in other subsystem processes in addition to the Privileged Time in the application. Switching to the subsystem process causes one Context Switch in the application thread. Switching back causes another Context Switch in the subsystem thread.

Index: 146   Default Scale: 0.01

Counter Type: PERF_COUNTER_COUNTER   Counter Size: 4 bytes

Elapsed Time   *Advanced*

The total elapsed time (in seconds) this thread has been running.

Index: 684   Default Scale: 0.0001

Counter Type: PERF_ELAPSED_TIME   Counter Size: 8 bytes

ID Process   *Wizard*

ID Process is the unique identifier of this process. ID Process numbers are reused, so they only identify a process for the lifetime of that process.

Index: 784   Default Scale: 1

Counter Type: PERF_COUNTER_RAWCOUNT   Counter Size: 4 bytes

ID Thread   *Wizard*

ID Thread is the unique identifier of this thread. ID Thread numbers are reused, so they only identify a thread for the lifetime of that thread.

Index: 804   Default Scale: 1

Counter Type: PERF_COUNTER_RAWCOUNT   Counter Size: 4 bytes

Priority Base   *Advanced* ·

The current base priority of this thread. The system may raise the thread's dynamic priority above the base priority if the thread is handling user input, or lower it towards the base priority if the thread becomes compute bound.

Index: 682   Default Scale: 1

Counter Type: PERF_COUNTER_RAWCOUNT   Counter Size: 4 bytes

Priority Current   *Advanced*

The current dynamic priority of this thread. The system may raise the thread's dynamic priority above the base priority if the thread is handling user input, or lower it towards the base priority if the thread becomes compute bound.

Index: 694   Default Scale: 1

Counter Type: PERF_COUNTER_RAWCOUNT   Counter Size: 4 bytes

Start Address   *Wizard*

Starting virtual address for this thread.

Index: 706   Default Scale: 1

Counter Type: PERF_COUNTER_RAWCOUNT   Counter Size: 4 bytes

Thread State   *Wizard*

Thread State is the current state of the thread. It is 0 for Initialized, 1 for Ready, 2 for Running, 3 for Standby, 4 for Terminated, 5 for Wait, 6 for Transition, 7 for Unknown. A Running thread is using a processor; a Standby thread is about to use one. A Ready thread wants to use a processor, but is waiting for a processor because none are free. A thread in Transition is waiting for a resource in order to execute, such as waiting for its execution stack to be paged in from disk. A Waiting thread has no use for the processor because it is waiting for a peripheral operation to complete or a resource to become free.

Index: 046   Default Scale: 1

Counter Type: PERF_COUNTER_RAWCOUNT   Counter Size: 4 bytes

Thread Wait Reason   *Wizard*

Index: 336   Default Scale: 1

Counter Type: PERF_COUNTER_RAWCOUNT   Counter Size: 4 bytes

Thread Wait Reason is only applicable when the thread is in the Wait state (see Thread State). It is 0 or 7 when the thread is waiting for the Executive, 1 or 8 for a Free Page, 2 or 9 for a Page In, 3 or 10 for a Pool Allocation, 4 or 11 for an Execution Delay, 5 or 12 for a Suspended condition, 6 or 13 for a User Request, 14 for an Event Pair High, 15 for an Event Pair Low, 16 for an LPC Receive, 17 for an LPC Reply, 18 for Virtual Memory, 19 for a Page Out; 20 and higher are not assigned at the time of this writing. Event Pairs are used to communicate with protected subsystems (see Context Switches).

Thread Details Object

Object: Thread Details   Index: 816   *Wizard*

Thread Details object contains the thread counters that are time consuming to collect.

User PC   *Wizard*

Current User Program Counter for this thread.

Index: 708   Default Scale: 1

Counter Type: PERF_COUNTER_RAWCOUNT   Counter Size: 4 bytes

UDP Object

Object: UDP   Index: 658   *Advanced*

The UDP Object Type includes those counters that describe the rates that UDP datagrams are received and sent by a certain entity using the UDP protocol. It also describes various error counts for the UDP protocol.

Datagrams No Port/sec   *Advanced*

Datagrams No Port/sec is the rate of received UDP datagrams for which there was no application at the destination port.

Index: 664   Default Scale: 0.1

Counter Type: PERF_COUNTER_COUNTER   Counter Size: 4 bytes

Datagrams Received Errors   *Advanced*

Datagrams Received Errors is the number of received UDP datagrams that could not be delivered for reasons other than the lack of an application at the destination port.

Index: 666   Default Scale: 1

Counter Type: PERF_COUNTER_RAWCOUNT   Counter Size: 4 bytes

Datagrams Received/sec   *Advanced*

Datagrams Received/sec is the rate that UDP datagrams are delivered to UDP users.

Index: 446   Default Scale: 0.1

Counter Type: PERF_COUNTER_COUNTER   Counter Size: 4 bytes

Datagrams Sent/sec   *Advanced*

Datagrams Sent/sec is the rate that UDP datagrams are sent from the entity.

Index: 442   Default Scale: 0.1

Counter Type: PERF_COUNTER_COUNTER   Counter Size: 4 bytes

Datagrams/sec   *Advanced*

Datagrams/sec is the rate that UDP datagrams are sent or received by the entity.

Index: 438   Default Scale: 0.1

Counter Type: PERF_COUNTER_COUNTER   Counter Size: 4 bytes

Registry Value Entries

This appendix lists value entries from the Windows NT Registry that can have an effect on system performance. These values are set to appropriate defaults when Windows NT is installed, and in almost all cases you do not need to change them.

Each section of this appendix represents a key or subkey in the Registry. Not all values in each subkey are listed. Only those values that may have a significant effect on system performance are shown. For a complete reference of Registry entries, see the *Microsoft Windows NT Resource Guide*.

Caution Using Registry Editor incorrectly can cause serious problems, including corruptions that may make it necessary to reinstall Windows NT. Wherever possible, you should use Control Panel and the applications in the Administrative Tools program group to make changes to the system configuration.

Not all entries that appear here may be found in the Registry for a particular computer. For many entries, the system uses the default value unless you add the entry to the Registry and specify another value.

In general, if you change values for any entries in the CurrentControlSet, you must restart the computer for the changes to take effect.

If you change values for entries under HKEY_CURRENT_USER using Registry Editor, you may have to log off and log back on for the changes to take effect.

The information in this appendix appears in the following format:

> **Entry Name** **REG_*type*** *Range for value entry*
> A description of the entry, usually including the conditions under which you might change the value.
>
> Default: *value*
> (For value ranges that are Boolean, the value can be **1** for true or "enabled," or **0** for false or "disabled.")

CurrentControlSet\Control Subkeys

This key contains parameters that control system startup, such as subsystems to load, the size and location of paging files, and so on.

Note The system must be restarted for any changes in the Control key to take effect.

The Control subkey itself can contain the following value entries:

RegistrySizeLimit **REG_DWORD** *Size in bytes*
Specifies the total amount of space that can be consumed by Registry data.

The system ensures that the value for **RegistrySizeLimit** is at least 4 MB and no greater than about 80 percent of the size of **PagedPoolSize.** Setting **RegistrySizeLimit** to 0xffffffff sets the value to be as large as 80 percent of **PagedPoolSize** (under the Control\Session Manager\MemoryManagement key). You can allow for a bigger Registry by setting the initial **PagedPoolSize,** or you can set the value of **RegistrySizeLimit.** If you want a very large Registry, you want to set both. However, for all but a few domain controllers, **RegistrySizeLimit** never needs to be changed.

RegistrySizeLimit must have a type of REG_DWORD and a data length of 4 bytes, or it will be ignored.

Default: 8 MB (That is, 25 percent of the default **PagedPoolSize.**)

Memory Management Control Entries

The Memory Management subkey defines paging options under the following Registry path:

```
HKEY_LOCAL_MACHINE\SYSTEM\CurrentControlSet\Control
    \Session Manager\Memory Management
```

LargeSystemCache   **REG_DWORD**   *Number*

Specifies, for a nonzero value, that the system favor the system-cache working set rather than the processes working set. Set this value by choosing the Windows NT Advanced Server installation base.

Default: 0

WOW Startup Control Entries

The following values control startup parameters that affect MS-DOS–based applications and applications created for 16-bit Windows 3.1. The Registry path for these values is the following:

```
HKEY_LOCAL_MACHINE\SYSTEM\CurrentControlSet
    \Control\WOW
```

Size   **REG_SZ**   *Number in megabytes*

Defines the amount of memory to be given to each individual MS-DOS VDM. The default of 0 gives the VDM as much memory as Windows NT determines is necessary, depending upon the memory configuration.

To change this value, change the related value in the PIF file for the application.

Default: 0

Wowsize   **REG_SZ**   *Up to 16 megabytes*

For RISC-based computers, defines the amount of memory provided in a VDM when a WOW session is started. This value is not used on *x*86-based computers, where Windows NT allocates the memory needed when it is asked for.

The default size chosen for a RISC-based computer depends on the amount of system memory on the computer. For each MB specified, the system uses 1.25 MB, so setting **Wowsize** to 4 MB causes the VDM to allocate 5 MB, although applications can only use 4 MB. You can override the following defaults:

System memory size	Default VDM size
Less than 12 MB (small)	3 MB
12–16 MB (medium)	6 MB
More than 16 MB (large)	8 MB

Caution Setting **Wowsize** to a value lower than 3 MB will cause most applications to fail.

Default: Depends on RISC-based computer's system memory

Serial Subkey Entries in the CurrentControlSet\Services Subkey

The following subkey and value can be found under the following key:

```
HKEY_LOCAL_MACHINE\System\CurrentControlSet\Services\Serial
```

The Serial subkey contains a subkey named Parameters, under which is a set of subkeys typically named Serial*X* where *X* is a whole number. A system administrator must place these subkeys and values into the Registry. You can only define and manipulate these values by using Registry Editor.

For example, under the Serial2 subkey, the following optional value entry can appear, and does affect system performance.

ForceFifoEnable   REG_DWORD   *0 or 1*

If the value is 1 and the hardware supports a FIFO buffer (for example, the NS 16550AFN), the driver enables the FIFO. Not all FIFOs are reliable. If the application or the user notices lost data or no data transmission, it is recommended that this value be set to 0.

Default: 1

Mouse and Keyboard Driver Entries

Parameters in this section are for the mouse and keyboard class and port drivers, including these drivers:

Busmouse	Inport	Mouclass
i8042prt	Kbdclass	Sermouse

Microsoft Bus Mouse Port Driver Entries

The following value entry for the Microsoft bus mouse are found in this subkey:

`HKEY_LOCAL_MACHINE\SYSTEM\CurrentControlSet\Services\Busmouse\Parameters`

MouseDataQueueSize   REG_DWORD   >= *0x1*

Specifies the number of mouse events to be buffered internally by the driver, in nonpaged pool. The allocated size, in bytes, of the internal buffer is this value times the size of the MOUSE_INPUT_DATA structure (defined in NTDDMOU.H). Consider increasing the size if the System log in Event Viewer frequently contains this message from the Busmouse source: "The ring buffer that stores incoming mouse data has overflowed (buffer size is configurable via the Registry)."

Default: 0x64 (100)

Intel 8042 Port Driver Entries

The i8042prt driver handles the keyboard and mouse port mouse (also known as a PS/2-compatible mouse) for the Intel 8042 controller. These value entries are found in the following subkey:

`HKEY_LOCAL_MACHINE\SYSTEM\CurrentControlSet\Services\i8042prt\Parameters`

KeyboardDataQueueSize   REG_DWORD   >= *0x1*

Specifies the number of keyboard events to be buffered internally by the driver, in nonpaged pool. The allocated size, in bytes, of the internal buffer is this value times the size of the KEYBOARD_INPUT_DATA structure (defined in NTDDKBD.H). Consider increasing the size if the System log in Event Viewer contains the following message from the i8042prt source: "The ring buffer that stores incoming keyboard data has overflowed (buffer size is configurable via the Registry)."

Default: 0x64 (100)

MouseDataQueueSize   REG_DWORD   >= *0x1*

Specifies the number of mouse events to be buffered internally by the driver, in nonpaged pool. Consider increasing the size if the System log in Event Viewer contains the following message from the i8042prt source: "The ring buffer that stores incoming mouse data has overflowed (buffer size is configurable via the Registry)."

Default: 0x64 (100)

Microsoft InPort Bus Mouse Port Driver Entries

The value entries for the Microsoft InPort® bus mouse are found in the following subkey:

HKEY_LOCAL_MACHINE\SYSTEM\CurrentControlSet\Services\Inport\Parameters

MouseDataQueueSize   REG_DWORD   >= *0x1*

Specifies the number of mouse events to be buffered internally by the driver, in nonpaged pool. The allocated size, in bytes, of the internal buffer is this value times the size of the MOUSE_INPUT_DATA structure (defined in NTDDMOU.H). Consider increasing the size if the System log in Event Viewer contains the following message from the InPort source: "The ring buffer that stores incoming mouse data has overflowed (buffer size is configurable via the Registry)."

Default: 0x64 (100)

Microsoft Serial Mouse Port Driver Entries

The value entries for the Microsoft serial mouse are found in the following subkey:

HKEY_LOCAL_MACHINE\SYSTEM\CurrentControlSet\Services\Sermouse\Parameters

MouseDataQueueSize   REG_DWORD   >= *0x1*

Specifies the number of mouse events to be buffered internally by the driver, in nonpaged pool. The allocated size, in bytes, of the internal buffer is this value times the size of the MOUSE_INPUT_DATA structure (defined in NTDDMOU.H). Consider increasing the size if the System log in Event Viewer contains the following message from the Sermouse source: "The ring buffer that stores incoming mouse data has overflowed (buffer size is configurable via the Registry)."

Default: 0x64 (100)

Mouse Class Driver Entries

The value entries for the mouse class driver are found in the following subkey:

```
HKEY_LOCAL_MACHINE\SYSTEM\CurrentControlSet\Services\Mouclass\Parameters
```

MouseDataQueueSize   REG_DWORD   >= *0x1*

Specifies the number of mouse events to be buffered internally by the driver, in nonpaged pool. The allocated size, in bytes, of the internal buffer is this value times the size of the MOUSE_INPUT_DATA structure (defined in NTDDMOU.H). Consider increasing the size if the System log in Event Viewer frequently contains the following message from the Mouclass source: "The ring buffer that stores incoming mouse data has overflowed (buffer size is configurable via the Registry)."

Default: 0x64 (100)

Keyboard Class Driver Entries

The value entries for the keyboard class driver are found in the following subkey:

```
HKEY_LOCAL_MACHINE\SYSTEM\CurrentControlSet\Services\Kbdclass\Parameters
```

KeyboardDataQueueSize   REG_DWORD   >= *0x1*

Specifies the number of keyboard events to be buffered internally by the driver, in nonpaged pool. The allocated size, in bytes, of the internal buffer is this value times the size of the KEYBOARD_INPUT_DATA structure (defined in NTDDKBD.H). Consider increasing the size if the System log in Event Viewer contains the following message from the Kbdclass source: "The ring buffer that stores incoming keyboard data has overflowed (buffer size is configurable via the Registry)."

Default: 0x64 (100)

SCSI Miniport Driver Entries

The basic SCSI miniport driver entries in the Registry are found under subkeys in the following path:

```
HKEY_LOCAL_MACHINE\System\CurrentControlSet\Services
```

Each subkey's name is the same as the driver's filename minus the .SYS filename extension; for example, FD8XX, which is the entry for all Future Domain 800-series SCSI adapter. The Registry includes entries for at least the following SCSI miniport device drivers:

Driver name	Description
Aha*xxx*	Adaptec™ 154x and 174x SCSI adapters
DptScsi	DPT SCSI adapter
Fd16_700, Fd7000ex, Fd8xx	Future Domain MCS 600/MCS 700, TMC-7000ex, and 800-series SCSI adapters
Ncr53c9x, Ncrc700, Ncrc710	NCR SCSI controller and adapters
Oliscsi	Olivetti® SCSI adapter
Sparrow	SCSI adapter
Spock	SCSI adapter
T128 and T13B	Trantor SCSI adapters
Ultra*xxx*	UltraStor 124, 14f, and 24f SCSI adapters
Wd33c93	Maynard SCSI adapter

The contents of a SCSI miniport subkey are standard for all SCSI miniport drivers, with these basic value entries:

Value entry	Value
ErrorControl	0x01—which is the preferred value for **ErrorControl**. With a value of 0x01, the startup process continues if the SCSI miniport driver fails to initialize.
Group	SCSI Miniport.
Start	0x00 (Auto Start).
Tag	Optional (determines the load order of SCSI miniport drivers).
Type	0x01 (device driver).

For each SCSI miniport key, there can be one or more subkeys named Parameters\Device or Parameters\Device$N$, where N = 0, 1, 2, and so on. The value of N corresponds to the SCSI host adapter number. If the subkey name is Device, the value is globally defined. If the subkey name is Device$N$, the value only pertains to the particular SCSI host adapter.

The SCSI miniport driver recognizes the following optional value entries, which are used to fix problems such as device time-outs or controller detection errors but will reduce I/O performance. These value entries can be abbreviated. For example, a value entry of **Disable** will cause **DisableSynchronousTransfers, DisableTaggedQueuing, DisableDisconnects,** and **DisableMultipleRequests** to be set.

Note   The system must be restarted before these options take effect.

BreakPointOnEntry   REG_DWORD   *0 or 1*

A DbgBreakPoint() call is immediately made inside of SpParseDevice. This is used for debugging.

Default: 0 (disabled)

DisableDisconnects   REG_DWORD   *0 or 1*

Disables disconnects on the SCSI bus. It causes all requests to be executed sequentially.

Default: 1 (enabled)

DisableMultipleRequests   REG_DWORD   *0 or 1*

Prevents the SCSI miniport driver from sending more than one request at a time per SCSI device.

Default: 1 (enabled)

DisableSynchronousTransfers   REG_DWORD   *0 or 1*

Disables synchronous data transfers on the SCSI bus.

Default: 1 (enabled)

DisableTaggedQueuing   REG_DWORD   *0 or 1*

Disables SCSI-II tagged command queuing on the host adapter.

Default: 1 (enabled)

DriverParameter   *Data type is specific to driver*   *A string*

A pointer to this data is passed to the SCSI miniport driver in a miniportFindAdapter routine. It is the fourth parameter, ArgumentString. A miniport driver uses this data to define the IRQ number for the SCSI host adapter, but other applications for the data are possible.

The data type for this value is defined by the specific SCSI miniport driver developer. If the data type is REG_SZ, the Unicode string is converted to an ANSI string before transferring it to the SCSI miniport driver.

The following drivers currently use the **DriverParameter** value entry:

Driver	Values	Meaning
Wd33c93	**IRQ=**xx; **DMA=**yy	xx is the IRQ the card should use. Valid values are: 3, 4, 5, 10, 11, 12, and 15. The default is 10. yy is the DMA channel the card should use. Valid values are: 5, 6, and 7. The default is 6.
Aha154x	**BusOnTime=**xx	xx is the bus on time in microseconds for the card. Valid values are 2–15. The default is 7. The value is usually adjusted downward when DMA transfers from the Adaptec card are interfering with other DMA transfers.
FD8XX	**IRQ=**xx	xx is the IRQ the card should use. Valid values are 0, 3, 4, 5, 10, 11, 12, 14, 15. This value should match the jumper settings on the card. Numbers 0, 3, and 5 are for the short cards (850, 845); the rest are for the 885 card only. A value of 0 indicates the card should not use any interrupts and will poll. The default is 5.
T128	**IRQ=**xx	xx is the IRQ the card should use. Valid values are: 0, 3, 5, 7 , 10, 12, 14, and 15. This value should match the jumper settings on the card. Numbers greater than 7 are for the T128F card only. A value of 0 indicates the card should not use any interrupts and will poll. The default is 5.
T13B	**IRQ=**xx	xx is the IRQ the card should use. Valid values are 0, 3, 5, and 7. This value should match the jumper settings on the card. A value of 0 indicates the card should not use any interrupts and will poll. The default is 5.
TMV1	**IRQ=**xx	xx is the IRQ the card should use. Valid values are: 2, 3, 4, 5, 6, 7, 10, 11, 12, and 15. The default is 10.

Video Device Driver Entries

This section describes the entries for video device drivers under the DeviceMap subkey and under the CurrentControlSet\Services subkeys for specific video drivers.

Video Driver Entries in the Services Subkey

The port driver portion of the video driver is hardware-independent and contains operating system-specific code. Therefore, the port driver, VIDEOPRT.SYS, can support one or more video devices. The Services\Videoprt subkey has no added parameters, and its standard entries are the following:

Value entry	Default value
ErrorControl	0x1 (Normal)
Group	Video
Start	0x1 (system)
Type	0x1 (Kernel driver)

The specific subkey for each video driver contains all the information required to initialize and program the device properly. If several adapters can be handled by a single driver, the subkeys Device1, Device2, and so on will contain information for the other devices. The Registry path looks like this, where *VideoDriverName* is the name of a specific video device driver:

```
HKEY_LOCAL_MACHINE\SYSTEM\CurrentControlSet\Services
    \VideoDriverName\Device0
```

The *VideoDriverName* subkeys for drivers in Windows NT include the following. This is not an exhaustive list:

Ati	S3	Wdvga
ET4000	Trident	Xga
Jazzg*xxx*	Vga	

For example, the following subkey contains information for the first logical device of type VGA:

```
HKEY_LOCAL_MACHINE\SYSTEM\CurrentControlSet\Services\Vga\Device0
```

The following values, which can be set in a video driver subkey, affect system performance.

DefaultSettings.BitsPerPel   REG_DWORD   *Number of bits per pixel*

Contains the number of colors for the mode requested by the user. For example, for the v7vram miniport, the following value yields a 256-color mode:

```
DefaultSettings.BitsPerPel = 8
```

DefaultSettings.XResolution   REG_DWORD   *Number of pixels*

Contains the width of the mode requested by the user. For example, for the et4000 miniport:

```
DefaultSettings.Xresolution = 1024
```

DefaultSettings.YResolution   REG_DWORD   *Number of pixels*

Contains the height of the mode requested by the user. For example, for the et4000 miniport:

```
DefaultSettings.Yresolution = 768
```

Registry Entries for Network Services

This section describes parameters for Windows NT services under the HKEY_LOCAL_MACHINE\SYSTEM\CurrentControlSet\Services subkey.

Some of these services also have configuration information stored under HKEY_LOCAL_MACHINE\SOFTWARE. These values are described in "NetRules Subkey Entries," earlier in this chapter.

Note Wherever possible, choose the Services icon in Control Panel or use Server Manager in Windows NT Advanced Server to change values for these services.

AppleTalk and MacFile Service Entries for SFM

Services For Macintosh (SFM) does not appear in the Registry until you install SFM using the Network icon in Control Panel. After installation, the SFM value entries appear under several Services subkeys: AppleTalk®, MacFile, MacPrint, and MacSrv. You should let the system maintain entries in the MacPrint or MacSrv service. However, the AppleTalk and MacFile services contain definable parameters described in this section.

You should use the Network icon in Control Panel to configure SFM, and use File Manager to administer file services, Server Manager to administer server services, and Print Manager to administer print services for SFM.

Adapter Card Entries for AppleTalk

The entries for AppleTalk that are specific to network adapter cards are found under the following Registry path:

```
HKEY_LOCAL_MACHINE\SYSTEM\CurrentControlSet\Services
    \AppleTalk\Adapters\adapter_name
```

There is one subkey for each adapter that is AppleTalk-compatible on the computer. These entries are found in each *Adapter_Name* subkey.

For changes to take effect, you must restart the File Server for Macintosh® using the Devices icon in Control Panel.

AarpRetries   REG_DWORD   *Number*

Specifies the maximum number of AppleTalk address-resolution protocol packets to be sent by the AppleTalk protocol.

Default: 0xa

DdpCheckSums   REG_DWORD   *0 or 1*

Tells the AppleTalk protocol whether to compute checksums in the DDP layer. If this entry is 1, the AppleTalk protocol uses sums in the DDP layer.

Default: 0

MacFile Entries for SFM

The MacFile subkey contains the main entries for the AppleTalk File Protocol (AFP) server. All configuration information for the file server is in the following subkey:

```
HKEY_LOCAL_MACHINE\SYSTEM\CurrentControlSet\Services\MacFile
```

The MacFile\Parameters subkey includes Type_Creators, Icons, and Extensions subkeys. You should let the system maintain entries in the Icons or Extensions subkeys. This section describes value entries for the Parameters subkey.

MacFile Parameters Entries

The Registry path for MacFile parameters is the following:

```
HKEY_LOCAL_MACHINE\SYSTEM\CurrentControlSet\Services\MacFile\Parameters
```

The following value entries specify server options, which can be set from the Server Manager. All other entries are added to the Registry when changes to the default values occur.

For information about the Macintosh codepage, see the entry for MacCP in the NLS\CodePage subkey.

For changes to take effect, you must restart the computer.

MaxSessions   REG_DWORD   *1 to unlimited (0xffffffff)*
Specifies the maximum number of user sessions that the file server for Macintosh can accommodate.
Default: 0xff (255 in decimal)

PagedMemLimit   REG_DWORD   *1000K to 256000K*
Specifies the maximum amount of page memory that the file server for Macintosh uses. Performance of the MacFile service increases with an increase in this value. However, the value should not be set lower than 1000 KB. It is especially important that you are well acquainted with memory issues before changing this resource parameter. You cannot change this value from Server Manager.
Default: 0x4e20 (20000 in decimal)

NonPagedMemLimit   REG_DWORD   *256K to 16000KB*
Specifies the maximum amount of RAM that is available to the file server for Macintosh. Increasing this value helps performance of the file server, but decreases performance of other system resources.
Default: 0xfa0 (4000 in decimal)

DiskPerf Service Entries

The DiskPerf subkey entries determines whether disk performance statistics are maintained by the system. If the **Start** value is 0 (boot), then statistics are counted and are reported by Performance Monitor and similar tools. Collecting disk performance statistics can take up to 1.5 percent of the disk throughput on a system with a slow processor (such as an 20 MHz 80386 computer) but should have negligible impact on a system with a faster processor (such as a 33 MHz i486 and above).

Turn DiskPerf on or off only by using the Diskperf utility; for example, type **diskperf -y** at the command prompt.

The Registry path is the following:

```
HKEY_LOCAL_MACHINE\SYSTEM\CurrentControlSet\Services\DiskPerf
```

There are no parameters that users can set. The following are the default values for the standard entries:

Value entry	Value
ErrorControl	0x1 (Normal)
Group	Filter
Start	0x4 (disabled)
Type	0x1 (Kernel driver)

EventLog Service Entries

The Services subkey for EventLog contains at least three subkeys for the three types of logs—Application, Security, and System. Each of the three *Logfile* subkeys for the EventLog service can contain the value entry described in this section. The Registry path is the following, where *logfile* is System, Application, or Security.

```
HKEY_LOCAL_MACHINE\SYSTEM\CurrentControlSet\Services
    \Eventlog\logfile
```

This entry is included for informational purposes only. This information is usually maintained by Event Viewer. New keys under the Application key can only be added in meaningful ways by using the Win32 Registry APIs.

MaxSize   REG_DWORD   *Number in kilobytes*

Specifies the maximum size of the log file. This value can be set using the Event Viewer.

Default: 512

NBF (NetBEUI) Transport Entries

The startup parameters for the NetBEUI (NBF) transport are found under the following subkey:

```
HKEY_LOCAL_MACHINE\SYSTEM\Services\NBF\Parameters
```

The Init*xxx* entries for NBF define the initial allocation and the size of free memory for items. The Max*xxx* entries define the upper limits. Within these ranges, the system autotunes performance. By default, the NBF service uses all the resources necessary to handle client requests, and when it is not actively working, it doesn't use many resources. Set Init*xxx* values to control initial allocation, which can make the system a little faster when you know a server will be busy. Set the Max*xxx*values to control limits when you don't want the server to be too busy or to use too much memory for networking.

With Registry Editor, you can modify the following startup parameters for the NBF transport:

DefaultT1Timeout   REG_DWORD   *100-nanosecond units*

Specifies the initial value for the T1 timeout. T1 controls the time that NBF waits for a response after sending a logical link control (LLC) poll packet before resending it. Adjust this parameter only if NBF will be connecting over slow networks or to slow remote computers (although NBF does adapt).

Default: 6000000 (600 milliseconds)

DefaultT2Timeout   REG_DWORD   *100-nanosecond units*

Specifies the initial value for the T2 timeout. T2 controls the time that NBF can wait after receiving an LLC poll packet before responding. It must be much less than T1; one-half or less is a good general rule. Adjust this parameter only if NBF will be connecting over slow networks or to slow remote computers.

Default: 1500000 (150 milliseconds)

DefaultTiTimeout   REG_DWORD   *100-nanosecond units*

Specifies the initial value for the Ti timeout. Ti is the inactivity timer. When it expires, NBF sends an LLC poll packet to ensure that the link is still active. Adjust this parameter only if NBF is connecting over networks with unusual reliability characteristics, or over slow networks or to slow computers.

Default: 300000000 (30 seconds)

InitAddresses   REG_DWORD   *1 or higher; 0 = no limit*

Specifies the number of initial addresses to allocate within any memory limits that might imposed on NBF. Addresses correspond to NetBIOS names. An address is for the actual name, and an address file is for a TDI (Transport Driver Interface) client using that name; so usually you have the same number, but if two users open the same address, that is two address files but only one address.

Set this parameter if you know that a large number of addresses are needed. Otherwise, the system automatically allocates space for addresses as needed.

Default: 0 (no limit)

InitAddressFiles   REG_DWORD   *1 or higher; 0 = no limit*

Specifies the number of initial address files to allocate within any memory limits that might imposed on NBF. Set this parameter if you know that a large number of address files are needed. Otherwise, the system automatically allocates space for address files as needed.

Default: 0 (no limit)

InitConnections   REG_DWORD   *1 or higher; 0 = no limit*

Specifies the number of initial connections (NetBIOS sessions) to allocate within any memory limits that might imposed on NBF. Set this parameter if you know that a large number of connections are needed. Otherwise, the system automatically allocates space for connections as needed.

Default: 1

InitLinks   REG_DWORD   *1 or higher; 0 = no limit*

Specifies the number of initial LLC links to allocate within any memory limits that might imposed on NBF. Typically, you have one connection per LLC link to another network adapter card, because the redirector puts all links to a computer into one connection. However, you may have more if two computers are communicating with each other or if a NetBIOS application is running. Set this parameter if you know that a large number of links are needed. Otherwise, the system automatically allocates space for links as needed.

Default: 2

InitReceiveBuffers   REG_DWORD   *1 or higher; 0 = no limit*

Specifies the number of initial receive buffers to allocate. Receive buffers are used by NBF when it calls NDIS TransferData for received datagrams. Usually, this value is allocated as needed, but you can use this parameter to preallocate memory if you know a large number of datagram frames will be received.

Default: 5

InitReceivePackets   REG_DWORD   *1 or higher; 0 = no limit*

Specifies the number of initial receive packets to allocate. Receive packets are used by NBF when it calls NDIS TransferData for received data. Usually, this value is allocated as needed, but you can use this parameter to preallocate memory if you know a large number of UI frames will be received.

Default: 10

InitRequests   REG_DWORD   *1 or higher; 0 = no limit*

Specifies the number of initial requests to allocate within any memory limits that might imposed on NBF. Requests are used for in-progress connect requests, remote adapter status requests, find name requests, and so on. Set this parameter if you know that a large number of requests are needed. Otherwise, the system automatically allocates space for requests as needed.

Default: 5

InitSendPackets   REG_DWORD   *1 or higher; 0 = no limit*

Specifies the number of initial send packets to allocate. Send packets are used by NBF whenever it sends connection-oriented data on behalf of a client. Usually, this value is allocated as needed, but you can use this parameter to preallocate memory if you know a large number of data frames are needed or if you see a lot of "send packets exhausted" messages when using Performance Monitor.

Default: 30

InitUIFrames   REG_DWORD   *1 or higher; 0 = no limit*

Specifies the number of initial UI frames to allocate. UI frames are used by NBF to establish connections and for connectionless services such as datagrams. Usually, this value is allocated as needed, but you can use this parameter to preallocate memory if you know a large number of UI frames are needed.

Default: 5

LLCMaxWindowSize   REG_DWORD   *Number of frames*

Specifies the number of LLC I-frames that NBF can send before polling and waiting for a response from the remote. Adjust this parameter only if NBF is communicating over a network whose reliability often changes suddenly.

Default: 10

LLCRetries   REG_DWORD   *1 or higher; 0 = no limit*

Specifies the number of times that NBF will retry polling a remote workstation after receiving a T1 timeout. After this many retries, NBF closes the link. Adjust this parameter only if NBF is connecting over networks with unusual reliability characteristics.

Default: 8

MaxAddresses   REG_DWORD   *1 or higher; 0 = no limit*

Specifies the maximum number of addresses that NBF allocates within any memory limits that might imposed on NBF. Addresses are NetBIOS names that are registered on the network by NBF. An address is for the actual name, and an address file is for a TDI client using that name.

Use this optional parameter to fine-tune use of NBF memory. Typically this parameter is used to control address resources with an unlimited NBF.

Default: 0 (no limit)

MaxAddressFiles   **REG_DWORD**   *1 or higher; 0 = no limit*

Specifies maximum number of address files that NBF allocates within any memory limits that might imposed on NBF. Each address file corresponds to a client opening an address.

Use this optional parameter to fine-tune use of NBF memory. Typically this parameter is used to control address files with an unlimited NBF.

Default: 0 (no limit)

MaxConnections   **REG_DWORD**   *1 or higher; 0 = no limit*

Specifies the maximum number of connections that NBF allocates within any memory limits that might imposed on NBF. Connections are established between NBF clients and similar entities on remote computers.

Use this optional parameter to fine-tune use of NBF memory. Typically this parameter is used to control connection resources with an unlimited NBF.

Default: 0 (no limit)

MaximumIncomingFrames   **REG_DWORD**   *1 or higher; 0 = off*

Used in some cases to control how many incoming frames NBF will receive before it sends an acknowledgment to a remote machine. In general, NBF automatically senses when to sends acknowledgments, however when communicating with some Microsoft LAN Manager or IBM LAN Server remote computers configured with a very low value for **maxout**, this parameter can be set to an equal or lower value to improve network performance. (This parameter corresponds roughly to the Microsoft LAN Manager **maxin** parameter.) A value of 0 turns off this hint, causing NBF to revert to usual behavior. For communication with most all remotes, this parameter isn't used.

Default: 2

MaxLinks   **REG_DWORD**   *1 or higher; 0 = no limit*

Specifies the maximum number of links that NBF allocates within any memory limits that might imposed on NBF. Links are established for every remote adapter to which NBF communicates.

Use this optional parameter to fine-tune use of NBF memory. Typically this parameter is used to control link resources with an unlimited NBF.

Default: 0 (no limit)

MaxRequests   REG_DWORD   *1 or higher; 0 = no limit*

Specifies the maximum number of requests that NBF allocates within any memory limits that might imposed on NBF. Requests are used by NBF to control send, receive, connect, and listen operations.

Use this optional parameter to fine-tune use of NBF memory. Typically this parameter is used to control request resources with an unlimited NBF.

Default: 0 (no limit).

NetBIOSAddNameQueryRetries   REG_DWORD   *Number*

Specifies the number of times that NBF will retry sending ADD_NAME_QUERY and ADD_GROUP_NAME_QUERY frames. Adjust this parameter only if NBF is registering addresses on a network that drops many packets.

Default: 3

NetBIOSAddNameQueryTimeout   REG_DWORD   *100-nanosecond units*

Specifies the time-out between NBF sending successive ADD_NAME_QUERY and ADD_GROUP_NAME_QUERY frames. Adjust this parameter only if NBF is registering addresses on a network with slow computers or over a slow network.

Default: 5000000

NetBIOSGeneralRetries   REG_DWORD   *Number*

Specifies the number of times that NBF will retry sending STATUS_QUERY and FIND_NAME frames. Adjust this parameter only if NBF is operating on a network that drops many packets.

Default: 3

NetBIOSGeneralTimeout   REG_DWORD   *100-nanosecond units*

Specifies the time-out between NBF sending successive STATUS_QUERY and FIND_NAME requests. Adjust this parameter only if NBF is operating on a network with slow computers or over a slow network.

Default: 5000000

NetBIOSNameQueryRetries   REG_DWORD   *Number*

Specifies the number of times that NBF will retry sending NAME_QUERY frames. Adjust this parameter only if NBF is connecting to computers over a network that drops many packets.

Default: 3

NetBIOSNameQueryTimeout   **REG_DWORD**   *100-nanosecond units*

Specifies the time-out between NBF sending successive NAME_QUERY frames. Adjust this parameter only if NBF is connecting to slow computers or over a slow network.

Default: 5000000

NetLogon Service Entries

The Registry path for the parameters for the NetLogon service is the following:

```
HKEY_LOCAL_MACHINE\SYSTEM\CurrentControlSet\Services\Netlogon\Parameters
```

PulseInterval   **REG_DWORD**   *60 to 3600 seconds*

Specifies how long a domain controller waits before sending each update notice to Windows NT Advanced Servers.

When this value is not specified in the Registry, NetLogon determines optimal values depending on the domain controller's load.

Default: 300

Randomize   **REG_DWORD**   *15 to 120 seconds*

Specifies the amount of time a Windows NT Advanced Server domain controller uses to stagger requests sent to the domain controller. This value is used by every server in the domain. When the domain controller sends update message to the servers, it includes the **Randomize** value in the message. The servers receiving that message will wait a maximum of that many seconds before responding to that message.

When this value is not specified in the Registry, NetLogon determines optimal values depending on the domain controller's load.

Default: 30

NWLink Transport Entries (IPX/SPX)

NWLink is an implementation of the IPX/SPX protocols popular in NetWare networks. In addition, the module NWNBLink provides support for the Novell implementation of the NetBIOS protocol.

Caution   All entries have reasonable defaults that usually should not need to be modified. Be careful when modifying an entry, because any change can easily affect the performance of a conversation between the sender and receiver.

The NWLink keys do not appear in the Registry unless this service is installed using the Network icon in Control Panel. After the service is installed, not all entries appear by default in the Registry. If the entry is not there, the default value for that entry is used.

NWNBLink Entries for Microsoft Extensions to Novell NetBIOS

The Microsoft Extensions to Novell NetBIOS are included to enhance the performance of the traditional Novell NetBIOS protocol. NWNBLink can detect automatically whether it is talking to a Novell NetBIOS implementation that does not understand these extensions; in such a case, NWNBLink will fall back to the standard Novell NetBIOS protocol currently used in NetWare networks. However, significant performance gains can be realized if the extensions are used (for example, if the NetBIOS conversation occurs between two Windows NT computers).

The Registry path for these value entries is the following:

```
HKEY_LOCAL_MACHINE\SYSTEM\CurrentControlSet
    \Services\NWNBLink\Parameters
```

AckDelayTime   REG_DWORD   *50 to 65535 milliseconds*
Determines the value of the delayed acknowledgment timer.

Default: 250 (no entry = default)

AckWindow   REG_DWORD   *0 to 65535 frames*
Specifies the number of frames to receive before sending an acknowledgment. The **AckWindow** entry is used as a clocking mechanism on networks in which the sender is networked on a fast LAN, but the receiver is networked on the other side utilizing a slower link. By automatically forcing acknowledgments, the sender can keep sending frames continually. If both the sender and receiver are located on a fast link, you can set **AckWindow** to 0 to turn off sending an acknowledgment to the sender. Alternatively, NWNBLink can be set to dynamically determine whether to use the **AckWindow** parameter based on the setting of **AckWindowThreshold**. Related parameter: **AckWindowThreshold.**

Default: 2 (no entry = default)

AckWindowThreshold   REG_DWORD   *0 to 65535 milliseconds*

Specifies the threshold value for the round-trip time that defines when **AckWindow** will be ignored. The round trip time is an estimate of how long it takes for a frame to be sent and received from a workstation. NWNBLink determines this estimate and uses it as a basis for determining whether it is necessary to send automatic acknowledgments. If **AckWindowThreshold** is set to 0, NWNBLink relies on the **AckWindow** entry. Related parameters: **AckWindow.**

Default: 500 (no entry = default)

EnablePiggyBackAck   REG_DWORD   *0 or 1*

Allows the receiver to piggyback acknowledgments. Piggybacking acknowledgments can occur when the receiver has detected the end of a NetBIOS message. When the sender and receiver are not participating in two-way NetBIOS traffic, you should set **EnablePiggyBackAck** to 0. An example of one-way traffic is a stock update application, where a server constantly sends NetBIOS messages to clients but the client does not need to respond.

If **EnablePiggyBackAck** is set to 1 but there is no back traffic, NWNBLink waits the number of milliseconds determined by **AckDelayTime** before sending the acknowledgment, and then it turns off support for piggybacking acknowledgments. If the workstation at some point starts sending as well as receiving data, NWNBLink turns support back on for piggybacking acknowledgments. Related parameter: **AckDelayTime.**

Default: 1 (true—enable piggybacking acknowledgments; no entry = default)

Extensions   REG_DWORD   *0 or 1*

Specifies whether to use NWNBLink extensions discussed in this section.

Default: 1 (true; no entry = default)

RcvWindowMax   REG_DWORD   *1 to 49152 frames*

Specifies the maximum number of frames the receiver can receive at one time. The value specified by **RcvWindowMax** is sent to the sender during session initialization to give the sender an upper bound on the number of frames that can be sent at one time. Related parameters: **AckDelayTime, AckWindow, AckWindowThreshold, EnablePiggyBackAck,** and **RcvWindowMax.**

Default: 4 (no entry = default)

NWLink Entries for IPX/SPX:
NWLink Parameters for the Network Adapter Card

This parameter is specific for each binding of NWLink to a network adapter card. The Registry path for these value entries is the following:

```
HKEY_LOCAL_MACHINE\SYSTEM\CurrentControlSet\Services
    \NWLinkIPX\NetConfig\Driver01
```

MaxPktSize   REG_DWORD   *0 to 65535*

Specifies the maximum frame size the network adapter card should be allowed to transmit. If this number is 0, NWLink will get this information from the card driver. This parameter allows the administrator to make the maximum transmit size for a card smaller than the card driver allows. A scenario in which you might want to change this entry is in an environment in which the network adapter card on one side of a conversation is on a link that has a larger frame size than the link on the other side of a conversation—for example, if the sending station is linked to a 16 Mbps Token Ring and the receiving station is linked to an Ethernet network.

Default: 0

NWLink Entries for IPX/SPX:
Global IPX Parameters

The following parameters are global for the entire transport. The Registry path for these value entries is the following:

```
HKEY_LOCAL_MACHINE\SYSTEM\CurrentControlSet
    \Services\NWLinkIPX\Parameters
```

ConnectionCount   REG_DWORD   *1 to 65535*

Specifies the number of times the probe will be sent when SPX is trying to connect to a remote node. If no response is received after the probes are sent, an error will occur. Related parameter: **ConnectionTimeout**.

Default: 10

ConnectionTimeout   REG_DWORD   *1 to 65535 half-seconds*

Specifies the time between connection probes when SPX is trying to connect to a remote node. Related parameter: **ConnectionCount**.

Default: 2 (1 second)

KeepAliveCount   REG_DWORD   *1 to 65535*

Specifies how many times to send a keep-alive probe before timing out if there is no response. Related parameter: **KeepAliveTimeout**.

Default: 8

KeepAliveTimeout   REG_DWORD   *1 to 65535 half-seconds*

Specifies the time that the local side should wait before sending a probe to the remote to verify that the SPX connection is still alive. Related parameter: **KeepAliveCount**.

Default: 12 (6 seconds)

RipAgeTime   REG_DWORD   *1 to 65535 minutes*

IPX maintains an RIP cache in order to locate computers on a remote network. The **RipAgeTime** entry informs IPX how long to wait before requesting an RIP update for an entry. This timer is reset when an RIP announcement is received for an entry in the RIP cache.

Default: 5 minutes

RipCount   REG_DWORD   *1 to 65535*

When the RIP protocol layer is trying to find a route on the network, this parameter specifies how many times to send a request before giving up. Related parameter: **RipTimeout**

Default: 5

RipTimeout   REG_DWORD   *1 to 65535 half-seconds*

Specifies the timeout between RIP request packets being sent out when the RIP protocol layer is trying to find a route on the network. Related parameter: **RipCount**.

Default: 1 (1 half-second)

RipUsageTime   REG_DWORD   *1 to 65535 minutes*

IPX maintains a RIP cache in order to locate computers on a remote network. The **RipUsageTime** entry informs IPX how many minutes to wait before an entry in the RIP cache will be deleted from the cache. This timer is reset when a packet is sent to the remote computer.

Default: 15 minutes

SourceRouteUsageTime   REG_DWORD   *1 to 65535 minutes*

Range: Specifies the number of minutes an unused entry can remain in the Token Ring source routing cache before it is flushed.

Default: 10

WindowSize   REG_DWORD   *1 to 10 SPX packets*

Specifies the window to use in the SPX packets. SPX uses the Allocation field of the SPX packet to tell the remote how many receives are available for receiving data. The **WindowSize** entry specifies what value to put in the SPX Allocation field.

Default: 4

Redirector (Rdr) Service Entries

The subkey for the Rdr (redirector) service has the following Registry path:

```
HKEY_LOCAL_MACHINE\SYSTEM\CurrentControlSet\Services\Rdr\Parameters
```

LowerSearchThreshold   REG_DWORD   *Number of kilobytes*

Specifies the number of bytes below which the redirector will request a search of **LowerSearchBufferSize.** If the search size is larger than this (but below the **UpperSearchBufferSize**), the redirector will use the **UpperSearchBufferSize**.

Default: 16K

Remote Access Service (RAS) Entries

The RemoteAccess subkey is created in the Registry when you install RAS on a server, using the Network icon in Control Panel. The default values in RemoteAccess and its subkeys work well for all Windows NT operations such as copying files, using network resources, and sending and receiving electronic mail. However, for some systems, you may want to adjust individual parameters to suit your particular performance and security needs.

Initially, there are no value entries in the Registry for the Remote Access key or its subkeys until you add them with new settings.

RAS NetBIOSGateway Subkey Entries

The Registry path for these entries is the following:

```
HKEY_LOCAL_MACHINE\SYSTEM\CurrentControlSet\Services
    \RemoteAccess\Parameters\NetbiosGateway
```

MaxDynMem   **REG_DWORD**   *131072 to 4294967295*

Sets the amount of virtual memory used to buffer NetBIOS session data for each remote client.

Because the Remote Access server is a gateway between the slow line and the LAN, data is stored (buffered) in its memory when coming from the fast line (LAN) before it is forwarded to the slow line (asynchronous line).

The Remote Access server minimizes the usage of the system's physical memory by locking only a minimal set of pages (about 64K per client) and making use of virtual memory (up to **MaxDynMem**) to buffer the rest of the data. So, as long as there is enough space on the hard disk to expand PAGEFILE.SYS, you can increase this value if needed.

If you have an application with a LAN (fast) sender and an asynchronous (slow) receiver, and if the sender is sending more data at a time than the Remote Access server can buffer in **MaxDynMem**, the Remote Access server tries to apply a form of NetBIOS level flow control by not submitting NCB.RECEIVE on the session until it has enough buffer space to get incoming data. For this reason, if you have such an application, you should increase your NetBIOS SEND/RECEIVE timeouts so that the fast sender can keep pace with the slow receiver.

Default: 655350

MultiCastForwardRate   **REG_DWORD**   *−1 (disabled); 0 to 32,676 seconds*

Governs the multicasting of group name datagrams to all remote workstations. This parameter filters datagrams sent on group names by forwarding them at a specified time interval.

The value −1 disables forwarding. The value 0 guarantees delivery of group name datagrams. The value n forwards datagrams every n seconds, when $1 \leq n \leq 32,676$.

If the **EnableBroadcast** parameter is set to 0, broadcasts are not forwarded even if the **MultiCastForwardRate** parameter is set to a positive number (in this case, only multicast datagrams are forwarded). The line becomes overloaded. If **MultiCastForwardRate** is set to –1, broadcasts are still not forwarded even if **EnableBroadcast** is set to 1. See also **EnableBroadcast**.

To save bandwidth for session traffic, filter the datagrams. However, if you have an application based on multicast datagrams, set this parameter to 0. This value guarantees delivery of all datagrams sent on group names from the LAN to the remote client.

Default: 5

NumRecvQueryIndications   REG_DWORD   *1 to 32*

Allows a Remote Access client to initiate multiple network connections simultaneously. If a remote client is running a NetBIOS application that does multiple NCB.CALL commands simultaneously, increase this parameter to improve performance.

Default: 3

RcvDgSubmittedPerGroupName   REG_DWORD   *1 to 32*

Determines the number of NetBIOS commands of the type Receive Datagram that can be submitted simultaneously per group name on the LAN stack. Keep this setting as small as possible to minimize the amount of memory consumed by system resources. Each datagram command received locks about 1.5K of physical memory in the system.

Default: 3

SizWorkBufs   REG_DWORD   *1024 to 65536*

Sets the size of work buffers. The default setting is optimized for the server message block (SMB) protocol, the protocol between the workstation and the server running on the Windows NT Advanced Server system.

Default: 4500

RAS AsyncMAC Subkey Entries

The Registry path for these entries is the following:

```
HKEY_LOCAL_MACHINE\SYSTEM\CurrentControlSet\Services
    \AsyncMacn\Parameters
```

For changes to take effect, you must restart the computer.

MaxFrameSize   REG_DWORD   *576 to 1514*

Determines the maximum frame size. Use smaller frames for noisy links. A lower setting sends less data per frame, slowing performance. Do not change this parameter for previous versions of the Remote Access service. The value is negotiated between the server and Windows NT clients.

Default: 1514

Server Service Entries

With Registry Editor, you can modify the startup parameters for the Server service. Unless otherwise noted, these parameters are found in this path:

```
HKEY_LOCAL_MACHINE\SYSTEM\CurrentControlSet\Services
   \LanmanServer\Parameters
```

AlertSched   REG_DWORD   *1 to 65535 minutes*

Specifies in Microsoft LAN Manager and in Windows NT how often the server checks alert conditions and sends needed alert messages.

Default: 5

Announce   REG_DWORD   *1 to 65535 seconds*

Specifies how often a nonhidden server announces itself to the network. More frequent announcements keep client server tables more up to date, but cost network overhead and processing on client computers, because clients must process every announcement.

Default: 240

AnnDelta   REG_DWORD   *0 to 65535 milliseconds*

Specifies the time by which the announcement period can vary. This helps to prevent several servers from continuously announcing simultaneously, thereby reducing network load peaks.

Default: 3000

Disc   REG_DWORD   *0 to infinite minutes*

Specifies the amount of idle time that a circuit is allowed before being disconnected. If the virtual circuit has any open files or searches, it is not automatically disconnected. If this parameter is set to a low value, it saves server resources but hinders performance because of clients' overhead in reconnecting. This is equivalent to **autoDisconnect** in Microsoft LanManager.

Default: 15 minutes

DiskSpaceThreshold   REG_DWORD   *0 to 100 percent*

Specifies the percentage of free disk space remaining before an alert is sent.

Default: 10 percent

EnableFCBopens   REG_DWORD   *0 or 1*

Specifies whether MS-DOS File Control Blocks (FCBs) are folded together, so multiple remote opens are performed as a single open on the server. This saves resources on the server.

Default: 1 (true)

EnableOplocks   REG_DWORD   *0 or 1*

Specifies whether the server allows clients to use oplocks on files. Oplocks are a significant performance enhancement, but have the potential to cause lost cached data on some networks, particularly wide-area networks.

Default: 1 (true)

EnableRaw   REG_DWORD   *0 or 1*

Specifies whether the server processes raw Server Message Blocks (SMBs). If enabled, this allows more data to be transferred per transaction and improves performance. However, it is possible that processing raw SMBs can impede performance on certain networks. This parameter is automatically tuned by the server.

Default: 1 (true)

Hidden   REG_BINARY   *0 or 1*

If this parameter is disabled, the server's name and comment can be viewed by others on the domain. If enabled, the server's name and comment will not be announced.

Default: 0 (False)

InitConnTable   REG_DWORD   *1 to 128*

Specifies the initial number of tree connections to be allocated in the connection table. The server automatically increases the table as necessary, so setting the parameter to a higher value is an optimization.

Default: 8

InitWorkItems   REG_DWORD   *1 to 512*

Specifies the initial number of receive buffers, or work items, used by the server. Allocating work items costs a certain amount of memory initially, but not as much as having to allocate additional buffers later.

Default: (depends on configuration)

MaxFreeConnections   **REG_DWORD**   *2 to 8 items*

Specifies the maximum number of free connection blocks maintained per endpoint.

Default: Depends upon configuration

MaxLinkDelay   **REG_DWORD**   *0 to 100,000 seconds*

Specifies the maximum time allowed for a link delay. If delays exceed this number, the server disables raw I/O for this connection.

Default: 60

MaxKeepSearch   **REG_DWORD**   *10 to 10000 seconds*

Specifies the maximum time during which an incomplete MS-DOS search will be kept by the server. Larger values ensure better interoperability with MS-DOS utilities such as tree-copy and delete-node. However, larger values can cause unusual local behavior (such as a failure of a local directory-delete operation) and higher memory use on the server.

Default: 1800

MaxMpxCt   **REG_DWORD**   *1 to 100 requests*

Provides a suggested maximum to clients for the number of simultaneous requests outstanding to this server. A higher value can increase server performance but requires higher use of server work items.

Default: 50

MaxNonpagedMemoryUsage   **REG_DWORD**   *1 MB to infinite bytes*

Specifies the maximum size of nonpaged memory that the server can have allocated at any time. Adjust this parameter if you want to administer memory quota control.

Default: (depends on system and server configuration)

MaxPagedMemoryUsage   **REG_DWORD**   *1 MB to infinite bytes*

Specifies the maximum size of pageable memory that the server can have allocated at any time. Adjust this parameter if you want to administer memory quota control.

Default: (depends on system and server configuration)

MaxWorkItems   **REG_DWORD**   *1 to 512 items*

Specifies the maximum number of receive buffers, or work items, the server can allocate. If this limit is reached, the transport must initiate flow control at a significant performance cost.

Default: (depends on configuration)

MinFreeWorkItems   REG_DWORD   *0 to 10 items*

Specifies the minimum number of available receive work items that are needed for the server to begin processing a potentially blocking SMB. A larger value for this parameter ensures that work items are available more frequently for nonblocking requests, but it also increases the likelihood that blocking requests will be rejected.

Default: 2

MinRcvQueue   REG_DWORD   *0 to 10 items*

Specifies the minimum number of free receive work items needed by the server before it begins allocating more. A larger value for this parameter helps ensure that there will always be work items available, but a value that is too large is simply inefficient.

Default: 2

NumBlockThreads   REG_DWORD   *1 to 10 threads*

Specifies the number of threads set aside by the server to service requests that can block the thread for a significant amount of time. Larger values can increase performance but use more memory. A value that is too large can impede performance by causing excessive task switching.

Default: (depends on configuration)

RawWorkItems   REG_DWORD   *1 to 512 items*

Specifies the number of special work items for raw I/O that the server uses. A larger value for this parameter can increase performance but costs more memory.

Default: (depends on configuration)

ScavTimeout   REG_DWORD   *1 to 300 seconds*

Specifies the time that the scavenger remains idle before waking up to service requests. A smaller value for this parameter improves the response of the server to various events but costs CPU cycles.

Default: 30

ScavQosInfoUpdateTime   REG_DWORD   *0 to 100,000 seconds*

Specifies the time that can pass before the scavenger goes through the list of active connections to update the link information.

Default: 300

SessConns   REG_DWORD   *1 to 2048 connections*

Specifies the maximum number of tree connections that can be made on the server via a single virtual circuit.

Default: 2048

SessOpens   REG_DWORD   *1 to 2048 files*

Specifies the maximum number of files that can be open on a single virtual circuit.

Default: 2048

SessUsers   REG_DWORD   *1 to 64 users*

Specifies the maximum number of users that can be logged on to a server via a single virtual circuit.

Default: 32

SizReqBuf   REG_DWORD   *512 to 65536 bytes*

Specifies the size of request buffers that the server uses. Small buffers use less memory; large buffers may improve performance.

Default: 4356

ThreadCountAdd   REG_DWORD   *0 to 10 threads*

The server uses one worker thread per processor for the computer it is running on. This parameter indicates how many additional threads the server should use. More threads can improve performance but cost memory. Too many threads can hurt performance by causing excessive task switching.

Default: (depends on configuration)

ThreadPriority   REG_DWORD   *0, 1, 2, or 15*

Specifies the priority of all server threads in relation to the base priority of the process. Higher priority can give better server performance at the cost of local responsiveness. Lower priority balances server needs with the needs of other processes on the system. Values 0 to 2 are relative to normal or background processes. The default value of 1 is equivalent to the foreground process. A value of 15 runs the server threads at real-time priority—which is not recommended.

Default: 1

TCP/IP Transport Entries

The various TCP/IP keys do not appear in the Registry unless TCP/IP is installed using the Network icon in Control Panel.

TCP/IP Parameters Subkey Entries

The entries for TCP/IP parameters appear under the following Registry path:

```
HKEY_LOCAL_MACHINE\SYSTEM\CurrentControlSet\Services\Tcpip\Parameters
```

ArpCacheLife   **REG_DWORD**   *Number of Seconds*

Determines the default lifetime for entries in the ARP cache table. Once an entry is placed in the ARP cache, it is allowed to remain there until its lifetime expires or until its table entry is reused because it is the oldest entry.

Default: 600 (10 minutes)

ArpCacheSize   **REG_DWORD**   *Number*

Determines the maximum number of entries that the ARP cache table can hold. The ARP cache is allowed to grow dynamically until this size is reached. After the table reaches this size, new entries can only be added by replacing the oldest entries that exist.

Default: 62

IpReassemblyTimeout   **REG_DWORD**   *Number of seconds*

Determines how long IP accepts fragments when attempting to reassemble a previously fragmented packet. That is, if a packet is fragmented, all of the fragments must make it to the destination within this time limit; otherwise, the fragments will be discarded and the packet will be lost.

Default: 60 seconds

TcpDisableReceiveChecksum   **REG_DWORD**   *0 or 1*

Specifies whether Checksums is disabled on receive.

Default: 0 (false, that is, checksums will be checked on receives)

TcpDisableSendChecksum   **REG_DWORD**   *0 or 1*

Specifies whether Checksums is disabled on send.

Default: 0 (false, that is, checksums will be generated on sends)

TcpKeepCnt   REG_DWORD   *Number in seconds*

Specifies how often TCP/IP will generate keep-alive traffic. When TCP/IP determines that no activity has occurred on the connection within the specified time, it generates keep-alive traffic to probe the connection. After trying **TcpKeepTries** number of times to deliver the keep-alive traffic without success, it marks the connection as down.

Default: 120

TcpKeepTries   REG_DWORD   *Number*

Specifies the maximum number of times that TCP/IP will attempt to deliver keep-alive traffic before marking a connection as down.

Default: 20

TcpMaxConnectAttempts   REG_DWORD   *Number*

Specifies the maximum number of times TCP/IP attempts to establish a connection before reporting failure. The initial delay between connection attempts is 3 seconds. This delay is doubled after each attempt.

Default: 3

TcpMaxRetransmissionAttempts   REG_DWORD   *Number*

Specifies the maximum number of times that TCP/IP attempts to retransmit a piece of data on an established connection before ending the connection. The initial delay before retransmitting is based on the current estimate TCP/IP makes of the round-trip time on the connection. This delay is doubled after each retransmission. Acknowledgment of the data results in a recalculation of the estimate for the round-trip time.

Default: 7

TcpSendSegmentSize   REG_DWORD   *Bytes*

Specifies the maximum send segment size.

Default: 1460

TcpWindowSize   REG_DWORD   *Number*

Sets the size of the TCP send and receive windows, which is the amount of data that can be accepted in a single transaction. This parameter is important in transferring files between a client and a server and is critical for performance for one-way traffic, such as for FTP.

Default: 8192

UdpDisableReceiveChecksum   REG_DWORD   *0 or 1*

Specifies whether Checksums is disabled on receive.

Default: 0 (false, that is, checksums will be checked on receives)

**UdpDisableSendChecksum   REG_DWORD   *0 or 1*

Specifies whether Checksums is disabled on send.

Default: 0 (false, that is, checksums will be generated on sends)

Adapter Card Parameters for TCP/IP

These parameters for TCP/IP are specific to individual network adapter cards. These appear under the following Registry path, where *adapter name#* refers to the Services subkey for the specific adapter card:

```
HKEY_LOCAL_MACHINE\SYSTEM\CurrentControlSet\Services
  \adapter name#\Parameters\Tcpip
```

**MTU   REG_DWORD   *Number in octets*

Specifies the maximum transmission unit size of an interface. Each interface used by TCP/IP may have a different MTU value specified. The MTU is usually determined through negotiation with the lower driver, using that lower driver's value. However, that value may be overridden.

Ideally, the MTU should be large enough to hold any datagram in one frame. The limiting factor is usually the technology making the transfer. Some technologies limit the maximum size to as little as 128; Ethernet limits transfers to 1500; and proNet-10 allows as many as 2044 octets per frame.

Datagrams larger than the MTU value are automatically divided into smaller pieces called fragments; size is a multiple of eight octets. Fragmentation usually occurs somewhere through which the traffic must pass whose MTU is smaller than the encapsulated datagram. If fragmentation occurs, the fragments travel separately to the destination computer, where they are automatically reassembled before the datagram is processed.

Default: 0 (That is, use the value supplied by the adapter.)

**RouterMTU   REG_DWORD   *Number in octets*

Specifies the maximum transmission unit size that should be used when the destination IP address is on a different subnet. Each interface used by TCP/IP may have a different **RouterMTU** value specified. In many implementations, the value of **RouterMTU** is set to 576 octets. This is the minimum size that must be supported by any IP node. Because modern routers can usually handle MTUs larger than 576 octets, the default value for this parameter is the same value as that used by **MTU**.

Default: 0 (That is, use the value supplied by the lower interface.)

FTP Server Service Entries for TCP/IP

The following Registry path contains parameters that affect the behavior of the FTP server service component:

```
HKEY_LOCAL_MACHINE\SYSTEM\CurrentControlSet\Services\Ftpsvc\Parameters
```

The Ftpsvc subkey does not appear until you install the FTP service using the Network icon in Control Panel. Also, you must restart the FTP server service (Ftpsvc) using the Services icon in Control Panel for any changes to these values to take effect.

ConnectionTimeout   REG_DWORD   *Seconds*

Specifies the time to allow clients to remain idle before forcibly disconnecting them. This prevents idle clients from consuming server resources indefinitely.

This value may be set to 0 if time-outs are not to be enforced. If set to 0, idle clients may remain connected indefinitely.

Default: 600 (10 minutes)

LogAnonymous   REG_DWORD   *0 or 1*

When this value is 1, all successful anonymous logins are logged to the system event log.

Default: 0 (false —do not log successful anonymous logins)

LogNonAnonymous   REG_DWORD   *0 or 1*

When this value is 1, all successful non-anonymous logins are logged to the system event log.

Default: 0 (false, that is, do not log successful non-anonymous logins)

MaxConnections   REG_DWORD   *0 or 1*

Specifies the maximum number of simultaneous clients the server will service. This value may be set to 0 if there is to be no limit on simultaneous clients.

Default: 20

NBT Parameters for TCP/IP

NBT is the NetBIOS over TCP/IP service. Parameters for TCP/IP are also configured under NBT in the following Registry path:

```
HKEY_LOCAL_MACHINE\SYSTEM\CurrentControlSet\Services\NBT\Parameters
```

MaxPreload   REG_DWORD   *Number*

Specifies the maximum NBT number of entries for LMHOSTS that are preloaded into the NBT NetBIOS name cache. LMHOSTS is a file located in the directory specified by **DatabasePath.**

Default: 100

Streams Parameters for TCP/IP

The TCP/IP parameter for Streams are found under the following Registry path:

```
HKEY_LOCAL_MACHINE\SYSTEM\CurrentControlSet\Services\Streams\Parameters
```

MaxMemoryUsage   REG_DWORD   *Number of bytes*

Specifies the maximum amount of memory that can be allocated to the Streams environment. Once this limit is reached, Streams will fail allocation requests made by Streams-based drivers.

Default: No limit

Workstation Service Entries

You can modify the startup parameters for the Workstation service using the Registry Editor. Unless otherwise indicated, these value entries are found in the following Registry path:

```
HKEY_LOCAL_MACHINE\SYSTEM\CurrentControlSet\Services
    \LanmanWorkstation\Parameters
```

BufFilesDenyWrite   REG_DWORD   *0 or 1*

Specifies whether the redirector should cache files that are opened with only FILE_SHARE_READ sharing access. Usually, if a file is opened with FILE_SHARE_READ specified, the file cannot be buffered because other processes may also be reading that file. This optimization allows the redirector to buffer such files. This optimization is safe because no process can write to the file.

Disable this parameter if it is necessary to preserve the strict semantics of the sharing modes specified.

Default: 1 (true)

BufNamedPipes   REG_DWORD   *0 or 1*

Indicates whether the redirector should buffer character-mode named pipes.

Disable this parameter to guarantee that all pipe write operations are flushed to the server immediately and to disable read ahead on character-mode named pipes.

Default: 1 (true)

BufReadOnlyFiles   REG_DWORD   *0 or 1*

`\CurrentControlSet\Services\LanmanWorkstation`

Specifies whether the redirector should cache files that are read-only. Usually, if a read-only file is opened, the file cannot be buffered because other processes may also be reading that file. This optimization allows the redirector to buffer such files. This optimization is safe because no process can write to the file. However, another user can modify the file to enable writing to the file, causing loss of data.

Disable this parameter if it is necessary to preserve the strict semantics of the sharing modes specified.

Default: 1 (true)

CacheFileTimeout   REG_DWORD   *Number of seconds*

Specifies the maximum time that a file will be left in the cache after the application has closed the file.

Increase the value of this parameter if you are performing operations on the server that could cause files to be reopened more than 10 seconds after the application has closed them. For example, if you are performing a build over the network, you should increase this parameter's value.

Default: 10

CollectionTime   REG_DWORD   *0 to 65535000 milliseconds*

Specifies the maximum time that write-behind data will remain in a character-mode pipe buffer.

Changing this value may cause a named pipe application's performance to improve (but it does not affect SQL Server applications).

Default: 250

KeepConn   REG_DWORD   *1 to 65535 seconds*

Specifies the maximum amount of time that a connection can be left dormant. This parameter is the redirector equivalent of the **Disc** parameter in the Services\LanmanServer\Parameters subkey.

As a general rule, try increasing this value if your application closes and opens UNC files to a server less frequently than 10 minutes apart. This decreases the number of reconnections made to a server.

Default: 600

LockMaximum   REG_DWORD   *Number of milliseconds*

Used to configure the lock backoff package. This parameter exists to prevent an errant application from "swamping" a server with nonblocking requests where there is no data available for the application.

Default: 500

LockQuota   REG_DWORD   *Bytes of data*

Specifies the maximum amount of data that is read for each file using this optimization if the **UseLockReadUnlock** parameter is enabled.

Increase this value if your application performs a significant number of lock-and-read style operations. (This means performing lock operations and immediately reading the contents of the locked data.) It is conceivable that you could cause the system to run out of paged pool, but only by increasing this value to a few megabytes and by using an application that locks millions-of-byte ranges.

Default: 4096 (bytes)

LogElectionPackets   REG_DWORD   *0 or 1*

Specifies whether the Browser should generate events when election packets are received.

Default: 0 (false)

MailslotBuffers   REG_DWORD   *Number of buffers*

Specifies the maximum number of buffers available to process mailslot messages. If your application uses many mailslot operations, set this higher to avoid losing mailslot messages.

Default: 5

MaxCmds REG_DWORD *0 to 255*

Specifies the maximum number of work buffers that the redirector reserves for performance reasons.

Increase this value to increase your network throughput. If your application performs more than 15 simultaneous operations, you might want to increase this value. Because this parameter actually controls the number of execution threads that can be simultaneously outstanding at any time, your network performance will not always be improved by increasing this parameter. Each additional execution threads takes about 1K of nonpaged pool if you actually load up the network. Resources will not be consumed, however, unless the user actually makes use of them.

Default: 15

NumIllegalDatagramEvents REG_DWORD *Number of events*

Specifies the maximum number of datagram events to be logged within the span of time specified by the **IllegalDatagramResetTime** parameter. Because Windows NT logs all illegal datagrams, the event log can be filled with a proliferation of these in a short time. This entry and the **IllegalDatagramResetTime** entry work together.

Default: 5

PipeIncrement REG_DWORD *Number of milliseconds*

Controls the rate at which the redirector "backs off" on failing nonblocking pipe reads.

This parameter is used to prevent an errant application from swamping a server with nonblocking requests where there is no data available for the application. You can use the backoff statistics to tune this parameter to be more efficient for an application that uses nonblocking named pipes (except for SQL Server applications).

Default: 10

PipeMaximum REG_DWORD *Number of milliseconds*

Controls the maximum time at which the redirector "backs off" on failing non-blocking pipe reads.

This parameter exists to prevent an errant application from swamping a server with nonblocking requests where there is no data available for the application. You can use the backoff statistics to tune this parameter to be more efficient for an application that uses nonblocking named pipes (except for SQL Server applications).

Default: 500

ReadAheadThroughput   REG_DWORD   *Kilobytes per second*

Specifies the throughput required on a connection before the cache manager is told to enable read ahead.

Increase this value if you think that the use of read-ahead is lowering the response time of the network. This should only be a problem on a wide-area network.

Default: 0xffffffff

SizCharBuf   REG_DWORD   *64 to 4096 bytes*

Specifies the maximum number of bytes that will be written into a character-mode pipe buffer. Adjusting this value may improve performance for a named-pipe application (but it will not affect SQL server applications).

Default: 512

UseLockReadUnlock   REG_DWORD   *0 or 1*

Indicates whether the redirector uses the lock-and-read and write-and-unlock performance enhancements.

When this value is enabled, it generally provides a significant performance benefit. However, database applications that lock a range and don't allow data within that range to be read will suffer performance degradation unless this parameter is disabled.

Default: 1 (true)

UseRawRead   REG_DWORD   *0 or 1*

Enables the raw-read optimization. This provides a significant performance enhancement on a local area network

Default: 1 (true)

UseRawWrite   REG_DWORD   *0 or 1*

Enables the raw-write optimization. On a LAN, this provides a significant performance enhancement.

Default: 1 (true)

UseUnlockBehind   REG_DWORD   *0 or 1*

Indicates whether the redirector will complete an unlock operation before it has received confirmation from the server that the unlock operation has completed. Disable this parameter only to isolate problems or to guarantee that all unlock operations complete on the server before completing the application's unlock request.

Default: 1 (true)

UseWriteRawData   **REG_DWORD**   *0 or 1*

Enables the raw-write-with-data optimization. This allows the redirector to send 4 KB of data with each write-raw operation. This provides a significant performance enhancement on a local area network.

Default: 1 (true)

UtilizeNtCaching   **REG_DWORD**   *0 or 1*

Indicates whether the redirector uses the cache manager to cache the contents of files. Disable this parameter only to guarantee that all data is flushed to the server immediately after it is written by the application.

Default: 1 (true)

Registry Entries for Microsoft Mail

The parameters used by the Microsoft Mail application provided with Windows NT appear under this subkey:

```
HKEY_CURRENT_USER\Software\Microsoft\Mail
```

Many of the entries in the subkeys of this key have default values and won't be present. To change the appearance and behavior of the Mail application, use the Mail menu commands instead of editing the Mail entries directly. Some of the options that you specify in the Mail application are stored in your mail message file (.MMF) instead of the Mail Registry entries.

These keys are created in HKEY_CURRENT_USER when you first run Mail. If your system previously contained a Windows for MS-DOS version of MSMAIL.INI, its contents are migrated to the Registry when you first run Mail under Windows NT.

Microsoft Mail Entries

This subkey is used to define the appearance and behavior of the Mail program. This is the Registry path for this subkey:

```
HKEY_CURRENT USER\Software\Microsoft\Mail\Microsoft Mail
```

This key also appears under HKEY_USERS\.DEFAULT, but its only contents are **MigrateIni and MigrateIniPrint.**

These are the value entries that can appear in this key:

ForceScanInterval   REG_SZ   *seconds*

Affects the mail spooler's latency checking, which is intended to prevent the spooler background processing from interfering with foreground work. If the designated length of time passes without the spooler getting an opportunity to do outstanding work, idle time is requested more frequently (based on the value of **ScanAgainInterval**), and eventually idle time is used whenever it can.

Default: 300 seconds (5 minutes)

IdleRequiredInterval   REG_SZ   *seconds*

Affects the mail spooler's latency checking, which is intended to prevent the spooler's background processing from interfering with foreground work. The spooler defers its work temporarily if the system has serviced an interactive request such as a keyboard entry or mouse movement within this interval, to avoid starting a transfer when the user is busy.

Default: 2 seconds

NetBios   REG_SZ   *0 or 1*

Enables NetBIOS notification of new mail delivery. When NetBIOS notification is used, the Windows NT computer sending a mail message to another Windows NT computer sends a NetBIOS notification message to the destination computer to tell the Mail program running on that machine that a new mail message was sent to the computer. The Mail program on the destination computer can then check the workgroup postoffice for the new mail message. This entry set to 1 to enable NetBIOS notification also provides quicker response to the arrival of new mail from users on your local postoffice. If this entry is 0 to disable NetBIOS notification, the Mail client needs to regularly check for the arrival of new mail messages on the postoffice.

Default: 1

NewMsgsAtStartup   REG_SZ   *0 or 1*

Specifies whether Mail is to check for new mail messages in the foreground as soon as the user logs in. Set this entry to 1 to have Mail download new messages as quickly as possible when it is started. If this entry is 0, Mail checks for new messages in the background (as is usually the case when the Mail application is being used).

Default: 0

PollingInterval   REG_SZ   *minutes*

Gives the default for the Check for New Mail Every *n* Minutes option in the Mail Options dialog box. The value the user enters in the dialog box is written to the user's mail message file (.MMF)—this value is used to define how often the Mail spooler checks for new mail messages.

Default: 10

PumpCycleInterval   REG_SZ   *seconds*

Permits the spooler to check for new mail more often than once per minute, or to override the polling interval value defined in the user's mail message file.

Default: 60 seconds, or the number of minutes specified in the Mail Options dialog box

ScanAgainInterval   REG_SZ   *seconds*

Affects the mail spooler latency checking to prevent spooler background processing from interfering unduly with foreground work. When the spooler defers work because of higher priority, interactive tasks, it rechecks the availability of the system at this interval.

Default: 2

MMF Entries for Mail

Most entries under this key affect automatic compression of the Mail message file, which by default has the filename extension of .MMF. When enabled, automatic compression uses idle time on your PC to recover disk space freed by the deleted messages and returns the disk space to the file system. You should not need to change the default values for entries in this subkey.

This is the Registry path for this subkey:

```
HKEY_CURRENT_USER\Software\Microsoft\Mail\MMF
```

Kb_Free_Start_Compress   REG_SZ   *kilobytes*

Background compression starts when at least this much recoverable space is detected in your message file. Both **Percent_Free_Start_Compress** and this entry are always active. The first entry to trigger starts the compression.

Default: 300

Kb_Free_Stop_Compress   REG_SZ   *kilobytes*

Background compression stops when there is less than the indicated amount of recoverable space in your message file. This avoids the unnecessary difficulty in trying to recover the last little bit of free space. Both this entry and **Percent_Free_Stop_Compress** are always active. The first entry to trigger stops the compression.

Default: 100.

No_Compress   REG_SZ   *0 or 1*

Specifies whether background compression is to be disabled. A value of 1 disables background compression of the .MMF message store.

Default: 0 (That is, background compression is enabled.)

Secs_Till_Fast_Compress   REG_SZ   *seconds*

The background compression algorithm has a fast mode and a slow mode. Background compression begins in the slow mode to avoid slowing system response time. After a number of seconds of system inactivity indicated by this entry, the compression switches to fast mode. Any user activity changes the setting back to slow mode.

Default: 600 seconds (That is, ten minutes of system inactivity.)

See also the entry for **AppInit_DLLs** in "Windows Software Registration Entries."

APPENDIX C

Using Response Probe

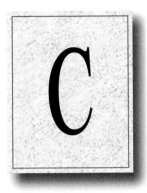

We created Response Probe so we could place pure, synthetic workloads on Windows NT to verify its algorithms and its fundamental performance characteristics. It has also proven useful for calibrating maximum throughputs for various workloads. We included Response Probe on the floppy disk provided with this book so that you can quickly assess the performance of various components of your own computer equipment.

Testing components with Response Probe reveals what we call the multidimensional *response surface*, which characterizes the performance of every computer. Each hardware component represents a separate dimension.

In this appendix we describe the structure of Response Probe and how you alter its parameters to create a wide variety of synthetic workloads to suit your needs.

Why You Would Use Response Probe

A Response Probe workload is pure—it is completely controlled and specified by the experimenter. Systematic changes to the workload produce corresponding changes in the response by the computer's hardware and software. By placing a series of known workloads on the computer, Response Probe can characterize overall computer performance in an application-independent fashion.

Response Probe experiments are relatively short. Because you can place a pure workload on the computer, the experiments are highly repeatable.

Response Probe has limitations, however. It doesn't test the graphics subsystem. To evaluate this area, you must use other benchmarks. Even more important, you must keep in mind that unless you really understand your applications, it is a significant leap from understanding the computer's response surface to predicting the performance of applications. This is because only measuring the actual applications with Performance Monitor will reveal which computer components are used by various applications, and in what proportions. Complicating the matter is that these proportions change when the hardware is changed.

The approach to using Response Probe, therefore, can take on at least two forms. One is to chart the whole response surface, varying one parameter at a time (such as record size) in a systematic way while keeping all other parameters fixed, to yield a response surface chart. This is the method we use throughout this book. You can then measure your applications and match their characteristics to the charts of the response surface to see how they are affected by hardware changes. Another approach is to measure your application to form a picture of the application's use of the computer. Then use Response Probe to mimic the application's behavior as closely as possible, and apply that synthetic load to the various types of hardware you will use.

Response Probe Design

The Response Probe workload simulates an actual use of the computer by a user: cycles of idle time (user think time) followed by some processing. The idle time or user think time state (THINK state) allows simulation of interactive use of the computer (using word processors, spreadsheets, and so on). The processing state consists of two sub-states: one state to access a file (ACCESS state) and another one to consume processor time (COMPUTE state). The following diagram shows a complete probe cycle.

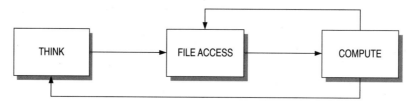

Figure C.1 Complete Response Probe cycle

Normal Distribution

You specify the amount of time to spend in each phase of the interaction cycle. Each parameter is an independent dimension of the workload. The values actually used to apply the workload in each dimension from one cycle to the next are normally distributed based on two simple parameters that you supply. The normal distribution (better known as the bell-shaped curve), has some good characteristics for applying known workloads.

When a workload has a normal distribution, about two-thirds of the samples are within plus or minus one standard deviation of the mean. About 95% of the samples are within plus or minus two standard deviations of the mean. And about 99% of the samples are within plus or minus three standard deviations of the mean. A standard deviation of zero causes the mean workload equal to be applied constantly. So (you guessed it), you supply the mean and the standard deviation of the each phase and, voilà, a purely defined workload.

Response Probe uses a folded normal distribution for some of its parameters. Actually there is no such thing in statistics, so we invented it. That is because some of the dimensions have upper and lower boundaries. None of the dimensions can realistically be negative, for example. (That's what we need; negative compute time so we'd be done before we start. Now that's fast!) And Response Probe will not access a file beyond its beginning or end. So if a computation of a workload parameter ends up beyond the boundary of the dimension, it is arithmetically folded back towards the mean. If it then happens to go past the boundary of the dimension on the other side, it is again folded back towards the mean, and this process continues until a value within the boundaries of the dimension is returned.

For example, suppose a dimension has boundaries of 1 and 100. If the computation of a parameter is 102, is folded back into the boundary and becomes 98. If a computation yields 205, it becomes 5 when folded back within the boundary.

Response Probe uses the following formula to calculate normally distributed values. If the result is beyond the boundaries, it is folded back into the specified range as described previously.

*Normal = Mean + (-7 + Sum(14 Random Numbers [0..1])) * Standard Deviation*

To get some idea of how the parameters to a normal distribution work, take a look at Figure C.2. This shows how access to a file with 1000 records is distributed when the mean is placed at record 500, and various standard deviations are supplied. When the standard deviation is one-third of the mean (166 = 500/3), we get the familiar bell-shaped curve. By the time the standard deviation is equal to the mean, at 500 records, we get a nearly uniformly random distribution of access across the file. If this were a pure normal distribution, this would look instead like the central two-thirds of the bell shaped curve. Since the access that would fall beyond the ends of the file are folded back into the file around the endpoints, the random distribution results instead.

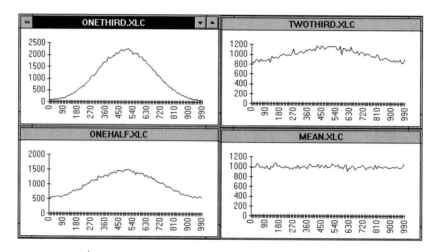

Figure C.2 Normally distributed curves produced by various standard deviations

If we had selected a standard deviation of 0, all the access would have been to record 500 of the file.

Now let's take a look at the operation of the various phases of Response Probe.

THINK State

User think time during interactive use of the computer is simulated during this state. The Response Probe thread just goes idle during this state. The length of the idle time is a normally distributed value based on the supplied mean and standard deviation (in milliseconds).

After the simulated user think time, a normally distributed value is generated for the number of file access phases to execute before thinking again.

FILE ACCESS State

During this state, the access to the file is a read, or a write, or (if you like) a series of these actions that you specify. For random mode, a normally distributed seek value is used to move the file pointer before the first record is accessed. For sequential mode, the record number from the last FILE ACCESS phase is used. In this case the file system is told of the sequential access at open time so the read-ahead by the cache manager is maximized.

You can also specify access as using BUFFERED, UNBUFFERED, or MAPPED. Buffered access operations use the file system cache. Unbuffered access operations do not use the cache. Mapped access does not use the file system at all, but instead accesses the file as an array of records in memory. See Chapter 6, "Detecting Cache Bottlenecks," for more information.

After the file is accessed, Response Probe generates the milliseconds of processor time to compute based on the mean and standard deviation supplied.

COMPUTE State

During this state, processor time is consumed for the amount of time you specify. When Response Probe begins, it calibrates itself to the processor to determine the amount of processor cycles executed per unit of real time. Thereafter, when you specify Response Probe to consume the processor for a certain amount of time, it does so by consuming the appropriate number of processor cycles. Processor calibration is done at High Priority class.

During the processor time consumption period, code and data pages are touched. Response Probe simulates code pages by reading during computation a file you create. To simulate data pages, Response Probe uses a section of virtual memory backed by the paging file that is written during computation.

The pages being touched (both code pages and data pages) are selected as normally distributed values based on the supplied mean and standard deviation for code and data pages. These values control the paging activities during the compute state.

Response Probe Input Files

Text script files are used to specify the exact workload applied to the computer being probed. This allows for a highly flexible method of applying various loads on the computer. The high-resolution performance counter discussed at the end of Chapter 12, "Writing a Custom Windows NT Performance Monitor," is used to measure response times.

All the input arguments and script parameters are checked against possible error conditions. Probing starts once all the required processes and their corresponding threads launch successfully and are ready to probe. Measurements are taken by each thread once the computer reaches a steady state. Steady state is reached when increasing the time limit on the trial has no significant effect on the threads' response times. Currently, each thread begins taking measurements with the first probe cycle to start after 50% of the trial time has expired.

In the script file, you supply values for the mean and standard deviation. These values generate the normally distributed values needed during the probe cycles.

Once any of the threads is done probing, all other threads are forced to stop the probe operation. Test results are printed to the designated output file, as discussed in the following section.

Performing Response Probe Experiments

To perform a Response Probe experiment, create the script file containing the experiment parameters. Then type the following:

Probe *ProbeFileScr Time [ProbeOutFile]*

ProbeFileScr is the .SCR script file containing information about the processes in the experiment. The following sections of this chapter discuss the possible contents and format of the .SCR file, and the contents and format of the .SCP and .SCT script files that the .SCR file can refer to. *Time* is the total trial time in seconds. *ProbeOutFile* is the name of the Response Probe's output file. *ProbeOutFile* is optional—if you don't specify a filename for *ProbeOutFile*, *ProbeFileScr*.OUT is used as the default.

Script Files

All scripts that drive Response Probe are tiny text files. There are three types of script files:

- .SCR files for creating processes in Response Probe runs. For each Response Probe run, there is exactly one .SCR file.
- .SCP files for creating threads for processes.
- .SCT files for setting parameters for the threads.

You can create any number of processes and threads in this way, and these processes and threads can be similar or different in any way you want.

*.SCR File Format

This script file is used as the first input argument to the probe program. It contains all process script file names. For each PROCESS line specified in the file, a process is created with the following parameters:

- Script file name
- Data memory pages size (in number of pages)
- "Code" memory pages

The format of each PROCESS line in the .SCR file is:

```
[REPEAT N] PROCESS ParameterFileName.SCP DataSize CodePagesFileName
[ProcessName [PriorityClass]]
```

ParameterFileName is the name of the .SCP file for this process. *DataSize* is the amount of virtual memory (in pages) allocated as the paging file that simulates data pages. *CodePagesFileName* is the name of the file (that you must have created) to be used to simulate code pages. You can use the **createfil** utility to create *CodePagesFileName*. The size of this file determines how large the code space is. The process maps virtual memory to the size of the code pages file. "REPEAT N" creates the PROCESS within the same line N times, creating N processes.

ProcessName and *PriorityClass* are optional, but if you specify a *PriorityClass* you must also specify a *ProcessName*. The default for *ProcessName* is PROBEPRC.EXE. Changing this makes it possible to have child processes with different names so they can be identified by the Performance Monitor. You'll copy PROBEPRC.EXE to files with these names before running. *PriorityClass* is one of the following: Idle, Normal (the default), High, and Realtime. You need supply only the first letter of the priority class (I, N, H, or R).

To include a comment in the .SCR file (or in a .SCP or .SCT file), begin that line with a # character.

Here is an example .SCR file that creates one process and then three more:

```
PROCESS  LikeMine.scp 500 SomeCode.dat MyProg.exe H
REPEAT 3 PROCESS  LikeHis.scp 300 OtherCod.dat HisProg.exe N
```

The first line creates a process with the process parameter file LIKEMINE.SCP. The data space in the paging file is 500 pages. The file for simulating the code space is SOMECODE.DAT. You have copied PROBEPRC.EXE to MYPROG.EXE for this process. It executes at High Priority class.

The next line creates three identical processes. Their parameters are in the LIKEHIS.SCP file. They each allocate 300 private pages of paging file. They will share the "code" pages in the OTHERCOD.DAT file. The three processes each have the name HISPROG.EXE (you must have copied PROBEPRC.EXE to this filename), and you will see data from only one of them in the Performance Monitor. They will run at Normal Priority class.

*.SCP File Format

This script file contains the names of the thread script files. For each THREAD line, a thread is created using the parameters in another specified script file..

The format of each THREAD line is as follows:

```
[REPEAT N] THREAD ThreadFileName.SCT [ThreadPriority]
```

ThreadFileName is the name of the .SCT file containing the parameters for this thread. *ThreadPriority* is optional. If it is specified, it must be one of the following: TimeCritical, Highest, AboveNormal, Normal (the default), BelowNormal, Lowest, and Idle. Only the first letter of the thread priority is significant and need be supplied.

"REPEAT N" creates N identical threads.

*.SCT File Format

This script file contains all the information required for the operation of Response Probe threads. Supplied mean and standard deviation values may not be negative numbers.

Here is the format of the .SCT file. The parameter lines can be in any order. The units for each parameter on the right are not part of the specification of the workload, but are indicated here for reference. We actually include them in each .SCT file for reference since they don't hurt anything by hanging around out there on the end of each line.

```
THINKTIME        Mean  SDev                (milliseconds)
CYCLEREADS       Mean  SDev                (number)
FILESEEK         Mean  SDev                (records)
CPUTIME          Mean  SDev                (milliseconds)
DATAPAGE         Mean  SDev                (pages)
CODEPAGE         Mean  SDev                (pages)
FILEACCESS       FileAccessName            (name)
[FILEATTRIBUTE   {RANDOM | SEQUENTIAL}]    (R | S)
[FILEACCESSMODE {MAPPED | BUFFERED | UNBUFFERED}]    (M | B | U)
[RECORDSIZE      Bytes]                    (default: 4096 bytes)
[FILEACTION {R | W}*]                      (read/write pattern)
```

The commands FILEATTRIBUTE, FILEACCESSMODE, RECORDSIZE, and FILEACTION are optional. All others are required. Defaults for the optional commands are Random, Buffered, 4096, and 1 Read respectively.

If UNBUFFERED is selected as FILEACCESSMODE, then the RECORDSIZE must be a multiple of the disk sector size.

A few of these parameters deserve some additional explanation. CYCLEREADS indicates the number of times that FILEACTION followed by CPUTIME are executed before the next THINK cycle is carried out. The name CYCLEREADS is a holdover from early versions of Response Probe. Forgive us just this once.

FILESEEK is how you distribute random access on the FILEACCESS file. It specifies a mean and standard deviation of the record to be accessed. It is typical to place the mean at the central record of the file; for example, at record 500 in a 1000-record file.

DATAPAGE and CODEPAGE also specify a mean and standard deviation of the page to be accessed, except that they are in units of pages.

If the FILEACCESS method is SEQUENTIAL, FILESEEK is ignored. If SEQUENTIAL mode is specified, access starts at the beginning of the file again when the end of the file is reached. We defined FILEACCESSMODE already. If you can't remember how it works you have to read this appendix again as a punishment.

RECORDSIZE is the size of each file access to the FILEACCESS file. If you change this, you might want to adjust FILESEEK to get the same access pattern since it is in units of records, and the record that is the center record in a file will change as you modify the RECORDSIZE. Tricky, huh?

FILEACTION is the most fun parameter. Here you specify a string of reads and writes with R and W. Here is an example FILEACTION:

```
FILEACTION  RRWRR
```

In this case, FILESEEK is performed first if access is RANDOM, otherwise it accesses the next sequential record in the file. That record is read, and then so is the next record. The second record that was read is then written. In other words, writes that follow reads write the last record that was read, much as an application would. Then the third record in the sequence is read, and then the fourth. Now this FILEACTION is over, and a COMPUTE phase executes, and then another [FILESEEK /] FILEACTION occurs as long as the number of CYCLEREADS computed for this cycle has still not decremented to zero. This permits the simulation of a wide variety of file access patterns, although certainly not all possible patterns.

Sample .SCT Files

Here are some sample .SCT files. The first one does nothing, and you'll get a near zero response time from it because Response Probe has calibrated its overhead and subtracted it from each cycle.

```
THINKTIME        0  0            (milliseconds)
CYCLEREADS       0  0            (number)
FILESEEK         0  0            (records)
CPUTIME          0  0            (milliseconds)
DATAPAGE         0  0            (pages)
CODEPAGE         0  0            (pages)
FILEACCESS       access.dat      (name)
```

Here's one that reads a single record, 1024 bytes long, from the start of the ACCESS.DAT file 100 times, without using the file system cache:

```
THINKTIME        0  0            (milliseconds)
CYCLEREADS       100 0           (number)
FILESEEK         0  0            (records)
CPUTIME          0  0            (milliseconds)
DATAPAGE         0  0            (pages)
CODEPAGE         0  0            (pages)
FILEACCESS       access.dat      (name)
RECORDSIZE       1024            (default: 4096 bytes)
FILEATTRIBUTE    RANDOM          (R | S)
FILEACCESSMODE   UNBUFFERED      (B | U | M)
FILEACTION       R               (read/write pattern)
```

Finally, here is an example of a workload that, during its 1000 milliseconds of computation, repeatedly reads the first DWORD of a page in a 4-MB code page file. The page reads will occur in a normal distribution. Four megabytes is 1024 pages on a machine with 4096-byte pages, so the central page is number 512. One third of 512 is about 170, so to stretch the bell-shaped curve across the file we specify 170 as the standard deviation.

```
THINKTIME        0   0          (milliseconds)
CYCLEREADS       0   0          (number)
FILESEEK         0   0          (records)
CPUTIME          1000  0        (milliseconds)
DATAPAGE         0   0          (pages)
CODEPAGE         512  170       (pages)
FILEACCESS       access.dat     (name)
```

If we had specified 512 and 170 for DATAPAGE instead of CODEPAGE, during computation Response Probe would have written to the first DWORD of a page selected with the normal distribution from the paging file section of 1024 pages that we had specified in the .SCP file for the experiment.

These code and data page references occur once in each basic computation loop. The number of basic processor loops per millisecond on the processor in question is given by the Relative Processor Speed in the .OUT file described in the next section. The basic computation loop computes the result for these two normal distributions, checks to see if it is time to stop computing, and that's about it.

Output Format

Output appears in the following format in a text file named as indicated previously in "Performing Response Probe Experiments." For each thread in the experiment, one data line is printed.

```
Multi-Processor Response Probe.
Copyright 1990-1993 Microsoft Corporation.
Version 2.0 (93.06.24)
Wed Jun 24 15:36:02 1993
Script File : pb01_01a.scr
Trial Time : 100 seconds
Stable interval : [50%..100%] of Trial Time == [50..100] (50 seconds)
Relative Processor Speed:    11.37
(All times are in milliseconds)
```

PID	TID	File Mode	Rec Size	Total Time	Resp Time	Resp Count	Mean	SDev	Min	Max
72	71	S U	4096	100049	46235	941	49	0	49	50

Think Mean	Think SDev	Reads Mean	Reads SDev	CPU Mean	CPU SDev	DataPg Mean	DataPg SDev	CodePg Mean	CodePg SDev
0	0	0	0	50	0	1	0	1	0

(In the actual output file, the columns from "PID" to "CodePg SDev" all appear in one wide row.)

The really interesting number here is the "Mean" response time to the workload that you have devised. This is in the eighth column from the left. In addition to all the Performance Monitor data you may collect when you run your experiment, this number can be revealing. Keep an eye on it.

You want to be sure your experiment is long enough that the "Mean" response time for the action you specified is repeatable. Keep increasing the length of your experiment until this is true. The larger the number of threads and the more file or paging activity you generate, the longer your experiments will have to be.

"PID" is the Process ID of the thread, and "TID" is the thread ID. "Total Time" is the experimentally observed total time for this thread. "Resp Time" is the time during which the thread actually observed its own response time. It should be the last half of the total time. "Resp Count" is the number of complete cycles observed in the response time computation. "Mean" is the average response time to the Resp Count cycles. "Sdev," "Min," and "Max" are the standard deviation, minimum, and maximum of the response time observed in the Resp Cycles. The remaining columns specify some of the input parameters to the experiment, in case you lose your .SCT file.

Response Probe should help you get a good idea of how your equipment can handle workloads of various types, as well as how changes to your equipment have affected its capacity. What a tool!

Index

Russ Blake

Russ Blake is a graduate of Antioch College (BA, Philosophy) and holds an MS degree in Computer Science from the University of Wisconsin, Madison. He has been involved in the construction of operating systems and performance monitoring tools since joining the HP3000 development team at Hewlett Packard in the early 70's. He invented and authored the Xray performance monitor for Tandem Computers. After a stint in robotics and its real-time performance concerns, he joined Sun Microsystems as Director of Operations for the Software Products Division. For the last five years, he has been Manager of Advanced Operating Systems Performance at Microsoft Corporation. He designed and led the construction of Windows NT Performance Monitor, and created the other principal performance tools used to tune the Windows NT operating system and Windows NT applications.

Microsoft® Win32™ Programmer's References

This is the official documentation for the Microsoft Win32 Software Development Kit (SDK).
It's the resource material that you'll need to turn to during the design and development of a
Win32-based application. The *Programmer's References* contain overview material on systems, services,
Window management, and the Graphics Device Interface, as well as the alphabetical Application
Programming Interface (API) references and information about messages, structures, and data types.

Microsoft® Win32™ Programmer's Reference, Vol. 1
Window Management and Graphics Device Interface
896 pages, softcover $20.00 ($26.95 Canada)   ISBN 1-55615-515-8

Microsoft® Win32™ Programmer's Reference, Vol. 2
System Services, Multimedia, Extensions, and Application Notes
1040 pages, softcover $20.00 ($26.95 Canada)   ISBN 1-55615-516-6

Microsoft® Win32™ Programmer's Reference, Vol. 3
Functions (A-G)
768 pages, softcover $20.00 ($26.95 Canada)   ISBN 1-55615-517-4

Microsoft® Win32™ Programmer's Reference, Vol. 4
Functions (H-Z)
800 pages, softcover $20.00 ($26.95 Canada)   ISBN 1-55615-518-2

Microsoft® Win32™ Programmer's Reference, Vol. 5
Messages, Structures, and Macros
704 pages, softcover $20.00 ($26.95 Canada)   ISBN 1-55615-519-0

Solid Programming Advice

Programming Windows™ 3.1, 3rd ed.

Charles Petzold

*"If you're going to program for Windows, buy this book.
It will pay for itself in a matter of hours."*   **Computer Language**

The programming classic for both new Windows 3.1 programmers
and owners of previous editions. It's packed with indispensable reference
data, tested programming advice, keen insight, and page after page of
sample programs. This edition includes two disks that contain
the source code and associated files from the book.

1008 pages, softcover with one 1.44-MB 3.5-inch disk
$49.95 ($67.95 Canada)   ISBN 1-55615-395-3

Code Complete

Steve McConnell

This practical handbook of software construction covers the art and
science of the entire development process, from design to testing. Examples
are provided in C, Pascal, Basic, Fortran, and Ada—but the focus is on programming techniques. Topics includ upfront planning, applying good design
techniques to construction, using data effectively, reviewing for errors, managing
construction activities, and relating personal character to superior software.

880 pages, softcover $35.00 ($44.95 Canada)· ISBN 1-55615-484-4

Writing Solid Code
Microsoft Techniques for Developing Bug-Free C Programs

Steve Maguire

*Foreword by Dave Moore,
Director of Development, Microsoft Corporation*

Written by a former Microsoft developer and troubleshooter, this book
is an insider's view of the most important aspect of the development process:
preventing and detecting bugs. Maguire identifies the places developers typically
make mistakes and offers practical advice for detecting costly mistakes.
Includes proven programming techniques for producing clean code.

228 pages, softcover $24.95 ($32.95 Canada)   ISBN 1-55615-551-4

Essential Resources from Microsoft Press

Microsoft® Visual C++™ Run-Time Library Reference
Microsoft Corporation

This official run-time library reference provides detailed information on more than 550 ready-to-use functions and macros designed for use in C and C++ programs and is an up-to-date complement to the Visual C++ online reference. The book provides a superb introduction to using the run-time library and to the library's variables and types. It also covers the important details for each function in the run-time library: syntax; meaning of each argument; include files; return value; cross-references to related functions; and compatibility notes. Covers version 1.0 of the Standard and Professional editions of Visual C++.

704 pages, softcover $35.00 ($44.95 Canada)   ISBN 1-55615-559-X

The Microsoft® Windows™ 3.1 Developer's Workshop
Dr. John Butler, Bob Chiverton, John Clark Craig,
William S. Hall, Ray Patch, and Alok Sinha

This is a winning collection of articles on significant Windows 3.1 programming issues—from the best programming minds in the business. The book covers internationalizing software for Windows ■ programming Windows for Pen Computing ■ the GDI device transform ■ NetBIOS programming ■ developing virtual device drivers ■ Visual Basic as a professional tool. The accompanying disk contains all the source code and executable (EXE) files in the book.

350 pages, with one 1.44-MB 3.5" disk
$34.95 ($47.95 Canada)   ISBN 1-55615-480-1

The Peter Norton PC Programmer's Bible
Peter Norton, Peter Aitken, and Richard Wilton
"Admirably explains the inner workings with no loss of detail."
Computer Book Review

This is *the* ultimate reference to the IBM PC and compatible hardware and systems software. This new edition of *The Peter Norton Programmer's Guide to the IBM PC & PS/2* is packed with unmatched, authoritative programming advice, solid technical data, and key information. This book is designed to teach programmers the fundamental concepts of PC hardware, MS-DOS system calls (current through version 6.0), essential ROM BIOS services, and graphical programming with Windows, Windows NT, and OS/2.

608 pages, softcover $29.95 ($39.95 Canada)   ISBN 1-55615-555-7

IMPORTANT — READ CAREFULLY BEFORE OPENING SOFTWARE PACKET(S).
By opening the sealed packet(s) containing the software, you indicate your acceptance
of the following Microsoft License Agreement.

Microsoft License Agreement

MICROSOFT LICENSE AGREEMENT
(Resource Kit Companion Disks)

This is a legal agreement between you (either an individual or an entity) and Microsoft Corporation. By opening the sealed software packet(s) you are agreeing to be bound by the terms of this agreement. If you do not agree to the terms of this agreement, promptly return the unopened software packet(s) and any accompanying written materials to the place you obtained them for a full refund.

MICROSOFT SOFTWARE LICENSE

1. GRANT OF LICENSE. Microsoft grants to you the right to make and use copies of the Microsoft software program included with this book (the "SOFTWARE") for your internal use. The SOFTWARE is in "use" on a computer when it is loaded into temporary memory (i.e.. RAM) or installed into permanent memory (e.g., hard disk, CD-ROM, or other storage device) of that computer.

2. COPYRIGHT. The SOFTWARE is owned by Microsoft or its suppliers and is protected by United States copyright laws and international treaty provisions. Therefore, you must treat the SOFTWARE like any other copyrighted material (e.g., a book or musical recording). You may not copy the written materials accompanying the SOFTWARE.

3. OTHER RESTRICTIONS. You may not rent or lease the SOFTWARE, but you may transfer the SOFTWARE and accompanying written materials on a permanent basis provided you retain no copies and the recipient agrees to the terms of this Agreement. You may not reverse engineer, decompile, or disassemble the SOFTWARE. If the SOFTWARE is an update or has been updated, any transfer must include the most recent update and all prior versions.

DISCLAIMER OF WARRANTY

The SOFTWARE (including instructions for its use) is provided "AS IS" WITHOUT WARRANTY OF ANY KIND. MICROSOFT FURTHER DISCLAIMS ALL IMPLIED WARRANTIES INCLUDING WITHOUT LIMITATION ANY IMPLIED WARRANTIES OF MERCHANTABILITY OR OF FITNESS FOR A PARTICULAR PURPOSE OR AGAINST INFRINGE-MENT. THE ENTIRE RISK ARISING OUT OF THE USE OR PERFORMANCE OF THE SOFTWARE AND DOCUMENTA-TION REMAINS WITH YOU.

IN NO EVENT SHALL MICROSOFT, ITS AUTHORS, OR ANYONE ELSE INVOLVED IN THE CREATION, PRODUCTION, OR DELIVERY OF THE SOFTWARE BE LIABLE FOR ANY DAMAGES WHATSOEVER (INCLUDING, WITHOUT LIMITATION, DAMAGES FOR LOSS OF BUSINESS PROFITS, BUSINESS INTERRUPTION, LOSS OF BUSI-NESS INFORMATION, OR OTHER PECUNIARY LOSS) ARISING OUT OF THE USE OF OR INABILITY TO USE THE SOFTWARE OR DOCUMENTATION, EVEN IF MICROSOFT HAS BEEN ADVISED OF THE POSSIBILITY OF SUCH DAMAGES. BECAUSE SOME STATES/COUNTRIES DO NOT ALLOW THE EXCLUSION OR LIMITATION OF LIABILITY FOR CONSEQUENTIAL OR INCIDENTAL DAMAGES, THE ABOVE LIMITATION MAY NOT APPLY TO YOU.

U.S. GOVERNMENT RESTRICTED RIGHTS

The SOFTWARE and documentation are provided with RESTRICTED RIGHTS. Use, duplication, or disclosure by the Government is subject to restrictions as set forth in subparagraph (c)(1)(ii) of The Rights in Technical Data and Computer Software clause at DFARS 252.227-7013 or subparagraphs (c)(1) and (2) of the Commercial Computer Software — Restricted Rights 48 CFR 52.227-19, as applicable. Manufacturer is Microsoft Corporation/One Microsoft Way/Redmond, WA 98052-6399.

If you acquired this product in the United States, this Agreement is governed by the laws of the State of Washington.

Should you have any questions concerning this Agreement, or if you desire to contact Microsoft Press for any reason, please write: Microsoft Press/One Microsoft Way/Redmond, WA 98052-6399.

08/03/93   32100017.DOC